Law and Investment in China

The Chinese market is appealing, but the Chinese legal system is very complicated. A basic understanding of Chinese law is absolutely crucial for companies investing in this fast-growing and potentially huge market. Since China is moving toward a socialist market economy and is increasingly integrated into the world market, some aspects of China's commercial law are different from, while others are moving into line with, those of mature market economies. This book introduces the Chinese legal system relating to foreign direct investment, and highlights recent government policies and measures undertaken to intensify economic reforms so as to meet various challenges arising from China's accession to the World Trade Organization.

Vai Io Lo specializes in Asian and comparative law, especially American, Chinese, and Japanese laws. Currently, she is teaching at the International University of Japan. She is the author of various articles in law journals and the book *Law and Industrial Relations: China and Japan after World War II*.

Xiaowen Tian specializes in Chinese business and economics, especially foreign direct investment in China. He is currently teaching at the University of Nottingham. He is the author of various articles in referred international journals and the book *Dynamics of Development in an Open Economy: China since 1978*.

Law and Investment in China

in China

The legal and business environments after WTO accession

Vai Io Lo and Xiaowen Tian

RoutledgeCurzon
Taylor & Francis Group
LONDON AND NEW YORK

First published 2005
by RoutledgeCurzon
2 Park Square, Milton Park, Abingdon, Oxon OX14 4RN

Simultaneously published in the USA and Canada
by RoutledgeCurzon
270 Madison Ave, New York, NY 10016

Typeset in Times by
Graphicraft Limited, Hong Kong
Printed and bound in Great Britain by
Antony Rowe Ltd, Chippenham

British Library Cataloguing in Publication Data
A catalogue record for this book is available
from the British Library

Library of Congress Cataloging in Publication Data
A catalog record for this book has been requested

ISBN 0–415–32479–3

Contents

Preface

With China's accelerated economic reforms and accession to the World Trade Organization (WTO), foreign investors are finding it increasingly necessary to understand the regulatory environment of this potentially huge market. To provide handy reference, this book is an introduction to the legal framework of doing business in China. The intended readers are law students, business students, students majoring in Chinese studies, lawyers practicing international transactions, and management consultants.

This book is organized from the general to the specific. It commences with an overview of China's current legal system. Chapters 2 and 3 examine the legal framework of business entities in China, including both domestic and foreign investment enterprises. Chapters 4 to 9 cover substantive areas of law on business operations, including contracts, intellectual property, labor and employment, consumer protection, taxation, banking, securities, and dispute resolution. The closing chapters, Chapter 10 and 11, discuss China's WTO commitments and policies on the development of its western region and highlight new business opportunities for foreign investors. In its entirety, this book provides readers with a basic understanding of the pertinent issues on foreign direct investment in China. However, the material on each topic can also stand on its own, and the basic knowledge of a specific area of law may be obtained by focusing on the relevant chapter.

Since China has carried out legal reforms for fewer than three decades, its regulatory environment is relatively dynamic because new laws and regulations are frequently enacted while existing ones are often amended or repealed. Moreover, China is a large country with diverse physical, economic, and social circumstances. Accordingly, the Chinese central government enacts laws, regulations, and rules that are applicable nationwide, whereas local authorities implement them by enacting local regulations, or when there are no national laws or regulations dealing with certain issues, enact local regulations to address important concerns. Taking page limit and manageability into consideration, this book discusses mainly laws, administrative regulations, and government rules that have general applicability. When foreign investors make business decisions, they must also consult local regulations and industry-specific laws or regulations.

In preparing the case materials for this book, we have employed both translation and editing. Therefore, the court decisions discussed in this book are not verbatim opinions actually written by Chinese judges. The original opinions of almost all of these cases in Chinese can be read on the respective Web sites of the courts. To facilitate reading, we report each case by following this format: "Heading", "Facts", "Reasoning", and "Judgment" or "Ruling". The "Heading" section contains the names of the parties, the docket number of the case, the name of the court that delivered the judgment, and the date when the opinion was issued. The "Facts" section provides the pertinent factual background and discusses the lower court's decision rendered in the case. The "Reasoning" section explains the basis on which the court has reached the judgment or ruling. The "Judgment" or "Ruling" section provides a summary of the court's judgment or ruling, namely, what the court decision is.

Given China's complicated regulatory framework of foreign direct investment, our aim here is to present the most relevant information in a concise and accessible manner. Readers who are interested in studying more in-depth legal analyses or wish to know how legal theories have been put into practice may consult the articles cited in the Further Reading section of each chapter. We hope that readers will find this book useful as well as informative.

V.I.L.
X.T.
March 2004

1 An overview of the Chinese legal system

In December 2001, China acceded to the World Trade Organization (WTO). This event is significant not only for the Chinese, but also for foreign investors who want to establish a presence in China. It is expected that China's entry into the WTO will result in trade liberalization, and, thus, increased investment opportunities for foreign investors. To enter the Chinese market, foreign investors must understand the business and legal environments in which they will operate. Accordingly, this book aims to introduce the legal framework to conducting business in China, with emphasis on business organizations, investment vehicles, contracts, labor and employment, intellectual property, consumer protection, tax considerations, securities, banking, and dispute resolution. Before delving into specific issues, however, it is imperative to have an overview of the Chinese legal system.

1 The Chinese legal system from 1949–78

To understand the present, one must know the past. Having defeated the Kuomintang (国民党), who subsequently fled to Taiwan, the Chinese Communist Party (the Party) established the People's Republic of China in 1949. The new regime first abolished Kuomintang's legal system, which was considered to have supported "semi-feudal" or "semi-colonial" rule. Thereafter, it removed most of the judges who had been appointed by the Kuomintang government. In addition, the Party initiated several mass campaigns, such as the Land Reform Movement and the Movement against "Three Evils,"[1] to prepare the masses for a new political order. During those campaigns, "mass trials" were conducted to try "enemies"[2] before assembled crowds. In terms of formal legal norms, only a handful of laws were enacted during this period, such as the Marriage Law, the Trade Union Law, and the Land Reform Law. Meanwhile, the government under the leadership of the Party carried out nationalization and collectivization measures. Consequently, large private industrial and commercial establishments were converted into state-owned enterprises, while medium-sized and small industrial and commercial concerns were grouped together to become collectives.

As China followed the Soviet Union in adopting a command economy, efforts were also undertaken to develop a legal system based on the Soviet model. From 1953, the government launched several legislative projects with the help of Soviet jurists. As a result, the first Constitution was promulgated in 1954, followed by laws relating to the state structure. The drafting of a criminal code, civil code, and criminal procedure code was also begun. Moreover, legal institutions were strengthened. For example, the concept of judicial independence was introduced and law schools were set up to train judges and lawyers. Nevertheless, the efforts in constructing a socialist legal system did not last long. From the mid-1950s, a series of political events in China and the Maoist ideology in great measure immobilized the construction of a legal system.

In 1956, the Party launched the Hundred Flowers Movement, encouraging people to express views and criticisms. In response, many people spoke out and criticized the Party. Thereafter, the Party launched the Anti-Rightist Campaign to purge its critics. Hundreds of people, especially lawyers and judges who had been quite outspoken, were sentenced to "re-education through labor" (劳改) without any formal court proceedings. These two mass campaigns triggered the weakening of legal institutions. For instance, lawyers stopped practicing law, and law schools were switched to teach politics. Furthermore, according to Mao Zedong (Mao), there were two basic types of social contradictions – "contradictions among the people" and "contradictions against the people." Simply stated, "contradictions among the people" were day-to-day conflicts among ordinary people, whereas "contradictions against the people" were conflicts between the people and the enemies. To resolve conflicts among ordinary citizens, education and persuasion through mediation was the preferred means. To resolve conflicts between the people and the enemies, legal institutions, such as formal trial proceedings, were employed. Since the majority of conflicts were among the people, the construction of a legal system was not an exigency. Although the drafting of the Criminal and Criminal Procedure Codes was resumed in the early 1960s, laws and legal institutions were relegated to oblivion during the subsequent Cultural Revolution.

The notorious Cultural Revolution began in 1966, when Mao launched a mass campaign to purge counterrevolutionaries, revisionists, and "people on the capitalist road" with the assistance of the Red Guards, who consisted mainly of students and young people. Numerous people were persecuted, factories were closed down, and political meetings were the order of the day. Many contemporary scholars and commentators view the Cultural Revolution as a power struggle between the pragmatists and radicals in the Party. Whatever the real cause, law was denounced as a legacy of capitalism and a restraint on the revolutionary masses. As a result, law schools were closed down, lawyers were persecuted, and courts were combined with public-security bureaus under military control. With the abolition of legal institutions, "politics was in command." After Mao died in September 1976, the Gang of Four (radicals) was arrested and put on trial. The downfall of the Gang of Four led to the demise of the Cultural Revolution. As the Cultural

Revolution ended, the country faced the urgent tasks of enacting legal norms and restoring legal institutions.

2 Economic and legal reforms in the late 1970s and early 1980s

During the Cultural Revolution, political struggles put the country's economic and legal developments completely on hold. In the late 1970s, the new leadership headed by Deng Xiaoping decided to modernize the country's industry, agriculture, national defense, and science and technology. Toward this end, China implemented economic reforms and opened its door to the outside world. Economic reforms commenced with the decollectivization of agricultural production. Prior to 1979, agricultural production in China was collective. The agricultural hierarchy consisted of communes, brigades, production teams, and individual households. Farming households were to complete production orders from their production teams. In return, the team leader would give farming households grains and other coupons. Farming households could also keep a small portion of their produce for consumption. At the end of the 1970s, the household responsibility system was implemented. This system allowed farming households to contract with their production teams. Once they had fulfilled the agreed-upon quotas of production, they could keep whatever was left. In addition, they were allowed to engage in sideline production or planting cash crops. Consequently, farming households became much more productive, and their income substantially increased.

Owing to the success of the household responsibility system, the leadership decided to implement economic reforms in industrial production. As mentioned above, China had adopted a command economy. In this economy, the central government promulgated five-year plans and made annual economic decisions, on the basis of which regional authorities formulated their respective economic programs. Moreover, production from state-owned enterprises was under the supervision of their respective departments-in-charge, and their economic performance was evaluated in terms of output rather than profit. Since the state routinely meted out subsidies to loss-making enterprises, many state-owned enterprises suffered from inefficiency and low productivity. Hence, in the early 1980s, the central government decentralized economic decision-making. Local governments and enterprises were given more autonomy to make economic and production decisions. In addition, enterprise directors became accountable for profits and losses.

To attract foreign capital, technology, and management expertise, China passed its first foreign investment law, the Law on Sino-Foreign Equity Joint Ventures, in 1979. Moreover, the government established four Special Economic Zones (SEZs) – Shenzhen, Zhuhai, Shantou, and Xiamen – where investment incentives, such as preferential tax treatment, were offered to foreign investors. Subsequently, the government designated 14 Open Coastal Cities, such as Dalian, Fuzhou, Guangzhou, Shanghai, Ningbo, Qingdao, and Tianjin, to increase the inflow of foreign capital and technology. This open-door policy encouraged many foreign investors and overseas Chinese from Hong Kong, Macau, and Taiwan to invest in China, and thus, contributed to the country's rapid economic growth. Calculated at the 1978 constant price, China experienced an average annual GDP growth rate of 9.3 percent in the period of 1978–98.[3]

The preceding economic reforms led to the increased complexity of commercial transactions. In particular, the successful absorption of foreign investment depended on an effective legal system in which the rights and interests of foreign investors would be protected. Most importantly, the leaders at that time, many of whom had suffered persecution during the Cultural Revolution, believed that a sound legal system was indispensable to protecting citizens' basic rights and contributing to the country's political and social stability. Hence, efforts were undertaken to rebuild a socialist legal system. For example, the Ministry of Justice was restored in 1979, legal education was revived, and courts were reopened.

This chapter and the remainder of this book introduce you to the contemporary Chinese legal system, namely, what has been accomplished in a span of less than 30 years. In implementing economic and legal reforms, China has taken an incremental approach. That is, without years of accumulated experiences, China has often adopted economic measures and enacted legislation on a trial basis before any fully fledged implementation. For years, scholars and commentators from countries having relatively developed legal systems have criticized the Chinese legal system for various deficiencies, such as ambiguous legal provisions and weak enforcement. Having joined the WTO, China will have to accelerate its efforts in reforming and refining its legal system. Like the study of many other legal systems, our study of Chinese law also commences with the Constitution.

3 Constitution and state structure

China's Constitution is the fundamental law of the state and has supreme legal authority. Since its establishment in 1949, China has promulgated four Constitutions – 1954, 1975, 1978, and 1982 Constitutions. As of March 2004, the 1982 Constitution, the latest Constitution, had been revised four times.[4] The Constitution outlines the basic structure of the state by delineating the rights and responsibilities of major government organs. Accordingly, the following discussion will first highlight the important provisions of the 1982 Constitution and then introduce the various constituents of the state.

The 1982 Constitution

According to the Preamble of the 1982 Constitution, the basic task of the nation is to concentrate its efforts on "socialist modernization construction" (社会主义现代化建设) along the road of Chinese-style socialism. The Chinese people are to work diligently and self-reliantly to modernize the country's industry, agriculture, national defense, and science and technology. Moreover, the five principles of foreign policy consist of:

1   mutual respect for sovereignty and territorial integrity;
2   mutual non-aggression;
3   mutual noninterference with internal affairs;
4   equality and mutual benefit; and
5   peaceful coexistence in developing diplomatic relations and economic and cultural exchanges with other countries.

Hence, the Preamble outlines the directions the country is to take and the bases on which China will handle foreign affairs.

Chapter One of the Constitution contains general principles. Apparently, the Constitution avows the rule of law because the state upholds the uniformity and dignity of the socialist legal system; all state organs, armed forces, political parties, social organizations, enterprises, and institutions must abide by the Constitution and the law; and no organization or individual is privileged to be above the Constitution or the law. In addition, China is a socialist country because the means of production is owned by the whole people or collectively owned by the working people; and land in the city is owned by the state, while land in the rural and suburban areas is owned by collectives. No organization or individual may appropriate, buy, sell, or unlawfully transfer land, but the right to the use of the land, which is referred to as land use right (土地使用权), may be transferred in accordance with the law.

On the economic side, China is to adopt a socialist market economy. Public ownership is the principal component, but diverse forms of ownership may coexist. In fact, the non-public sectors of the economy, such as the individual sector (个体经济) and the private sector (私营经济), are important components of, the socialist market economy. Citizens have the inviolable right to private property, and compensation must be made for any expropriation or requisition. Moreover, China permits foreign investment, and the rights and interests of foreign enterprises, foreign economic organizations, and Sino-foreign equity joint ventures are protected under Chinese law.

Chapter Two of the Constitution enunciates the fundamental rights and duties of Chinese citizens. The Chinese version of the Bill of Rights includes freedom of speech, of the press, of assembly, of association, of procession, and of demonstration (article 35); freedom of religious belief (article 36); freedom of person (article 37); personal dignity (article 38); no unlawful search of residence (article 39); and freedom and privacy of correspondence (article 40). Nonetheless, these rights are not absolute because the exercise of such rights may not infringe upon the interests of the state, society, and the collective and upon the lawful freedoms and rights of other citizens (article 51).

Chapter Three of the Constitution outlines the structure of the state, which will be discussed in the subsequent sections of this chapter. In comparing the Chinese Constitution with those of the U.S.A. and the Soviet Union, Professor Jones makes the following observations.[5] First of all, the structures of the U.S. Constitution and the Chinese Constitution are similar. That is, in both Constitutions, the powers of the most important government organs are depicted in general terms, and the government organs (the legislative, the executive, and the judicial) are also similar. Moreover, both China and the U.S.A. have a Bill of Rights. Nonetheless, the Chinese Constitution differs from the U.S. Constitution in that China has additional institutions (the Central Military Commission and the Procuratorate), and China is a unitary rather than a federal state. On the other hand, the basic similarities between the Chinese Constitution and the Soviet Constitution are the inclusion of ideological statements and the clear recognition of Marxism as the official doctrine of the state. Besides, the Chinese procuratorate is of Soviet origin, and the use of standing committees of large government organs to do the real work is common to both countries.

The overall state structure

In China, state power is divided among five constituents. The Communist Party has political power, people's congresses have legislative power, the State Council and its ministries and commissions have executive power, the people's courts have judicial power, and the people's procuratorates have procuratorial power. The state hierarchy consists of the central, provincial, municipal, county, township, and village levels. There are 23 provinces, five

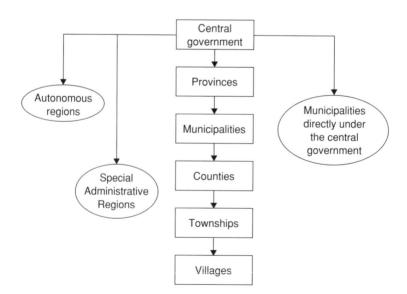

Figure 1.1 Administrative hierarchy

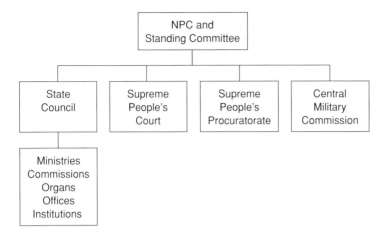

Figure 1.2 Central level

autonomous regions,[6] four municipalities directly under the central government,[7] and two Special Administrative Regions[8] (see Figure 1.1).

At the central level, the National People's Congress (NPC) has the highest power. The State Council, Supreme People's Court, Supreme People's Procuratorate, and the Central Military Commission are accountable to the NPC. Under the State Council, there are ministries, commissions, organs, offices, and institutions. Accordingly, the question is whether China has the doctrine of separation of power. On one hand, one may argue that China maintains separation of power because various governmental organs hold different types of power and perform different functions. On the other hand, one may assert that China does not practice separation of power because, first, the NPC has the highest power and supervises the State Council, Supreme People's Court, and Supreme People's Procuratorate, and, second, the power to interpret laws belongs to the NPC Standing Committee (see Figure 1.2).

At the local levels of province, municipality, county, township, and village, the preceding structure is replicated. The people's congress has the highest power. The local governments, people's courts, and people's procuratorates are accountable to the local people's congresses. Moreover, higher-level governments, people's courts, and people's procuratorates have supervisory power over lower-level governments, people's courts, and people's procuratorates. For example, a municipal government is accountable to the provincial government, and a people's procuratorate at the municipal level is accountable to a procuratorate at the provincial level (see Figure 1.3).

The Chinese Communist Party was founded in 1921. With the NPC at the top, Party congresses at the levels of province, autonomous region, municipality directly under the central government, and other municipalities provide leadership and establish national policies. However, the Chinese

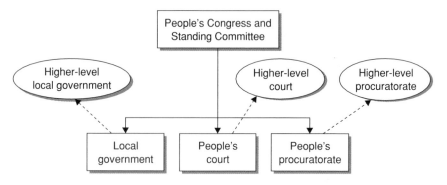

Figure 1.3 Local level

People's Political Consultative Conference, "a broadly representative organization of the united front," has members from minority parties.

The National People's Congress

The NPC and local people's congresses at various levels are the organs through which citizens exercise power. The NPC is the highest organ of state power and the highest legislative body. The NPC is composed of deputies elected by the provinces, autonomous regions, municipalities directly under the central government, and the armed forces. There are about 3,000 deputies to the NPC. The NPC is elected for a term of five years. The NPC meets in session once a year for a period of one to three weeks. The 10th NPC commenced in March 2002.

The major functions and powers of the NPC include the following. It amends the Constitution and supervises its implementation. It enacts and amends basic laws concerning criminal offenses, civil affairs, the state organs, and other matters. It appoints and removes top officials of the highest state organs, such as the President, the Premier, and the President of the Supreme People's Court. It examines and approves national economic and social development plans and the state budget. It approves the establishment of provinces, autonomous regions, municipalities directly under the central government, and Special Administrative Regions.

The NPC has nine Special Committees: Ethnicity; Law; Foreign Affairs; Overseas Chinese; Internal and Judicial Affairs; Finance and Economics; Education, Science, Culture, and Public Health; Environmental and Resources Protection; and Agriculture and Rural Affairs. The main work of these committees is to examine, discuss, and draw up relevant bills and draft resolutions. When the NPC is not in session, these committees work under the direction of the NPC Standing Committee.

The NPC Standing Committee is the permanent body of the NPC. Members of the Standing Committee are elected by the NPC for the same term as the NPC. Currently, the NPC Standing Committee has more than 130 members. The Chairperson and Vice-Chairperson of the Standing Committee cannot serve more than two consecutive terms. Nobody on the Standing Committee can hold office in any of the administrative, judicial, or procuratorial organs. The Standing Committee meets in session once every two months.

The major functions and powers of the Standing Committee are as follows. It interprets the Constitution and supervises its enforcement. It enacts and amends laws, except for those that should be enacted by the NPC. It supplements or amends laws enacted by the NPC when the NPC is not in session. It interprets laws. It supervises the work of the State Council, the Central Military Commission, the Supreme People's Court, and the Supreme People's Procuratorate. It annuls administrative regulations, decisions, and decrees of the State Council that contravene the Constitution or laws. It annuls local regulations or decisions that contravene the Constitution, laws, or administrative regulations or resolutions. It appoints and removes the vice-presidents and judges of the Supreme People's Court, members of its Adjudicative Committee, and the President of the Military Court at the suggestion of the President of the Supreme People's Court. It decides on the ratification or abrogation of treaties.

The State Council

The State Council is the highest organ of state administration. The Premier, vice-premiers, state councilors, ministers in charge of ministries, ministers in charge of commissions, the Auditor-General, and Secretary-General comprise the State Council. The working organ of the State Council is its General Affairs Office. The term of office of the State Council is the same as that of the NPC. The Premier, vice-premiers, and state councilors cannot serve more than two consecutive terms. Since its restructuring in 2003, the State Council is composed of 22 ministries, 4 commissions, the People's Bank of China, and the State Audit Office. Examples of ministries and commissions are the Ministry of Commerce, Ministry of Finance, Ministry of Justice, Ministry of Foreign Affairs, Ministry of Land and Resources, State Development and Reform Commission, and State Ethnic Affairs Commission.

Moreover, there are various administrative organs, offices, and institutions under the unified leadership of the State Council. For instance, the State Administration of Taxation, State Administration for Industry and Commerce, State Statistics Bureau, State Administration of Press and Publication, and State Intellectual Property Office are administrative organs directly under the State Council; the Overseas Chinese Affairs Office and Legislative Affairs Office are administrative offices directly under the State Council; and the Xinhua News Agency, China Securities Regulatory Commission, and China Academy of Social Sciences are institutions directly under the State Council. Apart from these government entities, there are various bureaus overseen by the ministries and commissions.

The State Council exercises the following major functions and powers. It adopts administrative measures, enacts administrative regulations, and issues decisions and orders in accordance with the Constitution and laws. It submits proposals to the NPC or its Standing Committee. It exercises unified leadership over the work of local organs of state administration at different levels. It formulates and implements plans for national economic and social development and the state budget. It administers work concerning urban and rural development, education, science, culture, public health, civil affairs, public security, judicial administration, foreign affairs, national defense, etc. It amends or annuls inappropriate orders, directives, and rules issued by ministries or commissions.

The Supreme People's Procuratorate

The Supreme People's Procuratorate is the highest state organ of judicial supervision. It is responsible to the NPC and its Standing Committee. It has the powers of legal supervision and administration of justice. It directs the work of local people's procuratorates, which supervise judicial proceedings in criminal cases, investigate criminal cases and decide whether or not to prosecute the suspect, lodge protests to people's courts against effective, but incorrect, judgments or rulings, and handle cases of officials' misconduct in office. The term of office of the Procurator-General of the Supreme People's Procuratorate is the same as that of the NPC. The Supreme People's Procuratorate provides interpretations of questions concerning specific applications of laws in procuratorial work and formulates regulations regarding such work.

4 Legislation

Since China commenced legal reforms in the late 1970s, numerous laws, regulations, rules, and decrees have been promulgated. Notwithstanding the sheer volume of legal norms, lawmaking in China has been plagued with problems. For instance, people's congresses at various levels were criticized for being "rubber stamps." In addition, different lawmaking entities issued inconsistent legal norms on the same or related subjects, and laws and regulations passed at various times contained conflicting provisions on the same subject. Thus, it was unclear which legal provision should govern. Furthermore, government rules were issued, amended, or repealed without immediate or widespread publication, which made it difficult to tell whether a certain subject was being regulated or a particular rule was still in effect. In view of these problems, the NPC enacted the Legislation Law in 2000.[9] Together with the Constitution, the Legislation Law provides clear and uniform guidance on legislative activities.

Types of legal norms and lawmaking entities

In China, legal norms consist of the Constitution (宪法), basic laws (基本法), administrative regulations (行政法规), government rules (部门规章 or 地方政府规章), local regulations (地方性法规), and self-governing or specific regulations (自治条例 or 单行法).

As mentioned above, the NPC adopts and amends the Constitution. The NPC also has the power to enact and amend basic laws (or laws) relating to criminal matters, civil matters, and government organs, as well as other types of basic laws. Moreover, the Standing Committee of the NPC has the power to enact and amend laws other than those made by the NPC, and while the NPC is not in session, to supplement and amend those laws made by the NPC. Specifically, the following matters are to be regulated by means of law: sovereignty issues; the establishment, organization, and powers of people's congresses, people's governments, people's courts, and people's procuratorates at various levels; systems relating to the self-governance of ethnic areas and grassroots organizations[10] or to Special Administrative Regions; crimes and punishments; deprivation of political rights; compulsory measures and punishments restricting freedom of person; governmental expropriation of non-state-owned property; the basic system of civil affairs; basic systems relating to economics, fiscal policy, taxes, customs, finance, and foreign trade; and litigation and arbitration systems. Some examples of basic laws are the Criminal Law, Trade Union Law, Marriage Law, Law on the Organization of the People's Procuratorates, and Civil Procedure Law.

To perform its mission, the State Council is empowered to enact administrative regulations to implement basic laws as well as regulations regarding matters falling within its administrative power. An example of this type of administrative regulation is the Regulations on the Administration of Broadcasting Television. Moreover, the NPC and its Standing Committee can authorize the State Council to enact administrative regulations on those matters for which laws have not been made, except for crimes and punishments, deprivation of political rights, compulsory measures and punishment restricting freedom of person, and judicial system. The Provisional Regulations on Private Enterprises is an example of this type of administrative regulation. In this connection, it is noteworthy that the NPC may also authorize the people's congress and its standing committee of the province or city where a SEZ is located to enact regulations to be implemented within the zone. One example of this type of regulation is the Regulations of the Shenzhen Special Economic Zone on Commodity Market.

Ministries and commissions under the State Council, the People's Bank of China, the State Audit Office, and administrative organs directly under the central government may enact ministerial and departmental rules (部门规章) on matters falling within their respective administrative powers in order to implement laws as well as the State Council's administrative regulations, resolutions, and decrees. One example of this type of government rule is the Rules on the Administration of Patent Agencies. If a matter falls within the powers of two ministries or departments, it should be submitted to the State Council for the enactment of an administrative regulation, or the relevant ministries or departments jointly should make a government rule on such subject. For instance, the Ministry of Labor and the Ministry of Foreign Trade and Economic Cooperation have promulgated jointly the Rules on Labor Management in Foreign Investment Enterprises. Likewise, the people's governments of provinces, autonomous regions, municipalities directly under the central government, and larger cities may enact local government rules (地方政府规章) to implement basic laws, administrative regulations and local regulations, and to deal with concrete administrative matters within their respective administrative districts. One good example is the Notice of the Zhejiang People's Government concerning the Establishment of a Government Procurement System. Since these two types of rules are similar and ranked the same in the hierarchy of legal norms (discussed below), they are collectively termed "government rules" here.

Furthermore, people's congresses and their standing committees of provinces, autonomous regions, and municipalities directly under the central government may enact local regulations in light of the actual circumstances and practical needs of their respective administrative districts. Cities where the people's governments of autonomous regions are located, SEZs, and larger cities approved by the State Council may enact local regulations, subject to the approval of the standing committees of the provincial or autonomous-regional people's congresses. Apart from local affairs, local regulations may be enacted to implement laws and administrative regulations. Moreover, except for matters that must be regulated by laws, provinces, autonomous regions, municipalities directly under the central government and larger cities may enact local regulations if no laws or administrative regulations dealing with the same subjects exist. One example of local regulations is the Measures of the Anhui Province on the Handling of Water Traffic Accidents.

Finally, the people's congresses of ethnic autonomous areas may enact self-governing or specific regulations in light of local political, economic, and cultural characteristics. The self-governing or specific regulations of autonomous regions become effective upon the approval of the NPC Standing Committee. The self-governing or specific regulations of an autonomous prefecture or autonomous county become effective upon the approval of the standing committee of the people's congress of the province, autonomous region, or city directly under the central government. In implementing laws and administrative regulations by means of self-governing or specific regulations, autonomous areas may make adaptations in accordance with local circumstances, but not in contradiction of the basic principles of the laws or administrative regulations. One example of self-governing regulation is the

Measures of Ningxia Hui Autonomous Region on the Management of Sports Competition.

Hierarchy of legal norms

As previously mentioned, the Constitution is the supreme law of the country. Therefore, basic laws, administrative regulations, government rules, local regulations, and self-governing or specific regulations cannot contravene the Constitution. In addition, administrative regulations must be made in accordance with the Constitution and basic laws; local regulations cannot contradict the Constitution, basic laws, and administrative regulations; and government rules are enactments of ministries or commissions under the State Council or local governments. Accordingly, basic laws take precedence over administrative regulations, local regulations, and government rules; and administrative regulations take precedence over local regulations and government rules. Furthermore, local regulations take precedence over government rules enacted by the same-level or lower-level government. Finally, government rules made by the people's government of a larger city are subordinate to those made by the provincial or autonomous regional government. In short, the Constitution is at the top of the legal hierarchy. The laws adopted by the NPC or its Standing Committee and administrative regulations enacted by the State Council rank second and third, respectively.

Inconsistencies between legal norms

In the case of conflicting provisions in laws, administrative regulations, local regulations, self-governing regulations, specific regulations, or government rules made by the same entity, the specific takes precedence over the general, and the new takes precedence over the old. Moreover, conflicting provisions between two laws are to be determined by the NPC Standing Committee, while conflicting provisions between two administrative regulations are to be determined by the State Council. Similarly, conflicting provisions between new and old government rules made by the same government organ are to be determined by the government organ. However, conflicting provisions between local regulations and government rules issued by ministries or departments under the State Council should be referred to the State Council. In that case, the State Council may decide either to apply the local regulation in the relevant locality, or to submit to the NPC Standing Committee for a determination. Furthermore, if there are conflicting provisions between government rules issued by different ministries or departments under the State Council, or conflicting provisions between government rules issued by ministries or departments and government rules issued by local governments, the State Council should make a determination. Finally, conflicting provisions between laws and regulations based on delegated power are to be determined by the NPC Standing Committee.

Interpretation of legal norms

Depending on the interpretive entity, there are three types of legal interpretation in China – legislative, administrative, and judicial. As regards legal significance, legislative interpretation has the greatest weight, while judicial interpretation appears to have the least, and administrative interpretation falls somewhere in the middle. The Standing Committee of the NPC is authorized to interpret laws where it is necessary to give more concrete meaning to the law, and where new circumstances have arisen since the enactment of the law and it is necessary to clarify the appropriate legal basis. The interpretations of the Standing Committee have the same legal effect as laws.

In 1981, the NPC Standing Committee adopted a resolution,[11] allowing the State Council and departments-in-charge to interpret laws or decrees[12] with respect to their non-trial or non-procuratorial application. This resolution, however, does not deal with the interpretation of administrative regulations or government rules. For years, the State Council and its subordinates have been the exclusive interpreters of administrative regulations or government rules. In a circular to local people's governments, ministries and commissions, and administrative organs directly under the central government,[13] the State Council maintains that it has the power to supplement and clarify the limits of administrative regulations, and that departments-in-charge are to interpret administrative regulations with respect to their specific application. Thus, it is common for the State Council and ministries to indicate in administrative regulations or government rules which entity has the power to interpret the provisions therein. For example, the Ministry of Labor and Social Security is to interpret the Regulations on the Handling of Labor Disputes in Enterprises. In interpreting administrative regulations or government rules, the people's courts always defer to the relevant ministries or departments.

In China, the people's court is the judicial organ of the state, and the people's procuratorate is the state organ for legal supervision. The Constitution does not authorize people's courts to interpret laws and regulations. To facilitate the uniform application of laws by courts across the country, the 1981 Resolution also authorizes the Supreme People's Court to interpret laws or decrees relating to their specific application at trial. Even so, the interpretive power of the Supreme People's Court should be limited because no constitutional or statutory provisions provide that judicial interpretations have the same legal effect as laws. However, in a 1997 circular,[14] the Supreme People's Court maintained that its interpretations had legal effect. If lower courts base their judgments or rulings on judicial interpretations, they should cite both the legal rules and judicial interpretations. Moreover, the Supreme People's Court has often issued interpretations in reply to legal questions raised by lower courts. For instance, in November 2000, the Supreme People's Court issued to Jilin Province High People's Court the

Reply Concerning Questions in the Trial of a Criminal Case with an Incidental Civil Action. Furthermore, the Supreme People's Court has issued opinions or circulars in order to provide a complete set of answers to questions with respect to the application of a particular statute. These general interpretations often supplement broad, ambiguous, or vague provisions in existing laws, and thus, become a source of law. One example of this type of judicial interpretation is the Interpretations Concerning Several Questions about the Application of the Securities Law.

The 1981 Resolution also authorizes the Supreme People's Procuratorate to interpret laws or decrees relating to their application in procuratorial work. Like the Supreme People's Court, the Supreme People's Procuratorate also maintains that its interpretations have the same effect as laws.[15] If the interpretation provided by the Supreme People's Court conflicts with that of the Supreme People's Procuratorate, both interpretations must be submitted to the NPC Standing Committee for interpretation or determination.

5 The judicial system

Since the late 1970s, China has undertaken various efforts to rebuild or revitalize its judicial system. Nonetheless, in the last two decades, the Chinese judicial system has been much criticized, especially on the poor quality of judges, lack of judicial independence, and weak enforcement. Therefore, this section first introduces the Chinese court system and then explains the controversy over the lack of judicial independence.

Levels of court

In China, there are four levels of general jurisdiction courts. At the national level, there is the Supreme People's Court. At the level of province, autonomous region, or municipality directly under the central government, there are high people's courts (about 30). In districts or municipalities within provinces or autonomous regions as well as municipalities directly under the central government, there are intermediate people's courts (about 380). At the level of county, municipality, or district within a municipality, there are basic people's courts (about 3,000). Moreover, China adopts a two-trial system, namely, one trial at the court of first instance and one appeal at the court of second instance. In each court, there are various divisions. Most courts have the criminal division, civil division, and administrative division. Some courts also have other divisions, such as the economic division, intellectual property division, and bankruptcy division. The criminal division deals with crimes, the civil division hears civil disputes, and the administrative division processes complaints against administrative actions. Furthermore, China has special people's courts, such as military courts, maritime courts, railway transportation courts, and forest courts (see Figure 1.4).

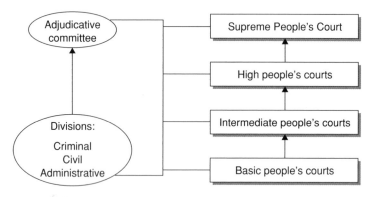

Figure 1.4 Courts

The Supreme People's Court is accountable to the NPC and its Standing Committee. The NPC elects the President (院长) of the Supreme People's Court. The term of office of the President of the Supreme People's Court is the same as that of NPC. Upon recommendation of the President of the Supreme People's Court, the NPC Standing Committee appoints the Vice-President (副院长), chief judge of a division (庭长), deputy chief judge of a division (副庭长), judges (审判员), and the members of the adjudicative committee (审判委员会). The Constitution mandates that the Supreme People's Court supervise the administration of justice by local people's courts and special courts at all levels. As already mentioned, the Supreme People's Court provides interpretations of questions concerning specific applications of laws at trial.

The people's courts at various levels are accountable to the organs of state power that created them, that is, people's congresses. The court president of a local people's court is elected by the local people's congress. If the people's congress is not in session and the standing committee wants to replace the president of a people's court, it may do so by submitting to the standing committee of the people's congress at the next higher level for approval. The vice-president, members of the adjudicative committee, chief judge of a division, deputy chief judge of a division, and judges are appointed by the standing committee of the people's congress. Assistant judges (助理审判员) are appointed by the president of the people's court.

Jurisdiction

According to the Organic Law of the People's Courts,[16] basic people's courts are courts of first instance in criminal and civil cases. However, the basic people's court may request to have a case transferred to the intermediate people's court if it thinks that the case is significant. In addition, basic people's courts are to handle civil disputes that do not need a court session or minor criminal offenses, as well as direct the work of people's mediation committees. Intermediate people's courts are courts of first instance as stipulated in laws or decrees. Moreover, intermediate people's courts handle appeals against judgments or rulings made by basic people's courts as well as protests lodged by people's procuratorates against effective, but incorrect, judgments or rulings. The intermediate people's court may also request to have an important civil or criminal case transferred to the high people's court. Similarly, high people's courts are courts of first instance as stipulated in laws or decrees. They also handle appeals or protests against judgments or rulings made by lower people's courts. The Supreme People's Court is the court of first instance as stipulated in laws or decrees or if it deems appropriate. The Supreme People's Court handles appeals against judgments and rulings made by high people's courts or special people's courts, as well as protests lodged by the Supreme People's Procuratorate.

Judges

After the Cultural Revolution, courts were reopened, but very few qualified judges were available. In addition, retired military personnel were often appointed as judges in local people's courts. As a result, the competency of many judges was questionable. In 1995, China passed its Judges Law,[17] outlining the qualifications as well as the rights and duties of judges. Specifically, the Judges Law provides that judges cannot be dismissed without cause or without legal procedure; the wages of judges are to be increased at fixed intervals; and the performance of judges is to be evaluated annually.

To become a judge or an assistant judge, a Chinese citizen must:

1   be at least 23 years old;
2   have graduated with a degree in law or a degree in another area of specialization (but having professional knowledge in law) from an institution of higher education and have engaged in legal work for two years (or three years for those who will become judges in the high people's court and the Supreme People's Court), or have obtained a master's or doctorate degree in law or a master's or doctorate degree in another area of specialization (but having professional knowledge in law) from an institution of higher education and have engaged in legal work for one year (or two years for those who will become judges in the high people's court and the Supreme People's Court);
3   have not been criminally punished or dismissed from public office; and
4   have passed a judge examination administered by the Supreme People's Court, etc.

In addition, a judge cannot serve concurrently as a member of the standing committee of a people's congress; work for an administrative or procuratorial organ, enterprise, or institution; or practice as a lawyer.

Judicial independence

In many countries, such as the U.S.A. and Japan, judicial independence means that a judge independently makes decision in an individual case without any interference. In China, however, judicial independence has a somewhat different meaning. Article 126 of the Chinese Constitution states that people's courts exercise judicial power independently and are not subject to interference by any administrative organs, social organizations, or individuals. Hence, judicial independence refers to the independence of the court as a collective entity vis-à-vis other state organs or external bodies.

Moreover, an adjudicative committee is to be established in each court. The adjudicative committee is composed of the court president and some judges appointed by the standing committee of the people's congress upon the recommendation of the court president. Its mission is to summarize trial experiences and to discuss important or difficult cases as well as other questions relating to trial work. A court may claim independence, but an individual judge or a collegiate bench does not act independently when deciding important cases. This is because the adjudicative committee may direct the individual judge or collegiate bench as to what verdict should be given, and the collegiate bench just implements the decision of the committee.

Given that judicial independence in China refers to the independence of the court vis-à-vis other entities, judicial independence may not be achieved for at least two reasons. First, local people's courts at various levels are supported financially by local governments. Thus, there is a strong incentive for local people's courts to protect local interests. Second, the appointment or removal of judges is subject to the approval of local people's congresses and their standing committees. Hence, judges may be susceptible to the influence of the deputies to local people's congresses. In other words, local protectionism and personal interest may have a negative impact on judicial independence.

Judicial reform

In 1999, the Supreme People's Court promulgated a five-year reform program. Based on the general guidelines of the Supreme People's Court, lower people's courts would formulate implementation plans in light of their particular circumstances. Xiao Yang, the President of the Supreme People's Court, discussed the following reform measures during an interview in 2000.[18] First, various measures would be adopted to enhance the quality of judges. For example, a system for appointing the presiding judge of a collegiate bench and a sole judge through competitive selection would be established. Judges at higher-level courts would be selected from among prominent judges at lower-level courts and among lawyers or high-level legal personnel. In addition, judges would be selected through a strict procedure, and the appointment of judges for all courts would be fixed. Accordingly, persons who were disqualified as judges would be transferred to do supportive work or assigned to other administrative posts.

Apart from the quality of judges, individual judges would be given more responsibility. As discussed above, judges who directly handled cases sometimes did not have the power to make a decision, but those who were in the adjudicative committee did. To correct this problem, the presiding judge of a collegiate bench or the sole judge who directly handled a case would be responsible for signing the relevant legal documents. In this way, the responsibility of individual judges would be strengthened. At the same time, the adjudicative duty of the court president and the chief judge of a division would be restored. Thus, the court president and the chief judge would not be engrossed only in administrative duties and would be able to contribute their expertise to the trial of cases. Finally, a new system would be established in every province for managing, directing, and coordinating the enforcement of court decisions on a unified basis.

6 The legal profession

After the Cultural Revolution, lawyers began to reappear and law schools were reopened or formed. Initially, Chinese lawyers worked for the government. Over the years, lawyers have become the advocates for private individuals, private law firms have increased steadily, and the self-regulating All China Lawyers Association has been established.

Lawyers

For 16 years, the Chinese legal profession was regulated under a provisional regulation. In 1996, the Lawyers Law[19] was promulgated, providing guidance on the rights and duties of lawyers, qualification requirements, law firms, lawyer associations, legal aid, and disciplinary measures. Subsequently, detailed rules for its implementation have also been issued, covering such areas as legal service fees and the bar examination.

To practice law, one must obtain the necessary qualifications and be granted a practicing license. To qualify as a lawyer, one must take the uniform bar examination. According to the Lawyers Law, any person who holds a degree in law or a degree in another area of specialization (but having professional knowledge in law) from an institution of higher education may take the bar examination. However, those who have obtained a law degree, have engaged in legal research or teaching, and have worked in high-level posts or obtained equivalent professional level may also obtain the lawyer qualification with the approval of the judicial administration department of the State Council, that is, the Ministry of Justice. Once a person has been qualified as a lawyer and has undergone one full year's apprenticeship in a law firm, he or she may be issued a practicing license.

A lawyer may practice with one law firm, but cannot associate concurrently with two law firms. A lawyer must join the local lawyers association, and thus, become a member of the All China Lawyers Association. A law firm must have its own name, domicile, and articles of association; Renminbi (RMB) 100,000 or more in capital; and qualified lawyers. Moreover, law firms can be formed as state-owned enterprises, cooperatives, or partnerships. With respect to legal service fees, the Ministry of Justice is authorized to formulate measures, subject to the approval of the State Council.

Foreign law firms

According to the Regulations on the Administration of Representative Offices of Foreign Law Firms in China,[20] foreign law firms are allowed to establish representative offices in China if they meet certain requirements and receive permission from the Ministry of Justice. The requirements are as follows:

1   The foreign law firm must have lawfully practiced law in its own country and have not been punished for any violation of professional ethics or disciplinary measures.
2   The representatives of the foreign law firm in China must be duly licensed lawyers and members of the relevant lawyers association, have practiced law outside China for at least two years, and have never been criminally punished or punished for violating professional ethics or disciplinary measures.
3   The chief representative must have practiced law outside China for three years and be a partner of the foreign law firm.
4   The law firm has practical needs to establish a representative office in China.

Once the foreign law firm has obtained the necessary permission, it must register with the local judicial administration department at the level of province, autonomous region, or municipality directly under the central government. The representative office and the representatives must register every year; and any merger, division, or addition of representatives must be approved. Currently, foreign law firms can advise clients on the laws of their home countries; advise clients on international treaties and customary rules; take instructions from clients or Chinese law firms and act on their behalf in their home jurisdiction; give instructions to Chinese law firms on behalf of their foreign clients; conclude contracts with Chinese law firms to maintain a long-term agency relationship; and provide information relating to China's legal environment.

Nevertheless, the representative office cannot hire Chinese lawyers, and its Chinese assistants cannot provide legal services. Moreover, a foreign lawyer must stay in China for at least six months per year. If the foreign lawyer stays in China for less than six months, he or she will not be able to register the following year. Likewise, if the foreign lawyer's Chinese license is revoked, he or she will not be able to represent foreign law firms in China for five years. Furthermore, a foreign lawyer may not serve concurrently as the representatives of two foreign law firms in China.

Although the representative offices of law firms from Hong Kong and Macao are regulated separately, their scope of activities is similar to that of the representative offices of foreign law firms. In 2003, mainland China and Hong Kong and Macao entered respectively into the Closer Economic Partnership Arrangements (CEPA). A Hong Kong or Macao law firm that has already established a representative office in China and a qualified Chinese law firm within its locality may now form a jointly operated enterprise in China to provide separate legal services.

Challenges facing the legal profession

During an interview in 2001, Gao Zongze, the President of the All China Lawyers Association, discussed the challenges facing the legal profession.[21] According to Gao, although the number of lawyers has been on the rise, the legal profession itself does not have the prestige that it deserves. This can be exemplified by the frequent incidents of discrimination and harassment against lawyers. In addition, certain rights and functions that should belong to lawyers are not separated from administrative organs, thus preventing the emergence of a unified market for legal services. At the same time, many local lawyers associations do not hold meetings regularly, which makes it difficult for lawyers to unite. Besides, the overall quality of lawyers is still far from satisfactory.

Accordingly, Gao concluded that the Chinese legal profession should take the following reform measures. First, the standard of a pass at the bar examination should be raised. Second, a multifaceted, multi-layered business organization for the legal profession, with partnership being the main operational model for law firms, should be established. Along with that, both general and specialized practices should be offered. Third, as government provision of legal services has reduced gradually, the legal profession should decide the supply of legal service market. Fourth, it is imperative to assist and train lawyers and law firms that are adept at international competition. Fifth, owing to regional developmental disparities, flexible management tactics should be applied to lawyers in different areas.

Further reading

Jones, William C., "The Constitution of the People's Republic of China," *Washington University Law Quarterly* 63, 1985, pp. 707–35.

Lubman, Stanley, "Bird in a Cage: Chinese Law Reforms after Twenty Years," *Northwestern Journal of International Law and Business* 20, 2000, pp. 383–423.

Peerenboom, Randall, "The X-Files: Past and Present Portrayals of China's Alien 'Legal System'," *Washington University Global Studies Law Review* 2, 2003, pp. 37–95.

Notes

1 The "three evils" were corruption, waste, and bureaucratism in the Party, government agencies, and state-owned enterprises.
2 Generally, "enemies" referred to counterrevolutionaries, landlords, and criminals.
3 This figure is derived from State Statistics Bureau, *China Statistical Yearbook 1999*, Beijing: China Statistics Press, 1999, pp. 55 and 58.
4 The Constitution of the People's Republic of China, adopted at the 5th Session of the 5th National People's Congress on 4 December 1982 and amended at the 1st Session of the 7th National People's Congress on 12 April 1988, the 1st Session of the 8th National People's Congress on 29 March 1993, the 2nd Session of the 9th National People on 15 March 1999, and the 2nd Session of the 10th National People's Congress on 14 March 2004, respectively.
5 See William C. Jones, "The Constitution of the People's Republic of China," *Washington University Law Quarterly* 63, 1985, p. 707, nn. 1 and 2.
6 Examples of autonomous regions, where ethnic minorities reside, are Xinjiang, Tibet, Inner Mongolia, and Ningxia.
7 Municipalities directly under the central government are Beijing, Tianjin, Shanghai, and Chongqing.
8 Special Administrative Regions are Hong Kong and Macao.
9 The Legislation Law of the People's Republic of China, adopted at the 3rd Session of the 9th National People's Congress on 15 March 2000.
10 Examples of grassroots organizations are residents' committees in the urban areas and villagers' committees in the rural areas.
11 The Resolution Regarding the Strengthening of Legal Interpretative Work, promulgated by the 19th Session of the Standing Committee of the 5th National People's Congress on 10 June 1981.
12 The NPC Standing Committee sometimes passes a resolution or a decree instead of enacting a law, especially on a matter having only one or a few issues.
13 The Notice Concerning Questions about the Procedures and Powers in the Interpretation of Administrative Regulations, promulgated by the State Council on 3 March 1993 and 10 May 1999.
14 The Several Provisions Concerning Judicial Interpretations, promulgated by the Supreme People's Court on 23 June 1997.
15 The Provisional Regulations on Legal Interpretive Work of the Supreme People's Procuratorate, promulgated by the Supreme People's Procuratorate on 9 December 1996.
16 The Organic Law of the People's Courts of the People's Republic of China, adopted at the 2nd Session of the 5th National People's Congress on 1 July 1979 and amended at the 2nd Session of the Standing Committee of the 6th National People's Congress on 2 September 1983.
17 The Judges Law of the People's Republic of China, adopted at the 12th Session of the Standing Committee of the 8th National People's Congress on 28 February 1995 and amended at the 22nd Session of the 9th National People's Congress on 30 June 2001.

18 See Yan Fa, "Program Designed to Promote Reform of the System of People's Courts," *China Law*, February 2000, pp. 55–8.

19 The Lawyers Law of the People's Republic of China, adopted at the 19th Session of the Standing Committee of the 8th National People's Congress on 15 May 1996 and amended at the 25th Session of the Standing Committee of the 9th National People's Congress on 29 December 2001.

20 The Regulations on the Administration of Representative Offices of Foreign Law Firms in China, promulgated by the State Council on 19 December 2001.

21 See "Retrospect and Prospect: Legal Profession in China," *China Law*, February 2001, pp. 56–9.

2   Business organizations

Having a sound business plan is only the beginning. The plan needs to be put into practice. The available means of doing business vary among different economies. In China, a business idea can be materialized in various forms, depending on the type of ownership. For decades, there were virtually only two kinds of business entities in China – state-owned enterprises and collectively owned enterprises – because China had a command economy and private property rights were not recognized. However, as China has adopted various economic reforms and embarked on developing a socialist market economy, gradually other types of business entities have emerged.

At the early stage of reform, the Chinese government allowed individuals to become *getigongshanghu* (个体工商户). A *getigongshanghu*, which literally means an individual industrial or commercial household and is thus akin to an entrepreneur, was permitted to engage in certain types of business activities with the assistance of his or her household. Subsequently, individuals were allowed to employ a few workers and engage in a larger scope of permissible business activities. Nevertheless, the private economy did not prosper because, absent formal recognition, private enterprises encountered difficulties in securing approvals, loans, raw materials, etc. In 1988, private enterprises were formally recognized with the passage of the Provisional Regulations on Private Enterprises.[1] According to these regulations, a private enterprise (私营企业) is a for-profit economic organization having private ownership and employing eight or more workers. Moreover, certain categories of individuals, such as villagers, the urban unemployed, retired people, and *getigongshanghu*, are authorized to establish private enterprises in the form of a sole proprietorship, a partnership, or a limited liability company.

In the 1990s, with the intensification of economic reforms, including the reformation of state-owned enterprises, the expansion of foreign investment, and the increasing significance of private enterprises in the national economy, China enacted a series of basic laws and accompanying implementation regulations and/or rules, providing detailed guidance on sole proprietorship, partnership, limited liability companies, and companies limited by shares. The promulgation of these legal rules not only established a basic framework for regulating business organizations in China, but also made Chinese business entities more in line with those in other market economies.

At present, business entities in China can be subsumed in three main groups – domestic enterprises; enterprises formed by investors from Hong Kong, Macao, and Taiwan; and enterprises established by foreign investors.[2] In the domestic group, there are state-owned enterprises, collectively owned enterprises, stock cooperative enterprises, jointly operated enterprises, limited liability companies, companies limited by shares, private enterprises, etc. In the Hong Kong-Macao-Taiwan group and the foreign group, there are equity joint ventures, cooperative joint ventures, wholly foreign-owned enterprises, foreign companies limited by shares, etc. In other words, business entities in China are classified in accordance with their respective types of ownership and the nationalities or domiciles of their owners.

Although business organizations in China have various denominations, the available business forms for a private enterprise are sole proprietorship, partnership, limited liability company, and company limited by shares. Moreover, foreign investors will most likely establish a limited liability company or invest in a company limited by shares. Accordingly, this chapter focuses on depicting sole proprietorship, partnership, limited liability companies, and companies limited by shares. Nonetheless, since foreign investors will inevitably deal with other types of business organizations, whether in considering them as business partners or in concluding contracts with them, section 1 provides a succinct account of the state-owned enterprise, collectively owned enterprise, stock cooperative enterprise, and jointly operated enterprise.

1 A state-owned enterprise, a collectively owned enterprise, a stock cooperative enterprise, and a jointly operated enterprise

According to the Law on Industrial Enterprises Owned by the Whole People,[3] an industrial enterprise owned by the whole people (全民所有制工业企业), or in common parlance, a state-owned enterprise (国营企业 or 国有企业), is an economic organization owned by the state and engaged in the socialist production and operation of commodities.[4] Having the status of a legal person,[5] a state-owned enterprise bears civil liability with the property that the state has authorized it to use and manage. Unlike its predecessor, a state-owned enterprise nowadays is to be run in accordance with the principle of separation of ownership and management. That is, although the state is its owner, a state-owned enterprise autonomously makes business decisions, bears responsibility for profits and losses, practices independent accounting, and has the right to possess, use, and dispose of its property.

Generally, the management of a state-owned enterprise is effected through the implementation of the *chengbao* (承包) or *zulin* (租赁) responsibility system. In the *chengbao* (contracting out) mode, the state-owned enterprise (the contractor) contracts with the relevant government department (the party awarding the contract) to accomplish within the contract term specific goals, including the amount of profit to be remitted, the completion of technical improvement tasks, and the linkage of economic benefits with the total amount of wages. In the *zulin* (leasing) mode, the state-owned enterprise (the lessee) signs a lease with the relevant governmental unit (the lessor) for three to five years. During the lease term, the lessee is to reach the annual business target and to remit rents to the lessor.

In either the contract or lease case, the key player is the "operator of the enterprise," who can be an individual, a group, or another enterprise. If the "operator of the enterprise" is an individual, he or she will be the enterprise director. If the "operator of the enterprise" is a group or another enterprise, it will appoint or dispatch the enterprise director. Under the director responsibility system, the enterprise director is the legal representative of the enterprise, and with the assistance of a management committee, administers the enterprise's operations. Basically, a state-owned enterprise may engage in any business activities within its approved and registered scope of operations.

On the other hand, the Regulations on Collectively Owned Enterprises in Cities and Towns[6] define a collectively owned enterprise (集体企业) as a socialist economic organization, the property of which belongs to the working people and in which the principles of joint labor and distribution according to work are implemented. Since a collectively owned enterprise is a legal person, it bears civil liability with its property. As regards management, a collectively owned enterprise practices "democratic management," that is, the congress of staff and workers is its organ of power, electing and recalling managerial personnel, as well as making decisions on important operations issues. However, a collectively owned enterprise also implements the director responsibility system. Depending on the ownership structure, the director of a collectively owned enterprise can be elected or recruited by the congress of staff and workers, or appointed and removed by the enterprise's joint economic organization or its department-in-charge.[7] As the legal representative of a collectively owned enterprise, the director can deal with third parties on behalf of the enterprise.

In a similar vein, a stock cooperative enterprise (股份合作企业) is an economic organization in which the staff and workers jointly contribute capital and own its stock, while, at the same time, the enterprise absorbs a certain amount of capital from society at large.[8] Basically, a stock cooperative enterprise makes business decisions autonomously, bears responsibility for profits and losses, practices democratic management, makes distributions according to work, and allots dividends in proportion to the amount of stock. Although the stock cooperative enterprise is designed to promote cooperation among workers, legal rules on stock cooperative enterprises vary among cities, provinces, and economic sectors. When the government has amassed enough experience in the stock cooperative enterprise, a national law or regulation will probably be enacted to provide more uniform and detailed guidance.

Finally, a jointly operated enterprise (联营企业) is an economic organization in which two or more legal-person enterprises (those engaged in for-profit activities) or legal-person institutions (those engaged in nonprofit activities) have the same or different types of ownership jointly invested according to the principles of voluntaries, equity, and mutual benefit.[9] Currently, jointly operated enterprises can be divided into four groups: state, collective, state-collective, and others. In the state group, state-owned enterprises form jointly operated enterprises with other state-owned enterprises. In the collective group, collectively owned enterprises form jointly operated enterprises with other collectively owned enterprises. In the state-collective group, state-owned enterprises form jointly operated enterprises with collectively owned enterprises. In the "others" group, a state-owned enterprise forms a jointly operated enterprise with a private enterprise; a collectively owned enterprise forms a jointly operated enterprise with a private enterprise; or a jointly operated enterprise is formed among a state-owned, a collectively owned, and a private enterprise.

2 A sole proprietorship

As defined in the Sole Proprietorship Law,[10] a sole proprietorship (个人独资企业) is an economic entity established within China, the capital of which is contributed by a natural person and the property of which is owned by the sole proprietor, who bears unlimited liability for the debts of the enterprise to the extent of his or her personal property. The Sole Proprietorship Law, together with the Measures on the Administration of Registration of Sole Proprietorships,[11] outlines the formation, rights and liabilities, and dissolution of a sole proprietorship. Nonetheless, the Sole Proprietorship Law does not apply to a wholly foreign-owned enterprise, which will be discussed in Chapter 3.

Formation

To establish a sole proprietorship, the following requirements must be met. First, the investor is a natural person. Second, the enterprise has a lawful name. Third, there exists the capital as declared by the investor. Fourth, the enterprise has a fixed production or operation place as well as the necessary conditions for production and operation. Fifth, the enterprise has the necessary personnel.

Procedurally, the investor or its authorized agent should submit an application, together with proofs of the identity of the investor and of the enterprise's production and operation site, to the Administration for Industry and Commerce (AIC) of the place where the sole proprietorship will be located. If an agent is appointed to file the application, the agent should also produce the power of attorney (i.e. document indicating authorization) and proof of its legality. If the business of the sole proprietorship requires government approval(s), the approval document(s) issued by the relevant department(s) should also be submitted. On the application form, the following items should be clearly stated:

1   the name and domicile of the enterprise;
2   the name and residence of the investor;
3   the amount and form of capital contribution; and
4   the scope of business.

If the necessary documents are in order, the local AIC will register the sole proprietorship and issue a business license within 15 days of the receipt of the application. If registration is denied, the AIC will provide a written response together with the reasons.

The date of issue of the business license is the establishment date of the sole proprietorship. The sole proprietor cannot engage in any business activities prior to the issue of the business license. The principal place of business of a sole proprietorship is its domicile. If the sole proprietorship wants to establish a branch, the sole proprietor or its agent should apply for registration with the AIC of the place where the branch will be located. Within 15 days of the registration of the branch, the sole proprietor must report the registration to the AIC that has jurisdiction over the sole proprietorship, namely, the original AIC, for the record.

During its existence, if there are any changes in registration items, such as change of enterprise name, revision of the scope of business, or the modification of the form of capital contribution, the sole proprietorship should apply to the AIC for change of registration within 15 days of its decision to change. The AIC will issue either a new business license or a notice of change of registration, or it will disapprove the requested change. A sole proprietorship is subject to an annual review by the AIC. If a sole proprietorship, without legitimate reasons, does not start business within six months of its establishment, or ceases operations for six or more consecutive months, its business license will be revoked.

Rights and liabilities

Fist and foremost, the sole proprietor has ownership rights over the property of the enterprise, which can be transferred or inherited. The sole proprietor can self-manage the business, or he or she can authorize or hire someone with the capacity to engage in civil acts to run the business. In appointing or hiring someone to manage the business, the sole proprietor must sign a written contract with the agent or employee, detailing the entrusted matters and the scope of authorization. Any restriction placed by the sole proprietor on the power of the agent or employee cannot be used as a defense against a third party in good faith. Correspondingly, the agent or employee must act in good faith and with due diligence. Moreover, the sole proprietorship may borrow loans, acquire land use rights, and enjoy other rights provided by laws and administrative regulations.

At the same time, the sole proprietor bears unlimited liability for the debts of the enterprise to the extent of his or her personal property. If, at the time of application, the sole proprietorship explicitly declares any property jointly owned by his or her family as capital contribution, he or she will bear unlimited liability to the extent of such property. In addition, the sole proprietorship must make social security contributions for its staff and workers and pay taxes in accordance with the law.

Dissolution and liquidation

A sole proprietorship will dissolve if:

1   the investor decides to dissolve;
2   the investor died or is declared dead, and there are no heirs or the heirs have relinquished inheritance;
3   its business license has been revoked in accordance with the law; or
4   any other circumstances prescribed by laws and administrative regulations have occurred.

In dissolving a sole proprietorship, the investor can self-liquidate its assets, or the creditors can apply to the people's court for a designated liquidator.

Upon the dissolution of the sole proprietorship, the investor is still liable for the debts incurred during its existence. However, if the creditors do not assert claims within five years of the dissolution, the sole proprietor's liabilities will be eliminated. In addition, the creditors shall be paid in the following order of priority: unpaid wages and social security premiums, unpaid taxes, and other debts. The sole proprietor cannot transfer or conceal the property of the sole proprietorship before its debts are paid off. If the assets of the sole proprietorship cannot fully satisfy its liabilities, the sole proprietor shall use his or her other personal property to pay off the balance. After the sole proprietorship has been liquidated, the sole proprietor or the designated liquidator should prepare a liquidation report and apply for cancellation of registration within 15 days.

To apply for cancellation of registration, the sole proprietor should turn in the business license and submit an application form signed by the sole proprietor or the liquidator; the liquidation report signed by the sole proprietor or the liquidator; and other documents as required by the State Administration for Industry and Commerce. The sole proprietorship terminates upon the cancellation of registration.

3 A partnership

According to the Partnership Law,[12] a partnership (合伙企业) is a profit-making organization wherein the partners have concluded a partnership agreement; jointly manage the business, contribute capital, share profits, and bear risks; and jointly and severally bear unlimited liability for the debts of the enterprise. Coupled with the Measures on the Administration of Registration of Partnerships,[13] the Partnership Law provides the basic framework for operating a partnership in China.

Formation

For the establishment of a partnership, the following requirements must be met. First, there are two or more partners, both/all of whom bear unlimited liability in accordance with the law. Second, there is a written partnership agreement. Third, there is the capital actually contributed by each partner. Fourth, the enterprise has a name. Fifth, the enterprise has an operation site and the necessary conditions for running the partnership. Specifically, the partners must be persons having full capacity to engage in civil acts, and they can make capital contributions in the forms of cash, tangible goods, land use rights, intellectual property, service, and other proprietary rights.

To apply for registration of establishment, a representative of, or an agent appointed by, all the partners shall submit the following documents to the AIC of the place where the partnership will be located:

1   the application for registration signed by all the partners;
2   proof of identity of all the partners;
3   the power of attorney;
4   the partnership agreement;
5   proof of ownership of the capital contributions;
6   proof of the operation site; and
7   any other required documents.

If the business of the partnership requires government approval(s), the approval document(s) issued by the relevant department(s) should also be submitted. If one or more partners are entrusted with the execution of partnership affairs, the power of attorney should also be presented. The local AIC will approve the application, register the partnership, and issue a business license within 30 days of the receipt of the application. If registration is denied, the AIC will provide a written response together with the reasons.

The date of issue of the business license is the establishment date of the partnership. The partners cannot engage in any business activities prior to the issue of the business license. If the partnership wants to establish a branch, it should apply to the AIC of the place where the branch will be located for registration and issue of a business license. Within the term of the partnership, if there are any changes in registration, such as admission of a new partner, withdrawal of a partner, or revision of the partnership agreement, the partnership should apply to the AIC for change of registration within 15 days of the decision to change or the occurrence of the event. In any event, a partnership is subject to an annual review by the AIC.

A partnership agreement

A partnership agreement must be in writing and contain the following items:

1 the name of the partnership and its principal place of business;
2 the objective of the partnership and its scope of business;
3 the names and domiciles of the partners;
4 the form, amount, and time limit of capital contribution by each partner;
5 the method for distributing profits and allocating losses;
6 the execution of the partnership business;
7 joining of and withdrawal from the partnership;
8 the dissolution and liquidation of the partnership; and
9 liabilities in the case of breach.

In addition, a partnership agreement may stipulate the duration of the partnership and dispute resolution mechanisms. Nonetheless, a partnership agreement may be amended or supplemented only if all the partners have consented to do so.

Rights and liabilities

During the partnership, capital contributions made by the partners and profits obtained in the name of the partnership are the property of the partnership, which shall be jointly managed and used by the partners. More-over, the partners share profits and losses in accordance with the ratio stipu-lated in the partnership agreement. If the partners fail to stipulate the ratio, profits and losses will be shared equally among them. Nevertheless, the partnership agreement should not provide that all profits will be distributed to certain partners, or that certain partners will bear all losses. Within the term of the partnership, the partners may, based on the partnership agree-ment or their unanimous decision, increase the capital in order to expand operations or cover losses.

The partners may jointly execute, or appoint one or more partners to conduct, partnership affairs. In dealing with third parties, the managing partner(s) represent(s) the partnership. The non-managing partners, how-ever, have the rights to supervise the managing partner(s) and to examine the partnership's state of affairs. Indeed, every partner has the right to inspect the partnership books in order to understand the operating and financial conditions of the partnership. However, any restrictions imposed on the partners in connection with the execution of partnership affairs or representation of the partnership cannot be used as defenses against a third party who acts in good faith and is unaware of the restriction.

On the other hand, the partnership agreement may provide, or all the partners may decide, that the partners shall execute partnership affairs sep-arately. In that case, a partner may object to another partner's execution of a partnership affair, and the execution of such affair will be suspended upon objection. Moreover, the partners may unanimously consent to hire someone to manage the partnership. If the manager has acted beyond the scope of authorization or has caused losses to the partnership either willfully or due to gross negligence, he or she will be civilly liable to the partnership.

The partnership must first pay its debts with all of its assets. If the partnership property is not sufficient to pay the mature debts, the partners will be jointly and severally liable. Having paid the debts, a partner may seek indemnification from other partners for any amount exceeding his or her proportion as stipulated in the partnership agreement. Individually, a partner may not, either on his or her own or in cooperation with others, engage in any competitive activities against the partnership. Moreover, a partner may not conduct any business transactions with the partnership. Indeed, the creditor of any partner may not offset its debts owed to the partnership by its claim against the partner. Similarly, the creditor of any partner may not subrogate for the partner to exercise his or her rights in the partnership.

Admission and withdrawal

A partner may transfer his or her partnership interest, in whole or in part, to a third party with the consent of all other partners. Partners other than the assignor have the preemptive right to purchase the partnership interest under the same conditions. In addition, the admission of a new partner requires the consent of all the partners and the conclusion of a written admission agreement. The new partner enjoys rights and bears liabilities equally with the original partners, unless the admission agreement provides otherwise. The new partner is also jointly and severally liable for the debts incurred by the partnership prior to his or her admission.

If the partnership has a specific duration, a partner may withdraw under one of the following circumstances:

1   a ground for withdrawal as stipulated in the partnership agreement has arisen;
2   the withdrawal is consented by all the partners;
3   an event has occurred, rendering the partner's continuous participation in the partnership difficult; or
4   other partners have seriously breached their contractual duties.

If the partnership does not specify a term, a partner may withdraw if the withdrawal will not adversely affect the partnership and the partner has given a 30-day advance notice. If a partner unilaterally withdraws without giving the advance notice and in the absence of the aforementioned circumstances, the withdrawing partner shall compensate the other partners for any losses sustained.

Additionally, a partner must withdraw under one of the following circumstances:

1 the partner is dead or judicially declared dead;
2 the partner is declared to be without capacity to engage in civil acts;
3 the partner becomes insolvent; or
4 the partner's interest in the partnership has been attached by the court.

However, the legal heir of a deceased partner may, as provided in the partnership agreement or with the consent of all the partners, become a partner as of the date of succession. Furthermore, a pledge of partnership interest without the consent of all other partners is invalid and, thus, will be treated as a withdrawal from the partnership.

At the time of withdrawal, the other partners should conduct settlement with the withdrawing partner in light of the conditions of the partnership business. The other partners shall, in accordance with the partnership agreement or based on the decision of all the partners, return to the withdrawing partner his or her partnership share in cash or in kind. If the assets of the partnership are less than its liabilities at the time of withdrawal, the withdrawing partner shall share losses with other partners. Moreover, the withdrawing partner is jointly and severally liable for the debts of the partnership incurred prior to his or her withdrawal.

Dissolution and liquidation

A partnership will be dissolved under one of the following circumstances:

1 the partnership term has expired and the partners are unwilling to continue its operations;
2 a cause for dissolution as stipulated in the partnership agreement has occurred;
3 all the partners decide to dissolve the partnership;
4 the number of partners falls below the legal requirement;
5 the objective of the partnership has been achieved or cannot be reached;
6 the business license of the partnership is revoked in accordance with the law; or
7 any other reason as prescribed by laws and administrative regulations has arisen.

Upon dissolution of the partnership, the partners should conduct liquidation and inform the creditors by notice or public announcement. All the partners should serve as liquidators. However, if all the partners are unable to serve as liquidators, a majority of the partners may agree, within 15 days of the dissolution, that one or more partners, or a third party, will be designated or appointed as liquidator(s). If no liquidator is appointed within the 15 days, the partners or other interested persons may petition the people's court for a designated liquidator. The liquidator(s):

1   separately prepares a balance sheet and a schedule of the partnership's assets;
2   handles any unsettled affairs related to liquidation;
3   pays all taxes due;
4   sorts out the partnership's credits and debts;
5   disposes of the partnership's residuary property; and
6   participates in civil lawsuits on behalf of the partnership.

Prior to liquidation, the partners cannot request the division of partnership property, except if otherwise provided in the Partnership Law. Moreover, if the partners presumptuously transfer or dispose of any partnership property prior to liquidation, the partnership cannot assert such transfer or disposition as a defense against a third party who acts in good faith and has no knowledge of the unauthorized act. After liquidation and payment of the related expenses, the assets of the partnership shall be distributed in the following order: unpaid wages and social security premiums, unpaid taxes, debts, and return of the partners' capital contributions. If there is any surplus after these payments, it shall be distributed in accordance with the ratio stipulated in the partnership agreement or equally in the absence of stipulation. After the dissolution of the partnership, the partners will still be jointly and severally liable for the debts incurred during the existence of the partnership. However, if the creditors do not assert claims within five years of the dissolution, the partners' liabilities will be eliminated.

Together with the application for cancellation of registration, a liquidation report with the signatures and seals of the partners should be filed with the local AIC within 15 days of the liquidation. At the same time, the partnership should return its business license and submit any other documents required by the AIC. Once the registration of the partnership is cancelled, the partnership will cease to exist.

4 A limited liability company and a company limited by shares

Having embarked on developing a socialist market economy, China enacted its Company Law in 1993.[14] The Company Law and its accompanying regulations, such as the Regulations on the Administration of Registration of Companies,[15] the Provisional Rules on the Administration of Registration of Corporate Registered Capital,[16] and the Rules on Several Issues Regarding the Registration of Companies,[17] provide the basic framework for regulating companies in China. Nonetheless, the Company Law states that if the laws on Sino-foreign equity joint ventures, Sino-foreign cooperative joint ventures, and wholly foreign-owned enterprises, which will be discussed in

Chapter 3, provide otherwise, the provisions of such laws will apply. Thus, in establishing business entities in China, foreign investors should consult the Company Law in conjunction with the relevant laws on foreign investment enterprises.

At present, China allows two types of companies: limited liability companies (有限责任公司) and companies limited by shares (股份有限公司), both of which are legal-person enterprises. In a limited liability company, each shareholder is liable to the company to the extent of the amount of its capital contribution, while the company is liable for its debts to the extent of all of its assets. The shareholders are also entitled to receive dividends in proportion to their respective capital contributions. When the company wants to increase its capital, the shareholders have a preemptive right to make contributions. Besides, the shareholders may also transfer, in whole or in part, their capital contributions among themselves. However, to transfer its shares to a third party, a shareholder must obtain the consent of more than half of the other shareholders, and the other shareholders have a preemptive right to purchase the shares on the same terms.

In a company limited by shares, which has also been translated as a joint stock company, the entire capital is divided into shares of equal value. Each shareholder is liable to the company to the extent of the number of shares it holds, while the company is liable for its debts to the extent of all of its assets. Except for those shares held by incumbent directors, supervisors, and managers; or those shares held by the promoters within three years of the founding of the company, the shares of a company limited by shares are freely assignable. However, a company limited by shares may not repurchase its own shares except in the case of merger or for the purpose of reducing capital through cancellation of shares.

As China intensifies its reform of state-owned enterprises, an increasing number of state-owned enterprises have been converted into wholly state-owned limited liability companies or state-controlled companies. Wholly state-owned limited liability companies are those established by investment organs or government departments authorized by the state. In a state-controlled company, whether it is a limited liability company or company limited by shares, the state is the majority shareholder. Since the focus of this book is on foreign direct investment, the following discussion will not highlight those provisions specifically applicable to wholly state-owned limited liability companies or state-owned companies.

Requirements

To establish a limited liability company or a company limited by shares, the investors must satisfy the following requirements. First, the number of shareholders or promoters should meet the legal requirement. For a limited liability company, there must be two to fifty shareholders, except for a wholly state-owned limited liability company of which the state is only the shareholder.

For a company limited by shares, there is no ceiling on the number of shareholders. However, there must be at least five promoters, and more than half of them must be domiciled in China, regardless of whether the company is to be established by means of sponsorship or subscription. In the case of sponsorship, the promoters offer to buy all the shares to be issued by the company. In the case of subscription, the promoters subscribe to 35 percent of the shares and the public subscribes to the remainder.

Second, the capital contributed by the shareholders or the capital paid by the promoters and from public subscription should meet the minimum amount required by law. If the investors want to establish a limited liability company, the minimum amount will depend on the nature of its business. For a manufacturing company, the minimum amount is RMB 500,000; for a wholesaler of commodities, RMB 500,000; for a commercial retailer, RMB 300,000; and for a company engaged in the development of science and technology, consultancy, or services, RMB 100,000. For limited liability companies in specially designated industries, higher minimum amounts of registered capital are prescribed in separate laws and regulations. The shareholders may contribute capital in the form of cash, tangible goods, industrial property rights, non-patented technologies, and land use rights. However, capital contributions in the form of industrial property rights and non-patented technologies cannot exceed 20 percent of the registered capital, except otherwise specified by the state in the case of high and new technologies. The value of contributions other than cash must be properly appraised. On the other hand, the minimum amount of registered capital for a company limited by shares is RMB 10 million. Higher minimum amounts of registered capital may be prescribed in separate laws and regulations. The promoters may pay cash, make in-kind contributions, or transfer industrial property rights, non-patented technologies, and land use rights. Nonetheless, capital contributions in the form of industrial property rights and non-patented technologies cannot exceed 20 percent of the registered capital.

Third, to establish a limited liability company, the shareholders should have jointly formulated the articles of association. In a company limited by shares, the articles of association formulated by the promoters should have been adopted by the founding meeting. Fourth, the company should have a name and have set up an organizational structure in compliance with the requirements for establishing a limited liability company or a company limited by shares. Fifth, there should be a fixed production and operation site and the necessary conditions for production and operations. Sixth, in the case of a company limited by shares, the issue of shares and related preparatory work should conform to the requirements of law.

Articles of association

Basically, the articles of association of a company contain provisions required by the Company Law and those agreed upon voluntarily by the shareholders. In the case of a limited liability company, the articles of association must clearly state:

1 the name and domicile of the company;
2 the business scope of the company;
3 the registered capital of the company;
4 the names or titles of the shareholders;
5 the rights and obligations of the shareholders;
6 the form and amount of capital contributions;
7 the conditions for transferring capital contributions;
8 the organs of the company, the way of establishing them, and their powers and rules of procedure;
9 the legal representative of the company;
10 the grounds for dissolution and the means for liquidation; and
11 any other matters which the shareholders consider it necessary to provide.

In a similar fashion, the articles of association of a company limited by shares must clearly provide:

1 the name and domicile of the company;
2 the business scope of the company;
3 the way of establishing the company;
4 the total number of shares, par value per share, and registered capital of the company;
5 the names or titles of the promoters and the number of shares subscribed by them;
6 the rights and obligations of the shareholders;
7 the composition, powers, term of office, and rules of procedure of the board of directors;
8 the legal representative of the company;
9 the composition, powers, term of office, and rules of procedure of the board of supervisors;
10 the means of distributing profits;
11 the grounds for dissolution and the means for liquidation;
12 the method of issuing company notices and announcements; and
13 any other matters which the shareholders consider it necessary to provide.

• *Registration procedure*

To establish a company, a representative selected, or an agent jointly appointed, by the shareholders or the promoters, must file an application for pre-approval of the company's name with the designated AIC.[18] Within 10 days of the receipt of the application, the AIC must approve or disapprove the name, and, in the case of approval, issue a notice on the pre-approval of the company name. For companies whose establishment or scope of business must be approved in accordance with laws and administrative regulations, they shall submit their applications for approval in the pre-approved name of the company.

If the shareholders of a limited liability company make capital contributions in the form of cash, they should deposit the money into a temporary bank account. For contributions in the form of tangible goods, industrial property rights, and land use rights, the shareholders shall go through the formalities of assignment in accordance with the law. If the shareholders contribute non-patented technologies, they shall conclude technology-transfer contracts with the company. After all the shareholders have made their capital contributions, a legally authorized capital-examination organ, namely, a duly registered accounting or audit firm, must verify the contributions and produce a certificate of capital verification.

To apply for registration of establishment, a representative selected, or an agent jointly appointed, by the shareholders shall submit the following documents to the designated AIC:

1   an application form signed by the chairperson of the board of directors;
2   the power of attorney of the representative or agent;
3   the articles of association;
4   the certificate of capital verification;
5   proof of the legal-person status or natural-person identity of the shareholders;
6   documents listing the names and domiciles of the directors, supervisors, and managers, and proof of their appointment or election;
7   proof of the employment and identity of the legal representative;
8   the notice of the pre-approval of the company name; and
9   proof of the domicile of the company.

However, if prior examination and approval by the relevant government organ(s) are required, the company must obtain the necessary approval(s) and, within 90 days, submit the application for registration together with the certificate(s) of approval. The date of the issue of the business license is the founding date of the limited liability company.

Conversely, the establishment of a company limited by shares requires the prior approval of a government department authorized by the State Council or of the provincial-level government.[19] Besides, when laws and administrative regulations require approval of the company's scope of business, the approval(s) of the relevant government organ(s) must also be obtained. If the company is to be set up by means of sponsorship, the promoters should elect the board of directors and board of supervisors after they have paid in full their subscribed shares. Thereafter, the board of directors shall apply, together with the articles of association, the certificate of capital verification, any required certificate(s) of approval, etc., to the designated AIC for registration of the establishment of the company. If the company is to be established by means of subscription, the promoters should obtain approval from the China Securities Regulatory Commission prior to the public offer. Specifically, the promoters should submit the following documents to the Commission:

1   document(s) approving the establishment of the company;
2   the articles of association;
3   the operating budget;
4   the names or titles of the promoters, the number of shares they subscribe, the types of capital contribution, and the certificate of capital verification;
5   the prospectus;
6   the names and address of banks that receive payment on behalf of the company; and
7   the names of the underwriters and the underwriting agreements.

Having secured the approval of the Commission, the promoters can offer the company's shares to the public for subscription. The procedural details for a public offer are discussed in Chapter 8. If the company cannot be established, the promoters will be jointly and severally liable for the refund of the subscribers' payments plus interest at the rate on bank deposits for the corresponding period.

After payments for all the subscribed shares have been made, the promoters must have a registered accounting or audit firm verify the capital contributions and produce a certificate of capital verification. Within 30 days of the issue of the certificate, the promoters shall convene a founding meeting, which is composed of subscribers representing at least half of the total number of shares. At the founding meeting, the attendees shall adopt the articles of association and elect members of the board of directors and the board of supervisors. The board of directors then shall apply for registration of establishment and obtain a business license from the designated AIC within 30 days of the founding meeting.

To support the application, the board of directors should submit:

1   certificate(s) of approval issued by the relevant government organ(s);
2   the minutes of the founding meeting;
3   the articles of association;
4   financial and auditing reports on the preparation for the establishment of the company;
5   certificates of capital verification;
6´ proof of the legal-person status or natural-person identity of the promoters;
7   documents listing the names and domiciles of the directors, supervisors, and managers, and proof of their appointment or election;

8 the name and domicile of the legal representative, and proof of his or
   her employment and identity;
9 the notice of the pre-approval of the company name; and
10 proof of the domicile of the company.

The AIC shall approve or disapprove the registration of a company limited
by shares within 30 days of application. The date of the issue of the business
license is the founding date of the company limited by shares. Upon its
establishment, the company shall make a public announcement. If the company is established by subscription, it must also file a report on the public
offer with the China Securities Regulatory Commission for the record.

The principal place of business of a company is its domicile. Every company is subject to an annual review by the AIC, which determines whether
the company has the qualifications for continuing its operations. If a company, without legitimate reasons, does not commence business within six
months of its establishment, or ceases operations for six or more consecutive months, its business license will be revoked. Moreover, a company may
establish a branch or branches at the time of or after its formation. Since a
branch does not have the status of a legal person, the parent company will
assume the branch's civil liabilities. However, if a company establishes a
subsidiary, the subsidiary itself will independently assume civil liabilities
because it has the status of a legal person. Furthermore, if a company wants
to amend its scope of business, increase or reduce registered capital, merge
with another company, divide the company, establish a branch, or become
bankrupt, or if the company is dissolved, it must apply for change of registration, registration of establishment, or cancellation of registration. In the
case of a company limited by shares, a public announcement must also be
made after the application for change of registration has been approved.

Corporate governance

The governance of a company has several constituent parts. The shareholders'
meeting is the organ of power, and the board of directors is the organ of
decision. The management, which is accountable to the board of directors,
is the organ of operations. As the organ of supervision, the board of supervisors is accountable to the shareholders and oversees the financial affairs of
the company as well as the conduct of directors and managers.

Shareholders

In a limited liability company, the shareholders' meeting is composed of all
the shareholders. There are two types of shareholders' meeting: general and
interim. General meetings must be convened on time in accordance with the
stipulations in the articles of association. Interim meetings may be convened
upon the request of a quarter of the shareholders or one-third of the directors

or supervisors. To convene a shareholders' meeting, the company must notify the shareholders 15 days in advance.

During the shareholders' meeting, shareholders exercise the powers to:

1 decide on the company's business policies and investment plans;
2 elect and replace directors and decide on matters relating to their remuneration;
3 elect and replace supervisors who represent the shareholders and decide on matters relating to their remuneration;
4 examine and approve the reports of the board of directors;
5 examine and approve the reports of the board of supervisors or individual supervisor(s);
6 examine and approve the company's annual financial budgets and final accounts;
7 examine and approve plans for the distribution of profits and recovery of losses;
8 decide on the increase or reduction of registered capital;
9 decide on the issue of corporate bonds;
10 decide on the transfer of capital contribution to a non-shareholder;
11 adopt resolutions on merger, division, change of corporate form, dissolution, liquidation, etc.; and
12 amend the articles of association.

The procedures for deliberation and voting are to be specified in the articles of association. With respect to merger, division, dissolution, amendment of the articles of association, expansion and reduction of the registered capital, and change of corporate form, the votes of at least two-thirds of the shareholders are required.

In a company limited by shares, a general shareholders' meeting must be convened once a year. However, an interim meeting must be convened within two months of any of the following events:

1 the number of directors being less than two-thirds of the legally required number or the number stipulated in the articles of association;
2 losses of the company that have not been recovered amounting to one-third of the company's total share capital;
3 shareholders holding 10 percent or more of the shares requesting a meeting;
4 the board of directors thinking it necessary to convene a meeting; or
5 the board of supervisors proposing that a meeting be convened.

Shareholders must be notified of the matters to be discussed 30 days in advance. If bearer shares have been issued, a public announcement about the matters to be discussed must be made 45 days in advance. In any case, shareholders may appoint proxies to attend the shareholders' meeting.

The shareholders of a company limited by shares exercise the same powers as those of the shareholders in a limited liability company, except for the fact that they do not decide on the transfer of shares to outsiders because shares are freely assignable, but that they make decisions on the issue of new shares. At the shareholders' meeting, shareholders have one vote per share. As a general rule, resolutions are to be adopted by more than half of the attending shareholders' votes.[20] However, regarding merger, division, dissolution, and amendment of the articles of association, at least two-thirds of the attending shareholders' votes are required. If any resolution adopted by the shareholders' meeting violates any laws or administrative regulations, or infringes upon the lawful rights and interests of the shareholders, a shareholder has the right to initiate a lawsuit in the people's court to request that such violation or infringement be ceased.

Board of directors

In a limited liability company, the board of directors should consist of three to thirteen members. The term of office of a director cannot be longer than three years, but the director may serve another term if re-elected. The method of selecting the chairperson and vice-chairperson(s) should be provided in the articles of association. The chairperson of the board is the legal representative of the company, who is to convene and preside over the board's meetings. However, one-third or more directors may also request that a meeting be convened. Notice of a board's meeting should be sent to all directors 10 days in advance. If the company has a relatively small number of shareholders and is on a relatively small scale, it may have one executive director rather than a board of directors. The executive director, who is the legal representative of the company, may concurrently serve as the company's manager.

Being accountable to the shareholders' meeting, the board of directors:

1   is responsible for convening shareholders' meetings and reporting its work to the shareholders;
2   implements resolutions of the shareholders' meeting;
3   decides on the company's business and investment plans;
4   formulates the company's annual financial budgets and final accounts;
5   formulates plans for distributing profits and recovering losses;
6   formulates plans for the expansion and reduction of registered capital;
7   drafts plans for the company's merger, division, change of corporate form, and dissolution;
8   decides on the company's internal management structure;
9   appoints or dismisses the company's general manager, appoints or dismisses deputy managers and financial officers pursuant to the general manager's nominations, and decides on their remuneration; and
10   formulates the company's basic management system.

In a company limited by shares, the board of directors should consist of five to nineteen members. The term of office of a director cannot be longer than three years, but the director may serve another term if re-elected. The chairperson, who is the legal representative of the company, and the vice-chairperson(s) are to be elected by the votes of more than half of all the directors. The board must meet at least twice a year, and notice of a board's meeting must be sent to all the directors 10 days in advance. For interim meetings, the board of directors may provide for a different means and time limit for notification. A board's meeting can be held only if half or more of all the directors are present.

The powers of the board of directors in a company limited by shares are the same as those of the board of directors in a limited liability company, except that the former also formulates plans for the issue of company bonds but does not draft plans for change of corporate form. It is because a company limited by shares may raise capital in the securities market, and a limited liability company can be converted into a company limited by shares, but not vice versa. Any resolution requires the affirmative votes of more than half of all the directors. If any resolution adopted by the board of directors violates any laws or administrative regulations, or infringes upon the lawful rights and interests of the shareholders, a shareholder has the right to initiate a lawsuit in the people's court to request that such violation or infringement be ceased. If any resolution adopted by the board of directors violates any laws, administrative regulations, or the articles of association, and makes the company sustain serious losses, the directors who voted affirmatively are liable to the company. If a director explicitly objected to the resolution and such objection was recorded in the minutes, such director would not be liable.

Board of supervisors

Large limited liability companies and all companies limited by shares must have a board of supervisors consisting of three or more members. If a limited liability company is small, it may have one or two supervisors instead of a full board. The board of supervisors is composed of representatives of shareholders and representatives of staff and workers. Directors, managers, and financial officers may not serve concurrently as supervisors. The term of office of a supervisor is three years, but the supervisor may serve another term if re-elected.

The board of supervisors is responsible for:

1   checking on the financial affairs of the company;
2   supervising the acts of directors and the general manager that may violate laws, regulations, and the articles of association while performing their corporate duties;
3   requesting rectification from directors and the general manager for any acts that are damaging to the company's interests;

4   proposing that interim meetings of shareholders be convened; and
5   any other powers provided by the articles of association.

Managers

The general manager of both a limited liability company and a company limited by shares:

1   takes charge of the company's production, operations, and management, and organizes the implementation of the resolutions of the board of directors;
2   organizes the implementation of the company's annual business and investment plans;
3   drafts plans for establishing the company's internal management structure;
4   drafts the company's basic management system;
5   formulates the company's specific regulations and rules;
6   recommends the appointment or dismissal of deputy managers and financial officers;
7   appoints or dismisses managerial personnel other than those who should be appointed or dismissed by the board of directors; and
8   has any other powers conferred by the articles of association or the board of directors.

In a company limited by shares, the board of directors may allow a director to serve concurrently as the general manager.

Fiduciary duties

Directors, supervisors, and managers must abide by the articles of association, faithfully perform their duties, safeguard the company's interests, and not exploit their posts and powers to advance their personal interests. In addition, they must not disclose the company's secrets except in accordance with the law or with the consent of the shareholders' meeting. If they violate laws, administrative regulations, or the articles of association and cause losses to the company, they will have to make reparations. Furthermore, directors and managers must not misappropriate company funds or loan such funds to other people. They must not open bank accounts in their own names or the names of other individuals with the company's assets. Likewise, they must not use the company's assets as collateral for the debts of shareholders or other individuals. They must not engage in any business similar to that of the company or activities damaging to the company's interests, either on their own or on behalf of others. The proceeds derived from such business or activities shall belong to the company. What is more, they cannot engage in self-dealing, that is, they cannot conclude contracts or conduct transactions with the company, unless the articles of association provide otherwise or with the consent of shareholders. Nonetheless, at present, there are no explicit provisions protecting the interests of minority shareholders against majority shareholders.

Financial affairs

At the end of each fiscal year, a company must prepare a financial statement and have it examined and verified in accordance with the law. A limited liability company shall deliver its financial statement to the shareholders within the time period specified in the articles of association. A company limited by shares shall place its financial statement at the company for inspection by the shareholders at least 20 days before the shareholders' annual general meeting. A company limited by shares established by means of subscription shall make its financial statement public.

While distributing its annual after-tax profits, a company must allocate 10 percent to the statutorily required common reserve fund, and 5 to 10 percent to the statutorily required common welfare fund. The common reserve fund is to be used for covering losses, expanding production and operations, or increasing capital. The common welfare fund is to be used for the collective welfare of the staff and workers. When the balance in the common reserve fund is 50 percent or more of its registered capital, the company does not need to make further allocations. If the common reserve fund is not sufficient to compensate for the previous year's losses, the current year's profits should be used to make up for the losses before allocations are made to the common reserve and common welfare funds. After the company has made up for its losses and allocated to the common reserve and common welfare funds, the residual profits should be distributed to the shareholders in proportion to their capital contributions or to the number of shares they hold. When the shareholders of a company limited by shares resolve to convert the common reserve fund into capital, the company may distribute new shares or increase the par value of each share. In such a case, the balance of the common reserve fund must not be less than 25 percent of the registered capital.

When a company wants to reduce its registered capital, it must prepare a balance sheet and a schedule of assets. The company must inform its creditors within 10 days of its decision to reduce capital and make a public announcement in a newspaper at least three times within 30 days of the decision. Within 30 days of the receipt of the notification, or within 90 days of the first public announcement, the creditors have the right to demand that the company pay off its debts or provide appropriate guarantee. The company must not reduce its registered capital below the statutory minimum amount. When a limited liability company increases its registered capital by receiving new contributions from its shareholders, or when a company limited by shares issues new shares to increase its registered capital, the relevant procedural provisions on the payment of capital contributions for the establishment of a limited liability company, or on the subscription of shares for the establishment of a company limited by shares, should be followed.

Furthermore, a company may invest in other limited liability companies or companies limited by shares. The investing company will be liable to the invested company to the extent of the amount of capital contribution. Where a company invests in other companies, the aggregate amount of its investment cannot exceed 50 percent of its net assets, except for investment companies and holding companies designated by the State Council. However, the 50 percent limit does not apply to any increase in the capital of the invested companies as a result of the conversion of profits of these companies into capital.

Merger and division

The shareholders' meeting decides on the merger or division of a company. For a company limited by shares, its merger or division requires the approval of the government department authorized by the State Council or of the provincial-level government. The merger of two companies may be done by means of absorption or establishment of a new company. Where one company absorbs another company, the absorbed company is dissolved. Where two or more companies merge into one company, all the participating companies are dissolved. The parties to a merger must conclude a merger agreement and prepare a balance sheet and a schedule of assets. The companies must notify their creditors within 10 days of the decision to merge and make a public announcement in a newspaper at least three times within 30 days of the decision. Within 30 days of the receipt of the notification, or within 90 days of the first public announcement, the creditors have the right to demand that the company pay off its debts or provide appropriate guarantee. If the debts are not paid off or no guarantee is provided, the merger will not be allowed. The respective credits and debts of the participating companies are to be assumed by the company that survives the merger or the newly established company.

When a company is divided, it must prepare a balance sheet and a schedule of assets. The company must inform the creditors within 10 days of its decision to divide and make a public announcement in a newspaper at least three times within 30 days of the decision. Within 30 days of the receipt of the notification, or within 90 days of the first public announcement, the creditors have the right to demand that the company pay off its debts or provide appropriate guarantee. If the debts are not paid off or no guarantee is provided, the company will not be allowed to divide. Any pre-division debts are to be assumed by the post-division companies in accordance with the relevant agreement.

Dissolution and liquidation

A company may be dissolved if:

1   its term has expired or one of the grounds for dissolution as provided in the articles of association has occurred;
2   the shareholders adopt a resolution to dissolve it; or
3   dissolution becomes necessary upon its merger or division.

In addition, a company must be dissolved if it is declared bankrupt by a people's court or is closed down due to violation of laws or administrative regulations. When a company is dissolved, a liquidation committee must be set up. If the company is dissolved due to the expiration of its term or in accordance with the articles of association or the shareholders' resolution, a liquidation committee should be set up within 15 days of its dissolution. If the company is dissolved as a result of bankruptcy, the people's court will organize the shareholders, relevant organs, and appropriate professionals to establish a liquidation committee. If the company is closed down due to violation of laws or administrative regulations and, thus, must be dissolved, the organ-in-charge shall organize the shareholders, relevant organs, and appropriate professionals to form a liquidation committee.

The liquidation committee of a limited liability company is composed of its shareholders. The members of the liquidation committee of a company limited by shares are to be determined by the shareholders' meeting. The liquidation committee:

1   checks on the company's property and makes a balance sheet and a schedule of assets;
2   sends notices to the company's creditors or makes a public announcement;
3   completes the company's unfinished business;
4   pays the taxes due;
5   sorts out the credits and debts of the company;
6   disposes of residual property after the company has paid off its debts; and
7   represents the company in civil proceedings.

The liquidation committee must inform the creditors within 10 days of its establishment or make a public announcement in a newspaper at least three times within 60 days of its establishment. Within 30 days of the receipt of the notification, or within 90 days of the first public announcement, the creditors must submit their claims to the liquidation committee.

Having prepared a balance sheet and a schedule of assets, the liquidation committee shall formulate a liquidation plan and present it to the shareholders' meeting or the organ-in-charge. If the company has sufficient assets to satisfy its debts, it shall pay in the following order: liquidation expenses; wages and labor insurance premiums; unpaid taxes; and debts. If there are any residual assets after these payments have been made, they shall be distributed in proportion to the shareholders' capital contributions or the numbers of shares they hold. If a member of the liquidation committee intentionally or through gross negligence causes the company or its creditors to sustain losses, he or she shall be liable for compensation. If the company's assets are insufficient to satisfy its debts, the liquidation committee shall apply to the people's court for a declaration of bankruptcy. Once the company is declared bankrupt, it shall transfer any matters pertaining to liquidation to the people's court.

When liquidation proceedings are completed, the liquidation committee shall prepare a liquidation report and present it to the shareholders' meeting or the organ-in-charge for confirmation. Together with the liquidation report, the company shall apply to the AIC for cancellation of registration and publicly announce the company's termination. Once the application for cancellation of registration is approved, the company ceases to exist.

5 Selected cases

Zhang Zhongshan v. Yan Guoping *(2000)* 民终字第8号, *Supreme People's Court, 24 July 2000*

Facts

Longyao County Automatic Door Factory (hereinafter the factory), located at the Nanbaishe Village, was a small casting enterprise established by Zhang Zhongshan (hereinafter ZZ). In April 1994, ZZ and Yan Guoping (hereinafter YG) verbally agreed to run the factory as a partnership, stipulating that ZZ and YG shared equally (50:50) in the distribution of profits and assumption of risks. In addition, they agreed that ZZ should be responsible for production and daily management, whereas YG would be responsible for sales. During the period of the partnership, Yan Guoan, the brother of YG, was employed as the accountant, while Wang Yongqin, the wife of ZZ, was employed as the cashier. Both of them were responsible for the financial affairs of the partnership.

From the establishment of the partnership, neither party drew any profit, except for their monthly wages. At the end of each year, they distributed profit on the books pursuant to the ratio of 50:50 and reinvested it as capital for next year so as to expand the production. In March 1998, ZZ withdrew from the management of the partnership. From that point, YG was in charge of both production and management of the partnership. Subsequently, disputes arose between ZZ and YG. In September 1998, ZZ filed a lawsuit with the court of first instance, requesting that the court terminate the partnership relationship, distribute the joint property of the partnership in accordance with the law and contractual provisions, and let him own about RMB 5,000,000 worth of assets that should belong to him. In October 1998, ZZ amended his claims on the basis that there were errors in the business report produced by the accountant. ZZ alleged that after auditing the relevant documents relating to the initial investments of the parties, the total amount of investment made by him and YG were RMB 283,809.85 and RMB 36,300, respectively. Therefore, he claimed that the assets of the partnership should be distributed according to the ratio of their capital contribution, that is, more than RMB 7,000,000 worth of assets of the partnership should belong to him.

In August 1998, YG and Yan Guoan, the accountant, were not in the enterprise for objective reasons. Thus, Wang Yongqin controlled the funds in the current account of the partnership for that month. The funds had remained in ZZ's hands since the filing of this lawsuit. The court of first instance decided to have both parties reconcile their accounts in order to clarify this matter; however, ZZ disagreed. According to the report on business operations for the year ended 31 December 1997, which was submitted by ZZ, the capital of the partnership that was actually received was RMB 4,304,602.95, the profits were RMB 3,636,758.55, and the amount to be paid for worker welfare was RMB 59,064.65. The total amount was RMB 8,000,426.15, which YG had already confirmed. Moreover, the balance sheet of the partnership, submitted by YG, showed that the capital of the partnership that was received as of 31 July 1998 was RMB 7,885,861.48, the realized profits from January to July 1998 were RMB 2,170,389.96, and the amount to be paid for worker welfare was RMB 176,496.75. The total amount was RMB 10,232,748.19. At the trial of first instance, both parties agreed that the aforementioned figures should form the basis for calculating the total assets of the partnership. Besides, based on the average profit from January to July 1998, the profits from August to December 1998 were reckoned. Therefore, by the end of 1998, the total amount of assets of the partnership was RMB 11,783,026.69 [10,232,748.19 + (2,170,389.96/7) × 5]. Since both parties agreed to terminate their partnership relationship, but asked to retain the factory and continue its operations, the court of first instance conducted mediation several times, as well as using bidding, but without avail.

The court of first instance found that since the parties jointly ran the factory based on the meeting of their minds and joint investments, their conduct was lawful and their rights to enjoy the assets of the partnership should be protected by law. Although neither party had a written contract in respect of the means, amount, and proportion of their initial investments, the initial investment accounts indicated that both parties had already fulfilled their investment obligations. Prior to the lawsuit, ZZ had announced to the public many times that he was a 50 percent shareholder. In addition, both parties had distributed the profits pursuant to the 50:50 ratio for many years. Hence, there was sufficient evidence to conclude that the parties were to enjoy the assets of the partnership pursuant to the 50:50 ratio.

ZZ claimed that he was cheated by YG, and that since both parties did not make equal amounts of investment, the assets of the partnership should be distributed according to the proportion of their investments. Nonetheless, ZZ could not substantiate his claims with evidence, nor could he prove the causal relationship between the proportion of investment and the proportion of asset distribution. Besides, the time for ZZ to file a lawsuit had already lapsed. Thus, ZZ's claims were untenable and were dismissed. Both parties now requested that the partnership relationship be terminated due to various disputes, but indicated their respective intentions to continue to run the factory. For the sake of fairness, the court of first instance used bidding to solve the problem. However, since ZZ did not agree to the 50:50 ratio for asset distribution, and the parties submitted different conditions during bidding, the method of bidding was futile. Considering both parties' actual ability to run the business and the important impact of the sales of the products upon the existence and development of the partnership, and ensuring that ZZ's legal rights and interests would be adequately protected, the court held that YG could retain and continue to run the factory but must pay ZZ by installments an amount equal to one-half of the assets of the partnership within a reasonable time. This judgment, as the court stated, could adequately protect the legal rights and interests of both parties and facilitate the continuous operation and development of the partnership. Accordingly, the court held as follows:

1   The partnership relationship between ZZ and YG was terminated, and the factory was to be owned and operated by YG.
2   YG had to pay ZZ RMB 5,891,513.345 for ZZ's one-half share in the total assets of the partnership as of the end of 1998. For the period from January 1999 to the effective date of this judgment, YG had to pay ZZ one-half of RMB 310,055.70 (the average monthly profit for 1998) each month. With respect to ZZ's one-half share, YG should pay ZZ RMB 3,500,000 within three months of the effective date of this judgment and the balance within the next two years.
3   ZZ had to return to YG the funds that he drew from the factory during August 1998 within 10 days of the effective date of this judgment.
4   ZZ's other claims were dismissed.

Neither party was satisfied with the judgment of the court of first instance and appealed to the court. ZZ alleged that since the court of first instance did not audit the initial capital contributions and the current total amount of assets of the partnership, the basic facts had not been clearly ascertained. Since YG's investment did not match the required amount, the current total assets could be distributed only in accordance with their respective proportions of investment. In addition, it was obviously unfair, regardless of their respective amounts of investment, to distribute the profits of the partnership pursuant to the 50:50 ratio. Therefore, ZZ sought the reversal of the judgment of the court of first instance, termination of the partnership relationship, permission to continue to operate the factory, re-auditing and reassessment of the initial capital contributions and the current total assets of the partnership, and distribution of the assets of the partnership pursuant to the actual investment proportion.

On the other hand, YG alleged that when the court of first instance determined the assets of the partnership prior to 31 July 1998, it did not consider deducting the tax payable and the fee for worker welfare; thus, these expenses should be subtracted from the total assets. Under the circumstance that the partners did not even know whether the partnership would earn profit or incur loss, the court of first instance flatly determined that the partnership would be profitable and the period of profit was from January 1999 to the effective date of the judgment. Likewise, the court of first instance lacked any legal basis to hold that the average monthly profit was RMB 310,055.70. Therefore, YG requested that the court ascertain the facts and amend the total amount of assets in accordance with the law.

During this trial, ZZ submitted the accounts and vouchers of the partnership for August 1998. YG found that there were many blank items in the vouchers; however, YG was unwilling to confront ZZ in court and to confirm it. YG indicated that only after ZZ returned the RMB 2,300,000 drawn from the partnership during August 1998, would he be able to make available the financial and account statements of the partnership for the months subsequent to September 1998. ZZ disagreed with the view of YG.

Reasoning

Although there was no written partnership agreement between ZZ and YG, both parties acknowledged their partnership relationship. Moreover, other requirements for a partnership were met. Thus, the court affirmed the partnership relationship between ZZ and YG, and held that the accumulated assets of the partnership should be jointly owned by ZZ and YG. Both parties agreed that, during the partnership, they were to share profits and assume risks in accordance with the 50:50 ratio. In practice, they had distributed on the books the profits of the partnership pursuant to such a ratio and reinvested them as capital, on the basis of which they also made the annual financial statements. ZZ had never objected to such arrangement. Hence, there was no basis for ZZ to assert that the profits should be distributed in accordance with their respective proportions of investment.

At the trial of first instance, both parties agreed to use RMB 10,232,748.19 as stated in the financial reports to calculate the total assets of the partnership prior to 31 July 1998. Although ZZ wanted to retract his agreement during this trial, he could not substantiate his request with contrary evidence. Regarding the issue that the court of first instance estimated the profits from August to December 1998 on the basis of the average profit from January to July 1998, because both parties agreed to such calculation during trial, ZZ did not provide the funds of the partnership for August 1998, and YG did not provide the accounts of the partnership after September 1998, the court of first instance made no error.

In respect of YG's objection to the profits after January 1999 estimated by the court of first instance, because YG declared that he had not fabricated the accounts and could not substantiate his objection with contrary evidence, the court did not support him. Concerning YG's claim that tax expenses, etc. should be deducted, as these expenses had not actually been made, and the court handled only the distribution of assets after the termination of the partnership relationship, the parties should pay tax separately in accordance with the relevant regulations. The court of first instance ordered ZZ to return the funds drawn from the partnership during August 1998 to YG, which was beyond the scope of YG's claims, and the amount of the funds was unclear. Thus, the court held that such order should be rectified.

Judgment

According to article 153(1)(i) and (iii) of the Civil Procedure Law,[21] the court held that items 1, 2 and 4 of the judgment of the court of first instance were affirmed and item 3 was reversed.

This judgment was final.

Zhuo Xiaoqin *v.* Li Xianli and Wang Li *(2000)* 一中经终字 第1663号, *Beijing City No. 1 Intermediate People's Court, 26 September 2000*

Facts

On 12 July 1995, Zhuo Xiaoqin, Li Xianli, Wang Li and Gong Zhizhong (hereinafter ZX, LX, WL and GZ, respectively) signed an investment contract to establish Beijing Yishipo Beauty Ltd. (hereinafter YSP). YSP was to be a limited liability company, and its scope of business included beauty services and plastic surgery. The registered capital of YSP was RMB 300,000. ZX was to contribute RMB 50,000; LX, RMB 120,000; WL, RMB 50,000; and GZ, RMB 80,000. The contract stipulated the parties' rights and obligations, such as the sharing of residual assets after the dissolution of YSP and the payments of their respective contributions on time. In addition, the contract stipulated the duration of YSP (20 years), the circumstances under which YSP could be terminated, the organizational and management systems of YSP, financial management, distribution of profits, liabilities for breach, etc. On 11 August 1995, ZX, LX, WL and GZ formulated the articles of association stipulating the scope of business and confirming the shareholder status and the amounts and means of investments of ZX, LX, WL and GZ. Moreover, the shareholders' meeting, the organ of power, had to include all shareholders. Corporate matters, such as the dissolution of YSP, must be adopted at the shareholders' meeting by two-thirds of all the shareholders who had voting rights. The articles of association also stipulated the rights and duties of the shareholders, the requirements for transferring shares, the organization and financial affairs of YSP, distribution of profits, the circumstances under which YSP could be dissolved, etc.

On 22 February 1998, LX, WL and GZ convened an interim shareholders' meeting and adopted a resolution in which they agreed to dissolve YSP. LX, WL and GZ together formed a liquidation team to settle the assets and liabilities of YSP. On 28 April 1998, LX, WL and GZ together signed a liquidation report for YSP with a list of assets. They decided to distribute YSP's residual assets to shareholders in proportion to their investments. ZX's share only amounted to RMB 72,058.90. On 23 May 1998, LX, WL and GZ convened an interim shareholders' meeting and unanimously adopted a liquation report made by the liquidation team. On 2 June 1998, the AIC canceled the registration of YSP and made a public announcement. On 9 August 1998, ZX's father received a notice that ZX was asked to go back to the former address of YSP to obtain his share of the residual assets on 8 August or 9 August 1998. Eventually, ZX did not receive his share. During interrogation, LX, WL and GZ admitted that they unanimously agreed to place ZX's share of YSP's residual assets at the former site of YSP and until now had not given it to ZX. ZX filed a lawsuit against LX and WL, but not against GZ because he had not actually run the business.

The court of first instance found that since ZX, LX, WL and GZ jointly signed the articles of association and established YSP, they lawfully obtained the status of shareholders. LX, WL and GZ convened shareholders' meetings and signed resolutions to dissolve YSP, form the liquidation team, and adopt the liquidation report, which complied with the relevant requirements of the Company Law. Hence, the decisions of the shareholders' meetings were binding upon all shareholders. After YSP had been liquidated, and the liquidation expenses, wages and labor insurance premiums, unpaid taxes and debts had been paid, the residual assets were distributed to all shareholders in proportion to their investments. Since the property of the company became the property of the shareholders, ZX should be able to receive his share in accordance with the liquidation report. ZX's claim was based on both factual and legal grounds and thus should be supported. As members of the liquidation team, LX, WL and GZ did not carry out their duties to give ZX his share to which he was entitled, but instead deprived ZX of his rights to his share. Therefore, they should be jointly and severally liable. Since ZX did not name GZ as a defendant and LX and WL did not raise any objection, the court of first instance did not object either. Alleging that ZX tried to seize YSP's assets without permission, LX and WL refused to give ZX his share to which he was entitled. Since LX and WL could not provide convincing evidence, the court of first instance did not support their claim. As a result, the court of first instance held that within 10 days of the effective date of the judgment, LX had to give ZX RMB 72,058.90, and that WL was jointly and severally liable. LX and WL appealed to the court to have the original judgment reversed and ZX's claim dismissed on the following grounds:

1   While a director and manager of YSP, ZX used his private funds to set up "Beijing Yitonglian Communications and Technology Ltd.," which had the same scope of business as that of YSP. This act violated the relevant provisions of the Company Law, so the board of directors decided to penalize ZX RMB 30,000.
2   ZX seized the assets of YSP without permission and caused the shareholders a loss of RMB 117,086. Therefore, that amount should be deducted from ZX's share.
3   GZ was a necessary party to the lawsuit, but the court of first instance did not add him as a litigant. The omission of GZ as a defendant impaired their interests.
4   While they were trying to produce evidence and prepare to file a counterclaim, the court of first instance had made the judgment hastily and, thus, had impaired their legal rights and interests.

On the other hand, ZX was willing to accept the judgment of the court of first instance because:

1   he denied the facts and reasons of the allegations 1 and 2 of LX and WL;
2   since GZ did not really run the business, he did not name GZ as a defendant; and
3   LX and WL did not raise any counterclaim at the court of first instance.

Reasoning

The court found that ZX, LX, WL and GZ jointly signed the investment contract, formulated the articles of association, established YSP in accordance with the law, and obtained the status of shareholders. In addition, LX, WL and GZ convened the interim shareholders' meetings, signed the resolution to dissolve YSP, formed the liquidation team to conduct liquidation, produced the liquidation report, and confirmed the liquidation report with their signatures. All of these acts were in conformity with the investment contract, the articles of association, and the relevant requirements of the Company Law. Thus, these acts were legally valid. Based on the Company Law, after YSP had been liquidated, and the liquidation expenses, wages and labor insurance premiums, unpaid taxes and debts had been paid, the residual assets should have been distributed to all shareholders in proportion to their investments. Accordingly, ZX had both factual and legal grounds to assert his claim for the share to which he was entitled. As members of the liquidation team, LX, WL and GZ did not carry out their duties to give ZX the share to which he was entitled, thus jointly infringing upon the ownership right of ZX. Hence, they should be jointly and severally liable. With respect to joint and several liability, the creditor had the right to ask one, several or all debtors, simultaneously or consecutively, in whole or in part, to perform their debt obligations. In this case, ZX sued only LX and WL, but not GZ, to which the court did not object. Therefore, the argument of LX and WL that GZ should be added as a joint litigant could not be supported. Furthermore, allegations 1 and 2 of LX and WL were not related to this case and should be separately handled. In sum, the appeal of LX and WL had no grounds. The judgment of the original court was based on clearly ascertained facts and correct application of law.

Judgment

According to article 153(1)(i) of the Civil Procedure Law,[22] the court held that the appeal was dismissed and the original judgment was affirmed.

This judgment was final.

Further reading

Gu, Minkang, "The Joint Stock Cooperative Enterprise: A New Independent Legal Entity in China," *Hastings International and Comparative Law Review* 23, 1999, 25–48.

Schipani, Cindy A. and Liu, Junhai, "Corporate Governance in China: Then and Now," *Columbia Business Law Review* 2002, 2002, 1–69.

Notes

1 The Provisional Regulations of the People's Republic of China on Private Enterprises, promulgated by the State Council on 25 June 1988.
2 See Rules on the Classification of Enterprise Registration, promulgated by the State Statistics Bureau and the State Administration for Industry and Commerce on 28 August 1998.
3 The Law of the People's Republic of China on Industrial Enterprises Owned by the Whole People, adopted at the 1st Session of the 7th National People's Congress on 13 April 1988.
4 The Law on Industrial Enterprises Owned by the Whole People is also applicable to state-owned enterprises in such industries as communications and transportation, post and telecommunications, construction, commerce, foreign trade, agriculture, and forestry.
5 According to article 37 of the General Principles of the Civil Law of the People's Republic of China, which was adopted at the 4th Session of the 6th National People's Congress on 12 April 1986, a legal person is established in accordance with the law; has necessary property and operating funds; has a name, organizational structure, and site; and can assume civil liability independently.

6 The Regulations of the People's Republic of China on Collectively Owned Enterprises in Cities and Towns, promulgated by the State Council on 9 September 1991.

7 A department-in-charge is the government department to which a state-owned enterprise or collectively owned enterprise is accountable.

8 See Rules on the Classification of Enterprise Registration, promulgated by the State Statistics Bureau and the State Administration for Industry and Commerce on 28 August 1998.

9 See Rules on the Classification of Enterprise Registration, promulgated by the State Statistics Bureau and the State Administration for Industry and Commerce on 28 August 1998.

10 The Sole Proprietorship Law of the People's Republic of China, adopted at the 11th Session of the Standing Committee of the 9th National People's Congress on 30 August 1999.

11 The Measures on the Administration of Registration of Sole Proprietorships, promulgated by the State Administration for Industry and Commerce on 13 January 2000.

12 The Partnership Law of the People's Republic of China, adopted at the 24th Session of the Standing Committee of the 8th National People's Congress on 23 February 1997.

13 The Measures of the People's Republic of China on the Administration of Registration of Partnerships, promulgated by the State Council on 19 November 1997.

14 The Company Law of the People's Republic of China, adopted at the 5th Session of the Standing Committee of the 8th National People's Congress on 29 December 1993 and amended at the 13th Session of the Standing Committee of the 9th National People's Congress on 25 December 1999.

15 The Regulations of the People's Republic of China on the Administration of Registration of Companies, promulgated by the State Council on 24 June 1994.

16 The Provisional Rules on the Administration of Registration of Corporate Registered Capital, promulgated by the State Administration for Industry and Commerce on 18 December 1995.

17 The Rules on Several Issues Regarding the Registration of Companies, promulgated by the State Administration for Industry and Commerce on 7 January 1998.

18 For example, the State Administration for Industry and Commerce is responsible for the registration of companies limited by shares that have been approved by departments authorized by the State Council; companies invested under the authorization of the State Council; limited liability companies established solely or jointly by investment organs or departments authorized by the State Council; foreign-invested limited liability companies; and any other companies that should be registered with the State Administration for Industry and Commerce in accordance with laws and administrative regulations.

19 A provincial-level government is the government of a province, an autonomous region, or a municipality directly under the central government.

20 According to the Company Law, a shareholders' meeting in a company limited by shares is composed of "shareholders" (art. 102). However, it is not clear whether the shareholders' meeting must be composed of all the shareholders, or how many shareholders constitute a quorum.

21 Article 153(1) of the Civil Procedure Law provides that the court of second instance should: "(i) dismiss the appeal and affirm the judgment of the court of first instance if the original judgment is based on clear facts and correct application of law, ... (iii) remand the case for retrial or amend the original judgment if the original judgment is based on erroneous or unclear facts or insufficient evidence".

22 Article 153(1)(i) of the Civil Procedure Law provides that the court of second instance should dismiss the appeal and affirm the judgment of the court of first instance if the original judgment is based on clear facts and correct application of law.

3　Foreign investment enterprises

For companies that want to expand overseas, an assortment of investment vehicles are at their disposal, depending on their business strategies, financial means, human resources, familiarity with the foreign market, and the legal environment of the host country. A manufacturer may just want to export its products, in which case, it will have to commit the least amount of resources and assume the least amount of risk. At the other end of the spectrum, the manufacturer may want to establish a wholly owned subsidiary in the foreign country, which will engage in production, distribution, and warranty services. In that case, the manufacturer will have to commit abundant resources and will be likely to encounter the greatest amount of risk. Taking the middle course, the manufacturer may find a local partner to form a joint venture, with the local partner taking responsibilities for sale and distribution while it concentrates on production. In such a case, the manufacturer will share control, profits, and risks with the local partner.

Since China opened its door to the outside world in 1979, there have been five major vehicles for foreign investors to do business in China: representative office, branch, Sino-foreign equity joint venture, Sino-foreign cooperative joint venture, and wholly foreign-owned enterprise. Without the status of Chinese legal persons, the first two investment vehicles are preparatory in nature and involve a relatively limited scope and amount of business activities. The latter three types of business entities, which are collectively referred to as foreign investment enterprises (外商投资企业) (FIEs), are Chinese legal persons and the core instruments for foreign direct investment in China. In recent years, China has also allowed foreign investors to establish foreign companies limited by shares. This relatively new investment vehicle has been gaining popularity among foreign investors. Accordingly, this chapter aims to highlight the important legal provisions on these six investment vehicles.

Over the years, China has enacted an array of laws, administrative regulations, and government rules on representative office, branch, and FIEs in order to attract foreign capital, technology, and management expertise. Apart from these general legal norms, the State Council and government ministries or departments have also enacted industry-specific regulations and rules, while governments of provinces, autonomous regions, municipalities directly under the central government, and SEZs have passed local regulations impacting on FIEs in their respective areas. For example, there are industry-specific regulations or rules on foreign-invested financial institutions, insurance companies, telecommunications enterprises, shipping companies, and leasing companies. Moreover, Shanghai, Tianjin, Shenzhen, Guangdong, Qinghai, Heilongjiang, etc. have enacted legal provisions on FIEs established under their jurisdictions. Since this chapter focuses on discussing national legal norms on FIEs, foreign investors should also consider industry-specific and local regulations when they make decisions to invest in China. Furthermore, it is noteworthy that laws, administrative regulations, and government rules on FIEs, in general, are also applicable to enterprises funded by overseas Chinese from Hong Kong, Macao, and Taiwan.

1 Representative office of a foreign enterprise

The governing rules on representative offices of foreign enterprises are the Provisional Regulations on the Administration of Resident Representative Offices of Foreign Enterprises,[1] the Measures on the Administration of Registration of Resident Representative Offices of Foreign Enterprises,[2] and the Detailed Implementation Rules on the Approval and Administration of Resident Representative Offices of Foreign Enterprises in China.[3] These three pieces of legislation outline the requirements and procedures for the establishment, registration, extension, modification, and termination of representative offices of foreign enterprises in China.

To establish a resident representative office, the foreign enterprise (外国企业) must be lawfully registered in its home country; have a sound business reputation; provide authentic and reliable documents and materials as required by law; and have gone through the application formalities in accordance with the law. However, to apply for approval, the foreign enterprise cannot go to the government directly. Instead, the foreign enterprise must entrust a company that has been approved by the government to engage in foreign economic and trade business, or a foreign-economic-and-trade organization or a foreign-affairs-service unit approved by the government, with the task of going through the application formalities.

In applying for approval, the foreign enterprise must submit the following documents and materials:

1   a written application signed by the chairperson of its board of directors or its general manager, providing a brief introduction of the enterprise, the purpose of establishing a representative office, the name of the representative office, the names of the chief representative and representatives, the business scope of the representative office, the duration of the representative office, and the location of the representative office;

2   a copy of the business certificate issued by the relevant authorities of its home country;

3   the original certificate of credit worthiness issued by a bank with which it does business;

4   the power of attorney signed by the chairperson of its board (the executive director if there is no board) or the general manager regarding the appointment of the chief representative and representatives,[4] the resumes of the representatives, and copies of proof of their identity;

5   a completed "Application Form for the Establishment of Resident Representative Office of Foreign Enterprise" and a completed "Application Form for Personnel of Resident Representative Office of Foreign Enterprise"; and

6   any other materials deemed necessary by the examination-and-approval organ.

With respect to traders, manufacturers, contractors, consulting companies, advertising companies, leasing companies, investment companies, etc., the examination-and-approval organ is the Ministry of Foreign Trade and Economic Cooperation (MOFTEC) (now the Department of Foreign Trade of the Ministry of Commerce) or its office in the relevant province, autonomous region, municipality directly under the central government, or separately planned city.[5]

Within 30 days of approval, the chief representative must register with the State Administration for Industry and Commerce or its office in the relevant province, autonomous region, municipality directly under the central government, or separately planned city. The major items to be registered are the name of the representative office, the address of the representative office, the number of representatives and their names, the business scope of the representative office, and the term of the representative office. To apply for registration, the foreign enterprise should complete the "Application Form for the Registration of Resident Representative Office of Foreign Enterprise" and submit the certificate of approval, items 1 to 4 of the list of materials required for application, and any other materials as required by the AIC. The date of registration is the founding date of the representative office. Having obtained the certificate of approval, the certificate of registration, and work permits (formerly called "certificates of representatives"), the representative office should also go through the necessary formalities with the public security, banking, customs, and tax authorities.

The maximum term of a representative office is three years, starting from the date of the issue of the approval certificate. If the representative office wants to continue operations after the expiration of its term, it can apply for an extension, via the original entrusted entity, 60 days before it expires. The certificate of registration is valid for one year and must be renewed within the 30 days prior to its expiration by submitting an annual report on the representative office's business operations and an application form. In the case where the representative office obtains an extension after the expiration of its term, it will have to submit the new certificate of approval issued by the original examination-and-approval organ and complete an application form for registration of extension. During its term, if the representative office has any changes to its name, responsible personnel, scope of business, duration, or address, it must obtain approval from the original examination-and-approval organ and apply for registration of change. If the representative office wants to change a representative, it should also submit the power of attorney issued by the foreign enterprise and the resume and proof of identity of the new representative.

The name of the representative office should include the following: "country + enterprise name + city name + representative office." The representative office of a foreign enterprise can engage in indirect business activities and, on behalf of the foreign enterprise and within its scope of business, conduct such business activities as business liaison, product introduction, market studies, and technical exchanges. In any event, the foreign enterprise assumes legal liability for all the business activities of the representative office. Given these constraints on business activities, a foreign enterprise establishes a representative office mainly to obtain a better understanding of the Chinese market or introduce itself to potential customers.

When the representative office terminates upon or prior to the expiration of its term, it must, via the original entrusted entity, submit an application for cancellation signed by the chairperson of its board or its general manager and report to the original examination-and-approval organ for the record 30 days in advance, and after settling its debts, taxes payable, and other relevant matters, go through the formalities of cancellation of registration, customs record, etc. Similarly, if the foreign enterprise has been declared bankrupt, the representative office must settle its debts and taxes payable and apply for cancellation of registration.

2 Branch of a foreign company

Articles 199 to 205 of the Company Law govern the establishment of branches of foreign companies. A foreign company, which is a company established and registered outside China in accordance with the law of a foreign country, may establish a branch or branches in China to engage in production and operations. To set up a branch, the foreign company shall file an application with the relevant Chinese authorities, together with its articles of association, the registration certificate issued by its home country and any other relevant documents.

Having secured the required approval, the company must register with and obtain a business license from the AIC. To apply for registration of establishment, the foreign company must submit the following documents:

1   a written application signed by the chairperson of its board of directors or its general manager;
2   a completed "Application Form for the Registration of Foreign Enterprise";
3   the certificate of approval issued by the examination-and-approval organ;

4   the business certificate issued by its home country;
5   a certificate of credit worthiness;
6   the power of attorney signed by the chairperson of its board or its general manager concerning the appointment of responsible personnel, and their resumes and proof of identity;
7   proof of allocation of operating funds to the branch, etc.[6]

The branch must indicate in its name the nationality of the foreign company and what type of liability the foreign company has. The articles of association of the foreign company must be available at the branch. Compared with a representative office, the branch of a foreign company is allowed to engage in a broader scope of business activities. However, since the branch of a foreign company does not have the status of a Chinese legal person, the foreign company assumes civil liabilities for the business activities of the branch. When a foreign company withdraws its branch from China, it shall repay the debts of the branch and conduct liquidation in accordance with the law. The property of the branch cannot be transferred overseas before its debts are repaid.

3   Equity joint ventures

With the passage of the Law on Sino-Foreign Equity Joint Ventures (Equity Joint Venture Law) in 1979, China opened its door to the outside world. To date, the Equity Joint Venture Law has been revised twice: in 1990 and 2001.[7] Coupled with the Regulations for the Implementation of the Law on Sino-Foreign Equity Joint Ventures,[8] the Equity Joint Venture Law provides the basic legal framework for equity joint ventures in China. Nevertheless, China has also passed a series of administrative regulations and government rules on various topics relating to FIEs, which are applicable to equity joint ventures, cooperative joint ventures, and wholly foreign-owned enterprises. Accordingly, the issues raised below are based on the relevant provisions in the Equity Joint Venture Law and its implementation regulations. If the provisions are taken from other legislative sources, they will be so noted.

Requirements

The Equity Joint Venture Law allows foreign companies, enterprises, economic entities, or individuals (the foreign party) to form Sino-foreign equity joint ventures (中外合资经营企业) with Chinese companies, enterprises, or economic entities (the Chinese party). An equity joint venture is to be established in the form of a limited liability company, and the capital contributed by the foreign party cannot be less than 25 percent of the registered capital of the joint venture. The registered capital (注册资本) refers to the total amount of capital contributions of the parties that is to be registered with the AIC for the establishment of the joint venture. During its term, the joint venture cannot reduce the registered capital. If it is necessary to reduce the registered capital due to changes in the total amount of investment and production or operation scale, the joint venture must obtain the approval of the examination-and-approval organ and go through the formalities of change of registration with the AIC.

Additionally, the proportion of the registered capital to the total amount of investment (投资总额) which is the sum of capital construction funds and cash flow needed for production as stipulated in the joint venture contract and the articles of association (including loans) should be as follows:

1   If the total amount of investment is US$3 million or less, the registered capital should be at least 70 percent of the amount of total investment.
2   If the total amount of investment is more than US$3 million but US $10 million or less, the registered capital should be at least 50 percent of the total amount of investment (if the total amount of investment is less than US$4.2 million, the registered capital cannot be less than US$2.1 million).
3   If the total amount of investment is more than US$10 million but US$30 million or less, the registered capital should be at least 40 percent of the total amount of investment (if the total amount of investment is less than US$12.5 million, the registered capital cannot be less than US$5 million).
4   If the total amount of investment is more than US$30 million, the registered capital should be at least 33 percent of the total amount of investment (if the total amount of investment is less than US$36 million, the registered capital cannot be less than US$12 million).[9]

Investment may be made in the form of cash, in-kind contributions (machinery, equipment, and materials), buildings, factory premises, industrial property rights, proprietary technologies, and the right to use a site. If the foreign party contributes cash in foreign currency or the Chinese party contributes cash in Renminbi, it shall be converted into Renminbi or foreign currency in accordance with the joint venture contract based on the standard exchange rate announced by the People's Bank of China on the day of payment. Apart from the right to use a site, the value of each contribution is to be appraised by the parties through joint consultation or can be evaluated by a third party agreed upon by the parties. If the foreign party contributes machinery, equipment, and materials, they must be necessary for the production of the joint venture, and their price must not be higher than the current international market prices for similar machinery, equipment, or materials. If the foreign party contributes an industrial property right or a proprietary technology, it must be capable of improving notably the performance and quality of existing products and raising productivity, or it should be capable of producing remarkable savings in raw materials, fuel, or power. In any event, the machinery, equipment, materials, industrial property right, etc. contributed by the foreign party is subject to the approval of the examination-and-approval organ.

If a joint venture needs to use a site, it must file an application with the municipal-level or county-level land administration department of the place where it is located. After obtaining the approval, the joint venture shall sign a contract, stipulating the area and location of the site, the purpose of use, the duration of the contract, the site-use fee, etc. In the case where the right to use a site is not part of the Chinese party's capital contribution, the joint venture will be required to pay a site-use fee to the government. If the right to use a site is part of the Chinese party's capital contribution, the monetary value of this right will be the same as the site-use fees required for similar sites. The standards of site-use fees shall be determined by the people's government of the province, autonomous region, or municipality directly under the central government where the joint venture is located with reference to such factors as the purpose of use, geographic and environmental conditions, expenses for requisition, demolition, and resettlement, and the joint venture's requirements with respect to infrastructure. Site-use fees as part of the investment of the Chinese party are not subject to adjustment during the contract term.

The parties must pay in full their respective contributions by the deadlines stipulated in the joint venture contract. If a party delays making a payment or has not paid in full, it shall pay interest for the arrears or a compensation for loss as stipulated in the joint venture contract. After the parties have made all the contributions, an accountant registered in China shall verify the contributions and produce a certificate of capital verification, on the basis of which the joint venture will issue certificates of investment.

If an equity joint venture is engaged in an investment project encouraged or permitted by the Chinese government, it may or may not have a fixed term. However, a joint venture must have a fixed term if it does business in one of the following industries or situations:

1   services, such as hotels, apartments, office buildings, recreation and entertainment, food and beverages, taxis, maintenance, and consultation;
2   land development and real estate;
3   prospecting and exploitation of natural resources;
4   investment projects restricted by the state; or
5   contracts requiring fixed terms as stated in other laws and regulations.[10]

Where an equity joint venture is required to have a fixed term, the term may be set differently, depending on the industry or the circumstances. An equity joint venture may apply for an extension with the examination-and-approval organ six months prior to the expiration of its term. The examination-and-approval organ will approve or reject the application within one month of the receipt of the application.

Rights and liabilities

In an equity joint venture, the parties share profits and bear risks and losses in proportion to their respective contributions to the registered capital. Before distribution of after-tax profits, the joint venture should allocate to the reserve fund, staff-and-worker bonus and welfare fund, and enterprise development fund. The proportion of allocations is to be determined by the board of directors. Money in the reserve fund can be used to cover losses, or, with the approval of the examination-and-approval organ, to increase the joint venture's capital for expansion of production. Nonetheless, profits must not be distributed before the losses of the previous year(s) have been covered.

If one party wants to transfer all or part of its equity, it must obtain the consent of all the other parties and the approval of the examination-and-approval organ, as well as going through the formalities of change of registration. The terms of the transfer given to a third party cannot be more favorable than those given to the other parties to the joint venture, and the other parties have the right of first refusal. Having fulfilled its obligations prescribed by laws or stipulated in agreement or contract, the foreign party may remit abroad its net profit and any funds it receives upon the expiration or discontinuation of the joint venture in the currency as specified in the joint venture contract. If the foreign party reinvests its net profit in China, it may apply for a refund of that portion of income tax paid. The wages and other legitimate incomes of expatriates may be remitted abroad after individual income taxes have been paid.

An equity joint venture may establish branches outside China. When a joint venture needs to purchase machinery, equipment, raw materials, fuel, parts, office supplies, transportation vehicles, etc., it has the right to decide whether to buy them in China or from abroad. Equity joint ventures are encouraged to sell products in the international market. They may export products on their own or sell products through their sales agents or China's foreign-trade companies on a commission basis. As regards prices for materials purchased in China and fees charged for such services as water, electricity, gas, heating, transportation of goods, labor, engineering design, consultation, and advertisement, equity joint ventures shall be treated equally with domestic enterprises. In addition, joint ventures are required to pay taxes in accordance with tax laws and regulations, which are discussed in Chapter 8. Nevertheless, taxes on machinery, equipment, parts, raw materials, etc. imported by the joint venture as part of the foreign party's investment or for production of export goods may be exempted or reduced.

Application procedure

To establish an equity joint venture, the parties must obtain approval from the MOFTEC (now the Department of Foreign Investment Administration of the Ministry of Commerce). However, the State Council also delegates to the people's governments in provinces, autonomous regions, and municipalities directly under the central government as well as relevant departments under it the power to examine and approve the establishment of equity joint ventures that meet two requirements:

1   The total amount of investment should be within the approval limit as set by the State Council, and the source of capital of the Chinese party must have been ascertained.
2   Additional allocations of raw materials by the state must not be needed, and the national balance of fuel, power, communications and transportation, and foreign trade export quotas, etc. would not be affected.

If the prospective joint venture meets these two requirements, it may need to obtain approval from one of the examination-and-approval organs and report to the Ministry of Commerce for the record.

In applying for approval, the parties must jointly submit the following documents to the examination-and-approval organ:

1   an application for the establishment of a joint venture;
2   a feasibility study report jointly prepared by the parties;
3   the joint venture agreement, joint venture contract, and articles of association signed by representatives authorized by the parties;
4   a list of candidates nominated by the parties for the posts of chairperson, vice-chairperson, and members of the board of directors; and
5   any other documents as required by the examination-and-approval organ.

Specifically, the joint venture agreement (合营企业协议) refers to the document agreed upon by the parties with respect to certain major points and principles governing the establishment of the joint venture. The joint venture contract (合营企业合同) refers to the document concluded by the parties with respect to their mutual rights and obligations. The articles of association (合营企业章程) refer to the document agreed upon by the parties delineating the objectives, organizational principles, management methods, etc. of the joint venture in accordance with the principles of the joint venture contract. If the joint venture agreement and joint venture contract have conflicts, the joint venture contract will prevail. If the parties agree to conclude only the joint venture contract and the articles of association, the joint venture agreement may be omitted.

Obviously, the joint venture contract is the centerpiece of all the required documents. The major items to be included in the joint venture contract include:

1   the names, countries of registration, and legal addresses of the parties, and the names, posts, and nationalities of their legal representatives;

2 the name, legal address, objective(s), business scope, and scale of the joint venture;
3 the joint venture's total amount of investment and registered capital, the amount, proportion, form, and time limit of each party's investment, and provisions regarding unpaid contributions and transfer of equity;
4 the proportion to be borne by each party with respect to profit distribution and liability for loss;
5 the composition of the board of directors, the distribution of the number of directors, and the responsibilities, powers, and means of appointment of the general manager, deputy general managers, and other senior managerial personnel;
6 the main production equipment and technology to be adopted and their sources of supply;
7 the methods of purchasing raw materials and of selling products;
8 the principles governing the treatment of finance, accounting, and auditing;
9 provisions on labor management, wages, welfare, labor insurance, etc.;
10 the duration of the joint venture, its dissolution, and the liquidation procedure;
11 liabilities for breach of contract;
12 the means and procedure for resolving disputes between the parties; and
13 the language used for the joint venture contract and the conditions for putting the contract into effect.

Moreover, the formation, validity, interpretation, performance of the joint venture contract and the resolution of any disputes over it are to be governed by Chinese law.

Likewise, the articles of association of an equity joint venture should contain:

1 the name and legal address of the joint venture;
2 the objective(s), business scope, and duration of the joint venture;
3 the names, countries of registration, and legal addresses of the parties to the joint venture, and the names, posts, and nationalities of their legal representatives;
4 the total amount of investment and registered capital of the joint venture, the amount and proportion of each party's capital contribution, provisions on transfer of equity, and the proportion to be borne by each party with respect to profit distribution and liability for loss;
5 the composition, powers, and rules of procedure of the board of directors, the term of office of directors, and the duties of the chairperson and vice-chairperson of the board;
6 the establishment of management organs and their rules for handling affairs, the responsibilities of the general manager, deputy general

managers, and other senior managerial personnel, and the means to appoint and dismiss these officers;

7   the principles governing the systems of finance, accounting, and auditing;
8   dissolution and liquidation; and
9   the procedure for amending the articles of association.

Thus, the contents of the joint venture contract and the articles of association are largely the same. In addition, the joint venture agreement, joint venture contract, and articles of association take effect upon the approval of the examination-and-approval organ.

Having received all the required documents, the examination-and-approval organ must approve or disapprove the joint venture within three months. Within one month of the receipt of the certificate of approval, the parties must apply for registration with the relevant AIC. The date of the issue of the business license is the founding date of the equity joint venture. During its term, if the equity joint venture has major changes, it must obtain approval from the examination-and-approval organ and go through the formalities of change of registration with the AIC.

Corporate governance

In an equity joint venture, the board of directors is the highest organ of power. The number of directors must be at least three, and the allocation of the number of directors is to be determined by the parties through consultation and with reference to the proportion of capital contributed. Each party is responsible for appointing and replacing its directors. The term of office of a director is four years, and each party may reappoint its director(s). The chairperson of the board of directors is the legal representative of the joint venture. The chairperson and vice-chairperson of the board of directors shall be chosen by the parties through consultation or be elected by the board of directors. If the chairperson of the board of directors is from one side, the vice-chairperson must be from the other side.

The board of directors must meet at least once a year. Interim meetings may be convened if one-third or more of the directors propose. A board meeting can be held only if two-thirds or more of the directors are present. If a director is unable to attend, he or she may send a proxy. The powers of the board of directors must be provided in the articles of association. The board of directors shall decide on the following important issues:

1   plans for development, production, and business operations;
2   budget;
3   distribution of profits;
4   labor and wage plans;
5   termination of operations;

6   the appointment, powers, and remuneration of the general manager, deputy general managers, chief engineer, chief accountant, and auditor; and

7   the increase or reduction of the registered capital.

For the amendment of the articles of association, termination and dissolution of the joint venture, expansion and reduction of the registered capital, and merger or division of the joint venture, there must be a unanimous vote of all the attendees. Resolutions on other matters shall be made in accordance with the rules of procedure provided in the articles of association.

A joint venture must establish a management organ that is responsible for the daily operations of the joint venture. The board of directors must appoint one general manager and several deputy general managers. The posts of general manager and deputy general managers are to be held separately by each side. The general manager is to implement the resolutions of the board of directors and is responsible for the daily management of the joint venture. Within the powers authorized by the board of directors, the general manager represents the joint venture externally and may appoint or dismiss subordinates. Directors may concurrently serve as the general manager, deputy general managers, and other senior managerial personnel of the joint venture. However, the general manager and deputy general managers must not concurrently serve as the general manager or deputy general managers of other economic entities and must not engage in any competitive activities of other economic entities against the joint venture.

Dissolution

An equity joint venture will be dissolved under one of the following circumstances:

1   expiration of the term of the joint venture;

2   inability to continue operations due to heavy losses;

3   inability to continue operations due to the failure of one party to fulfill its obligations prescribed in the joint venture agreement, joint venture contract, and articles of association;

4   inability to continue operations due to heavy losses caused by *force majeure*, such as natural disasters and wars;

5   failure to achieve the objectives of the joint venture and no prospects for future development; or

6   occurrence of other causes for dissolution stipulated in the joint venture contract and the articles of association.

In the case of points 2, 4, 5, and 6, the board of directors shall apply to the examination-and-approval organ for approval. In the case of point 3, the non-breaching party shall apply to the examination-and-approval organ for approval, and the breaching party will be liable for compensation for losses.

Upon dissolution, the joint venture must be liquidated. Members of the liquidation committee are generally selected from among the directors, but the joint venture may also appoint accountants and lawyers registered in China to the committee. The procedure for liquidation is discussed in section 9, "Liquidation of foreign investment enterprises," below. An equity joint venture is liable for its debts to the extent of all of its assets. After all the debts are paid off, the residual property will be distributed among the parties in proportion to their respective investments, unless otherwise provided by the joint venture agreement, joint venture contract, or articles of association. Furthermore, the equity joint venture shall apply for cancellation of registration with the AIC and the tax authority.

4 Cooperative joint ventures

Apart from equity joint ventures, foreign investors may also invest in China by means of Sino-foreign cooperative joint ventures (中外合作经营企业), which have also been translated as Sino-Foreign contractual joint ventures. The Law on Sino-Foreign Cooperative Joint Ventures (Cooperative Joint Venture Law)[11] and the Detailed Rules for the Implementation of the Law on Sino-Foreign Cooperative Joint Ventures[12] comprise the regulatory framework for cooperative joint ventures. As mentioned above, other administrative regulations and government rules on FIEs apply to cooperative joint ventures. Thus, the issues dealt with below are based on the relevant provisions in the Cooperative Joint Venture Law and its implementation rules. If the provisions are taken from other legislative sources, they will be so noted.

Requirements

The Cooperative Joint Venture Law allows foreign enterprises, other economic organizations, or individuals (the foreign party) to form cooperative joint ventures with Chinese enterprises or other economic organizations (the Chinese party). A cooperative joint venture can be a legal person or non-legal person. As mentioned in Chapter 2, a legal person is established in accordance with the law; has necessary property and operating funds; has a name, organizational structure, and site; and can assume civil liability independently.[13] If a cooperative joint venture meets the requirements of a legal person, it will be a limited liability company. In a non-legal-person cooperative joint venture, the parties operate as separate entities and bear liabilities independently, even though they may agree to jointly own all or parts of the investments (投资)[14] or cooperative means (合作条件).[15] However, the accumulated property of a non-legal-person cooperative joint venture is to be jointly owned by the parties. In essence, a non-legal-person cooperative joint venture is akin to a contractual arrangement between the parties.

If the cooperative joint venture is a legal person, the foreign party shall generally contribute not less than 25 percent of its registered capital. If the cooperative joint venture is not a legal person, the MOFTEC (now the Department of Foreign Investment Administration of the Ministry of Commerce) will prescribe specific requirements for the parties' investments and cooperative means. Indeed, the MOFTEC has explained that the foreign party's investment in a non-legal-person cooperative joint venture must not be less than 25 percent of the total amount of investment made by the Chinese and foreign parties.[16] In addition, the non-legal-person cooperative joint venture should register the investments or cooperative means contributed by the parties with the AIC.

Investments or cooperative means can be made in the form of cash, in-kind contributions, land use rights, industrial property rights, non-patented technologies, and other property rights. If the cooperative means furnished by the Chinese party are state-owned, they should be appraised in accordance with laws and administrative regulations. The parties must pay in full their investments or furnish the cooperative means on schedule. After the parties have made all the contributions, an accountant registered in China or a relevant organ shall verify the contributions and produce a certificate of capital verification, on the basis of which the cooperative joint venture will issue certificates of investment. The parties cannot mortgage or use as collateral in other situations their investments or cooperative means. During its term, the cooperative joint venture cannot reduce its registered capital. If it is necessary to reduce the registered capital due to changes in the total amount of investment and production or operation scale, the joint venture must obtain the approval of the examination-and-approval organ. The rules regarding the proportion of the registered capital to the total amount of investment in an equity joint venture also apply to cooperative joint ventures.[17]

The duration of a cooperative joint venture shall be determined by the parties through consultation and stipulated in the joint venture contract. There are no minimum or maximum requirements for the term of a cooperative joint venture. If the parties agree to extend the term of the joint venture, they must apply to the examination-and-approval organ 180 days before its expiration. The examination-and-approval organ will approve or disapprove the application within 30 days of its receipt. Where the foreign party has fully recovered its investment upon the expiration of the cooperative joint venture, the term of the joint venture shall not be extended. However, if the foreign party increases its investment and all the parties have reached a consensus, the cooperative joint venture may apply for an extension.

Rights and liabilities

As a limited liability company, a legal-person cooperative joint venture is liable for its debts to the extent of all of its assets. Likewise, the parties are liable to the cooperative joint venture to the extent of their respective investments or cooperative means, unless the joint venture contract provides otherwise. Indeed, the parties to a cooperative joint venture must stipulate in the joint venture contract such matters as investments made or cooperative means furnished by the parties, time limits for making investments or providing cooperative means, distribution of profits or products, sharing of risks and losses, management style, and ownership of the joint venture's property upon the expiration of its term. In other words, the parties to a legal-person cooperative joint venture may share profits and products as well as bear risks and losses in accordance with the joint venture contract.

Furthermore, if the parties stipulate in the joint venture contract that all the fixed assets of the joint venture will be given to the Chinese party upon the expiration of its term, they may also provide the means for the foreign party to recover its investment during the existence of the joint venture. Specifically, the foreign party may recover its investment during the term of the joint venture in one of the following ways:

1   According to distribution based on investments or cooperative means, the parties may agree in the joint venture contract to increase the profit sharing ratio of the foreign party.
2   Upon the examination and approval by the finance and tax authorities in accordance with relevant tax rules, the foreign party may recover its investment before income tax is paid by the joint venture.
3   The foreign party may use other means of investment recovery approved by the examination-and-approval organ as well as the finance and/or tax authorities.[18]

Nonetheless, the foreign party cannot recoup its investment in advance if the losses of the cooperative joint venture have not been covered. Where the foreign party may recover its investment during the term of the joint venture, both the Chinese and foreign parties are responsible for the debts of the cooperative joint venture in accordance with relevant laws and the stipulations in the joint venture contract.

If one party wants to transfer all or part of its rights in the cooperative joint venture to another party or an outsider, it must obtain the written consent of all the other parties and the approval of the examination-and-approval organ. In the case of a non-legal-person cooperative joint venture, the investments and cooperative means of the parties are subject to the joint venture's unified management and use, and no party may unilaterally dispose of them without the consent of the other parties. Having fulfilled its obligations prescribed by laws or stipulated in the joint venture contract, the foreign party may remit abroad its profits, other lawful incomes, and funds it receives upon the expiration of the joint venture. The wages and other legitimate incomes of expatriates may be remitted abroad after individual income taxes have been paid.

The Chinese government encourages the establishment of export-oriented or technologically advanced production-type cooperative enterprises. When a joint venture needs to purchase machinery, equipment, raw materials, fuel, parts and components, office supplies, etc., it may buy them in China or from abroad. Cooperative joint ventures may export products on their own or sell products through overseas sales agents or China's foreign-trade companies on a commission basis. Cooperative joint ventures may take out loans from financial institutions inside or outside China. However, the parties should each arrange any loans and their guarantee used as investment or cooperative means.

Application procedure

To apply for the establishment of a cooperative joint venture, the Chinese party must submit the following documents to the examination-and-approval organ:

1 a written proposal for the establishment of a cooperative project together with the document of consent of the department-in-charge;[19]
2 a feasibility study report jointly prepared by the parties together with the document of consent of the department-in-charge;
3 the joint venture agreement, joint venture contract, and articles of association signed by the legal representatives of the parties or the agents authorized by the legal representatives (the parties may agree to omit the joint venture agreement);
4 the business licenses or certificates of registration and certificates of credit worthiness of the parties, and valid proof of their legal representatives (where the foreign party is a natural person, valid proof of his or her identity, resume, and certificate of credit worthiness shall be provided);
5 a list of the chairperson, vice-chairperson and members of the board of directors, or a list of the head, deputy head and members of the joint management committee; and
6 any other documents required by the examination-and-approval organ.

The items to be included in the joint venture contract and articles of association of a cooperative joint venture are similar to those to be included in the joint venture contract and articles of association of an equity joint venture. However, since a cooperative joint venture may have a joint management committee rather than a board of directors and the parties to a cooperative joint venture may receive products rather than profits, provisions on corporate governance and profit distribution in the joint venture contract and articles of association of an equity joint venture should be included *mutatis mutandis* in the case of cooperative joint venture. In addition, the joint venture contract of a cooperative joint venture should also include arrangements for the revenue and expenditure of foreign exchange and the procedure for amending the joint venture contract, while its articles of association should also include provisions on labor management, such as hiring, training, labor contract, wages, social insurance, welfare benefits, and occupational safety. In any event, the formation, validity, interpretation, and performance of the joint venture contract and the resolution of any disputes over it are to be governed by Chinese law.

The examination-and-approval organ is either the MOFTEC (now the Department of Foreign Investment Administration of the Ministry of Commerce) or a department or local government authorized by the State Council. Under the following circumstances, a department or local people's government authorized by the State Council shall conduct examination and approval of an application:

1   The total amount of investment is within the investment amount to be approved by the department or local people's government.
2   The parties have raised capital on their own, and the state does not need to balance construction and production conditions.
3   The exportation of the joint venture's products does not require export quota and license to be issued by the relevant department(s)-in-charge, or if export quota and license are required, the consent of the relevant department(s)-in-charge has been obtained prior to the submission of the application.
4   Other situations in which departments or local governments authorized by the State Council shall examine and approve cooperative joint ventures as prescribed in laws and administrative regulations.

The examination-and-approval organ must approve or reject the application within 45 days of receipt of all the required documents.

For a cooperative joint venture approved by the Department of Foreign Investment Administration of the Ministry of Commerce or a department authorized by the State Council, the former shall issue the certificate of approval. For a cooperative joint venture approved by a local people's government, the certificate of approval shall be issued by the local government and be reported to the Department of Foreign Investment Administration of the Ministry of Commerce for the record. Within 30 days of the receipt of the certificate of approval, the cooperative joint venture should apply for registration with the relevant AIC and obtain a business license. The date of the issue of the business license is the founding date of the cooperative joint venture. Within 30 days of its establishment, the cooperative joint venture must also go through the registration formalities with the tax authority.

During the term of the cooperative joint venture, if the parties make major revisions to the joint venture contract, they must obtain approval from the examination-and-approval organ. If such revisions concern registration items, including change of name, change of domicile, transfer of equity, change of director or general manager, increase or reduction of registered capital, and establishment of a branch, the cooperative joint venture must go through the formalities of change of registration with the AIC.

Corporate governance

A cooperative joint venture must establish a board of directors or a joint management committee, which is its organ of power, to decide on important issues in accordance with the joint venture contract or the articles of association. Since a legal-person cooperative joint venture is a limited liability company, it should establish a board of directors. A non-legal-person cooperative joint venture, however, shall establish a joint management committee. The board of directors or the joint management committee must have at least three members, and the allocation of the number of members is to be determined by the parties through consultation and with reference to their investments or cooperative means. The directors or committee members shall be appointed or replaced by the parties. If the chairperson of the board of directors or the head of the joint management committee is from one side, the vice-chairperson or deputy head must be from the other side. The chairperson of the board of directors or the head of the joint management committee is the legal representative of the cooperative joint venture. The term of office of a director or committee member shall be stipulated in the articles of association, but each term cannot exceed three years. Upon expiration of his or her term, the director or committee member may serve another term if reappointed by the appointing party.

The board of directors or the joint management committee must meet at least once a year. A board or committee meeting may be convened if one-third or more of the directors or committee members propose. However, a board or committee meeting can be held only if two-thirds or more directors or members are present. If a director or committee member is unable to attend, he or she should authorize someone in writing to attend and cast the vote. A director or committee member who neither attends a meeting nor sends a proxy without any legitimate reasons shall be regarded as having attended the meeting and abstained from voting. The directors or committee members may also vote through communications.

The rules of procedure of the board of directors or the joint management committee shall be stipulated in the articles of association, unless otherwise provided in the implementation rules. Resolutions of the board of directors or the joint management committee shall be adopted with the affirmative votes of more than half of the directors or committee members. With respect to the following matters, a unanimous vote of all the attending directors or committee members is required:

1   the amendment of the articles of association;
2   the increase or reduction of the registered capital;
3   the dissolution of the joint venture;

4   the mortgage of the joint venture's assets;
5   the merger, division, or change of organizational form of the joint venture; and
6   any other matters agreed upon by the parties to be adopted only by a unanimous vote.

The board of directors or the joint management committee shall appoint a general manager to run the daily operations of the cooperative joint venture. The general manager is accountable to the board of directors or the joint management committee. Directors or committee members may concurrently serve as the general manager and other senior managerial personnel of the joint venture. After the formation of a cooperative joint venture, the board of directors or the joint management committee may unanimously agree to engage a third party to manage the business, in which case the joint venture must obtain approval from the examination-and-approval organ and the change must be registered with the AIC.

Dissolution

A cooperative joint venture will be dissolved under one of the following circumstances:

1   expiration of the term of the joint venture;
2   inability to continue operations due to its heavy losses or huge losses caused by *force majeure*;
3   inability to continue operations due to the failure of one party or several parties to fulfill its or their obligations stipulated in the joint venture contract and articles of association;
4   occurrence of other causes for dissolution stipulated in the joint venture contract and the articles of association; or
5   closing down of the joint venture due to violation of laws or administrative regulations.

In the case of points 2 and 4, the board of directors or the joint management committee shall apply to the examination-and-approval organ for approval. In the case of point 3, the non-breaching party or parties have the right to apply to the examination-and-approval organ for approval, and the breaching party or parties will be liable for compensation for losses.

Upon dissolution, the joint venture must be liquidated. The procedure for liquidation is discussed in section 9, "Liquidation of foreign investment enterprises," below. In addition, the cooperative joint venture shall apply for cancellation of registration with the AIC and the tax authority.

5 Wholly foreign-owned enterprises

Instead of equity joint ventures and cooperative joint ventures, foreign investors may establish wholly foreign-owned enterprises (外资企业 or 外商独资企业) in China. The Law on Wholly Foreign-Owned Enterprises[20] and the Detailed Rules for the Implementation of the Law on Wholly Foreign-Owned Enterprises[21] comprise the regulatory framework for wholly foreign-owned enterprises in China. As previously mentioned, other administrative regulations and government rules on FIEs apply to wholly foreign-owned enterprises. Hence, the issues dealt with below are based on the relevant provisions in the Law on Wholly Foreign-Owned Enterprises and its implementation rules. If the provisions are taken from other legislative sources, they will be so noted.

Requirements

Foreign enterprises, other economic organizations, or individuals (the foreign investor) may establish wholly foreign-owned enterprises in China. A wholly foreign-owned enterprise is 100 percent foreign-owned, but the proportion of its registered capital to the total amount of investment shall be the same as that of an equity joint venture.[22] The Chinese government encourages the establishment of export-oriented or technologyically advanced wholly foreign-owned enterprises, but wholly foreign-owned enterprises are prohibited or restricted in some industries. Those industries are listed in the Guidance Catalog of Industries with Foreign Investment, which will be discussed below. During its term, the wholly foreign-owned enterprise cannot reduce its registered capital. If it is necessary to reduce the registered capital due to changes in the total amount of investment and production or operation scale, the enterprise must obtain the approval of the examination-and-approval organ. Moreover, any increase or transfer of the registered capital is subject to the approval of the examination-and-approval organ and must be registered with the AIC.

The foreign investor may contribute convertible foreign currency, machinery, equipment, industrial property rights, or proprietary technologies. Subject to the approval of the examination-and-approval organ, it may also invest Renminbi profits obtained from other FIEs that it has established in China. If the foreign investor contributes machinery and equipment, such machinery and equipment must be necessary for the production of the wholly foreign-owned enterprise. The prices of such machinery and equipment cannot be higher than the current market prices of similar machinery and equipment on the international market. Indeed, a schedule of such machinery and equipment, including their names, types, quantity, and prices, must be attached as an appendix to the application filed with the examination-and-approval organ. When such machinery or equipment arrives at a Chinese port, the foreign investor should ask a Chinese commodity-inspection organ to inspect it and produce an inspection report. In addition, if the foreign investor contributes industrial property rights or proprietary technologies, it must be the owner of such rights or technologies. The principles used for capitalizing such rights or technologies should be the same as those used internationally, and the value of such rights or technologies cannot exceed 20 percent of the registered capital. The details of such rights or technologies must be attached as an appendix to the application filed with the examination-and-approval organ.

The time limits for investment shall be stipulated in the application form and the articles of association of the enterprise. The foreign investor may make capital contributions by installment. The first payment must be at least 15 percent and be paid within 90 days of the issue of the business license. The last payment must be made within three years of the issue of the business license. If the foreign investor has legitimate reason(s) to ask for an extension of the payment period, it must obtain the approval of the examination-and-approval organ and report it to the AIC for the record. After the foreign investor has made each installment, the wholly foreign-owned enterprise must engage an accountant registered in China to verify the investment and issue a certificate of capital verification, which must then be reported to the examination-and-approval organ and the AIC for the record.

With respect to its term, a wholly foreign-owned enterprise must obtain approval from the examination-and-approval organ. If the wholly foreign-owned enterprise wants an extension, it must file an application with the examination-and-approval organ 180 days prior to its expiration. The examination-and-approval organ must approve or reject the application within 30 days of its receipt. Within 30 days of the receipt of the approval document, the wholly foreign-owned enterprise must apply for change of registration with the AIC.

Rights and liabilities

A wholly foreign-owned enterprise is a limited liability company, or, with government approval, takes on another type of liability. If a wholly foreign-owned enterprise is a limited liability company, the foreign investor will be liable to the enterprise to the extent of its investment. If a wholly foreign-owned enterprise has another type of liability, the foreign investor's liability will be determined in accordance with Chinese laws and regulations.

If a wholly foreign-owned enterprise wants to mortgage or transfer its property or rights, it must obtain approval from the examination-and-approval organ and report the particulars to the AIC for the record. If a wholly foreign-owned enterprise reinvests its after-tax profits in China, it may apply for a refund of the income tax paid on the reinvested amount. A wholly foreign-owned enterprise must allocate at least 10 percent of its after-tax profits to the reserve fund and any percentage to the staff-and-worker bonus and welfare fund. It may cease allocation to the reserve fund if its accumulated amount reaches 50 percent of the registered capital. Nonetheless, it must not distribute profits if the losses of previous years have not been covered.

As regards use of land, the people's government at the county level or above of the place where the wholly foreign-owned enterprise will be located shall make arrangements in light of local circumstances. Within 30 days of the issue of the business license, the wholly foreign-owned enterprise must submit the certificate of approval and business license to the land-administration department of the people's government at the county level or above of the place where it is located to obtain a certificate of land use. The duration of land use is the same as the approved term of the wholly foreign-owned enterprise. The land use right cannot be transferred without approval, and the enterprise must pay a land use fee. If the land has been developed, the enterprise must also pay a land development fee. The land development fee may be levied as one-time payment or be paid in installments over a number of years. If the land has not been developed, the enterprise may develop the land on its own or entrust a development agency with the task. The construction of infrastructure, however, should be arranged uniformly by the people's government at the county level or above of the place where the enterprise is located.

If a wholly foreign-owned enterprise purchases in China machinery, equipment, raw materials, fuel, spare parts, office supplies, etc., it will, under the same conditions, be treated equally with a Chinese enterprise. A wholly foreign-owned enterprise may export products on its own or sell products through overseas sales agents or China's foreign-trade companies on a commission basis. Moreover, a wholly foreign-owned enterprise may remit abroad lawful profits, other legitimate incomes, and funds received upon its liquidation. The wages and other legitimate incomes of expatriates in a wholly foreign-owned enterprise may be remitted abroad after payment of individual income tax. Finally, taxes on machinery, equipment, parts, raw materials, etc. imported by the enterprise as part of the foreign investor's investment or for production of export goods may be exempted or reduced.

Application procedure

Before submitting an application for the establishment of a wholly foreign-owned enterprise, the foreign investor(s) must present to the local people's government at the county level or above of the place where the enterprise will be located a report, including such information as the objective(s) of the enterprise; its scope and scale of operations; products to be manufactured; technologies and equipment to be used; the area of land to be used and its requirements; the conditions and amounts for the use of water, electricity, coal, gas or other energies; and requirements in terms of public facilities. The people's government at the county level or above shall provide a written response within 30 days of the receipt of the report. Moreover, if the products of the wholly foreign-owned enterprise are subject to export licenses, export quotas or import licenses, or are restricted imports under the law, prior approval must be obtained from the relevant departments in charge of foreign trade and economy pursuant to their respective scopes of administrative power.

In applying for the establishment of a wholly foreign-owned enterprise, the foreign investor shall, through the local people's government at the county level or above in the place where the enterprise will be located, submit the following documents to the examination-and-approval organ:

1   a written application for the establishment of the enterprise;
2   a feasibility study report;
3   the articles of association;
4   a list of legal representative(s) or candidates for directors;
5   the registration certificate, names of the directors, three years' balance sheets, etc. of the foreign investor and a certificate of its credit worthiness, or, in the case of an individual, the nationality, identity, resume, and financial condition of the foreign investor;[23]
6   the written response of the people's government at the county level or above of the place where the enterprise will be located;
7   a list of materials needed to be imported; and
8   any other required documents.

If two or more foreign investors jointly apply for the establishment of the enterprise, a copy of the contract concluded between them must also be submitted.

On the application, the foreign investor shall state:

1   its name or title, domicile, and place of registration, and the name, nationality, and post of its legal representative;
2   the name and domicile of the proposed enterprise;
3   the business scope, product type(s), and production scale of the proposed enterprise;
4   the total amount of investment, registered capital, source of capital, method of investment, and time limits for investing in the proposed enterprise;
5   the organizational structure and the legal representative of the proposed enterprise;
6   the major production equipment to be used and its age, production technology, level of technology, and source of supply;
7   the direction, regions, channels, and means for the sale of products;
8   the arrangements made for foreign exchange income and expenditure;
9   the establishment of internal organs and their personnel, and matters regarding the recruitment, training, wages, welfare, insurance, labor protection, etc. of staff and workers;

10 the amount of environmental pollution likely to be caused and the solutions;
11 the site selected and the area of land to be used;
12 capital construction and the amount of capital, energy, and raw materials needed for production and operations as well as the measures to procure them;
13 progress plans on the implementation of the investment project; and
14 the term of the proposed enterprise.

Similarly, the wholly foreign-owned enterprise shall contain the following in its articles of association:

1 its name and domicile;
2 its purpose and business scope;
3 the total amount of investment, registered capital, and time limits for investment;
4 its organizational form;
5 the internal organs and their powers and rules of procedure, the legal representative, and the duties and powers of the general manager, chief engineer, and chief accountant;
6 the principles and systems regarding finance, accounting, and auditing;
7 labor management;
8 its duration, dissolution, and liquidation; and
9 the procedure for amending the articles of association.

The examination-and-approval organ is either the MOFTEC (now the Department of Foreign Investment Administration of the Ministry of Commerce) or the people's governments in provinces, autonomous regions, municipalities directly under the central government, separately planned cities, and SEZs authorized by the State Council. These local governments will examine and approve applications if the total amount of investment is within the investment amount to be approved by the local people's government; and the state does not need to allot raw materials, and the country's overall balance of energy, communications and transportation, foreign-trade export quotas, etc. will not be affected.

The foreign investor may authorize a Chinese FIE-service organ to go through the aforementioned formalities. The examination-and-approval organ will approve or disapprove the application within 90 days, and if the examination-and-approval organ is a local government, it should, within 15 days of the approval of an application, report the approval to the Department of Foreign Investment Administration of the Ministry of Commerce for the record. Within 30 days of the receipt of the certificate of approval, the wholly foreign-owned enterprise must apply for registration with the AIC and obtain a business license. The date of the issue of the business license is the founding date of the wholly foreign-owned enterprise. Within

30 days of its founding date, the wholly foreign-owned enterprise must also register with the tax authority.

In the case of division, merger, or significant change of capital, the wholly foreign-owned enterprise must engage an accountant registered in China to verify its capital and issue a certificate of capital verification, obtain approval from the examination-and-approval organ, and register the changes with the AIC. Moreover, a wholly foreign-owned enterprise must submit its annual balance sheets and profit-and-loss statements to the finance and tax authorities and report the details to the examination-and-approval organ and the AIC for the record.

Dissolution

A wholly foreign-owned enterprise will be dissolved under one of the following circumstances:

1   expiration of the term of the enterprise;
2   dissolution by the foreign investor due to poorly run operations and heavy losses;
3   inability to continue operations due to heavy losses caused by *force majeure*, such as natural disaster and war;
4   bankruptcy;
5   revocation of the enterprise's right to run the business due to violation of Chinese laws and regulations or impairment of public interest; or
6   occurrence of other causes for dissolution as stipulated in the articles of association.

In the case of points 2, 3, and 4, the wholly foreign-owned enterprise shall submit on its own an application for dissolution to the examination-and-approval organ for approval. The date of approval will be the date of the dissolution of the enterprise. If the enterprise is dissolved under point 1, 2, 3, or 6, it must, within 15 days of its dissolution, make a public announcement and notify its creditors. Within 15 days of the announcement, the enterprise must propose the procedures and principles for liquidation and nominate candidates for the liquidation committee. The liquidation committee shall be composed of the legal representative of the enterprise, a representative of its creditors, a representative of its department-in-charge, and accountants and lawyers registered in China. After the examination-and-approval organ has given its approval, the liquidation committee shall conduct liquidation. The procedure for liquidation is discussed in section 9, "Liquidation of foreign investment enterprises," below. A noteworthy point is that when a wholly foreign-owned enterprise liquidates its assets, Chinese enterprises or other economic organizations have the right of priority to purchase the assets on equal terms.

6 Foreign companies limited by shares

In 1995, the MOFTEC promulgated the Provisional Rules on Several Issues Concerning the Establishment of Foreign Companies Limited by Shares,[24] allowing foreign companies, enterprises, other economic organizations, or individuals (the foreign shareholder) to form foreign companies limited by shares (外商投资股份有限公司) with Chinese companies, enterprises, or other economic organizations (the Chinese shareholder). A foreign company limited by shares refers to a legal-person enterprise, whose total capital is composed of shares of equal value and whose foreign shareholder(s) contribute(s) 25 percent or more of its registered capital. The company bears liabilities with its total assets, while the shareholders bear liabilities in proportion to the number of their respective shares.

A foreign company limited by shares can be established by means of sponsorship or subscription. If the company is to be established by means of sponsorship, the promoters must meet the requirements stipulated in the Company Law, and there must be at least one foreign promoter. If the company is to be established by means of subscription, not only must the promoters meet the aforementioned requirements, but there must also be at least one promoter who has successively made profits in the last three years. Where this profit-making promoter is a Chinese shareholder, it must submit the last three years' financial and accounting statements audited by registered accountants in China. Where this profit-making promoter is a foreign shareholder, it must submit financial reports audited by registered accountants of the place where it is domiciled. The minimum amount of registered capital for a foreign company limited by shares is RMB 30 million. If a shareholder wants to transfer its shares, the consequential shareholding of the foreign shareholder must be at least 25 percent of the registered capital. In addition, the promoters can transfer their shares only if three years have passed since the registration of the company and the original examination-and-approval organ has given approval.

Having reached an agreement to establish a foreign company limited by shares, the promoters can entrust one promoter with the task of going through the application formalities. To begin with, the promoter must submit to the department-in-charge in the province, autonomous region, municipality directly under the central government, or separately planned city a written application, a feasibility study report, an asset-appraisal report, etc. On the application, the promoter must provide:

1   the names, domiciles, and legal representatives of the promoters;
2   the name, domicile, and objective(s) of the company;
3   the means of establishing the company, total amount of share capital, categories of shares, par value of each share, proportion of shares subscribed by the promoters, and scope and channels for the subscription of shares;

4 in the case of establishment by subscription, the production and operation situation of the promoters, including their production, assets and liabilities, and profits in the last three years;
5 details of how the capital will be invested and the business scope of the company;
6 the time of the application, signatures of the legal representatives of the promoters, and seals of the promoters; and
7 any other necessary items.

If the company is established by means of subscription, the promoter must also submit a prospectus.

After the department-in-charge has given its consent, it should transfer the aforementioned documents to the office of the MOFTEC (now the Department of Foreign Investment Administration of the Ministry of Commerce) in the province, autonomous region, municipality directly under the central government, or separately planned city for verification and approval. Having obtained the approval of these local offices, the promoters may sign a formal agreement and draw up the articles of association, which are sent to the MOFTEC (now the Department of Foreign Investment Administration of the Ministry of Commerce) for examination and approval. Within 90 days of the issue of the certificate of approval, the promoters must pay, in a lump sum, their respective subscribed shares. If the company cannot be established, the promoters will be jointly and severally liable for the expenses and debts incurred as a result of their promoting activities.

In the case of establishment by means of sponsorship, the promoters must set up a board of directors and a board of supervisors after they have paid in full their subscribed shares. The board of directors must then submit the certificate of approval, articles of association, and certificate of capital verification to the AIC to register the establishment of the company. In the case of establishment by means of subscription, the promoters must first pay in full their subscribed shares and then have a legally designated capital-verification organ verify their payments and produce a certificate of capital verification. Within 30 days of the issue of the certificate of capital verification, the promoters shall convene the founding meeting and elect a board of directors and a board of supervisors. The board of directors shall, within 30 days of the closing of the founding meeting, submit the certificate of approval, articles of association, certificate of capital verification, and minutes of the founding meeting to the AIC to apply for registration of establishment. Within 30 days of the receipt of all the required documents, the AIC must complete the registration formalities and issue a business license.

In 2001, the MOFTEC issued the Circular on Relevant Issues Concerning Foreign Companies Limited by Shares,[25] standardizing their listing on stock exchanges. To have its shares listed on stock exchanges, an existing foreign company limited by shares must meet the following requirements:

1   Upon application or after its shares have been listed, the company must abide by industrial policies on foreign investment.
2   The company should be an enterprise established or reformed in accordance with regulations and procedures.
3   After its shares have been listed, the proportion of non-listed foreign shares of the company must not be less than 25 percent of the total amount of share capital.
4   It should meet other conditions stipulated in the relevant regulations on listed companies.

In addition, the foreign company limited by shares must obtain the approval of the MOFTEC (now the Department of Foreign Investment Administration of the Ministry of Commerce).

7 A comparison of an equity joint venture, a cooperative joint venture, a wholly foreign-owned enterprise, and a foreign company limited by shares

As mentioned at the outset, what investment vehicles foreign investors choose depends on their business strategies, financial means, human resources, familiarity with the foreign market, and the legal environment of the host country. In China, foreign direct investment can be made in the form of an equity joint venture, a cooperative joint venture, a wholly foreign-owned enterprise, and a foreign company limited by shares. From the perspective of foreign investors, each of these investment means has advantages and disadvantages. This section is a succinct comparison of these investment vehicles. Nonetheless, the general advantages and disadvantages discussed here will not apply across the board because each foreign investor has its own set of circumstances.

In an equity joint venture, while contributing capital, technology, and know-how, the foreign party can draw on the Chinese party's distribution network, manufacturing capabilities, and access to raw materials. Moreover, the Chinese party better knows how to deal with bureaucracy and to obtain the necessary approvals. Nevertheless, since the foreign party must consult the Chinese party whenever it makes management and production decisions, it will not have complete control of the joint venture. Besides, if the foreign party makes capital contribution in the form of industrial property rights or know-how, the Chinese party will have access to the foreign party's technologies and trade secrets.

Compared with the equity joint venture, the cooperative joint venture provides the investors with more flexibility because the distribution of profits and assumption of risks need not be in strict proportion to a party's capital contribution, and the foreign party can recover its investment prior to the termination of the joint venture. Even so, the cooperative joint venture is more project-oriented and short-term. If the foreign investor wants to penetrate the Chinese market and maintain a more permanent establishment that constitutes a significant part of its overall business strategy in China, the cooperative joint venture will not be a good choice.

On the other hand, the foreign investor in a wholly foreign-owned enterprise does not need to share control with other partners. Not only does it have managerial autonomy, but it will also encounter less interference from the government because the Chinese party, often a state-owned enterprise, has obligations other than those in the equity or cooperative joint venture. In addition, the foreign investor does not need to reveal its technologies and know-how to a Chinese partner. Nevertheless, the logistics of setting up a wholly foreign-owned enterprise can be expensive and time-consuming because, without a Chinese partner, the foreign investor must build its own manufacturing plant, establish its own distribution network, and procure raw materials on its own. In other words, the foreign investor must commit abundant resources and will face more business risks.

A foreign company limited by shares may raise capital by offering its shares to the public. Thus, a foreign company limited by shares may rely more on equity than on debt to finance its operations. Moreover, since a foreign company limited by shares has more financial strength, it may operate on a larger scale and engage in a wider range of business activities. Nevertheless, the establishment of a foreign company limited by shares and the public offering of its shares require compliance not only with the Provisional Rules on Several Issues Concerning the Establishment of Foreign Companies Limited by Shares, but also laws and regulations on securities. Until 2003, the main legislation for foreign companies limited by shares has been the Provisional Rules on Several Issues Concerning the Establishment of Foreign Companies Limited by Shares. It is likely that when China gains more experience of this investment vehicle, a more comprehensive law or regulation on foreign companies limited by shares will be enacted.

8 Merger, division, and conversion of foreign investment enterprises

In the 1980s and early 1990s, most foreign investors chose to set up equity joint ventures and cooperative joint ventures. However, when foreign investors have disputes with their Chinese partners due to discrepancies in business objectives or management philosophy, they buy out the Chinese partner's interest and convert the joint venture into a wholly foreign-owned enterprise. In addition, equity joint ventures, cooperative joint ventures, wholly foreign-owned enterprises, and foreign companies limited by shares merge with other enterprises or split up for various strategic reasons. Accordingly, this section introduces the important provisions on the merger, division, and conversion of FIEs.

79

109

Merger and division

The Rules on the Merger and Division of Foreign Investment Enterprises[26] govern the merger or division of equity joint ventures, legal-person co-operative joint ventures, wholly foreign-owned enterprises, and foreign companies limited by shares. "Merger" refers to the consolidation of two or more companies through the conclusion of an agreement and in accordance with the relevant provisions of the Company Law. A merger can be achieved in one of two ways: absorption or establishment of a new company. "Division" refers to the splitting up of a company into two or more companies in accordance with the relevant provisions of the Company Law and the resolution of its highest organ of power. Likewise, division can be achieved in one of two ways: division with the continuous existence of the original company or division by the dissolution of the original company.

First and foremost, the merger or division of FIEs must not result in the establishment of wholly foreign-owned enterprises, companies with foreign-controlled shareholding, or companies with the predominance of foreign investors in those industries in which such companies are prohibited. If the merger or division of a company has caused changes in its line of business or business scope, such a merger or division must comply with the relevant laws, administrative regulations, and industrial polices, and the company must go through the formalities of examination and approval. Upon verification by the examination-and-approval organ and such authorities as customs and tax, the companies that have survived or emerged as newly established companies after the merger or division can continue to enjoy the FIE treatment given to the original companies. No merger or division shall be conducted before the investors of the companies have paid their investments or contributed the cooperative means in accordance with the joint venture contract or articles of association and the company has actually engaged in production or operation.

The merger or division of an FIE shall be examined and approved by the original examination-and-approval organ, and the registration formalities for the establishment, change, or cancellation of a company shall be completed with the relevant AIC. The company (companies) that is (are) to be dissolved due to a merger must apply to its (their) original examination-and-approval organ(s) for dissolution prior to the submission of application to the examination-and-approval organ if there are two or more original examination-and-approval organs involved. If the total amount of investment of the companies to be merged exceeds the amount to be approved by the original examination-and-approval organ or that of the examination-and-approval organ in the place where the merged company will be located, an examination-and-approval organ that has the appropriate amount of authority shall conduct the examination and approval. If one of the companies to be merged is a company limited by shares, the merger shall be examined and approved by the MOFTEC (now the Department of Foreign Investment Administration of the Ministry of Commerce). The views of the examination-and-approval organ in the place where the company to be dissolved or to be established is or will be located shall be solicited with respect to the dissolution of the original company or the establishment of new companies in other places. The merger or division of listed companies limited by shares must abide by the pertinent laws and regulations and the provisions issued by the State Securities Regulatory Commission and must go through the necessary formalities of examination and approval.

Moreover, the merger of an FIE and a domestic enterprise must conform to the relevant laws and regulations governing the use of foreign investment and with industrial polices, and must meet the following requirements:

1   The domestic company to be merged must be either a limited liability company or a company limited by shares.
2   The investors of the company emerging from the merger must satisfy the qualification requirements stipulated in the pertinent laws, regulations, and government rules on investors in the relevant industry.
3   The proportion of equity of the foreign investor(s) in the new company must be no less than 25 percent of its registered capital.
4   All the parties to the merger must ensure that the employees of the companies to be merged are fully re-employed or reasonably placed.

If the company that emerges from the merger is an FIE, its total amount of investment shall be the sum of the total amount of investment of the original FIE and the total amount of assets of the domestic company. The proportion of the registered capital to the total amount of investment must conform to the Provisional Rules on the Proportion of the Registered Capital to the Total Amount of Investment of Sino-Foreign Equity Joint Ventures,[27] unless otherwise approved by the MOFTEC (now the Department of Foreign Investment Administration of the Ministry of Commerce) and the State Administration for Industry and Commerce.

The company that is formed by the merger of two or more limited liability companies will be a limited liability company, and the company that is formed by the merger of two or more companies limited by shares will be a company limited by shares. The company that is formed by the merger of a listed company limited by shares and a limited liability company will be a company limited by shares, while the company that is formed by the merger of an unlisted company limited by shares and a limited liability company will be either a company limited by shares or a limited liability company. If a company limited by shares merges with another company limited by shares or the company emerging from the merger is a limited liability company, the post-merger registered capital shall be the sum of the amounts of registered capital of the original companies. The proportion of equity of the investors in the company that emerges from the merger shall be determined by the investors through consultation, or, based on the appraised value of the equity of the investors in the original companies, be stipulated in the contracts or articles of association. However, the proportion of equity of the foreign investor(s) in the company that is formed by merger must be no less than 25 percent of its registered capital. If a company limited by shares emerges from the merger of a limited liability company and a company limited by shares, its registered capital shall be the sum of the amount of equity into which the net assets of the original limited liability company have been converted and the amount of equity of the original company limited by shares.

Similarly, the amounts of registered capital of the companies emerging from the division of a company shall be determined by the highest organ of power of the original company in accordance with laws and regulations on FIEs as well as the relevant provisions issued by the State Administration for Industry and Commerce. The sum of the amounts of registered capital of the companies that are formed by the division shall be the registered capital of the original company. The proportion of equity of the investors in the companies that emerge from the division is to be determined by the investors in their contracts or the articles of association. Nonetheless, the proportion of equity of the foreign investor(s) in the company that emerges from the division shall be no less than 25 percent of its registered capital.

The examination-and-approval organ shall, within 45 days of the receipt of the required documents, make a preliminary written response as to whether it consents to the proposed merger or division. Within 10 days of the receipt of the preliminary response, the companies to be merged or the company to be divided shall send their (its) creditors notices explaining the succession plan for the current debts, and within 30 days, make three public announcements in nationally circulated newspapers at or above the provincial level. The creditors have 30 days after the notification, or 90 days after the first public announcement, to demand that the companies (company) revise the succession plan or to pay off the debts or provide appropriate guarantee. At the end of the 90-day period, the companies (company) must submit documents related to their (its) disposition of debts to the examination-and-approval organ, which will approve or disapprove the merger or division within 30 days.

The founding date of the company emerging from the merger will be that of the absorbing company if the company is formed by absorption. If the emerging company is formed by the establishment of a new company, the founding date of the company emerging from the merger will be the date on which the AIC approves the registration of its incorporation and issues the business license. The founding dates of the new companies formed as a result of the division of a company will be the date(s) on which the AIC approves the registration of their incorporation and issues the business licenses.

Conversion

If the foreign party wants to buy out the interest of the Chinese party and convert the equity joint venture into a wholly foreign-owned enterprise, it should consult the Rules on the Modification of Investors' Equities in Foreign Investment Enterprises.[28] According to these rules, if an equity joint venture is converted into a wholly foreign-owned enterprise, the parties must ensure that the wholly foreign-owned enterprise is allowed in the relevant industry and the requirements for establishment listed in the Detailed Rules for the Implementation of the Law on Wholly Foreign-Owned Enterprises are met. In industries where state-owned enterprises must be the controlling shareholders or take the predominant position, changes in the equities of investors must not lead to the control or predominance of foreign investors or non-state-owned enterprises.

The government organ to examine and approve the changes in equities is the examination-and-approval organ that has approved the establishment of the FIE. However, if the equity joint venture or cooperative joint venture will be converted into a wholly foreign-owned enterprise and this enterprise will do business in an industry in which wholly foreign-owned enterprises are restricted as stipulated in the Detailed Rules for the Implementation of the Law on Wholly Foreign-Owned Enterprises, the change of shareholding of the Chinese party must be approved by the MOFTEC (now the Department of Foreign Investment Administration of the Ministry of Commerce).

To obtain approval, the FIE should submit the following documents to the examination-and-approval organ:

1   a written application for the modification of the investors' equities;
2   the joint venture contract, articles of association, and the agreement on their revisions;
3   a duplicate of the certificate of approval for the establishment of the FIE and of its business license;
4   the resolution of the board of directors on the modification of the investors' equities;
5   a list of the directors after the modification of the investors' equities;
6   the agreement on the transfer of equity concluded between the transferor and the transferee and signed or confirmed in some written form by other investors; and
7   any other documents required by the examination-and-approval organ.

Specifically, the agreement on the transfer of equity should contain:

1   the names and domiciles of the transferor and transferee, and the names, posts, and nationalities of their legal representatives;
2   the amount and price of the equity to be transferred;
3   the time limit and means for completing the deal;

4   the rights and obligations to be assumed by the transferee in accordance with the contract and articles of association;
5   liabilities for breach of contract;
6   choice of law and resolution of disputes;
7   the effectuation and termination of the agreement; and
8   the time and place of the conclusion of the agreement.

Moreover, if the Chinese party has invested state-owned assets, the FIE must also submit the following documents to the examination-and-approval organ:

1   the signed opinion of the Chinese party's department-in-charge on the changes in equities;
2   the appraisal report on the equity to be transferred issued by the government organ responsible for evaluating state-owned assets; and
3   the letter of affirmation of the aforementioned report issued by the government department in charge of management of state-owned assets.

The examination-and-approval organ will approve or disapprove the application within 30 days of the receipt of all the required documents. The FIE must then go through the formalities of changing the certificate of approval with the examination-and-approval organ within 30 days of the approval of the modification. In addition, the FIE must, within 30 days of changing the certificate of approval, apply to the AIC for change of registration. In applying for change of registration, the FIE should submit the documents it has submitted to the examination-and-approval organ, the approval document issued by the examination-and-approval organ, and any other required documents. The agreement on the transfer of equity and the agreement on the revision of the original contract and articles of association will take effect on the date of the issue of the certificate of approval for modification.

Furthermore, according to the Provisional Rules on Several Issues Concerning the Establishment of Foreign Companies Limited by Shares, an equity joint venture, a cooperative joint venture, or a wholly foreign-owned enterprise may be converted into a foreign company limited by shares. To apply for conversion, the FIE must prove that it has made profits for the last three consecutive years. In addition, the original investors of the FIE should be the promoters either by themselves or with others. Specifically, the promoters should prepare:

1   the contract and/or articles of association of the original FIE;
2   the resolution of the board of directors on the reorganization of the FIE;
3   the resolution of the original investors of the FIE on the termination of the original contract and/or articles of association;

4   an appraisal report on the assets of the original FIE;
5   the agreement concluded by the promoters;
6   the articles of association of the prospective company;
7   the business license, certificate of approval, and financial statements of the last three consecutive years of the original FIE;
8   a written application for the establishment of the company;
9   certificates of credit worthiness of the promoters; and
10   a feasibility study report.

These documents must first be submitted to the examination-and-approval organ of the place where the FIE is located for initial approval, and then be transferred to the MOFTEC (now the Department of Foreign Investment Administration of the Ministry of Commerce) for examination and approval. After the certificate of approval has been issued and the promoters have paid in full their subscribed shares, the company must apply to the AIC for change of registration. Once the FIE becomes a foreign company limited by shares, it will have all the rights and obligations of the original FIE. The obligations of the parties stipulated in the contract and articles of association of the original FIE should also be included in the promoters' agreement and articles of association of the foreign company limited by shares.

Apart from FIEs, a state-owned enterprise, a collectively owned enterprise, or a company limited by shares may be converted into a foreign company limited by shares. Apart from the requirements listed in the Provisional Rules on Several Issues Concerning the Establishment of Foreign Companies Limited by Shares, three other requirements must be met:

1   In the case of a state-owned enterprise or a collectively owned enterprise, the enterprise must have been in business for at least five years and have made profits for the last three consecutive years (in the case of a company limited by shares, it is established with official approval of the state).
2   25 percent or more of the registered capital of the enterprise or the company limited by shares must have been purchased by foreign shareholders with convertible foreign currency.
3   The business scope of the enterprise or the company limited by shares must abide by the industrial policies on FIEs.

9 Liquidation of foreign investment enterprises

According to the Measures on the Liquidation of Foreign Investment Enterprises,[29] FIEs that are capable of organizing liquidation committees by themselves may conduct liquidation in accordance with the provisions on ordinary liquidation. If FIEs are not capable of organizing liquidation committees or have met obstacles in conducting ordinary liquidation, the board of directors, joint management committee, investors, or creditors may apply to the examination-and-approval organ to conduct special liquidation. Moreover, FIEs that have been ordered to close down should also conduct special liquidation.

With respect to ordinary liquidation, the liquidation should be started on the date of the expiration of the term of the FIE, the date of the dissolution of the FIE as approved by the examination-and-approval organ, or the date of the termination of the contract of the FIE as adjudged by the people's court or arbitrated by the arbitration commission. The duration of liquidation cannot exceed 180 days, beginning with the commencement of the liquidation and ending with the submission of the liquidation report to the examination-and-approval organ. When an extension of the liquidation period is necessary due to special circumstances, the liquidation committee should apply to the examination-and-approval organ 15 days before the expiration of the liquidation period. Even so, the extension cannot exceed 90 days.

The board of directors or the joint management committee of an FIE should organize a liquidation committee within 15 days of the commencement of the liquidation. The liquidation committee should consist of at least three members who are selected from and appointed by the board of directors or the joint management committee or are employed from relevant professions. The board of directors or the joint management committee is to appoint the chairperson of the liquidation committee. With the approval of the board of directors or joint management committee, the liquidation committee may employ other staff to perform specific tasks of liquidation. The liquidation committee has the power to:

1   sort out the FIE's assets, prepare a balance sheet and a schedule of assets, and formulate a liquidation plan;
2   make announcements to unknown creditors and send notices to known creditors;
3   settle the unfinished business of the FIE;
4   propose the basis for assessing and computing the value of property;
5   pay outstanding taxes;
6   settle credits and debts;
7   handle residual property after payment of debts; and
8   represent the FIE to participate in civil litigation.

The balance sheet, schedule of assets, basis for appraising and computing property, and the liquidation plan shall, after the affirmation of the board of directors or the joint management committee, be reported to the examination-and-approval organ for the record.

During the liquidation, the examination-and-approval organ and relevant government organs may send people to attend meetings and supervise the work of the liquidation committee. Within seven days of the commencement of the liquidation, the FIE should notify in writing the examination-and-approval organ, its department-in-charge, the bank with which it opens accounts, the customs, foreign exchange, tax, and registration authorities of its name and address, the reason(s) for liquidation, and the beginning date of the liquidation. If the FIE has state-owned assets, it should also notify the administrative department responsible for managing state assets. Within 10 days of its establishment, the liquidation committee shall send written notices to the known creditors to let them file claims. Within 60 days of its establishment, the liquidation committee shall make public announcements at least twice in a national newspaper and a local provincial or municipal newspaper. The first public announcement shall be published within 10 days of the establishment of the liquidation committee. Specifically, the announcement should state the name and address of the FIE, the reason(s) for liquidation, the starting date of the liquidation, and the correspondence address, names of the members, and the contact person(s) of the liquidation committee.

The creditors should file claims with the liquidation committee within 30 days of the receipt of the notices or within 90 days of the first public announcement. If the creditors fail to file claims within the time limit, the claims of known creditors will be liquidated; the claims of unknown creditors may be asserted and paid prior to the distribution of residual property, but will be considered abandoned after the distribution of residual property. If the creditors disagree with the liquidation committee over the assessment of their claims, they may ask the committee to re-examine their claims within 15 days of the receipt of the written notices. If the creditors still have objections after the re-examination, they may sue in the local people's court within 15 days of the receipt of the re-check notices. However, if the creditors and the FIE have agreed to settle disputes through arbitration, the creditors should submit their claims to arbitration. During any judicial or arbitration proceedings, the liquidation committee must not distribute any property in dispute.

Generally, the FIE shall satisfy its liabilities in the following order: liquidation expenses,[30] wages and labor insurance premiums, unpaid taxes, and debts. Nonetheless, secured creditors enjoy priority of repayment from the proceeds of the secured property. If the claim of a secured creditor cannot be satisfied fully with the proceeds of the secured property, the excess portion will be treated as unsecured debt. When the assets of the FIE are put on sale, the investors have priority to purchase them, and an asset will be sold to the one who gives the highest offer. The residual property of an FIE shall be distributed in proportion to the actual investments of its investors, unless otherwise stipulated in laws, administrative regulations, the joint venture contract, and the articles of association. If the FIE does not have sufficient assets to pay debts, the liquidation committee shall file for bankruptcy proceedings. In that case, liquidation shall be conducted in accordance with laws and administrative regulations on the liquidation of bankrupt enterprises.

During the liquidation period, neither the Chinese party nor the foreign party has the power to dispose of the FIE's property. With regard to any gains and losses found during the preparation of the inventory of property, sales, debts that the FIE has no ability to pay, loans that the FIE cannot recall, and any incomes and losses made during the liquidation period, the liquidation committee shall provide the board of directors or the joint management committee with written explanations and pertinent evidence and include them in liquidation gains and losses. The value of the assets of the FIE should be appraised in the following order of measures:

1   the stipulations in the joint venture contract and the articles of association;
2   the decisions of the parties through consultation, subject to the approval of the examination-and-approval organ;
3   the decisions made by the liquidation committee with reference to relevant regulations and the opinions of an asset-appraisal organ, subject to the approval of the examination-and-approval organ; or
4   the decision of the court or arbitration commission in the case of termination of contract.

In addition, the following actions of an FIE are invalid if they were done within 180 days prior to the commencement of the liquidation:

1   transfer of property without consideration;
2   sale of assets at abnormally low prices;
3   provision of property guarantee for debts which originally were not guaranteed;
4   repayment of debts prior to due dates; and
5   relinquishment of credits.

The liquidation committee shall prepare a liquidation report, which is to be affirmed by the board of directors or the joint management committee and filed with the examination-and-approval organ for the record. Within 10 days of the submission of the liquidation report, the liquidation committee must cancel the registration of the FIE with the customs and tax authorities. Within 10 days of such cancellation, the liquidation committee shall submit the liquidation report and the certificate of cancellation issued by the customs and tax authorities to the AIC to cancel the registration of the FIE and turn in its business license. Furthermore, the liquidation committee must make a public announcement of the termination of the FIE in a national newspaper and a local provincial or municipal newspaper.

As regards special liquidation, the commencement date shall be the date when the examination-and-approval organ approves special liquidation or when the FIE is ordered to close down by law. Unlike ordinary liquidation, a liquidation committee for special liquidation is to be organized by the examination-and-approval organ or a department with its authorization. The members of the liquidation committee consist of both Chinese and foreign investors, representatives of the relevant government organs, and professionals. During the liquidation, the chairperson of the liquidation committee, who is appointed by the examination-and-approval organ or a department authorized by it, exercises the powers of the legal representative of the FIE, while the liquidation committee exercises the powers of the FIE's power organ, namely, the board of directors or the joint management committee. In addition, the examination-and-approval organ is to affirm the liquidation plan and the liquidation report. Hence, the liquidation committee reports directly to the examination-and-approval organ.

The liquidation committee may convene meetings of the FIE's power organ or meetings of creditors to discuss the specific details of liquidation. All creditors are entitled to attend and vote in the meeting of creditors, except those who are secured creditors and have not given up their priority of repayment. The examination-and-approval organ or a department with its authorization shall also appoint the chairperson of the meeting of creditors from among the creditors who have the right to vote. The meeting of creditors has the power to examine the proof of claim, amount of claim, and collateral; and consider the circumstances of debt repayment and, based on such consideration and the liquidation plan, voice the creditors' opinions to the liquidation committee. In contrast, ordinary liquidation does not provide for the meeting of creditors, but creditors may initiate litigation or arbitration to protect their interests. Finally, if the provisions on special liquidation do not deal with an issue, the preceding provisions on ordinary liquidation will also apply.

10 Investment catalogs

Apart from meeting the respective requirements of an equity joint venture, a cooperative joint venture, a wholly foreign-owned enterprise, and a foreign company limited by shares, foreign investors must ascertain whether the Chinese government imposes any restrictions on the industry in which they plan to invest or what services or products the Chinese government encourages foreign investors to provide. In this regard, foreign investors should consult three investment catalogs: the Guidance Catalog of Industries with Foreign Investment, the Catalog of Encouraged High-Technology Products for Foreign Investment, and the Catalog of Advantageous Industries with Foreign Investment in the Middle and Western Regions. Together these three catalogs facilitate the application of policies on the examination and approval of FIEs and foreign investment projects.

First promulgated in 1995, the Regulations on Guiding the Direction of Foreign Investment and the Guidance Catalog of Industries with Foreign Investment (外商投资产业指导目录) provide foreign investors with investment guidelines and ensure that foreign investment corresponds with China's economic and development plans. In 2002, to fulfill its WTO commitments, China revised both the Regulations on Guiding the Direction of Foreign Investment[31] and the Guidance Catalog of Industries with Foreign Investment[32] to reduce investment restrictions and open up new industrial sectors. As the details of China's WTO commitments will be discussed in Chapter 10, this section focuses on outlining the contents of these two legal documents.

Foreign investment projects can be categorized into four types: encouraged, permitted, restricted, and prohibited. The Guidance Catalog of Industries with Foreign Investment lists only three categories: encouraged, restricted, and prohibited. Thus, anything not listed in the Guidance Catalog of Industries with Foreign Investment falls within the category of "permitted." A foreign investment project is "encouraged":

1   if it has new agricultural technologies, comprehensive agricultural development, or energy, communications and important raw materials;
2   if it offers high and new technologies or advanced application technologies that can improve product performance and increase technological and economic efficiency of enterprises, or offers the manufacture of new equipment and new materials which domestic production capacity is insufficient to produce;
3   if it is able to meet market needs, raise product grades, develop new markets, or increase the international competitiveness of products;
4   if it has new technologies and new equipment that can save energy and raw materials, comprehensively use resources and regenerate resources, and prevent environmental pollution;
5   if it can bring into play the manpower and resource advantages of the Middle and Western Regions and conform with the state's industrial policies; and
6   under any other circumstance as provided by laws and administrative regulations.

On the other hand, a foreign investment project is "restricted":

1   if its technologies lag behind;
2   if it is disadvantageous to saving resources and improving the ecological environment;
3   if it is engaged in the prospecting and exploitation of mineral resources that are protected by the state;
4   if it is one of the industries that the state opens gradually; and
5   under any other circumstance as provided by laws and administrative regulations.

Similarly, a foreign investment project is "prohibited":

1   if it jeopardizes the state's security or harms public interests;
2   if it pollutes the environment, destroys natural resources, or impairs human health;
3   if it occupies too much farmland and is unfavorable to the protection and development of land resources;

4 if it jeopardizes the security and usage of military facilities;
5 if it uses special Chinese crafts or technologies to manufacture products; and
6 under any other circumstance as provided by laws and administrative regulations.

Examples of encouraged, restricted, and prohibited projects are provided in Table 3.1.

Moreover, a foreign investment project may be "limited to equity and cooperative" or must have "the Chinese party as the controlling shareholder" or "the Chinese party as the relatively controlling shareholder." The phrase "limited to equity and cooperative" means that only Sino-foreign equity joint ventures and Sino-foreign cooperative joint ventures are permitted. "The Chinese party as the controlling shareholder" denotes that the investment ratio of the Chinese party (parties) in the project is 51 percent or more. "The Chinese party as the relatively controlling shareholder" means that the investment ratio of the Chinese party (parties) in the project is higher than that of any foreign party.

Apart from enjoying the preferential treatment provided by relevant laws and administrative regulations, encouraged projects that are engaged in the construction and operations of energy, communications, municipal infrastructure (coal, oil, natural gas, electricity, railways, highways, ports, airports, city roads, sewage disposition, garbage disposition, etc.) that require large amounts of investment and have long recovery periods may expand their related business scope with approval. In addition, permitted projects whose products are all exported directly will be regarded as encouraged projects. Similarly, restricted projects of which export sales account for 70 percent or more of their total sales may, with the approval of the people's governments of provinces, autonomous regions, municipalities directly under the central government, and separately planned cities or of the relevant ministry or department under the State Council, be regarded as permitted projects. Furthermore, the requirements may be relaxed for permitted and restricted projects that can really give the advantages of the Middle and Western Regions full play. In particular, those listed in the Catalog of Advantageous Industries with Foreign Investment in the Middle and Western Regions, which will be discussed below, may enjoy the preferential policies on encouraged projects.

In 2003, the Ministry of Science and Technology and Ministry of Commerce jointly promulgated the Catalog of Encouraged High-Technology Products for Foreign Investment (鼓励外商投资高新技术产品目录).[33] This catalog incorporates what is listed in the Catalog of Chinese High-Technology Products and adds the products that China urgently needs to develop as well as the products that show a big gap between China and the rest of the world in terms of technology and equipment. Based on technological domain, this catalog lists 917 items under 11 types, namely,

Table 3.1 The Guidance Catalog of Industries with Foreign Investment (excerpts)

Encouraged industries for foreign investment

I	Agriculture, forestry, animal husbandry, and fishery
8	Planting of natural rubber, sisal hemp, and coffee

II	Excavation
9	Prospecting and exploitation of copper, lead, and zinc mines (limited to equity and cooperative, but wholly foreign-owned enterprises permitted in the Western Region)

III	Manufacturing
1.1	Storage and processing of grain, vegetable, fruit, fowl, and livestock products
18.9	Design and manufacture of civil planes (with the Chinese party as the controlling shareholder)
21.1	Development and production of digital cameras and key components

IV	Production and supply of electricity, coal gas, and water
8	Construction and operations of water-supply plants in cities

VIII	Real estate
1	Development and construction of ordinary residential housing

XI	Education, culture and arts, broadcasting, film, and TV
1	Institutes of higher education (limited to equity and cooperative)

Restricted industries for foreign investment

I	Agriculture, forestry, animal husbandry, and fishery
1	Development and production of grain (including potato), cotton, and oil seed (with the Chinese party as the controlling shareholder)

II	Excavation
2	Prospecting and exploitation of precious metals (gold, silver, and platinum)

III	Manufacturing
1.1	Production of millet wine and spirits of famous brands

VII	Banking and insurance
4	Financial leasing companies

Prohibited industries for foreign investment

I	Agriculture, forestry, animal husbandry, and fishery
3	Fishing of aquatic products on the territorial seas and inland waters of China

III	Manufacturing
5.4	Production of enamel products

VI	Finance and insurance
1	Futures companies

electronics and information, software, aeronautics and astronautics, optomechatronics, biomedicine and medical equipment, new materials, new energy and efficient energy saving, environmental protection, geospace and ocean, nuclear applied technology, and modern agriculture. Hence, apart from the Guidance Catalog of Industries with Foreign Investment, foreign investors should also consult this catalog when making investment decisions in China.

Finally, the Chinese government has also promulgated the Catalog of Advantageous Industries with Foreign Investment in the Middle and Western Regions (中西部地区外商投资优势产业目录).[34] Based on the local circumstances of provinces, autonomous regions, and municipality directly under the central government in the Middle and Western Regions, such as Shanxi Province, Inner Mongolia, Anhui Province, Chongqing City, Sichuan Province, and Yunnan Province, this catalog lists the industries and products that have obvious advantages and potential due to the respective environments, resources, manpower, technology, markets, etc. of these localities. Any foreign investment projects listed in this catalog enjoy the various policies applicable to encouraged projects listed in the Guidance Catalog of Industries with Foreign Investment. A detailed discussion on the promotion of the development of the Western Region is provided in Chapter 11.

11 Foreign investment from 1979 to 2002

With the adoption of the Equity Joint Venture Law in 1979, foreign direct investment (FDI) started to flow into China. Since then, FDI inflows have grown rapidly, even though there have been some fluctuations due to changes in China's political and economic environments. In the 1980s, FDI grew gradually in China – about US$1.6 billion annually from 1979 to 1989. The FDI inflow began to slow down after the Tiananmen Incident in 1989, but soared after Deng Xiaoping called for the acceleration of economic reforms and further opening up in his much-publicized tour of Chinese southern provinces in early 1992. Consequently, most of the FDI flows in China occurred after 1992. In 2001, China received US$46.8 billion worth of FDI, accounting for about 33 percent of the FDI flows in developing countries and about 14 percent of FDI flows in the whole world. In 2002, the total FDI inflow reached over US$50 billion, close to 50 times the annual amount of FDI inflow in the 1980s.

Moreover, there were nearly half a million foreign investment enterprises in China, coming from more than 170 countries. Foreign investors mainly came from industrialized or newly industrialized economies in the Asia-Pacific Region. Until 2002, Hong Kong was the largest investor, accounting for 48 percent of the total FDI in China, followed by the United States (9 percent), Japan (8 percent), Taiwan (7 percent), Singapore (5 percent), Virgin Islands (5 percent), South Korea (3 percent), the United Kingdom (3 percent), Germany (2 percent), and France (1 percent). At the early stage of opening up, these foreign investors were more advanced than China in terms of production technology, to varying degrees and in various aspects. Western investors were, for instance, more advanced in high technology, whereas East Asian investors were more advanced in labor-intensive production technology. Apparently, China benefited greatly from the inflow of

FDI as evidenced by the rapid economic growth it has experienced in the last two decades.

The geographical distribution of FDI in China was quite uneven. As shown in Table 3.2, FDI was heavily concentrated in the Coastal Region, particularly in Guangdong Province. This came as no surprise. From the

Table 3.2 Regional distribution of pledged and actually used foreign direct investment in China 1979–2002

Region	Pledged FDI (%)	Realized FDI (%)
East	*86.4*	*85.96*
Beijing	4.49	4.09
Tianjin	3.99	3.90
Hebei	2.00	1.89
Liaoning	5.61	4.39
Shanghai	9.68	8.26
Jiangsu	13.41	12.81
Zhejiang	3.92	3.39
Fujian	9.27	9.47
Shandong	6.49	6.23
Guangdong	24.56	27.86
Hainan	1.62	1.69
Central	*7.58*	*8.78*
Shanxi	0.52	0.45
Jilin	0.83	0.82
Heilongjiang	0.84	1.01
Anhui	0.83	0.85
Jiangxi	0.70	0.79
Henan	1.20	1.21
Hubei	1.43	1.93
Hunan	1.12	1.53
West	*6.02*	*5.26*
Guangxi	1.88	1.85
Inner Mongolia	0.26	0.19
Chongqing	0.60	0.63
Sichuan	1.18	0.95
Guizhou	0.23	0.11
Yunnan	0.42	0.26
Tibet	0.00	0.00
Shaanxi	0.88	0.86
Gansu	0.16	0.13
Qinghai	0.08	0.01
Ningxia	0.07	0.04
Xinjiang	0.16	0.10
Total	*100.00*	*100.00*

Sources: *Almanac of Foreign Economic Relations and Trade of China* 1984–2003; *Statistical Yearbook of China* 1984–2003; *China Regional Economy: A Profile of 17 Years of Reform and Opening-Up.*

very beginning of the economic reform and opening-up, the Chinese government's foreign investment policy was to favor the coastal areas in order to take the geographical advantage of the coastal provinces and make use of their links with overseas Chinese business communities. As mentioned in Chapter 1, China first set up four SEZs in the Coastal Region – Shenzhen, Zhuhai, and Shantou, which are adjacent to Hong Kong and Macao, and Xiamen, which is only about 120 nautical miles from Taiwan – and granted foreign investors preferential policy treatment, such as tax incentives. In 1984, China opened up 14 more coastal cities, such as Dalian, Tianjin, Qingdao, Shanghai, Guangzhou, Yandai, and Fuzhou, to foreign investors who could enjoy preferential policy treatment similar to that in the SEZs. The preferential policy treatment was soon extended to other coastal areas, such as the Yangtze River Delta, Pearl River Delta, Liaodong Peninsula, Shandong Peninsula, and Bohai Rim. In late 1980s and early 1990s, Hainan was made the fifth SEZ in China, and Pudong was made a New Area to provide preferential policy treatment similar to that enjoyed by SEZs. Not until the 1990s were some limited inland areas opened up, providing preferential policy treatment.

In terms of sectoral distribution, FDI was first permitted only in oil exploration projects and such service sectors as tourist and hotel industries, and, after 1986, in such manufacturing sectors as textile and electronics industries. After Deng Xiaoping's southern tour in 1992, foreign investors began to have access to a wide range of industries, including retail sale, real estate, foreign trade, transportation, finance and banking. Until 2002, most FDI was made in the secondary industry (61 percent), while the remainder was in the tertiary industry (37 percent) and the primary industry (2 percent).

As mentioned above, the three most popular investment vehicles for foreign investors are the equity joint venture, the cooperative joint venture, and the wholly foreign-owned enterprise. During the period 1979–2002, 44 percent of FDI was in the form of equity joint ventures, 20 percent in the form of cooperative joint ventures, and 34 percent in the form of wholly foreign-owned enterprises.[35] Nonetheless, in recent years, FDI in the form of wholly foreign-owned enterprises steadily increased, while FDI in the form of cooperative joint ventures continually declined.

Notwithstanding the impressive inflow of FDI and China's aforementioned regulatory efforts, various problems existed in practice. For instance, since local authorities were eager to attract foreign investment, laws and regulations were not enforced consistently. Another common problem was that the parties to a joint venture were often unable to pay their subscribed investments or had to delay payment for various reasons. Sometimes FIEs were required to pay additional fees that were not explicitly prescribed by law, even though they enjoyed various tax exemptions and tax holidays. In addition, since FIEs received preferential tax and tariff treatments, domestic enterprises were disadvantaged.

With China's accession to the WTO, a new wave of FDI inflow will appear. In particular, three characteristics of the new wave of FDI inflow deserve close attention. First, an increasing number of large-scale multinational corporations will invest in China. Second, an increasing amount of FDI will move into the high-technology area and capital-intensive projects, such as petroleum, automobile, and large-scale integrated circuit. Third, an increasing amount of FDI will move into the tertiary industry, including securities, banking, telecommunications, transportation, and tourism. Furthermore, as competition increases, the Chinese government will have to level the playing field for domestic and foreign investment enterprises such that the former can compete with the latter on equal terms.

12 Selected cases

Hong Kong Huizhan Ltd. *v.* Head Office of Tianjin City Light Industrial Co. *(2001)* 民四提字第5号, *Supreme People's Court, 17 January 2002*

Facts

On 19 January 1994, Tianjin City Refrigerator Industrial Co. (hereinafter RIC) and Hong Kong Huizhan Ltd. (hereinafter HZL) signed an agreement to invest a total amount of US$28,000,000 to establish Xin Xing Guang International Building (Tianjin) Ltd. (hereinafter XIL). XIL planned to construct a skyscraper, Xin Xing Guang International Building (the building), with a total area of 30,800 m^2 at the site of Ke Nai Restaurant.

The investment of RIC included a 50-year land use right representing 26 percent of the total investment, whereas HZL contributed cash representing 74 percent of the total investment. Any profit was to be distributed according to the investment ratio. RIC should own 8,008 m^2 of the building. RIC retained 1,500 m^2 on the second floor for its own use. The other 6,508 m^2 was transferred to HZL at a price of RMB 7,000 per square meter. The total price was RMB 45,556,000. After deducting its previous payment, RIC had to pay HZL an actual amount of RMB 29,000,000. Both parties agreed that HZL should pay RIC RMB 1,000,000 within one week of the effective date of the agreement. In addition, within one week of the date when RIC completed the formalities for the transfer of the land use right and for the application of a business license for XIL, HZL should prepay RIC RMB 4,000,000. HZL should pay RIC a balance of RMB 24,000,000 within two and a half years of the effective date of the agreement. Moreover, both parties agreed that RIC was responsible for RMB 16,735,300, including the transfer price, the fee for transferring the land use right, accompanying fees (water, electricity, gas, communication, etc.), and the initial fees. Since RIC had a cash flow problem, HZL paid RMB 16,735,300 on its behalf. Such payment was to be deducted from the transfer price of RMB 45,556,000, which HZL owed RIC. HZL was responsible for all other fees.

On 16 June 1994, RIC and HZL signed an equity joint venture contract stipulating that they invest a total amount of US$2,300,000 to establish Tianjin San Le Development Ltd. (hereinafter SLL). HZL agreed to invest US$2,000,000 and owned 87 percent of the registered capital of SLL. RIC agreed to invest US$300,000 and owned 13 percent of the registered capital of SLL. In addition, they agreed that if one party wanted to transfer its equity in SLL, it must obtain the consent of the other party; when one party wanted to transfer its equity in SLL, the other party had the right of priority. Any transfer of registered capital had to be passed unanimously by the board of directors and approved by the original examination-and-approval organ. On 18 June 1994, RIC and HZL signed a supplementary contract that XIL would be converted to SLL. RIC completed the procedure for transferring the land use right of Ke Nai Restaurant by the end of June 1994. SLL would obtain the land use right. Furthermore, both parties agreed to pay HZL RMB 29,000,000 in full and to distribute the assets and profits after the second floor of the building was delivered. After the signing of the contract, HZL and RIC had paid in full their respective portions of registered capital: US$2,300,000 and US$300,000. HZL paid RIC RMB 8,000,000 and reimbursed it for the previously paid RMB 2,843,750 for the transfer of the land use right. On 28 June 1994, SLL obtained a certificate of land use. Meanwhile, the Tianjin San Jian Construction Ltd. (hereinafter SJL) had been contracted to build Jin Jie Building. Having completed portions of the building, SJL stopped the construction project in June 1998 due to financial hardship.

On 28 March 1996, the No. 2 Light Industry Bureau of Tianjin City (hereinafter LIB) transferred the entire equity of RIC in SLL and the project of Jin Jie Building to its subordinate company, Head Office of Tianjin City Light Industrial Company (hereinafter LIC). In addition, on 7 October 1996, RIC filed for bankruptcy. On 1 November 1996, the Tianjin City High People's Court declared RIC bankrupt. On 20 May 1997, LIC filed a lawsuit with the Tianjin City No. 2 Intermediate People's Court on the grounds that HZL did not make the required investment in full and the equity of RIC had been transferred to it. LIC requested that HZL return the land use right or continue to perform its contractual obligations.

The Tianjin City No. 2 Intermediate People's Court found that since it was a normal exercise of its power of office for LIB to transfer the equity of RIC in SLL and the project of Jin Jie Building to LIC six months before the Tianjin City High People's Court had accepted RIC's application for bankruptcy, LIC could assume the rights and obligations of RIC. Since the building had not been completed, LIC's request to have the 1,500 m^2 of land property delivered was denied. Accordingly, the Tianjin City No. 2 Intermediate People's Court held that:

1   The joint venture contract signed between RIC and HZL to construct the Jin Jie Building was valid, and LIC and HZL should continue to perform their obligations.
2   Within a month of the effective date of this judgment, HZL should pay LIC RMB 21,000,000 (the overdue penalty was 0.05 percent per day).
3   All other requests of both parties were dismissed.

HZL was not satisfied with the judgment and appealed to the Tianjin City High People's Court, which found that the contract and the supplementary contract signed between RIC and HZL were for the purpose of cooperation in constructing buildings. Being the department-in-charge of RIC, LIB transferred the rights and obligations of RIC in Jin Jie Building to LIC, which was an administrative means used by a state-asset management department to allocate state assets. Since RIC went bankrupt and its existence could not be restored, LIC should assume its contractual rights and obligations. As the ownership of the project of Jin Jie Building had already changed, the basis for continuing to perform the contract did not exist. Therefore, the judgment of the Tianjin City No. 2 Intermediate People's Court that the parties continue to perform the contract should be amended. Based on the aforementioned, the Tianjin City High People's Court held as follows:

1   Item 3 of the judgment of the Tianjin City No. 2 Intermediate People's Court was affirmed.
2   Item 2 of the judgment of the Tianjin City No. 2 Intermediate People's Court was amended. Within a month of the effective date of this judgment, HZL paid LIC RMB 21,000,000. The overdue interest was to be calculated using 200 percent of the lending rates set by the People's Bank of China for the corresponding period.
3   Item 1 of the judgment of the Tianjin City No. 2 Intermediate People's Court was also amended. The joint venture contract between RIC and HZL to construct the Jin Jie Building was terminated. HZL should make a one-time payment to LIC for the latter's interest in the 1,500 m^2 on the second floor of the Jin Jie Building. Based on the rate of RMB 7,000 per m^2, the total amount was RMB 10,500,000. The payment had to be made within 10 days of the effective date of this judgment. The overdue interest was to be calculated using 200 percent of the lending rates set by the People's Bank of China for the corresponding period.

HZL was dissatisfied with the judgment of the Tianjin City High People's Court. It appealed to the court for a retrial and dismissal of LIC's lawsuit on the following grounds:

1   LIB's transfer of equity in the joint venture by administrative means was legally ineffective. LIC was not qualified to be the plaintiff in this

case. Since HZL and LIC had no legal relationship, LIC should not name HZL as a defendant. The original courts incorrectly applied the law to name two civil entities without any legal relationship as parties.

2   The original courts omitted XIL as an important party in this case, which violated procedural law.
3   The joint venture contract and the supplementary contract between HZL and RIC should be terminated because RIC had already been declared bankrupt.
4   It was incorrect for the original courts to affirm that the land at issue and the building on it had been transferred to LIC (a third party).
5   HZL could not accept that the Tianjin City High People's Court ordered it to pay LIC nonexistent profits derived from an unfinished construction project.

LIC responded that the judgments of the original courts should be affirmed because they were based on clearly established facts and correct application of law. According to the Provisional Measures on the Determination of and the Handling of Disputes over State Property Rights, LIB had the right to transfer any state assets under its jurisdiction. LIC became a legally qualified shareholder based on LIB's document. Since LIC had all the rights and obligations of a shareholder, it could be a party of this case. Such transfer of equity was not for compensation, so the ownership still belonged to the state. Therefore, there was no breach of article 12 of the joint venture contract; the Equity Joint Venture Law and the Regulations for the Implementation of the Law on Sino-Foreign Equity Joint Ventures were inapplicable. This case was a lawsuit between the two investors (shareholders) of a joint venture, that is, the two parties of this case. HZL had a direct legal relationship with this case and should be a party. HZL had breached the contract many times by failing to make the required investment, thereby causing the Jin Jie Building to be unfinished even seven years after the conclusion of the contract and causing LIC serious economic losses. Thus, LIC requested that the court affirm the original judgment and dismiss HZL's appeal (*shensu*)[36] so as to prevent the loss of state assets.

Reasoning

The court held that the joint venture contract and the supplementary contract between RIC and HZL were legally valid because they represented the true intentions of both parties and their contents were lawful. The dispute in this case arose out of the performance of the contract, where the transfer of RIC's equity effected a change of shareholder of the joint venture. To ascertain whether the transfer of the equity of RIC had legal effect, the Equity Joint Venture Law and the Regulations for the Implementation of the Law on Sino-Foreign Equity Joint Ventures should be applied, not the Provisional Measures on the Determination of and the Handling of

Disputes over State Property Rights issued by the State Property Administration Bureau.

According to article 4(4) of the Equity Joint Venture Law, if one party wants to transfer its registered capital, it must obtain the consent of all the other parties. Moreover, article 24 of the Regulations for the Implementation of the Law on Sino-Foreign Equity Joint Ventures provides that any increase, transfer, or handling of the registered capital should be decided by the board of directors, approved by the original examination-and-approval organ, and registered with the original registering organ. With its own document, LIB, by administrative means, transferred the equity of RIC in the joint venture to LIC, a subordinate of LIB, thereby causing the legal consequence of a change of shareholder of the joint venture. Since the transfer of equity did not follow both procedural and substantive laws, had not been consented by HZL and decided by the board of directors, had not been approved by the original examination-and-approval organ, and had not gone through the formalities of changing registration, LIB's conduct violated the aforementioned provisions of the Equity Joint Venture Law and the Regulations for the Implementation of the Law on Sino-Foreign Equity Joint Ventures, as well as the relevant stipulations in the joint venture contract. Accordingly, the transfer of the equity of RIC was not legally effective.

Furthermore, since LIB was the department-in-charge of RIC, its unilateral change of a shareholder of the joint venture had no legal effect. Consequently, LIC did not obtain RIC's rights in the joint venture and other projects under RIC in accordance with the law. Because LIC had no right to be a plaintiff in lawsuits regarding disputes over matters of the joint venture, the court granted HZL's request to dismiss LIC's lawsuit. On the other hand, the court did not accept LIC's defenses. The determination of the original courts that LIC had the right to assume the rights and interests of RIC was based on erroneous application of law and thus should be rectified. The judgment of the Tianjin City High People's Court to terminate the performance of the contract and to order HZL to pay profits not yet earned from the unfinished construction work to LIC was also improper.

Ruling

According to article 4(4) of the Equity Joint Venture Law, article 24 of the Regulations for the Implementation of the Law on Sino-Foreign Equity Joint Ventures, and articles 108 and 153(1)(ii) of the Civil Procedure Law,[37] the court ruled that:

1 The judgments of the Tianjin City No. 2 Intermediate People's Court and the Tianjin City High People's Court were reversed.
2 The lawsuit of LIC was dismissed.

This ruling was final.

Hong Kong Xinmei Lianhe Water Cleaning Factory Ltd. *v.*
Nanjing City Jiangning District Dongshanqiao Township People's
Government *(2002)* 苏民三终字第060号, *Jiangsu Province High*
People's Court, 5 December 2002

Facts

On 14 January 1992, Hong Kong Xinmei Lianhe Water Cleaning Factory
Ltd. (hereinafter XML) and Jiangning County Sports Equipment Factory
(hereinafter JSF) signed a joint venture contract and established Nanjing
Dazhong Sports Equipment Ltd. (hereinafter NDL). Article 10 of the contract
stipulated that JSF and XML had to invest a total amount of US$300,000,
which was the registered capital of the joint venture. Specifically, each party
was to invest US$150,000 and own 50 percent of the registered capital.
Article 11 provided that JSF was to contribute the factory, machinery, and
other facilities, while XML was to contribute cash. Article 40 stipulated that
the duration of the joint venture was 15 years. Article 41 stated that when the
joint venture terminated prior to or upon the expiration of its term, it would
be liquidated according to the law, and that after liquidation, any assets
would be distributed in proportion to the parties' respective contributions.

On 20 January 1992, the former Jiangning County People's Government
approved the joint venture contract and articles of association of NDL.
On 29 January 1992, NDL was established with the approval of the State
Administration for Industry and Commerce. On 9 March 1992, NDL convened the first board meeting and decided to adopt the *chengbao* (承包)
responsibility system (contracting out), with JSF as the contractor. The
term of the *chengbao* contract was five years. In addition, the contractor
had autonomy in management, was accountable for profits and losses, would
be fully rewarded or liable, and was to be responsible for completing the
following basic tasks:

1   In the first two years of the operation, profits after tax were to reach
    US$300,000, that is, the total amount of the parties' investment, with
    40 percent being the return from the first year, which was US$120,000,
    and 60 percent being the return from the second year, which was
    US$180,000.
2   In the next three years of the operation, profits after tax, the amount of
    contracted work, and other matters should be decided by the board of
    directors in accordance with the business conditions of the previous two
    years.

After that contract had ended, NDL and JSF signed another *chengbao*
contract on 16 March 1995, stipulating that the contracting period would be
from April 1995 to April 2003. In this contract, JSF was to submit profits to
XML, be responsible for completing fixed amounts of work (but might

retain any excesses), and be fully liable for losses. The amount of profits submitted to XML for nine years was to be US$180,000, averaging US$20,000 per year. Every quarter JSF had to submit the profits and report to the board of directors. Upon the expiration of the contract term, all of XML's share capital in NDL would belong to JSF. The Nanjing City Jiangning County (now District) Dongshanqiao Township People's Government (hereinafter DSQ) was the guarantor of the contract, which was notarized by the Jiangning County Notary Office. Thereafter, Yang Jianguan, the legal representative of XML, requested that JSF perform the contract. He also requested that DSQ intervene, but to no avail. Therefore, XML filed a lawsuit with the court of first instance and requested the following:

1   The court terminate the joint venture and *chengbao* contracts.
2   JSF return the joint venture asset of US$100,000.
3   JSF pay *chengbao* fees (i.e. profits to be submitted) of US$80,000.
4   JSF, being liable as a result of the breach, compensate it RMB 150,000 for losses.
5   DSQ be responsible for settling JSF's credits and debts.
6   DSQ assume liability for its fault in the invalid guarantee of the *chengbao* contract.

Furthermore, since JSF and NDL did not undertake the annual review within the statutory period, the AIC revoked their legal-person enterprise business license and business license on 25 July 1998 and 8 November 1999, respectively.

The court of first instance found the following facts and reasons:

1   The contract between XML and JSF to establish NDL was legally valid. Both parties should exercise their rights and perform their obligations in accordance with the contract. Because JSF and NDL did not undertake their annual reviews within the statutory period, the AIC revoked their legal-person enterprise business license and business license. Thus, JSF and NDL ceased to have a legal status and were objectively unable to perform the contract with XML. Since XML's request to terminate the joint venture contract was based on facts and in conformity with the law, the court granted its request.
2   Having been established, NDL should engage in production and business activities pursuant to the relevant provisions of the Equity Joint Venture Law, within the scope approved by the State Administration for Industry and Commerce, and in accordance with the stipulations in the joint venture contract. After its establishment, absent any poor management, serious losses, or production or business activities, NDL undertook to contract out its work. This conduct violated the relevant statutory provisions. In addition, based on NDL's implementation of the *chengbao* responsibility system and the contents of its contract with

JSF, it could be concluded that the real purpose of the contracting out was to allow XML to recoup its investment. This disguise violated the relevant rules promulgated by the Ministry of Foreign Trade and Economic Cooperation and the State Administration for Industry and Commerce on the contracting out by Sino-foreign equity joint ventures. Hence, the *chengbao* contract was void from the very beginning.

3　According to the law, after the business license of NDL was revoked, the shareholders could, only after its assets were liquidated and its debts were paid off, distribute the residual assets in proportion to their investments. Under the circumstances that NDL had not been liquidated, and that JSF, as one of the investors of NDL, had no obligation to return the assets of NDL and was not a defendant in this case, XML lacked any legal basis to request JSF to return the joint venture asset of US$100,000.

4　Although the *chengbao* contract required JSF to pay XML *chengbao* fees, XML was not one of the parties to the contract. Since the business licenses of NDL and JSF, the parties to the contract, had been revoked, XML, being a nonparty to the contract, enjoyed no substantive rights vis-à-vis JSF and DSQ (the guarantor). In fact, JSF was not even a defendant in this case. Therefore, there was no legal basis for XML to request that JSF pay *chengbao* fees of US$80,000, to assume liability for breaching the contract, and to compensate RMB 150,000 as damages. Likewise, there was no legal basis for XML to request that DSQ be liable for being the guarantor of the void *chengbao* contract.

5　DSQ established JSF. After the business license of JSF was revoked, DSQ had the obligation to liquidate JSF according to the law. However, since there was no right-and-obligation relationship between XML and JSF, XML was not an interested party and had no right to request DSQ to liquidate JSF. Hence, there was no legal basis for XML to hold DSQ responsible for clearing up JSF's credits and debts.

Accordingly, based on article 3 of the Equity Joint Venture Law,[38] articles 22 and 106(1) of the Regulations for the Implementation of the Law on Sino-Foreign Equity Joint Ventures,[39] article 1 of the Rules Regarding the Contracting-Out with Sino-Foreign Equity Joint Ventures promulgated by the MOFTEC and the State Administration for Industry and Commerce[40] and article 128 of the Civil Procedure Law,[41] the court of first instance held that the joint venture contract between XML and JSF establishing NDL was terminated on 25 July 1998 and all other claims of XML were dismissed.

XML appealed to have the original judgment reversed and amended on the following grounds:

1　The court of first instance was confused about the nature of *chengbao* profits and investment return, and thus held the *chengbao* contract void and incorrectly applied the law.

2   Since DSQ's guarantee was ineffective, it should be liable for XML's losses.
3   The court of first instance deprived XML of its substantive right to file a lawsuit by reasoning that since XML was not a party to the *chengbao* contract, XML enjoyed no substantive rights vis-à-vis JSF and DSQ.
4   DSQ should be responsible for clearing up JSF's liabilities.
5   DSQ should return all the assets of NDL.

Conversely, DSQ requested to have the appeal dismissed and the original judgment affirmed on the following grounds:

1   The *chengbao* contract at issue was void, so JSF had no obligation to pay XML *chengbao* fees.
2   The fundamental reason for causing the guarantee to be ineffective was the invalidity of the *chengbao* contract.
3   XML had no right to hold DSQ responsible for settling the credits and debts of JSF.
4   After the business license of NDL was revoked, the liquidation organizer should have been the original examination-and-approval organ, not DSQ.
5   XML could not prove that the land of NDL was currently controlled by DSQ.

Furthermore, DSQ asserted that after the business license of NDL was revoked, the liquidation committee should be the one to institute a lawsuit against infringement, and XML had no standing to sue.

On appeal, both parties had no objection to the following facts established by the court of first instance:

1   NDL was a joint venture established by XML and JSF on 29 January 1992.
2   In March 1995, NDL and JSF signed a *chengbao* contract, allowing JSF to run NDL and making XML the beneficiary of *chengbao* fees, but dispute arose between XML and JSF over the performance of the *chengbao* contract.
3   Since JSF and NDL did not have the annual review within the statutory period, their legal-person enterprise business license and business license were revoked by the AIC on 25 July 1998 and 8 November 1999, respectively.

Hence, the court affirmed these facts. Nonetheless, the main issues before the court were:

1   whether the *chengbao* contract was effective, and whether JSF had the obligation to pay XML *chengbao* profits;

2   what kind of legal liability DSQ should assume as the guarantor of the *chengbao* contract;
3   what kind of responsibility with respect to JSF's debts DSQ should assume; and
4   after the business license of NDL was revoked, what kind of legal liability should DSQ assume.

Moreover, XML submitted the following new evidence:

1   The report on the actual capital contributions of NDL, proving that both parties had made the agreed-upon investments.
2   The certificate of capital verification issued to JSF, proving that DSQ was the investor of JSF.
3   The approval document issued by Jiangning County's Planning Committee and Foreign Trade and Economic Cooperation Committee regarding the feasibility study report on the establishment of "Nanjing Jianbao Feather Ltd." as a wholly foreign-owned enterprise, as well as the notice issued by the Nanjing City concerning the approval of the contract and articles of association of a FIE, proving that DSQ had leased the assets of NDL to a Taiwanese enterprise.

DSQ, however, did not submit any new evidence. The court found that evidence 1 was irrelevant to the present dispute and so should be discarded; DSQ raised no objection to evidence 2, so it should be adopted; and evidence 3 could only indicate that the Taiwanese enterprise had rented building(s) from DSQ, but could not prove that the factory rented to the Taiwanese enterprise was the one leased by DSQ to NDL.

Reasoning

The court reasoned and held as follows:

1   The *chengbao* contract was void, and JSF had no obligation to pay XML any *chengbao* profits. Article 4(3) of the Equity Joint Venture Law provides that the parties share profits and assume risks and losses in proportion to their respective contributions to the registered capital. In this case, *chengbao* was to be carried out in the following way: JSF was to submit profits to XML (the total amount of profits for nine years was to be US$180,000, averaging US$20,000 per year), complete fixed amounts of work, retain any excesses, and be fully responsible for losses. Obviously, by such a *chengbao* method, XML, being a party of the joint venture, simply enjoyed profits but did not bear any risks, thus shifting all business risks and losses to JSF, the other party of the joint venture. Hence, the *chengbao* contract violated article 4(3) of the Equity

Joint Venture Law and thus was void. Since the *chengbao* contract was void, the right-and-obligation relationship of the parties stipulated in the contract did not exist from the very beginning. For that reason, JSF had no obligation to pay XML any *chengbao* profits.

2 Being the guarantor of the *chengbao* contract, DSQ was not liable for any losses of XML. Although it was a mistake for DSQ to guarantee a void contract, since the contract at issue violated compulsory statutory provisions and thus was illegal, the losses sustained by XML as a result of the void contract were not protected by law and should be borne by XML.

3 XML had no right to hold DSQ responsible for settling the credits and debts of JSF. First, as mentioned above, JSF had no obligation to pay XML any *chengbao* profits. Second, XML did not submit evidence to prove that it had any other common interests with JSF. Therefore, XML was not an interested party vis-à-vis JSF. That being the case, after the business license of NDL was revoked, XML had no right to request DSQ, the founder of JSF, to assume the responsibilities for clearing up the credits and debts of JSF.

4 After the business license of NDL was revoked, DSQ had no duty to return the assets of NDL. According to articles 3, 36 and 62 of the Measures on the Liquidation of Foreign Investment Enterprises approved by the State Council,[42] after the business license of a joint venture is revoked, the original examination-and-approval organ should organize special liquidation, and any residual assets should be distributed in proportion to the investors' respective investments. Therefore, under the circumstance that after the business license of NDL had been revoked and liquidation had not been conducted, there was no legal basis for XML to request DSQ to return the assets of NDL.

Although the court of first instance incorrectly maintained that XML's reception of *chengbao* profits was a return on investment, and erroneously applied article 3 of the Equity Joint Venture Law, articles 22 and 106(1) of the Regulations for the Implementation of the Law on Sino-Foreign Equity Joint Ventures, and article 1 of the Rules Regarding the Contracting-Out with Sino-Foreign Equity Joint Ventures to affirm that the *chengbao* contract was void, these errors did not make a substantive difference to the judgment.

Judgment

In conclusion, XML's appeal could not be sustained. Based on article 153(1)(i) of the Civil Procedure Law,[43] the court held that the appeal be dismissed and the original judgment be affirmed.

This judgment was final.

Further reading

Chow, Daniel C.K., "Reorganization and Conversion of a Joint Venture into a Wholly Foreign-Owned Enterprise in China," *Tulane Law Review* 73, 1998, 619–52.

Chow, Daniel C.K., "The Limited Partnership Joint Venture Model in the People's Republic of China," *Law and Policy in International Business* 30, 1998, 1–45.

Zhang, Jim Jinpeng and Lowe, Jung Y. "Foreign Investment Companies Limited by Shares: The Latest Chinese Organization for Major International Ventures," *Journal of International Law and Business* 21, 2001, 409–33.

Notes

1 The Provisional Regulations of the People's Republic of China on the Administration of Resident Representative Offices of Foreign Enterprises, promulgated by the State Council on 30 October 1980.

2 The Measures on the Administration of Registration of Resident Representative Offices of Foreign Enterprises, promulgated by the State Administration for Industry and Commerce on 15 March 1983.

3 The Detailed Implementation Rules on the Approval and Administration of Resident Representative Offices of Foreign Enterprises in China, promulgated by the Ministry of Foreign Trade and Economic Cooperation on 13 February 1995.

4 The chief representative and representatives should be: foreign nationals holding general passports, excluding foreign students in China; or Chinese nationals who have obtained permanent residence in foreign countries; or compatriots from Hong Kong, Macao, and Taiwan who hold valid identification certificates; or Chinese nationals approved by the government.

5 However, financial and insurance enterprises should go to the People's Bank of China. Sea couriers or agents of sea transportation should go to the Ministry of Communications. Air couriers should go to the Civil Aviation Administration of China. (See note 9 on p. 323 for the definition of "separately planned city.")

6 The full list can be found on the Web site of the State Administration for Industry and Commerce.

7 The Law of the People's Republic of China on Sino-Foreign Equity Joint Ventures, adopted at 2nd Session of the 5th National People's Congress on 1 July 1979 and amended at the 3rd Session of the 7th National People's Congress on 4 April 1990 and at the 4th Session of the 9th National People's Congress on 15 March 2001.

8 The Regulations for the Implementation of the Law of the People's Republic of China on Sino-Foreign Equity Joint Ventures, promulgated by the State Council on 20 September 1983 and amended by the State Council on 15 January 1986, 21 December 1987, and 22 July 2001.

9 The Provisional Rules on the Proportion of the Registered Capital to the Total Amount of Investment of Sino-Foreign Equity Joint Ventures, promulgated by the State Administration for Industry and Commerce on 1 March 1987.

10 The Provisional Rules on the Duration of Sino-Foreign Equity Joint Ventures, promulgated by the Ministry of Foreign Trade and Economic Cooperation on 22 October 1990.

11 The Law of the People's Republic of China on Sino-Foreign Cooperative Joint Ventures, adopted at the 1st Session of the 7th National People's Congress on 13 April 1988 and amended at the 18th Session of the Standing Committee of the 9th National People's Congress on 31 October 2000.

12 The Detailed Rules for the Implementation of the Law of the People's Republic of China on Sino-Foreign Cooperative Joint Ventures, promulgated by the Ministry of Foreign Trade and Economic Cooperation on 4 September 1995.

13 See art. 37 of the General Principles of Civil Law.

14 "Investments" refer to currencies, buildings, machinery, industrial property rights, land use rights, etc. which are assigned prices and used as capital contributions of the parties. See the Explanations Concerning Several Articles in the Detailed Rules for the Implementation of Law of the People's Republic of China on Sino-Foreign Cooperative Joint Ventures, promulgated by the Ministry of Foreign Trade and Economic Cooperation on 22 October 1996.

15 "Cooperative means" refers to real estate and other property rights, such as land use rights, ownership of or right to use installations attached to buildings, and industrial property rights, which are not expressed in terms of currency. In a legal-person cooperative joint venture, cooperative means are owned by the joint venture and will be used to satisfy its debts. See the Explanations Concerning Several Articles in the Detailed Rules for the Implementation of Law of the People's Republic of China on Sino-Foreign Cooperative Joint Ventures, promulgated by the Ministry of Foreign Trade and Economic Cooperation on 22 October 1996.

16 See the Explanations Concerning Several Articles in the Detailed Rules for the Implementation of Law of the People's Republic of China on Sino-Foreign Cooperative Joint Ventures, promulgated by the Ministry of Foreign Trade and Economic Cooperation on 22 October 1996.

17 See the Provisional Rules on the Proportion of the Registered Capital to the Total Amount of Investment of Sino-Foreign Equity Joint Ventures, promulgated by the State Administration for Industry and Commerce on 1 March 1987.

18 According to the Ministry of Foreign Trade and Economic Cooperation, item 3 means that the foreign party may recover its investment in advance by amortizing the depreciation costs of the joint venture's fixed assets. If the assets of the joint venture reduce as a result of the amortization of depreciation costs, the foreign party must submit a letter of guarantee issued by a Chinese bank or financial institution or the branch of a foreign bank or financial institution established in China concerning the joint venture's ability to repay debts. See the Explanations Concerning Several Articles in the Detailed Rules for the Implementation of Law of the People's Republic of China on Sino-Foreign Cooperative Joint Ventures, promulgated by the Ministry of Foreign Trade and Economic Cooperation on 22 October 1996.

19 The department-in-charge of the cooperative joint venture, which provides coordination and assistance, is the department-in-charge of the Chinese party.

20 The Law of the People's Republic of China on Wholly Foreign-Owned Enterprises, adopted at the 4th Session of the 6th National People's Congress on 12 April 1986 and amended at the 18th Session of the Standing Committee of the 9th National People's Congress on 31 October 2000.

21 The Detailed Rules for the Implementation of the Law of the People's Republic of China on Wholly Foreign-Owned Enterprises, promulgated and amended by

the Ministry of Foreign Trade and Economic Cooperation on 12 December 1990 and 12 April 2001.

22 See the Provisional Rules on the Proportion of the Registered Capital to the Total Amount of Investment of Sino-Foreign Equity Joint Ventures, promulgated by the State Administration for Industry and Commerce on 1 March 1987.

23 See the Circular on the Explanation of Several Articles in the Detailed Rules for the Implementation of the Law of the People's Republic of China on Wholly Foreign-Owned Enterprises, promulgated the Ministry of Foreign Trade and Economic Cooperation on 6 December 1991.

24 The Provisional Rules on Several Issues Concerning the Establishment of Foreign Companies Limited by Shares, promulgated by the Ministry of Foreign Trade and Economic Cooperation on 10 January 1995.

25 The Circular on Relevant Issues Concerning Foreign Companies Limited by Shares, promulgated by the Ministry of Foreign Trade and Economic Cooperation on 17 May 2001.

26 The Rules on the Merger and Division of Foreign Investment Enterprises, promulgated and amended by the Ministry of Foreign Trade and Economic Cooperation and the State Administration for Industry and Commerce on 23 September 1999 and 22 November 2001, respectively.

27 See the Provisional Rules on the Proportion of the Registered Capital to the Total Amount of Investment of Sino-Foreign Equity Joint Ventures, promulgated by the State Administration for Industry and Commerce on 1 March 1987.

28 The Rules on the Modification of Investors' Equities in Foreign Investment Enterprises, promulgated by the Ministry of Foreign Trade and Economic Cooperation and the State Administration for Industry and Commerce on 28 May 1997.

29 The Measures on the Liquidation of Foreign Investment Enterprises, promulgated by the Ministry of Foreign Trade and Economic Cooperation on 9 July 1996.

30 Liquidation expenses include expenses incurred for the management, sale, and distribution of the FIE's property; expenses incurred for making public announcements, litigation, and arbitration; and any other expenses incurred during the liquidation proceedings.

31 The Regulations on Guiding the Direction of Foreign Investment, promulgated by the State Council on 11 February 2002.

32 The Guidance Catalog of Industries with Foreign Investment, promulgated by the State Development and Planning Commission, the State Economy and Trade Commission, and the Ministry of Foreign Trade and Economic Cooperation on 11 March 2002.

33 The Catalog of Encouraged High-Technology Products for Foreign Investment, promulgated by the Ministry of Science and Technology and the Ministry of Commerce on 2 June 2003.

34 The Catalog of Advantageous Industries with Foreign Investment in the Middle and Western Regions, promulgated by the State Development and Planning Commission, the State Economy and Trade Commission, and the Ministry of Foreign Trade and Economic Cooperation on 16 June 2000.

35 China did not provide statistics on foreign companies limited by shares until 2001. In 2001, foreign companies limited by shares accounted for 1.3 percent of the realized value of the total FDI in China. *China Business Review*, September/October, 2003, p. 56.

36 *Shensu* is an appeal after the original judgment becomes effective.

37 Article 108 of the Civil Procedure Law lists four requirements for filing a lawsuit: (1) the plaintiff should be a citizen, legal person, or other organization that has a direct interest in the case; (2) there should be a definite defendant; (3) there should be concrete claims with supporting facts and reasons; and (4) the case should be within the scope of civil litigation of a people's court and within the jurisdiction of the people's court with which the lawsuit is filed. Article 153(1)(ii) of the Civil Procedure Law provides that the court of second instance should amend the judgment if the original judgment is based on incorrect application of law.

38 Article 3 of the Equity Joint Venture Law provides that the parties to a joint venture must submit the joint venture agreement, joint venture contract, and articles of association to the MOFTEC (examination-and-approval organ) for approval, and that after approval, the joint venture should register with the State Administration for Industry and Commerce and obtain a business license.

39 Article 22 of the 1983 Regulations for the Implementation of the Law on Sino-Foreign Equity Joint Ventures provides that an equity joint venture must not reduce the registered capital during its term. Moreover, article 106(1) provides that an equity joint venture is liable for its debts to the extent of all of its assets, and that after all the debts are paid off, the residual property will be distributed among the parties in proportion to their respective investments, unless otherwise provided in the joint venture agreement, joint venture contract, or articles of association.

40 Article 1 of the Rules Regarding the Contracting-Out with Sino-Foreign Equity Joint Ventures provides that contracting out refers to the situation where the joint venture gives the contractor the entire or partial management right within a given period of time such that the contractor can run the joint venture business. During the contract term, the contractor bears risks and shares part of the profits. Moreover, contracting out is only a supplementary measure to solve the problems of serious losses and poor management in some joint ventures.

41 Article 128 of the Civil Procedure Law provides that after the conclusion of the debate in court, the court shall render a judgment; however, mediation may be conducted before a judgment is made.

42 Article 3 of the Measures on the Liquidation of Foreign Investment Enterprises provides that FIEs capable of organizing liquidation committees by themselves may conduct liquidation in accordance with the provisions on ordinary liquidation; that if they are not capable of organizing liquidation committees or have met obstacles in conducting ordinary liquidation, the board of directors, joint management committee, investors, or creditors may apply to the examination-and-approval organ for conducting special liquidation; and that if they have been ordered to close down, they should also conduct special liquidation. In addition, article 36 provides that a liquidation committee for special liquidation is to be organized by the examination-and-approval organ or a department with its authorization, and that the members of the liquidation committee consist of both Chinese and foreign investors, representatives of the relevant government organs, and professionals. The Measures on the Liquidation of Foreign Investment Enterprises do not have article 62; thus, this citation should be a typographical error. However, article 42 provides that the liquidation committee's liquidation plan and liquidation report must be affirmed by the examination-and-approval organ.

43 Article 153(1)(i) of the Civil Procedure Law provides that the court of second instance should dismiss the appeal and affirm the judgment of the court of first instance if the original judgment is based on clearly established facts and correct application of law.

4 Contracts

Contracts, whether oral or written, are indispensable to doing business in all market economies. In China, if a foreign company and a state-owned enterprise want to establish an equity joint venture or cooperative joint venture, they must first conclude a joint venture contract. If a multinational corporation wants to set up a wholly foreign-owned subsidiary in China, it must prepare to conclude various types of contracts, including a lease for the use of a manufacturing plant, a sale contract with a supplier, and labor contracts with Chinese employees. Similarly, if a high-tech company wants to license a technology to a state-owned enterprise in China, the parties must enter into a technology transfer contract. In other words, a basic understanding of Chinese contract law is a prerequisite for foreign investors who are planning to do business in China.

Prior to 1999, China had three contract laws, namely, the Economic Contract Law,[1] the Foreign Economic Contract Law,[2] and the Technology Contract Law, and various regulations on contracts, such as the Regulations on Loan Contracts and the Regulations on Contracts for Construction and Installation Projects. Since the regulatory framework was piecemeal and many repetitions existed among the three contract laws, China found it necessary to enact a unified and comprehensive contract law. In 1999, the Contract Law was passed,[3] repealing the previous three contract laws. The Contract Law consists of 428 articles and is divided into two parts: general principles and specific provisions. The specific provisions section deals with 15 particular types of contracts and contains the following chapters: purchase and sale; supply and use of electricity, water, gas, or heat; gift; loan; lease; financial leasing; work; construction project; transportation; technology; safe keeping; warehousing; mandate; brokerage; and intermediary.

To provide an overview of contract law, this chapter first discusses the general principles of the Contract Law, that is, what constitutes a legally enforceable contract in China, what rights and obligations the contracting parties have, and what remedies one party has if the other party breaches the contract. Subsequently, it highlights four specific types of contracts – sale, lease, work, and technology – because foreign investors frequently encounter them. Before studying the details, however, it is worth noting that the Contract Law does not apply to agreements on personal relationships, such as marriage, adoption, and guardianship.

1 General principles of the Contract Law

Although contract laws differ from country to country, they have many similarities and cover a number of common issues, including formation, performance, breach, and remedies. Focusing on these common issues, this section is designed to help foreign investors understand the basic ingredients of Chinese contract law. To begin with, the Contract Law provides that a contract is an agreement by which civil rights and obligations are established, modified, or terminated between natural persons, legal persons, and other economic organizations that are subjects of equal status. Nevertheless, it is imperative to know that not all agreements are legally enforceable contracts. A legally enforceable contract must meet certain requirements prescribed by the Contract Law.

Offer and acceptance

First of all, there must be an offer and an acceptance. An offer (要约) is the manifestation of the intention of one party (the offeror) to enter into a contract with another party (the offeree). The contents of the offer must be concrete and definite, and the offer must indicate that once the offeree accepts the offer, the offeror will be bound. In contrast, an invitation to offer is the manifestation of one's intention to be given an offer. Mailed price lists, auction announcements, bidding announcements, prospectuses, and commercial advertisements are only invitations to offer. Even so, if the contents of a commercial advertisement are in accord with the requirements of an offer, it will be viewed as an offer.

An offer becomes effective when it reaches the offeree. If a contract is to be concluded by means of data-telex (数据电文) and the recipient designates a specific system to receive the data-telex, the time at which the data-telex enters the designated system will be the time of arrival, but if no system is designated, the time at which the data-telex first enters any system of the recipient will be regarded as the time of arrival. Moreover, the offeror may withdraw (撤回) an offer by sending a notice of withdrawal to the offeree. The notice of withdrawal must reach the offeree before or at the same time at which the offer reaches the offeree (i.e. the offer has not yet become effective). Similarly, the offeror may revoke (撤销) an offer by sending a notice of revocation to the offeree. The notice of revocation must reach the offeree before the offeree dispatches its notice of acceptance. However, an offer cannot be revoked if the offeror has provided a fixed time for acceptance or otherwise expressly stated that the offer is irrevocable, or the offeree has reason to believe that the offer is irrevocable and has made preparation for performing the contract. Furthermore, an offer will become null and void if:

1   the notice of rejection sent by the offeree reaches the offeror;
2   the offeror revokes its offer in accordance with the law;
3   the offeree fails to accept the offer upon the expiration of the time limit; or
4   the offeree substantially alters the contents of the offer. *(counter offer ?)*

On the other hand, an acceptance (承诺) is the manifestation of the offeree's assent to an offer. Acceptance should be made by means of a notice, except when course of dealing or the offer indicates that acceptance may be made by the performance of an act. An acceptance must reach the offeror within the time limit specified in the offer. If the offer does not specify any time limit and the offer is made orally, the acceptance must be made immediately, unless otherwise agreed upon by the parties. If the offer does not specify any time limit and if the offer is made in a manner other than orally, the acceptance must reach the offeror within a reasonable time. If the offer is made by means of a letter or telegram, the time limit for acceptance commences at the date shown in the letter or the date when the telegram is handed in for dispatch. If no date is shown in the letter, the time limit for acceptance commences at the date postmarked on the envelope. If the offer is made by means of an express communication mode, such as telephone or fax, the time limit for acceptance will commence at the moment when the offer reaches the offeree.

An acceptance becomes effective when the notice of acceptance reaches the offeror. A contract is formed when the acceptance becomes effective. The offeree may withdraw an acceptance by sending a notice of withdrawal to the offeror. The notice of withdrawal must reach the offeror before or at the same time at which the acceptance reaches the offeror (i.e. the acceptance has not yet become effective). If the offeree accepts the offer beyond the time limit for acceptance, the acceptance will be treated as a new offer, unless the offeror promptly informs the offeree that the acceptance is effective. If the offeree dispatches the acceptance within the time limit for acceptance and the acceptance should have reached the offeror on time under normal circumstances, but for some reason(s) the acceptance reaches the offeror beyond the time limit, the acceptance will become effective, unless the offeror promptly notifies the offeree that it will refuse the acceptance.

In any event, the contents of the acceptance must be the same as those of the offer. If the offeree substantially modifies the contents of the offer, such as changing the subject matter, quantity, quality, price or remuneration, liabilities for breach, dispute resolution mechanisms, or the time limit, place, and manner of performance, the acceptance will be treated as a new offer. If the acceptance does not substantially change the contents of the offer, it will become effective and the contents of the contract will be based on the acceptance, unless the offeror promptly objects to the change(s) or the offer explicitly disallows modification.

Although the Contract Law mandates that there must be an offer and an acceptance, there is no mention of consideration. As mentioned above, the Contract Law contains one chapter on gifts. Thus, under Chinese law, consideration is not essential to the formation of a legally enforceable contract.

Subject matter

The parties to a contract determine its contents. In general, a contract should contain: the titles or names and domiciles of the parties; the object (标的物) of the contract; quantity; quality; price or remuneration; time limit, place and manner of performance; liabilities for breach; and dispute resolution mechanisms. With respect to the object of the contract, the parties can choose virtually anything, unless otherwise prohibited by law. Thus, a contract can concern the sale of tangible goods, transfer of intellectual property, or provision of services. Under Chinese law, a contract will become null and void if:

1   it is concluded through the use of fraud and coercion to impair the interests of the state;
2   it is concluded through malicious collusion to impair the interests of the state, a collective, or a third party;
3   it has an illegal purpose;
4   it is detrimental to public interests; or
5   it violates the mandatory provisions of laws and administrative regulations.

Similarly, a contract will be null and void if it exempts one party from liability for causing personal injury or property damage to the other party as a result of deliberate intent or gross negligence.

Capacity

Whether a contract is valid also depends on whether the parties have the legal capacity to enter into it. The contracting parties must be capable of possessing civil rights and engaging in civil conduct. Thus, when a person having limited capacity for civil conduct has concluded a contract, the contract will become effective only if his or her statutory agent ratifies it. Nonetheless, a contract that yields only profit or is appropriate to one's age, intelligence, or mental health conditions does not need ratification by the statutory agent. In any event, a bona fide party, that is, a person who acts in good faith,[4] has the right to revoke the contract before it is ratified.

If an agent enters into a contract in the name of its principal either beyond the scope of authorization or after the authorization has expired, and the other party has reason to believe that the agent has the power to act, the contract will be valid. Likewise, if the legal representative of a legal person exceeds his or her power and concludes a contract, the contract will be valid, unless the other party knew or should have known that the legal representative exceeded his or her power. Furthermore, if a person having no right disposes of another person's property, and the owner subsequently ratifies it or the person obtains the right after the conclusion of a contract, the contract will be valid.

Formalities

A contract may be concluded in writing, orally, or in another manner. If a contract is to be made in writing pursuant to law or administrative regulation or as agreed upon by the parties, the written form should be adopted. The written form refers to written contracts, letters, and data-telex (including telegram, telex, fax, EDI, and e-mail) that can show the contents in visible form. Even so, where the parties do not conclude a written contract in accordance with law or administrative regulation or their agreement, the contract will still be formed if one party has performed the principal obligation and the other party accepts it. If the parties want to conclude a contract by means of a letter or data-telex, they may request that a confirmation letter be signed before the conclusion of the contract.

In the case of a form contract, one party prepares standard terms (格式条款) in advance for repeated use, and the other party has not negotiated over them. When standard terms are used, the party supplying the standard terms should define the rights and duties of the parties in accordance with the principle of fairness, ask in a reasonable manner that the other party heed exclusions or restrictions on liability, and explain the terms as requested by the other party. If the party providing the standard terms exempts itself from liabilities, enhances the liabilities of the other party, or eliminates the major rights of the other party, the standard terms will be null and void. When dispute arises over the interpretation of a standard term, the term should be interpreted in accordance with general understanding. If there are two or more ways to interpret a standard term, an interpretation unfavorable to the party supplying the term should be used. Similarly, if there are inconsistencies between standard terms and nonstandard terms, the latter should be adopted.

The place where the acceptance becomes effective is the place where the contract is formed. Thus, if the contract is to be formed in writing, the place where the parties affix their signatures or seals to the contract will be the place of its formation. If the contract is to be formed by means of data-telex, the principal place of business of the recipient will be the place where the contract is formed, or if there is no principal place of business, the habitual residence of the recipient will be the place of formation, unless the parties agree otherwise.

Collateral conditions

If the parties want to conclude a written contract, the contract will be formed as soon as the parties sign or put their seals on it. If the parties want to conclude a contract by means of a letter or data-telex and request that a confirmation letter be signed before the conclusion of the contract, the contract will be formed as soon as the confirmation letter is signed. Nevertheless, if a contract requires approval or registration pursuant to law or administrative regulation, it will become effective upon approval or registration. Moreover, the parties may agree on collateral conditions with respect to the effectiveness of a contract. If the contract has a condition precedent, it will become effective when the condition occurs. Similarly, if the contract has a condition subsequent, its effectiveness will cease when the condition occurs. In any case, if one party, for its own interests, improperly prevents the condition precedent from happening or promotes the occurrence of the condition subsequent, the condition will be deemed satisfied or nonexistent.

Performance

The parties to a contract should exercise their rights and perform their obligations in accordance with the principle of good faith. If the parties have not agreed upon or have vaguely agreed upon such contractual terms as quality, price or remuneration, or place of performance, they may enter into a supplementary agreement. If they cannot reach a supplementary agreement, the terms will be determined in accordance with the relevant contractual clauses or their course of dealing. Nonetheless, if the aforementioned steps prove futile, the following provisions on quality, price or remuneration, expense, and place, time, and manner of performance will apply.

If quality is not clearly stipulated, the contract should be performed in accordance with state or trade standards. In the absence of state or trade standards, the contract should be performed pursuant to generally held standards or specific standards that are consistent with the purpose of the contract. If price or remuneration is not clearly provided, the market price of the place of performance at the time of the formation of contract should be applied, unless government-fixed or government-directed prices must be used under the law.[5] If the place of performance is not clearly stipulated, the contract should be performed in the place where the party receives payment of cash, where the real property is located, or where the obligor is domiciled. Likewise, if the time of performance is not clearly provided, the obligor may perform at any time, while the obligee may demand performance at any time provided that the obligor has the necessary time to make preparations. Moreover, if the manner of performance is not clearly provided, the contract should be performed in a way conducive to the achievement of the purpose of the contract. Indeed, if there are no clear provisions on performance expenses, they should be borne by the obligor.

The parties may agree that the obligor performs its obligations to a third party. If the obligor fails to do so or if its performance does not meet the terms of the contract, the obligor will be liable to the obligee for breach of contract. The parties may also agree that a third party performs the obligor's obligations to the obligee. If the third party fails to do so or the performance does not meet the terms of the contract, the obligor will be liable to the obligee for breach of contract. If both parties have obligations toward each other and there is no order of performance, they should perform simultaneously. Hence, one party has the right to reject the other party's request for performance before the other party performs, and one party has the right to reject the other party's corresponding request for performance if the other party's performance does not meet the terms of the contract. If there is an order of performance and the party that should perform first has not yet performed, the party that should perform later has the right to reject the former's request for performance. Likewise, if the performance of the party that should perform first does not meet the terms of the contract, the party that should perform later has the right to reject the former's corresponding request for performance.

Moreover, the party that should perform first may suspend performance if it has conclusive evidence that the other party is under any one of the following circumstances:

1   its business conditions are seriously deteriorating;
2   it transfers property and takes out capital to evade obligations;
3   it has lost business reputation; or
4   any other circumstances arise indicating that it has lost or may lose its ability to perform obligations.

If one party suspends performance, it should notify the other party promptly. However, it must resume performance if the other party provides appropriate guarantee. If the other party neither recovers its ability to perform nor provides appropriate guarantee, the party suspending performance may terminate the contract. In the case of division, merger, or change of domicile, if the obligee does not notify the obligor such that it becomes difficult for the obligor to perform its obligations, the obligor may suspend performance or have the object of the contract deposited.

The obligee may refuse advance performance by the obligor, unless the advance performance does not impair the interests of the obligee. Any additional expenses incurred by the obligee as a result of the advance performance shall be borne by the obligor. Similarly, the obligee may refuse partial performance by the obligor, unless the partial performance does not impair the interests of the obligee. Any additional expenses incurred by the obligee as a result of the partial performance shall be borne by the obligor. Moreover, if the obligor is indolent in exercising its claims as a creditor, thereby harming the interests of the obligee, the obligee may apply to the people's court for subrogation in its own name, unless the rights exclusively belong to the obligor. The necessary expenses incurred by the obligee in exercising subrogation shall be borne by the obligor.

If the obligor relinquishes its claims as a creditor or transfers its property without compensation, thereby harming the interests of the obligee, the obligee may ask the people's court to annul the obligor's act. If the obligor transfers its property for an obviously unreasonably low price, thus damaging the interests of the obligee, and the transferee knows about it, the obligee may request that the people's court annul the obligor's act. The necessary expenses incurred by the obligee in seeking annulment shall be borne by the obligor. In either case, the obligee must seek annulment within one year of the date when the obligee knew or should have known the grounds for annulment and within five years of the date when the act of the obligor took place; otherwise, its right will lapse.

Furthermore, if one party merges with a third party after the conclusion of the contract, the entity emerging from the merger will exercise the contractual rights and assume the contractual obligations. If one party is divided after the conclusion of the contract, the entities emerging from the division shall exercise the contractual rights and assume the contractual obligations jointly and severally, unless otherwise agreed upon by the parties.

Modification, assignment, and delegation

On their own initiative, the parties may agree to modify their contract. If laws or administrative regulations require approval, registration, etc. for the modification, the parties should go through the necessary formalities. If the items to be modified have not been made clear, the presumption will be that the contract is not to be modified. Also, one party has the right to ask the people's court or an arbitration tribunal to amend a contract if it is concluded as a result of serious misunderstanding; it is obviously unfair at the time of its formation; or it is concluded against the true intentions of one party due to the other party's fraud, coercion, or taking advantage of its plight.

The obligee may assign, wholly or partially, its rights under the contract to a third party, unless the rights cannot be assigned based on the nature of the contract; the parties have agreed that the rights under the contract cannot be assigned; or the rights cannot be assigned in accordance with the law. In assigning its rights, the obligee must notify the obligor; otherwise, the assignment will have no effect on the obligor. In addition, the obligee cannot revoke the notice of assignment, unless the assignee consents to do so. Through the assignment, the assignee also acquires the obligee's collateral rights, unless the collateral rights belong to the obligee exclusively. The obligor can assert its defenses against the obligee (assignor) against the assignee. Besides, if the obligor is a creditor of the assignee and its rights become due before or at the same time as its obligations toward the obligee (assignor) are due, it may offset the obligations by the credits.

In a similar vein, the obligor may delegate its obligations, wholly or partially, to a third party with the consent of the obligee. If the obligor delegates its obligations to a third party, the new obligor (delegatee) may assert defenses belonging to the original obligor (delegator) against the obligee. Through the delegation, the delegatee also assumes the original obligor's (delegator's) collateral obligations, unless the collateral obligations belong to the original obligor exclusively. Where laws or administrative regulations require approval, registration, etc. for the assignment or delegation, the necessary formalities must be completed.

Rescission and termination

One party has the right to ask the people's court or an arbitration tribunal to rescind a contract if it is concluded as a result of serious misunderstanding; it is obviously unfair at the time of its formation; or it is concluded against the true intentions of one party due to the other party's fraud, coercion, or taking advantage of its plight. Nonetheless, the court or arbitration tribunal will not rescind a contract if the party having the right to request rescission fails to do so within one year of the time at which it knew or should have known the grounds for rescission or waives such right by either word or act after it has learned the grounds for rescission.

If a contract is null and void or has been rescinded, it has no legal force from the beginning. However, if only parts of a contract are invalid, the unaffected parts of the contract will remain valid. In addition, a rescinded contract does not affect the validity of any dispute settlement provisions independently stipulated in the contract. If the parties have acquired property through the contract, they must return the property after its rescission. If the property cannot or need not be returned, it should be reimbursed at its estimated price. The party at fault shall compensate the other party for any losses incurred, but if both parties are at fault, the parties shall respectively bear their liabilities. In other words, the parties will be restored to their status quo (restitution) if the contract is rescinded.

As a rule, the rights and obligations of a contract will be discharged:

1   if the contractual obligations have been performed in conformity with the terms of the contract;
2   if the contract is terminated;
3   if the obligations have been offset against each other;
4   if the obligor has deposited the object of the contract in accordance with the law;
5   if the obligee has exempted the obligor's obligations;
6   if the rights and obligations are assumed by the same person, except for those involving the interests of a third party; or

7   if any other circumstances as stipulated by law or agreed upon by the parties have arisen.

Specifically, the parties may terminate the contract:

1   if the parties agree, after mutual consultation, to terminate the contract;
2   if the condition(s) stipulated in the contract for termination by one party has (have) arisen;
3   if the purpose of the contract cannot be achieved due to *force majeure*;
4   if one party indicates, either expressly or through its action and before the expiration of the performance period, that it will not perform its principal obligations;
5   if one party delays performing its principal obligations, and fails, after being urged, to perform them within a reasonable time;
6   if one party delays performing its obligations or commits an act in breach of the contract, thus rendering it impossible to achieve the purpose of the contract; or
7   if any other circumstances as stipulated by law have arisen.

In any event, the parties must exercise the right to terminate the contract either within the time limit prescribed by law or as agreed upon between them or within a reasonable time after being urged. The contract terminates upon the arrival of the notice of termination. If laws or administrative regulations require approval, registration, etc. for the termination, the parties must go through the necessary formalities. Upon termination, the contractual obligations that have not been performed will be discharged. If the contractual obligations have been performed, the parties, in light of the state of performance and the nature of the contract, may request that their status quo be restored or other remedial measures taken, and losses be compensated. Nonetheless, the discharge of contractual rights and obligations does not affect the validity of the contractual provisions on the settlement of accounts.

With respect to the canceling-out of obligations, if the parties have mutual obligations and the type and character of the obligations are the same, any party may offset its obligations against those of the other, unless the obligations cannot be offset according to the law or nature of the contract. The offset becomes effective when the notice of offset reaches the other party; however, it may not be attached by conditions or time limit. If the type and character of the mutual obligations are different, they can be offset against each other only after the parties have reached a consensus.

To deposit the object of the contract in accordance with the law, the obligor must experience difficulty in performing its obligations because:

1   the obligee refuses to accept its performance without legitimate reason(s);
2   the obligee is missing;

3 the obligee is dead and its heirs have not been determined, or the obligee has lost its ability to engage in civil conduct and its guardian has not been appointed; or

4 any other circumstances as stipulated by law have arisen.

However, if the object is not suitable to be deposited or the deposit expenses are excessively high, the obligor may auction or sell the object and deposit the proceeds instead. After the object has been deposited, the obligor must promptly notify the obligee (unless it is missing) or its heirs or guardian. The risks of damage, destruction, and loss as well as the expenses for keeping the object are to be borne by the obligee, but the profits derived from the object also belong to the obligee. The obligee may claim the deposited object at any time. However, if the obligee owes the obligor obligations, the deposit authorities should, upon the obligor's request and prior to the obligee's performance of obligations or provision of a guarantee, refuse to let the obligee claim the deposited object. The right to claim the deposited object will lapse if it is not exercised within five years of the date of deposit.

Liabilities for breach

During the negotiation of a contract, a trade secret may be learned, whether or not the contract will eventually be concluded. A party which causes the other party to sustain losses by disclosing or improperly using a trade secret shall be liable for damages. Likewise, a party will be liable for damages if it negotiates in bad faith, deliberately conceals material facts relating to the conclusion of the contract or provides false information, or commits any act in violation of the principle of good faith and causes the other party to incur losses.

After the conclusion of a contract, if one party indicates, either explicitly or through its actions, that it will not perform its obligations, the other party may demand it bear liability for breach even prior to the expiration of the performance period. If one party fails to perform its obligations or its performance fails to conform to the terms of the contract, it will be required to continue to perform, take remedial measures, compensate for losses, etc. Where the breaching party has performed or taken remedial measures, but the non-breaching party has other losses, the breaching party must also compensate for those losses. The amount of compensation shall be the losses caused by the breach, including the profits that can be obtained from performance, provided that the damages do not exceed the probable losses that the breaching party could foresee or should have foreseen at the time of the formation of the contract.

Nevertheless, the non-breaching party must adopt appropriate measures to prevent the increase of losses; otherwise, it cannot claim compensation for the increased losses. Any reasonable expenses incurred for preventing the increase will be borne by the breaching party. In the case of non-pecuniary obligations, the non-breaching party may request specific performance, unless the obligation cannot be fulfilled either in law or in fact, namely, impossibility of performance; the object of the contract is unsuitable for specific performance, or the performance cost is excessively high, in other words, commercial impracticability; or the obligee fails to request the performance within a reasonable time.

If the quality fails to conform to the terms of the contract, the breaching party must bear liability pursuant to the stipulations in the contract. If there are no contractual provisions on such an issue or if the provisions are not clear, and it cannot be determined with reference to state standards, trade standards, etc., the non-breaching party may, in light of the nature of the object of the contract and the degree of loss, reasonably choose to request that the breaching party provide such remedies as repair, replacement, remake, return, or reduction of the price or remuneration. Similarly, when a business operator commits fraud in supplying the consumer with goods or services, it must pay damages in accordance with the Law on the Protection of the Rights and Interests of Consumers, which is discussed in Chapter 7. Where one party's breach of contract infringes upon the other party's personal or property rights, the injured party is entitled to choose either remedies for breach of contract under the Contract Law or remedies for infringement under other laws.

On the other hand, the parties may agree on a fixed amount of damages or the method of calculating damages for any breach of contract. If the liquidated damages are smaller than the actual losses, the non-breaching party may request that the people's court or an arbitration tribunal increase the amount; if the liquidated damages are excessively greater than the actual losses, the breaching party may seek an appropriate reduction from the people's court or arbitration tribunal. Moreover, the parties may agree that one party pays a deposit to the other party as a guarantee. After the obligor has performed its obligations, the deposit must be returned or offset against the price. If the party paying the deposit fails to perform, it will have no right to reclaim the deposit; if the party accepting the deposit fails to perform, it will be required to refund twice the amount of deposit. If the parties agree on both damages and deposit, the non-breaching party may choose either one of these remedies.

If the contract cannot be performed due to *force majeure*, that is, unforeseeable, inevitable, and insurmountable objective circumstances, the liability will be exempted in part or in whole according to the impact of *force majeure*, unless otherwise provided by law. If *force majeure* occurs after one party has delayed performance, its liabilities will not be exempted. The party that is unable to perform because of *force majeure* must notify the other party promptly so as to reduce the probable losses to the other party and must provide evidence within a reasonable time.

Interpretation

With respect to disputes over the interpretation of contractual clauses, the true meaning of such clauses should be determined in accordance with the words and sentences used in the contract, the relevant clauses of the contract, the purpose of the contract, the course of dealing between the parties, and the principle of good faith. Moreover, if two or more languages are used in writing the contract and it is agreed that all texts are equally valid, it will be presumed that the terms and expressions in various versions have the same meaning. If the terms and expressions in different versions are inconsistent, they should be interpreted in conformity with the purpose of the contract.

Governing law

The general provisions will apply if a contract is not dealt with explicitly in the specific provisions section or elsewhere. However, the provisions in the specific provisions section that are most similar or other relevant laws may be applied *mutatis muntandis*. In addition, the parties to a foreign-related contract may choose the law governing the settlement of their disputes, except as otherwise prescribed by law. Simply stated, a contract is foreign-related if one of the parties is a foreign national, foreign enterprise, or stateless person; the object of the contract is located in a foreign country; the contract is to be performed in a foreign country; or the facts creating or terminating the contractual relationship between the parties have occurred outside China. If the parties fail to choose the governing law, the law of the country having the closest connection with the contract will be applied. Nevertheless, Chinese law must be applied to contracts of Sino-foreign equity joint ventures, contracts of Sino-foreign cooperative joint ventures, and Sino-foreign contracts involving the prospecting and exploitation of natural resources that are to be performed in China.

Furthermore, article 142 of the General Principles of the Civil Law[6] provides that if there are any inconsistencies between Chinese civil law and an international convention that China has concluded or joined, the international convention will prevail, except for those articles that China has made reservations. It also provides that if neither Chinese law nor the international convention has relevant provisions, international customary rules may be used. Since China is a signatory to the United Nations Convention on Contracts for the International Sale of Goods, the Contract Law supplements the Convention if the Convention expressly excludes coverage of certain areas or is silent with respect to issues addressed by the Contract Law. For instance, the Contract Law provides that the time limit for filing a lawsuit or applying for arbitration with regard to disputes over contracts involving the international sale of goods or the import and export of technology is four years, starting from the date when the party knew or should have known of the infringement of its rights. Thus, when a Chinese enterprise and an enterprise of another signatory enter into a sale contract, the parties should first consult the Convention.

Online contracting

Electronic commerce (e-commerce) generally refers to any commercial transaction involving the exchange of commodities, services, or information over the Internet. E-commerce between business and business (B2B) and business and consumer (B2C) has been growing rapidly all over the world. In most countries, the development of Cyber law has been trying to catch up with the advancement of information technology. In particular, confidentiality (privacy concerns), authenticity (identification issues), and integrity (alternation problems) are common among many countries. As of March 2004, China, like many other countries, had not yet enacted a national law or regulation on e-commerce. Although the Contract Law provides that contract can be formed by means of data-telex, including fax and e-mail, it does not deal with issues relating to electronic signature and the authenticity and integrity of e-documents. Therefore, a comprehensive set of rules regarding online contracting has yet to be developed. Nonetheless, Guangdong Province has taken the initiative to enact a set of regulations on electronic trade, which, among other things, provides for electronic signatures, electronic contracts, and certificate authorities.[7]

2 Specific contracts

As mentioned earlier, the Contract Law also contains provisions on 15 specific types of contracts. Since it will be an overwhelming task to examine the details of all 15 types of contracts, this section highlights only those most frequently encountered: sale, lease, work, and technology.

Sale contracts

A sale contract (买卖合同) is an agreement by which the seller transfers the ownership of an object to the buyer and the buyer pays a price for it. The seller must either own or have the right to dispose of the object for sale. Apart from the general contents of a contract mentioned above, a sale contract may provide for such matters as packaging, inspection means and standards, the method of account settlement, and the language to be used. The ownership of the object is transferred to the buyer upon delivery, unless otherwise provided by law or agreed upon by the parties. Even so, the parties may agree that if the buyer has not paid the price or performed other obligations, the ownership of the object belongs to the seller.

The seller is obliged to deliver to the buyer the object or the document to collect the object and to transfer the ownership of the object to the buyer. In addition, the seller should, pursuant to the contract or their course of dealing, deliver to the buyer relevant documents and materials other than the document to collect the object. The seller may deliver the object at any point during the agreed-upon time period. If the buyer has taken possession of the object before the contract is concluded, the delivery time will be the time when the contract becomes effective. The seller must also deliver the object to the designated place. If the parties have not agreed upon the place of delivery or have not made the place clear, and it cannot be determined by concluding a supplementary agreement or with reference to the relevant contractual clauses or course of dealing, the following rules should be observed:

1   If the object needs to be transported, the seller should deliver the object to the first carrier in order to give it to the buyer.
2   If the object does not need transportation and the parties know at the time of the formation of the contract where the object is located, such place should be the place of delivery; but if the place is unknown, the object should be delivered to the business place of the seller at the time of the formation of the contract.

Before the delivery of the object, the risks of damage, destruction, and loss are to be borne by the seller; after the delivery, the risks are to be borne by the buyer, unless otherwise provided by law or agreed upon by the parties. However, if the object cannot be delivered within the time limit because of the buyer, the buyer will have to bear the risks of damage, destruction, and loss, starting from the date of the breach. For an object that has been delivered by the seller to a carrier and is en route to the buyer, the risks of damage, destruction, and loss shall be borne by the buyer, starting from the time of the formation of the contract, unless otherwise agreed upon by the parties. After the seller has delivered the object to the first carrier because the parties have not agreed on the place of delivery or have not made the place clear, the risks of damage, destruction, and loss shall be borne by the buyer. Where the seller has put the object at the place of delivery in accordance with its agreement with the buyer, or, in the case of no agreement or unclear provisions, the place where the object is located or its place of business, but the buyer fails to collect the object in violation of the agreement, the risks of damage, destruction, and loss shall be borne by the buyer, starting from the date of the breach.

In addition, the seller should deliver the object packaged in a manner pursuant to its agreement with the buyer. If there is no agreement or the agreement is unclear, and the manner of packaging cannot be determined by concluding a supplementary agreement or with reference to the relevant contractual clauses or course of dealing, the seller should package the object by a common method, or, in the absence of a common method, by a means sufficient to protect the object. Moreover, the seller must guarantee that no third party has any rights in the object for sale, unless otherwise provided by law. Even so, if the buyer knew or should have known at the time of the formation of the contract that a third party had rights in the object for sale, the seller will have no obligation. Where the buyer has conclusive evidence that a third party may assert its rights in the object, it may suspend payment of the price, unless the seller has provided a guarantee.

On its part, the buyer must inspect the object within the agreed-upon inspection period. If no agreement has been made, the inspection should be done promptly. The buyer must notify the seller within the inspection period if the quantity or quality fails to conform to the terms of the contract. If the buyer is indolent in notifying the seller, the quantity or quality will be deemed satisfactory. If the parties have not agreed on the inspection period, the buyer should notify the seller within a reasonable time since it discovered or should have discovered that the quantity or quality did not meet the requirements of the contract. If the buyer does not notify the seller within a reasonable time or two years of its receipt of the object, the quantity or quality will be deemed satisfactory. Even so, if there is a warranty period for quality, such a warranty period should be applied. If the seller knew or should have known that the quantity or quality did not meet the terms of the contract, the buyer will not be subject to either of the time limits.

Furthermore, the buyer should pay the agreed-upon price at the designated place. If the parties have not agreed upon the place of payment or have not made the place clear, and it cannot be determined by concluding a supplementary agreement or with reference to the relevant contractual clauses or course of dealing, the buyer should pay at the business place of the seller. If payment is conditional upon delivery of the object or the document to collect the object, the buyer should pay at the place where the object or the document is delivered. Moreover, the buyer should pay at the agreed-upon time. If the parties have not agreed on the time of payment or have not made the time clear, and it cannot be determined by concluding a supplementary agreement or with reference to the relevant contractual clauses or course of dealing, the buyer should pay at the same time when it receives the object or the document to collect the object. If the buyer who is supposed to pay by installments fails to pay the price due and the amount unpaid reaches one-fifth of the whole price, the seller may demand that the buyer pay the whole price or terminate the contract. If the seller terminates the contract, it may request that the buyer pay for the use of the object.

If the quality of the object does not conform to the quality requirements, thereby rendering it impossible to achieve the purpose of the contract, the buyer may refuse to accept the delivery or terminate the contract. In that case, any risks of damage, destruction, and loss shall be borne by the seller. If the seller delivers more than the contract stipulates, the buyer may accept or reject the extra quantity. If the buyer accepts the excess, it should pay at the price stipulated in the contract. If the buyer rejects the excess, it should notify the seller promptly. If a contract is terminated because the principal part of the object does not meet the terms of the contract, the effectiveness of such termination will extend to the collateral part(s), but not vice versa. If the object of the contract is composed of several items and one item fails to meet the terms of the contract, the buyer may terminate the contract with respect to such an item. However, if the severance of such item from other items impairs the value of the object of the contract, the buyer may terminate the contract with respect to the other items.

Where the seller delivers the object in batches, if the seller fails to deliver one batch or the delivery fails to meet the terms of the contract, thus making it impossible for such a batch to achieve the purpose of the contract, the buyer may terminate the contract with respect to such a batch. If the seller fails to deliver one batch or the delivery fails to meet the terms of the contract, thereby making it impossible for subsequent batches to achieve the purpose of the contract, the buyer may terminate the contract with respect to such a batch and the subsequent batches. If the buyer has terminated the contract with respect to one batch and such a batch is indispensable to other batches, the buyer may terminate the contract with respect to all delivered or undelivered batches.

If a sale contract is concluded based on a sample of the object of the contract, the parties should seal up the sample and may make specifications regarding quality. The object delivered by the seller should be of the same quality as that of the sample and the specifications. If the buyer does not know that the sample has a hidden defect, even if the object delivered is the same as the sample, the object delivered must still meet the normal standards for that kind of object. Similarly, a sale contract may be concluded based on trial use. The parties may agree on the trial period, but if there is no agreement or such an agreement is unclear, and it cannot be determined by concluding a supplementary agreement or with reference to the relevant contractual clauses or course of dealing, the seller should decide on the period. During the trial use, the buyer may buy the object or refuse to buy it. Upon the expiration of the trial period, if the buyer fails to express whether or not it wants to buy the object, it will be deemed to have bought it.

Lease contracts

A lease contract (租赁合同) is a contract by which the lessor delivers the leased property to the lessee for use or generating proceeds and the lessee pays a rent. The contents of a lease contract should include such items as the title of the leased property, quantity, purpose of its use, lease term, rent and the time limit and method for payment, and maintenance. The term of a lease cannot exceed 20 years. If the term of a lease exceeds 20 years, the excess will be invalid. Upon the expiration of the lease term, the parties may extend the lease, but the extension cannot be more than 20 years. If the parties have not agreed on the lease term or their agreement is not clear, and it cannot be determined by concluding a supplementary agreement or with reference to the relevant contractual clauses or course of dealing, the lease will be regarded as one without a fixed term. A lease without a fixed term may be terminated at any time, but the lessor must give the lessee reasonably advance notice.

In the case of a lease for six months or more, the lease contract must be concluded in writing. If the lease contract is not concluded in writing, it will be deemed a lease without a fixed term. During the term of the lease, any changes in the ownership of the leased property do not affect the validity of the lease contract. If the lessee becomes dead, the co-inhabitants may continue the lease. After the expiration of the lease term, if the lessee continues to use the leased property and the lessor does not raise any objection, the original lease contract will continue to be effective, but the lease will become one without a fixed term.

The lessor must deliver the leased property to the lessee in accordance with the contract. During the term of the lease, the lessor must maintain the leased property for such use as stipulated in the contract. If the leased property needs repair, the lessee may request the lessor to do so within a reasonable time. If the lessor does not maintain and repair the leased property, the lessee can do so on its own, and the expenses will be borne by the lessor. If the repair work affects the lessee's use of the leased property, the lessor should reduce the rent or extend the lease term. In addition, if the leased property jeopardizes the safety or health of the lessee, the lessee may terminate the contract at any time even if it knew at the time of the conclusion of the contract that the leased property did not meet the quality requirements.

At the same time, the lessee must use the leased property pursuant to the manner as provided in the contract. Where there is no agreement or the agreement is not clear, and it cannot be determined by concluding a supplementary agreement or with reference to the relevant contractual clauses or course of dealing, the leased property should be used in conformity with its nature. If the lessee uses the leased property pursuant to its intended use or nature, which results in the wear and tear of the leased property, the lessee will not be liable for damages. If the lessee uses the leased property otherwise, which results in damage to the leased property, the lessor may terminate the lease contract and claim damages. Likewise, the lessee should keep the leased property properly. If improper storage causes damage, destruction, or loss to the leased property, the lessee will be liable for damages.

More importantly, the lessee must pay rent within the agreed-upon time limit. If the parties have not entered into any agreement or have not made the time limit clear, and it cannot be determined by concluding a supplementary agreement or with reference to the relevant contractual clauses or course of dealing, the lessee shall pay rent before the expiration of the lease term if the term is less than one year. If the lease term is one year or more, the lessee shall pay rent at the end of each year and upon the expiration of the lease term. In addition, if the lessee fails to pay or delays paying the rent without legitimate reason(s), the lessor may demand the lessee pay within a reasonable time. If the lessee fails to pay the rent within a reasonable time, the lessor may terminate the contract. Nonetheless, if the leased property is partly or wholly damaged, destroyed, or lost due to causes not attributable to the lessee, the lessee may request a reduction of the rent or not pay the rent at all. If the damage, destruction, or loss makes it impossible to achieve the purpose of the lease contract, the lessee may terminate the contract.

During the term of the lease, the lessee may keep any proceeds derived from the possession or use of the leased property, unless otherwise agreed upon by the parties. If the lessee cannot use or profit from the leased property due to the claims of a third party, it may request a reduction of the rent or not pay the rent at all. With the consent of the lessor, the lessee may improve the leased property or add things onto it. In the absence of consent, the lessor may request that the lessee restore the leased property to its original condition or pay damages. The lessee may also sublet the leased property to a third party if the lessor consents. In such a case, the lease contract between the lessee and the lessor continues to be effective, and the lessee will be liable for any damage caused by the third party. If the lessee fails to obtain consent, the lessor may terminate the lease contract. On the other hand, if the lessor sells the leased property, it must notify the lessee within a reasonable time prior to the sale. The lessee has the right of priority to purchase the leased property on equal terms.

Work contracts

A work contract (承揽合同) is a contract by which the contractor, in accordance with the requirements of the ordering party, completes the work and delivers the results and the ordering party pays it remuneration. The kinds of work to be contracted out include processing, repairing, duplicating, testing, and inspecting. A work contract should contain such items as the object of the contract, quantity, quality, remuneration, the method of work, the supply of materials, the time limit for performance, and the standards and means of inspection and acceptance. The ordering party may terminate the contract at any time, but it will be liable for damages if the contractor has incurred losses.

As a general rule, the contractor should use its own equipment, technology, and workforce to complete the principal part of the work, unless otherwise agreed upon by the parties. If the contractor delegates the principal part of the work to a third party for completion, the contractor will be liable to the ordering party with respect to the results of the third party's work. If the delegation is without the consent of the ordering party, the ordering party may also terminate the contract. Even if the contractor delegates only the auxiliary parts of the work to a third party for completion, it will still be liable to the ordering party with respect to the results of the third party's work. Similarly, if the ordering party changes the requirements of the work midway, thus causing losses to the contractor, the ordering party will be liable for damages. If the work needs the assistance of the ordering party, but the ordering party fails to provide assistance and causes the work to be unfinished, the contractor may urge the ordering party to provide assistance within a reasonable time and extend the performance period. If the ordering party fails to perform such an obligation within the time limit, the contractor may terminate the contract.

If the ordering party is to furnish the materials, it must supply the materials in accordance with the terms of the contract. The contractor must inspect the materials promptly, and if it discovers that they do not conform to the requirements of the contract, must notify the ordering party promptly so that the latter can replace them, supply what is missing or take other remedial measures. The contractor cannot unilaterally replace any materials furnished by the ordering party and cannot replace spare parts that need not be repaired. Indeed, the contractor must store the materials furnished by the ordering party and the results of the work properly, and if they are destroyed, damaged, or lost due to improper storage, the contractor will be liable for damages. Likewise, if the contractor provides the materials, it must select and use materials pursuant to the terms of the contract and allow inspection by the ordering party.

The contractor should accept the necessary supervision and inspection by the ordering party, even though the ordering party cannot obstruct the contractor's normal work activities. If the contractor discovers that the drawings supplied by the ordering party or its technical requirements are unreasonable, it should notify the ordering party promptly. The ordering party will be liable for damages if its indolence in responding causes the contractor to have sustained losses. When the contractor delivers the results of the work to the ordering party, it should submit the necessary technical material and relevant quality certificates. The ordering party should then examine and accept the results of the work. If they do not conform to the quality requirements, the ordering party may request the contractor to repair, remake, reduce remuneration, compensate for losses, etc.

Correspondingly, the ordering party must pay the remuneration within the agreed-upon time limit. If the parties have not agreed on the time limit or such an agreement is unclear, and it cannot be determined by concluding a supplementary agreement or with reference to the relevant contractual clauses or course of dealing, the ordering party should pay at the time at which the results of the work are delivered. If part of the results of the work is delivered, the ordering party should make a corresponding payment. In any case, if the ordering party fails to pay remuneration or the price for materials, etc., the contractor has the right to place a lien on the results of the work, unless otherwise agreed upon by the parties. On the other hand, the contractor should maintain confidentiality pursuant to the request of the ordering party and must not keep the duplicates or technical data without permission. The co-contractors will be jointly and severally liable to the ordering party, unless otherwise agreed upon by the parties.

Technology contracts

A technology contract (技术合同) is a contract by which the parties establish their rights and obligations with respect to technology development, technology transfer, and technical consultation and service. Accordingly, there are three types of technology contracts: technology development contracts, technology transfer contracts, and contracts for technical consultation and service. To provide a basic understanding of technology contracts, this section first discusses the general provisions that are applicable to all three types of technology contracts and then highlights important provisions on each specific type, especially the technology transfer contract.

In general, a technology contract should contain:

1 the title of the project;
2 the contents, scope, and requirements of the object of the contract;
3 the plan, schedule, time limit, place, region, and manner of performance;
4 the confidentiality of technical information and data;
5 an undertaking of risks;
6 the ownership of technological achievements and the method of sharing proceeds;
7 the standards and means of inspection and acceptance;
8 the price, remuneration or royalties and means of payment;
9 damages for breach of contract or the method for calculating the amount of compensation for losses;
10 dispute resolution mechanisms; and
11 interpretation of terms and technical expressions.

Moreover, relevant information, documents, and files, such as background information on technologies, reports on feasibility studies and technological appraisals, the project mission and plan, technological standards, and original designs, may be treated as part of the contract if agreed upon by the parties. In the case of a technology contract involving the use of a patent, the parties should indicate the title of the invention, the names of the patent applicant and the patentee, the date and number of the patent application, the patent number, and the term of validity of the patent.

With respect to the means of payment for the price, remuneration, or royalties, the parties may adopt one overall calculation and one-time payment, one overall calculation and payment by installments, proportionate payment, or proportionate payment plus an advance entry fee. If the parties agree on the method of proportionate payment, the amount of payment may be a certain percentage of the price of the product; the value-added after, or proceeds derived from, the exploitation of the patent or use of the know-how; the profits; the sales; or other methods as agreed upon by the parties. The percentage may be a fixed ratio or a ratio with a yearly progressive increase or decrease. In any event, a technology contract that monopolizes a technology, hinders technological advancement, or infringes upon the technological achievements of others is null and void.

Technology development contracts

The purpose of a technology development contract (技术开发合同) is to conduct research in and development of (R&D) new technologies, new products, new crafts, or new materials and their systems. A contract concluded for the purpose of applying or commercializing a technology that has value of industrial applicability should apply the provisions on technology development contracts *mutatis mutandis*. A technology development contract must be concluded in writing. There are two types of technology development contracts: commissioned development contracts and cooperative development contracts.

With respect to a commissioned development contract (委托开发合同), the commissioning party must, in accordance with the terms of the contract, pay the R&D expenses and remuneration, furnish technological material and original data, accomplish coordinating tasks, and accept the R&D results. Correspondingly, the commissioned party must formulate and implement the R&D plan, spend the R&D budget reasonably, complete the R&D work and deliver the R&D results on time, provide relevant technological material and necessary technical guidance, and assist the commissioning party in grasping the R&D results. If either party breaches the contract and causes a standstill, delay or failure in the R&D work, it will have to bear liability. The right to apply for a patent belongs to the commissioned party, unless otherwise agreed upon by the parties. However, the commissioning party may exploit the patent free of charge. If the commissioned party wants to transfer its right to apply for a patent, the commissioning party will have the right of priority to acquire such a right on equal terms.

As regards a cooperative development contract (合作开发合同), the parties should make investments in accordance with the terms of the contract, such as the contributing technologies, participating in the R&D based on division of labor, and cooperating with the other party in the R&D work. If one party breaches and causes a standstill, delay, or failure in the R&D work, it will have to bear liability. The right to apply for a patent is jointly owned by the parties, unless otherwise agreed upon by the parties. If one party wants to transfer its right, the other party will have the right of priority to acquire such right on equal terms. If one party relinquishes its right to apply for a patent, the other party may apply for a patent alone, but the party renouncing its right may exploit the patent free of charge. If one party does not agree to apply for a patent, the other party may not apply for it.

If the technology to be developed has been made public by others, thus making the performance of the contract meaningless, the parties may terminate the contract. The parties should agree on the liability for risks resulting from the failure or partial failure of the R&D work due to insurmountable technical difficulties. If there is no agreement or the agreement is unclear, and it cannot be determined by concluding a supplementary contract or with reference to the relevant contractual clauses or course of dealing, the risks should be shared by the parties in a reasonable manner. The party that is aware of a possible failure or partial failure of the R&D work should notify the other party promptly and take appropriate measures to mitigate losses.

Likewise, the parties should agree on the right to use or transfer know-how and the method of distributing its proceeds. If there is no agreement or the agreement is unclear, and it cannot be determined by concluding a supplementary contract or with reference to the relevant contractual clauses or course of dealing, either party has the right to use or transfer it. However, the commissioned party may not transfer the R&D results to a third party before delivering them to the commissioning party.

Technology transfer contracts

The subject matter of a technology transfer contract (技术转让合同) includes transfer of a patent, transfer of the right to apply for a patent, transfer of know-how, and licensing to exploit a patent. A technology transfer contract must be concluded in writing. The parties may agree on the scope of the exploitation of a patent or the use of a know-how provided that no restrictions may be imposed on technological competition and technological development. A contract for licensing is valid only within the term of validity of the patent right. In addition, the parties may stipulate the method of sharing technological improvements obtained from the exploitation of a patent or the use of a know-how in accordance with the principle of mutual benefit. If there is no agreement or the agreement is unclear, and it cannot be determined by concluding a supplementary contract or with reference to the relevant contractual clauses or course of dealing, one party will not have the right to share the technological improvements made by the other party.

To comply with the contract, the transferor should permit the transferee to exploit the patent, submit the technological material relevant to the exploitation of the patent, and provide the necessary technical guidance. Similarly, the transferor of know-how must furnish the technological material, conduct technical guidance, guarantee the applicability and reliability of the know-how, and undertake the obligation of maintaining confidentiality. In any case, the transferor must guarantee that it is the lawful owner of the furnished technology and that the technology is complete, without mistakes, effective, and capable of accomplishing the agreed-upon objective. Besides, if the transferor fails to transfer the technology, it must return the royalties in part or in whole and will be liable for breach. If the exploitation of the patent or use of a know-how by the transferee in accordance with the terms of the contract violates the legitimate rights and interests of a third party, the transferor will be liable, unless otherwise agreed upon by the parties.

On its part, the transferee must not allow any third party to exploit the patent, and must pay royalties in accordance with the terms of the contract. Likewise, the transferee of the know-how must pay the royalties and undertake the obligation of maintaining confidentiality. The transferee should, in accordance with the scope and the time limit agreed upon in the contract, maintain confidentiality of the portion of the technology that has not been publicly disclosed. Moreover, if the transferee exploits the patent or uses the know-how beyond the agreed-upon scope, unilaterally permits a third party to exploit the patent or use the know-how, or fails to maintain confidentiality, it will have to bear liability. Indeed, if the transferee fails to pay the royalties, it must make up for the arrears and pay damages for the breach pursuant to the contract. If the transferee does not pay, it must cease exploiting the patent or using the know-how and return the technological material, and will be liable for breach.

In the case of technology transfer between joint-venture partners, article 43 of the Regulations for the Implementation of the Law on Sino-Foreign Equity Joint Ventures provides that:

1   the licensing fees must be fair and reasonable;
2   unless otherwise agreed upon by the parties, the technology-exporting party must not impose any restrictions on the region of sale, quantity, and price of the products that will be exported by the technology-importing party;
3   the term of the contract generally should not exceed 10 years;
4   after the expiration of the technology transfer contract, the technology-importing party has the right to continue to use the technology;
5   the conditions for mutual exchange of technological improvements by both parties must be reciprocal;
6   the technology-importing party must have the right to buy the machinery, equipment, parts, and raw materials needed from whatever sources it deems suitable; and
7   the contract cannot include any unreasonably restrictive provisions that are prohibited by Chinese laws and regulations.

Contracts for technical consultation and service

A contract for technical consultation (技术咨询合同) is a contract by which feasibility studies, technological forecasts, technical investigations, and analytical evaluation reports are provided for a specific project. The commissioning party should explain the technical problem, furnish technical background information and relevant technological material and data, accept the results of the work, and pay the remuneration. If the commissioning party fails to provide the necessary material and data, thereby affecting the progress and quality of the consultation work, or does not accept the results of the work or accepts the results of the work beyond the time limit, the remuneration already paid may not be refunded, and the unpaid portion must be paid. On the other hand, the commissioned party must complete a consultation report or solve the technical problem within the agreed-upon time limit. If the commissioned party fails to submit the consultation report on time or the report does not meet the requirements of the contract, it will have to reduce or waive the remuneration. However, if the commissioning party makes decisions based on the report and advice of the commissioned party that meet the contractual requirements, any losses incurred will be borne by itself, unless otherwise agreed upon by the parties.

A contract for technical service (技术服务合同) is a contract by which one party undertakes to solve specific technical problems for the other party by using its technical expertise, excluding construction project contracts and work contracts. The commissioning party should furnish the conditions for service, accomplish coordinating tasks, accept the results of the work, and pay the remuneration. If the commissioning party fails to perform its obligations or the performance does not conform to the requirements of the contract, thereby affecting the progress and quality of the technical service, or does not accept the results of the work or accepts them beyond the time limit, the remuneration already paid may not be refunded, and the unpaid portion must be paid. On the other hand, the commissioned party should complete the service, solve the technical problem, guarantee the quality of its service, and convey to the commissioning party the knowledge of how to solve the technical problem. If the commissioned party fails to complete the service, it will have to waive the remuneration. Finally, any new technological achievements of the commissioned party accomplished by using the techno-logical material and work conditions furnished by the commissioning party belong to the commissioned party, but new technological achievements accomplished by the commissioning party based on the results of the work of the commissioned party belong to the commissioning party, unless other-wise agreed upon by the parties.

3 Selected cases

Shanghai Pepsi Cola Beverages Ltd. *v*. Xian City Jianfeng Trading Co. *(2000)* 沪一中经终字第896号, *Shanghai City No. 1 Intermediate People's Court, 13 September 2000*

Facts

On 29 September 1994, 24 April 1995, and 31 January 1996 Shanghai Pepsi Cola Beverages Ltd. (hereinafter PBL) and Xian City Jianfeng Trading Co. (hereinafter JTC) signed three contracts for the sale and purchase of products. In these three contracts, the supplier was PBL, while the buyer was JTC. The sales items (the object of the contract) were Pepsi Cola, 7-Up, and Miranda beverages (1.25-liter PET bottles and 355-ml cans). Moreover, PBL agreed that if the yearly sales of PET bottles reached 10,000 cases, PBL would give JTC an in-kind sales commission of 1 percent; 20,000 cases, 2 percent; 30,000 cases, 3 percent. In respect of canned beverages, if the yearly sales reached 10,000 cases, PBL would give JTC an in-kind sales commission of 1 percent; 30,000 cases, 2 percent; and 50,000 cases, 3 percent. The sales volume was to be accounted for at the end of each year.

The 1994 contract also stipulated that JTC, upon the conclusion of the contract, would remit RMB 300,000 into PBL's account as a security deposit against risk, and that by the end of 1995, PBL would repay JTC the RMB 300,000 principal plus the normal yearly interest. After the contract had been signed, JTC remitted RMB 300,000 into PBL's account on 2 December 1994. In addition, the 1995 contract stipulated that PBL and JTC agreed to charge the security deposit of RMB 300,000 against JTC's payment for goods. In 1995, PBL invoiced JTC for a total amount of RMB 3,009,414. At the end of 1996, the two parties reconciled their accounts and signed an account reconciliation statement, which indicated that, as of January 1996, PBL had given 506 cases of CAN1 and 123 cases of 1.25 PET as sales commission for the year of 1995. On 8 May 1997, Wang Jian Xin, an employee of PBL, issued a receipt, acknowledging the receipt of 168 cash-prize pull rings (125 of which were "Sunshine Vacation"), 9 drink-prize bottle caps, and 12 pull rings for the exchange of a prize of RMB 50. Furthermore, PBL and JTC signed an agreement on 26 June 1996, stipulating that PBL, on behalf of JTC, promised Northwest Airlines that if Northwest Airlines sold 20,000 or more cases of Pepsi Cola canned beverage series in 1996, JTC, on behalf of PBL, would pay Northwest Airlines an advertising fee of RMB 50,000. On the same day, JTC and Northwest Airlines signed a sale contract, stipulating that JTC would supply Northwest Airlines with 20,000 cases of Pepsi Cola products. Nonetheless, JTC subsequently supplied Northwest Airlines with fewer than 20,000 cases.

The court of first instance held that the contracts signed between JTC and PBL were valid. In addition, both the account reconciliation statement signed by JTC and PBL and the invoice with value-added tax issued by PBL could prove JTC's 1995 sales volume and number of cases awarded. Thus, PBL should carry out the award clause in the contract for the year of 1995 by giving JTC the awards in kind. Furthermore, since the employee of PBL had issued JTC a receipt, acknowledging that PBL had received from JTC prize pull rings and bottle caps, PBL should also pay JTC the corresponding cash award for those pull rings and bottle caps. Regarding the interest of the security deposit, since both parties in the 1995 contract agreed that the interest of the security deposit would be charged against payment for goods, PBL should pay JTC the interest accrued before then. In respect of the advertising fee, since both parties agreed that payment of an advertising fee required the selling of 20,000 or more cases, but PBL supplied JTC with fewer than 20,000 cases in 1996, and JTC could not produce evidence that it sold Northwest Airlines 20,000 cases of goods in 1996, the claim of JTC was denied. As to the losses alleged by JTC, since it had not made the payment for goods in accordance with the contract and could not substantiate the alleged losses with evidence, such a claim was not supported either. Concerning JTC's additional claims, the court would not accept them because JTC had not paid the corresponding litigation fee. Accordingly, the court of first instance held that for 1995 PBL gave JTC the awards in kind (506 cases of PBL's manufactured CAN1 and 123 cases of 1.25 PET), the "Sunshine Vacation" cash-prize of RMB 976.50, and the interest earned from the principal of RMB 300,000 security deposit according to the interest rates set by the People's Bank of China from 2 December 1994 to 24 April 1995.

After the judgment, both PBL and JTC were not satisfied and appealed. PBL alleged that JTC did not make the payment for goods on time and therefore could not require it to give JTC the awards in kind. In addition, since the RMB 300,000 security deposit had already been charged against JTC's purchase price, JTC had no legal basis to ask PBL to pay JTC interest on the deposit. On the other hand, JTC claimed that JTC had actually paid, on behalf of PBL, Northwest Airlines RMB 50,000 as advertising fees and had given Northwest Airlines a rebate of 600 cases of canned Pepsi Cola; therefore, PBL should pay JTC these two amounts of fees.

Reasoning

The court found that JTC and PBL did sign three sale contracts, which clearly stipulated JTC's annual rate of sales commission. Moreover, the subsequent account reconciliation statement signed by PBL and JTC confirmed the quantity of in-kind sale awards that JTC should be given. Therefore, PBL should carry out its duty to give JTC the awards in kind. In addition, the parties stipulated in the contracts that when PBL returned the security deposit, it would also pay interest. Indeed, before PBL charged the RMB 300,000 deposit against JTC's payment for goods, it had the use of the money. Hence, PBL should pay JTC the interest accrued during the period of use. Regarding JTC's claim of RMB 50,000 advertising fee to Northwest Airlines, the precondition stipulated in the contract was that JTC's sales to Northwest Airlines should reach 20,000 or more cases. Since JTC could not provide solid evidence as to the sales volume, its claim was denied. Similarly, JTC could not substantiate its alleged rebate of 600 cases of canned Pepsi Cola; therefore, the court denied JTC's claim. In fact, since JTC did not clearly state this claim at the original trial, the court would not consider it. The court of first instance made no mistake in handling the case because it had clearly ascertained the facts and correctly applied the law.

Judgment

According to articles 153(1)(i) and 107 of the Civil Procedure Law,[8] the court held that the appeal was dismissed and the original judgment was affirmed.

This judgment was final.

**Urumqi Taikang Food Industry Ltd. *v.* Beijing Xinsheng Science
and Technology Development Co.** *(2000)* 朝知初字第41号,
Beijing City Zhaoyang District People's Court, 10 June 2000

Facts

On 28 November 1999, Urumqi Taikang Food Industry Ltd. (hereinafter
TKL) and Beijing Xinsheng Science and Technology Development Co. (hereinafter XSC) signed a technology transfer contract. The contract stipulated
that XSC should transfer to TKL the production technologies for sugarless
grape wine, grainless sweet wine, soy sauce and vinegar, and TKL paid XSC
a transfer fee of RMB 16,000 before obtaining the production technologies.
Initially, TKL had to pay XSC RMB 3,800 for learning the techniques of
brewing sugarless grape wine and grainless sweet wine. Having received the
initial payment, XSC would provide all the technical information and train
one to two TKL technicians. The quality of the products should comply
with state standards or the samples provided by XSC. In transferring the
technologies, XSC guaranteed full delivery and comprehension until TKL
was satisfied and could manufacture the products independently. In addition, after TKL's technicians had finished the course, XSC would certify
their training. The production technologies were owned exclusively by XSC.
Having obtained the technologies, TKL had only the right to use, not the
right to transfer. Moreover, TKL could not disseminate or disclose the
know-how by any means; otherwise, TKL had to pay RMB 100,000 as
damages. At that time, XSC's production technologies were the most
advanced in the market. If there were any misrepresentations or inaccur-
ate cost accounting, XSC should compensate TKL RMB 100,000. XSC
would also compensate TKL for its total amount of investment in various
projects if XSC violated any of the preceding provisions.

When the contract was signed, TKL paid XSC RMB 3,800. XSC issued a
technical service fee invoice, which was used by the service industry at Beijing.
On the same day, TKL paid XSC RMB 368 for the purchase of grainless
yeast. XSC provided TKL with:

1   technical information for producing grainless wine and refining the
    taste with white wine;
2   technical information for producing grainless leavening wine (nutritious
    sweet wine);
3   technical information for producing millet wine;
4   copies of the examination report on grainless leavening wine issued by
    the State Food Quality Supervision and Examination Center;
5   copies of the state standards on strong-taste, light-taste and rice-taste
    white wine; and
6   advertising material on the three kinds of collaborations of the new
    production technology of grainless leavening wine.

Moreover, the production technology of grainless sweet wine was included in that of grainless leavening wine. At the same time, XSC also trained Song Ze, an employee of TKL, on the theory and practice of the production technology of grainless wine. However, XSC had not yet signed the certifying report. Nonetheless, both parties had not clearly itemized in the contract the amounts of transfer fees for the various production technologies, nor did they begin the training on the production technologies of soy sauce and vinegar.

TKL alleged that it signed a technology transfer contract with XSC on 28 November 1999. After TKL paid XSC the transfer fee, XSC instructed TKL on the production of grainless wine and on the production of sugarless grape wine by mixing millet wine and grape wine. However, it was impossible for TKL to produce sugarless grape wine by following XSC's instructions. Since XSC did not perform its contractual duty by transferring to TKL the technical information for producing grainless grape wine, TKL pleaded that the contract should be terminated; XSC should pay it RMB 100,000 as damages; and XSC should compensate it RMB 28,000 for the technology transfer fee, business travel expenses, loss of wages, legal expenses, etc.

XSC responded that it agreed with TKL on the transfer of four production technologies for the amount of RMB 16,000. TKL should pay XSC an initial amount of RMB 3,800 for learning the techniques of brewing sugarless grape wine and grainless sweet wine. On 28 November 1999, XSC had already given all the technical information on the production of grainless wine to TKL's staff, who had also been instructed on the spot. At the same time, XSC orally taught TKL's staff the technology of producing sugarless grape wine, even though XSC had not provided TKL with any written materials. However, TKL did not continue to pay XSC the transfer fee, nor did it dispatch its staff to Beijing for further training. As a result, the training was not complete. The transfer fee already paid by TKL was not even enough to cover the tuition for learning one of the two production technologies.

Although TKL denied XSC's claim that the technology of producing sugarless grape wine had been given orally, XSC did not produce any evidence to refute TKL's denial. On the other hand, TKL could not prove its claim that XSC instructed TKL on the production of sugarless grape wine by mixing millet wine and concentrated grape wine. XSC denied that such a technique was to be used for producing sugarless grape wine, and that it had not given such instructions. XSC confirmed that Song Ze came to Beijing on 18 November 1999 and left Beijing on 4 December 1999. During that period, Song Ze was engaged in the negotiation and signing of the technology transfer contract, as well as matters relating to technology learning. TKL paid travel expenses of RMB 3,833 for that trip which XSC did not deny. XSC also confirmed that TKL spent RMB 1,262 for a round-trip train ticket to Beijing for the lawsuit. However, TKL could not substantiate its other claims, including business travel expenses, loss of wages, and miscellaneous expenses.

Reasoning

The court found that the technology transfer contract between TKL and XSC was legally valid, so both parties should perform their contractual duties conscientiously. As the contract stipulated that TKL should pay XSC a transfer fee of RMB 3,800 for learning the techniques of brewing sugarless grape wine and grainless sweet wine, XSC should transfer to TKL the technical information of producing sugarless grape wine and grainless sweet wine after receiving the payment. Since TKL did not sue in respect of the production technology of grainless sweet wine, the court denied TKL's claim that it should be compensated for the purchase of the grainless yeast. XSC admitted that it had not transferred to TKL the production technology of sugarless grape wine after receiving the payment of RMB 3,800, but denied that the technology of mixing millet wine and concentrated grape wine to produce sugarless grape wine, as stated by TKL, was the technology it intended to transfer to TKL. Moreover, XSC did not produce evidence that it had taught TKL orally the production technology of sugarless grape wine. Therefore, the court concluded that XSC had not transferred to TKL the production technology of sugarless grape wine, which constituted a breach of contract.

Since the contract required an advance payment of RMB 3,800 by TKL before transferring the technologies of producing sugarless grape wine and grainless sweet wine, and XSC had not transferred the sugarless grape wine technology in accordance with the contract, XSC should return the corresponding transfer fee to TKL. Considering the fact that both parties did not stipulate the distributive proportion of the transfer fee of RMB 3,800 for the two technologies, the court, based on the principle of fairness, held at discretion that XSC should return to TKL RMB 1,900. Besides, both parties did not clearly indicate the amount of damages for breaching the contract, so TKL lacked the basis to plead damages. However, XSC should compensate TKL for any losses incurred resulting from its breach. XSC confirmed that the staff of TKL negotiated and signed the technology transfer contract as well as discussing matters relating to technology learning at Beijing from November 1999 to 4 December 1999. In addition, XSC did not dispute TKL's alleged amount of related expenses and confirmed the train fare spent for participating in the lawsuit. Hence, XSC should compensate TKL for the aforementioned expenses. In respect of other expenses, including business travel expenses, loss of wages and miscellaneous expenses, TKL could not produce sufficient evidence, and the court denied its claim. Given the fact that both parties did not fully perform their contractual duties, XSC breached the contract first, and TKL indicated its unwillingness to continue performance of the contract, the court granted TKL's request to terminate the contract. However, TKL had to keep the know-how confidential and could not use or transfer such know-how thereafter.

Judgment

According to articles 94(4) and 351 of the Contract Law,[9] the court held as follows:

1   Within 10 days of the effective date of this judgment, XSC had to return the transfer fee of RMB 1,900 to TKL.
2   Within 10 days of the effective date of this judgment, XSC should compensate TKL RMB 5,095.
3   The technology transfer contract between TKL and XSC was to be terminated on the effective date of this judgment.
4   TKL had to keep the know-how confidential and could not use or transfer such know-how.
5   XSC's other claims were dismissed.

If any party was not satisfied with this judgment, it might, within 15 days of the delivery of the judgment, submit an application for appeal to this court for the purpose of appealing to the Beijing City No. 2 Intermediate People's Court.

Further reading

Wang, Liming, "An Inquiry into Several Difficult Problems in Enacting China's Uniform Contract Law," (Translation by Keith Hand) *Pacific Rim Law and Policy Journal* 8, 1999, 351–92.
Zhang, Mo, "Freedom of Contract with Chinese Legal Characteristics: A Closer Look at China's New Contract Law," *Temple International and Comparative Law Journal* 14, 2000, 237–62.

Notes

1   Economic contracts are agreements made between enterprises, other economic organizations, *getigongshanghu*, and rural contracting households to pursue certain economic objectives.
2   Foreign economic contracts are agreements made between Chinese enterprises (or other economic organizations) and foreign enterprises (or other economic organizations or individuals) to pursue certain economic objectives. Since foreign investment enterprises are Chinese legal persons, their contracts with Chinese enterprises are to be governed by the Economic Contract Law.
3   The Contract Law of the People's Republic of China, adopted at the 2nd Session of the 9th National People's Congress on 15 March 1999.
4   Simply stated, good faith refers to honesty in belief, lack of intent to defraud, observance of reasonable commercial standards of fair dealing, etc.
5   If the government-fixed or government-directed price is adjusted during the time of delivery, the price at the time of delivery shall be used. If the seller has delayed delivery and the price has risen, the original price shall be used; but if the price has dropped, the new price shall be used. If the buyer has delayed payment or the

taking of possession and the price has risen, the new price shall be used; if the price has dropped, the original price shall be used.

6 The General Principles of the Civil Law of the People's Republic of China, adopted at the 4th Session of the 6th National People's Congress on 12 April 1986.

7 The Regulations of Guangdong Province on Electronic Trade, adopted by the 38th Session of the Standing Committee of the 9th Guandgong People's Congress on 6 December 2002.

8 Article 153(1)(i) of the Civil Procedure Law provides that the court of second instance should dismiss the appeal and affirm the judgment of the court of first instance if the original judgment is based on clearly established facts and correct application of law. Article 107 of the Civil Procedure Law concerns litigation fees in civil proceedings. In this case, each party was ordered to pay half of the court cost.

9 Article 94(4) of the Contract Law provides that if one party delays performing its obligations or commits an act in breach of the contract, thus rendering it impossible to achieve the purpose of the contract, the other party may terminate the contract. Article 351 of the Contract Law provides that if the transferor fails to transfer the technology, it must return the royalties in part or in whole and will be liable for breach, and that if the transferee exploits the patent or uses the know-how beyond the agreed-upon scope, or unilaterally permits a third party to exploit the patent or use the know-how, it will have to cease breaching the contract and bear liability.

5 Intellectual property

Nowadays, intangible assets feature prominently in the balance sheets of many companies, and intellectual property rights comprise a substantial portion of intangible assets. For that reason, it is imperative for businesses to understand intellectual property rights and to adopt appropriate measures to protect their intellectual property. In fact, intellectual property protection has been a major issue during bilateral or multilateral trade negotiations between China and other countries. This chapter is designed to provide an overview of the Chinese regulatory framework of intellectual property. Since patent, trademark, and copyright are the so-called "three pillars of intellectual property," the discussion here focuses on those three areas of intellectual property law. Nonetheless, as the protection of trade secrets has gained more attention, trade secrets will also be mentioned at the end of the chapter.

1 Overview

Prior to the introduction of economic reforms, most Chinese enterprises did not heed intellectual property rights because the absence of market competition under a centrally planned economy made the protection of intellectual property dispensable. Even so, there were regulations on trademark and patent. With the implementation of economic reforms and the opening-up of the country to the outside world in the late 1970s, China found it necessary to enact intellectual property laws and regulations. Thus, China enacted its Trademark Law[1] in 1982, Patent Law[2] in 1984, and Copyright Law[3] in 1990. Apart from domestic law, China also acceded to international conventions and became a member of international organizations that aimed at protecting intellectual property or establishing uniform guidelines for intellectual property rights. For instance, China joined the World Intellectual Property Organization in 1980, acceded to the Paris Convention for the Protection of Industrial Property in 1985, and joined the Madrid Agreement on the Registration of International Trademarks in 1989.

By the early 1990s, China had enacted laws and regulations covering the major aspects of intellectual property. Nevertheless, these laws and regulations were piecemeal, contained concepts reflective of a command economy, and had plenty of room for refinement. Moreover, although China had acceded to several international conventions on intellectual property, it was not a signatory to other important ones. Consequently, some aspects of China's intellectual property law were not in line with the international standards which existed at that time or which have been accepted subsequently. During his historical southern tour in 1992, Deng Xiaoping stressed the importance of complying with international standards on intellectual property.[4] Apparently, while encouraging greater efforts toward economic construction, Deng also realized that an internationalized intellectual property protection system was essential to the marketization of the Chinese economy and the attainment of scientific and technological advancement. Hence, the refinement of China's intellectual property system was indispensable.

Starting from 1992, China, on its own initiative, made various legislative enactments and amendments in order to meet the new demands of changing market conditions and to harmonize its domestic law with international standards. For example, in anticipation of the General Agreement on Tariffs and Trade (GATT) membership, China amended its Patent Law in 1992 to extend the duration of an invention patent to 20 years, revised its Trademark Law in 1993 to include service marks, and in 1997 added to the Criminal Law one section on intellectual property crimes.[5] Indeed, the enactment of intellectual property crimes was designed to meet the requirements of article 61 of the Agreement on Trade-Related Aspects of Intellectual Property Rights (TRIPS Agreement).

Meanwhile, China acceded to both the Berne Convention on the Protection of Literary and Artistic Works and the Universal Copyright Convention in 1992; the Convention for the Protection of Producers of Phonograms against Unauthorized Duplication of Phonograms in 1993; and the Patent Cooperation Treaty in 1994. As the United States exerted pressure on China to accelerate its enforcement efforts pertaining to intellectual property, the two countries also entered into three bilateral agreements: the Memorandum of Understanding on the Protection of Intellectual Property (1992); the Memorandum of Understanding Regarding the Enforcement of Intellectual Property Rights (1995); and the Report on Chinese Enforcement Actions under the 1995 Intellectual Property Rights Agreement, including the Annex Intellectual Property Enforcement and Market Access Accord (1996).

In anticipation of its WTO accession, China further revised its Patent Law, Trademark Law, and Copyright Law in 2000 and 2001. Subsequently, China promulgated a new set of Regulations on the Protection of Computer Software,[6] a new set of Measures on the Implementation of Administrative Punishment Regarding Copyright,[7] and a new set of Regulations on the Protection of Intellectual Property by the Customs.[8] Thus, China has undertaken efforts to harmonize many aspects of its intellectual property law with existing international standards. Nonetheless, since the incidence of infringement is high, China needs to enhance its enforcement efforts and to instill in the populace the importance of respecting intellectual property rights. Hopefully, China's intellectual property system will converge with international standards both in terms of legislation and enforcement.

2 Patents

In most countries, a patent may be granted on an invention, a utility model, or a design. Simply stated, an invention means any new technical solution relating to a product or a process. A utility model refers to any new technical solution relating to the shape and/or structure of a product. A design refers to any new, original, and ornamental design for a product that is fit for industrial use. A patent is a limited monopoly granted by the government to the inventor or designer for a period of time. In return, the inventor or designer discloses the invention, utility model, or design so that society as a whole will benefit from these innovations.

Apart from the Patent Law, the Chinese regulatory scheme of patent contains administrative regulations and government rules. For instance, there are the Detailed Regulations for the Implementation of the Patent Law[9] and the Measures on the Administration of Patent Agencies.[10] The following discussion, however, will highlight only the important provisions in the Patent Law and the Detailed Regulations for the Implementation of the Patent Law because these two pieces of legislation constitute the core of the regulatory system.

Requirements

According to the Patent Law, an invention-creation (发明创作) refers to an invention, a utility model, or a design. To obtain a patent for an invention or a utility model, the applicant must satisfy the requirements of novelty, inventiveness, and usefulness. Novelty means that, prior to the filing of the application, no identical invention or utility model:

1 has been publicly disclosed in domestic or foreign publications;
2 has been publicly used or made known to the public by any other means in the country; and
3 for which any other person has filed a patent application with the State Intellectual Property Office (SIPO), and such application has been recorded in patent application documents published after the filing date.

Even so, an invention-creation will not lose its novelty if one of the following circumstances has arisen within six months prior to the filing of the application:

1 it was exhibited for the first time at an international exhibition sponsored or recognized by the Chinese government;

2   it was disclosed for the first time at a prescribed academic or technical conference; or

3   it was divulged by any person without the consent of the applicant.

On the other hand, inventiveness means that, compared with the technologies existing before the filing date of the application, the invention has prominent substantive features and an obvious improvement, or the utility model has substantive characteristics and improvement. Usefulness means that the invention or utility model can be made or used and can produce positive results, in other words, has practical applicability. Similarly, for a design to be granted a patent, it must not be identical or similar to any design that, prior to the filing date of the application, has been publicly disclosed in domestic and foreign publications or has been publicly used in the country, and must not conflict with the legal rights and interests previously secured by others. Nonetheless, no patent will be granted to any invention-creation that violates the law, contravenes social morality, or impairs public interests. In particular, no patent will be granted to:

1   scientific discoveries;
2   rules and methods for mental activities;
3   methods for the diagnosis and treatment of diseases;
4   animal and plant varieties (except for processes used in producing such products); or
5   substances obtained by means of nuclear transformation.

Application procedure

In China, the right to apply for a patent or the patent right on an invention-creation is assignable. Thus, the applicant for a patent does not need to be the inventor. If the right to apply for a patent or the patent right is assigned, the parties must enter into a written contract and register it with the SIPO. The SIPO will then make a public announcement, and the assignment becomes effective on the date of registration. If a Chinese unit (单位), namely, entity, or individual wants to assign the right to apply for a patent or the patent right to a foreigner, it must first obtain the approval of the MOFTEC (now the Ministry of Commerce) and the Ministry of Science and Technology. Where an invention-creation is completed jointly by two or more entities or individuals, or is made by an entity or individual commissioned by another entity or individual, the right to apply for a patent belongs to the entity (entities) or individual(s) that made or jointly made the invention-creation, unless otherwise agreed upon between the parties. If two or more applicants separately file patent applications on the same invention-creation, the patent right will be granted to the person who filed first. In other words, China has the first-to-file system.

In filing a patent application for an invention or a utility model, the applicant must submit such documents as a written request, the specification and an abstract, and the patent claim(s). The written request must state the title of the invention or utility model, the name of the inventor, the name or title and address of the applicant, and other relevant matters. The specification must describe the invention or utility model in a manner sufficiently clear and complete such that an individual skilled in the art to which the invention or utility model pertains can make and use it, and if necessary, append drawings. The abstract should explain succinctly the technical essentials of the invention or utility model. The patent claim(s) should be based on the specification and explain the scope of patent protection requested. Similarly, in applying for a design patent, the applicant must submit a written request and the drawings or photographs of the design. In addition, the applicant must indicate the product on which the design is to be used as well as the classification of the product.

The date on which the SIPO receives the application materials is the filing date of the application. If the application is sent by post, the date of the postmark shall be the filing date. If the applicant, within 12 months of the date on which it first filed a patent application for an invention or a utility model in a foreign country, or within six months of the date on which it first filed a patent application for a design in a foreign country, files a patent application in China for the same subject matter, it may enjoy the right of priority in accordance with any treaty concluded between China and the foreign country, an international convention to which both China and the foreign country are signatories, or the principle of reciprocity. Likewise, if the applicant, within 12 months of the date on which it first filed a patent application for an invention or a utility model in China, files with the SIPO a patent application for the same subject matter, it may also enjoy the right of priority. To claim the right of priority, the applicant must make a written declaration at the time of filing and submit copies of the previous application materials in three months. If the applicant fails to do so, it will be deemed to have not made the claim.

Upon the receipt of a patent application for an invention, the SIPO conducts a preliminary examination to determine whether the application conforms to the requirements of the Patent Law. If everything is in order, the SIPO will publish the application 18 months after the filing date. The SIPO may also publish the application earlier upon the applicant's request. Within three years of the filing date, the SIPO may, upon the applicant's request at any time, conduct a substantive examination of the application. If the applicant fails to request a substantive examination within the time limit without any proper reason(s), the application will be deemed to have been withdrawn. Nonetheless, the SIPO may, on its own initiative, conduct a substantive examination of an application for an invention patent whenever necessary. In requesting a substantive examination of a patent application for an invention, the applicant shall furnish reference materials relating to the invention that were available prior to the filing date of the application. If the applicant has filed an application in a foreign country on the same invention, the SIPO may request that the applicant furnish, within a fixed period of time, materials obtained from any search made in connection with an examination in the foreign country or materials indicating the outcome of the examination. If these materials are not furnished without any valid reason(s), the application will be deemed to have been withdrawn.

Where the SIPO finds that an application for an invention patent does not conform to the requirements of the Patent Law, it shall ask the applicant to state its views or amend the application within a specific period of time. If the applicant fails to respond within the time limit without any valid reason(s), the application will be deemed to have been withdrawn. After the applicant has stated its opinions or amended the application, if the SIPO still finds that the application does not meet the requirements of the Patent Law, it shall reject the application. On the other hand, if the SIPO finds no cause to reject the application upon the completion of the substantive examination, it shall notify the applicant of the grant of a patent. The applicant must complete the registration formalities within two months of the receipt of the notification. After the registration has been completed, the SIPO shall issue a certificate of patent for the invention and announce the patent. The patent right of an invention becomes effective as of the date of announcement. Likewise, if the SIPO finds no cause to reject an application for a utility-model or design patent upon the completion of the preliminary examination, it shall issue a certificate of patent as well as registering and announcing the patent. The patent right of a utility model or design also becomes effective as of the date of announcement.

If the applicant does not agree with the decision of the SIPO to reject its application, it may request that the Patent Re-examination Board conduct a re-examination within three months of the receipt of the notification. The Patent Re-examination Board shall make a decision and notify the applicant. If the applicant is not satisfied with the decision of the Patent Re-examination Board, it may institute legal proceedings within three months of the receipt of the notification. This provision on judicial review was added in 2000 so as to meet the requirements of article 62(5) of the TRIPS Agreement, which mandates that final administrative decisions regarding acquisition and maintenance of intellectual property rights be subject to review by a judicial or quasi-judicial organ.

Where a foreign individual, enterprise, or organization having no regular place of dwelling or place of business in China files a patent application in China, the application is to be handled in accordance with any agreement concluded between the applicant's home country and China, any international treaty to which China and the applicant's home country are signatories, or the Patent Law on the basis of the principle of reciprocity. In this regard, it is noteworthy that since China is a signatory to the Paris Convention for the Protection of Industrial Property, foreign applicants from other member countries are entitled to receive national treatment. If a foreign individual, enterprise, or organization having no regular place of dwelling or place of business in China files a patent application or has other patent matters to handle, it must entrust a patent agency designated by the SIPO with the tasks. In fact, a Chinese entity or individual may also entrust a patent agency with the tasks of applying for a patent and handling other patent matters. Likewise, if a Chinese entity or individual wants to file a patent application in a foreign county for an invention made in China, it must first file a patent application with the SIPO and entrust a designated patent agency with the foreign application.

Patent rights

The term of a patent for an invention is 20 years, and 10 years for a utility model or design, starting from the filing date of the application. The patent holder is to pay an annual fee, beginning from the year in which the patent is granted. If the patentee does not pay the annual fee or relinquishes the patent right in writing, the patent will terminate prior to the expiration of its term.

After a patent is granted to an invention or a utility model, no entity or individual may, without the permission of the patent holder, exploit the patent, unless otherwise provided by law. In other words, no entity or individual may, for production or business purposes, make, use, promise to sell, sell, or import the patented product; use the patented process; or use, promise to sell, sell, or import products directly obtained by the patented process. Similarly, after a patent is granted to a design, no entity or individual may, without the permission of the patent holder and for production and business purposes, make, sell, or import products incorporating the patented design. Any entity or individual that wants to exploit the patent of another must conclude a written licensing contract with the patent holder and pay a royalty. However, the licensee does not have the right to permit anyone other than those stipulated in the licensing contract to exploit the patent. The licensing contract must be reported to the SIPO for the record within three months of its effective date. Furthermore, after the application for an invention patent has been publicly disclosed, the applicant may require any entity or individual that has exploited the invention to pay an appropriate amount of fee.

Invalidation

From the date on which the SIPO grants a patent, any entity or individual may request that the Patent Re-examination Board declare the patent invalid if the requestor thinks that the grant of such patent does not conform with the requirements of the Patent Law. An invalid patent is deemed to be nonexistent from the beginning. The decision invalidating a patent has no retroactive effect on any previous:

1   judgments or rulings regarding patent infringement that have been made and enforced by the people's courts;
2   decisions resolving patent infringement disputes that have been performed or enforced; or
3   contracts licensing the exploitation of the patent or assigning the patent that have been performed.

Nonetheless, if the non-restitution of the licensing fee or contract price is obviously unfair, the licensor or assignor will have to repay the whole or part of the licensing fee or contract price to the licensee or assignee. Moreover, if any party sustains damages as a result of the patentee's bad faith, the patentee will have to pay compensation.

The SIPO must register and announce any decisions invalidating patent rights. If any party is not satisfied with the decision of the Patent Re-examination Board to either invalidate or uphold the patent, it may file a lawsuit in the people's court within three months of the receipt of the notification. In such a case, the court shall inform the other party of the invalidation proceedings so that it can participate in the lawsuit as a third party.

Infringement and remedies

The scope of protection for an invention or utility-model patent is to be determined by the contents of the patent claim(s). In this connection, the specification and appended drawings may be used to interpret the patent claims. Similarly, the scope of protection for a design patent is to be determined by the product incorporating the patented design as shown in the drawings or photographs. The manufacture, use, promise to sell, sale, or import of a patented product for production and business purposes and without the permission of the patent holder constitutes patent infringement. Likewise, the use of a patented process or the use, promise to sell, sale, or import of products directly obtained by the patented process for production and business purposes constitutes patent infringement. If the infringement involves a patented process for the manufacture of a new product, any entity or individual manufacturing an identical product will have to prove that its manufacturing process is different from the patented process. If the infringement involves a utility model, the people's court and the department in charge of patent affairs may request that the patent holder provide the search report made by the SIPO.

Nonetheless, the following actions will not be deemed patent infringement:

1 the use, promise to sell, or sale of a patented product after it is made and imported by the patent holder or with the permission of the patent holder, or after the sale of a product directly obtained by a patented process;

2 the continuous manufacture of an identical product or the use of an identical process within its original scope by an entity or individual that, prior to the filing date of the patent application, had already made the identical product or used the same process, or had made the necessary preparations for such manufacture or use;

3 the use of a patent in its devices and equipment and for its own needs by a foreign vehicle of transportation that temporarily passes through the territorial land, waters, or airspace of China in accordance with any agreement concluded between China and its home county, any international treaty to which China and its home country are signatories, or the principle of reciprocity; and

4 the use of a patent solely for the purposes of scientific research and experimentation.

Moreover, the use or sale of a patented product or product obtained directly by a patented process for production and business purposes and without knowledge of its having been made and sold without the permission of the patent holder will not be liable for damages if it can be proven that the product comes from a lawful source. Thus, the burden is on the user or seller to prove that its product does not infringe upon the patented product or process.

Where a dispute involves patent infringement, the parties may resolve it through consultation. If the parties are unwilling or unable to resolve their dispute through consultation, the patent holder or any interested party may request that the department in charge of patent affairs handle the case or file a lawsuit in the people's court. The SIPO and local departments in charge of patent affairs are authorized to settle patent disputes and issue orders forbidding patent infringement. Specifically, if the department in charge of patent affairs finds patent infringement, it may order the infringer to stop the infringement immediately. If the infringer is dissatisfied with the injunctive order, it may file a lawsuit in the people's court pursuant to the Administrative Procedure Law within 15 days of the receipt of the notification. Upon the expiration of the 15-day period, if the infringer has neither filed a lawsuit nor ceased the infringement, the department in charge of patent affairs may seek enforcement from the people's court. Moreover, if the parties so request, the department in charge of patent affairs may conduct mediation regarding the amount of damages as a result of the patent infringement. If mediation is not successful, either party may file a lawsuit in the people's court pursuant to the Civil Procedure Law.

To protect its patent rights, the patent holder may also file a lawsuit directly. The amount of compensation shall be the losses suffered by the patent holder or the profits obtained by the infringer as a result of the infringement. If it is difficult to determine the amount of loss or profit, the damages will be determined reasonably based on a multiple of the licensing royalty. Where the patent holder or an interested party can prove that someone is infringing or is going to infringe its patent, and that its lawful rights and interests will suffer irreparable injury without timely prevention, it may apply to the people's court for a preliminary injunction and property preservation prior to the filing of a lawsuit. The time limit for filing a lawsuit regarding patent infringement is two years from the date on which the patent holder or an interested party knew or should have known about the infringement. Where the exploitation fee for an invention patent during the period from the publication of the application to the grant of the patent is not paid, the time limit for demanding payment is two years from the date on which the patent holder or an interested party knew or should have known of the exploitation. However, the statute of limitations runs from the date of the grant of the patent if the patent holder knew or should have known of the exploitation prior to the grant of the patent.

Apart from patent infringement, the Patent Law also prohibits the counterfeiting of a patent and the passing an unpatented product or process off as a patented product or process. Specifically, any of the following acts constitutes the counterfeiting of a patent:

1   marking the patent number of another on products manufactured or sold or on the packaging of the products without permission;
2   using the patent number of another in advertising or other propaganda materials without permission, thereby causing people to mistakenly believe that the technology involved is the patented technology;
3   using the patent number of another in a contract, thus causing people mistakenly to believe that the technology involved is the patented technology; or
4   forging or altering a certificate of patent, patent documents, or patent application documents of another.

If any entity or individual counterfeits the patent of another, in addition to civil liability, the department in charge of patent affairs shall order it to rectify the situation and confiscate any profits obtained illegally, and may, at the same time, levy a fine of no less than three times the unlawful earnings. If there are no illegal profits, a fine of RMB 50,000 or less may be imposed. If the infringement constitutes a crime, criminal liability will be pursued. Indeed, article 216 of the Criminal Law provides that if the counterfeiting of a patent is serious, the court may impose a fine and/or up to three years' imprisonment.

Similarly, any of the following acts constitutes the false representation of an unpatented product or process as a patented product or process:

1 the manufacture or sale of an unpatented product bearing a patent sign;
2 continuing to put a patent sign on products manufactured or sold after the patent has been declared invalid;
3 claiming an unpatented technology in advertising or other propaganda materials as a patented technology;
4 claiming in a contract an unpatented technology as a patented technology; or
5 forging or altering a certificate of patent, patent documents, or patent application documents.

If any entity or individual passes any unpatented product or process off as a patented product or process, the department in charge of patent affairs shall order the infringer to rectify the situation and publicly announce the decision, and may also levy a fine of RMB 50,000 or less.

Finally, where any party files a patent application in a foreign country without authorization, thus divulging an important state secret, the unit to which it belongs or the organ-in-charge at the next higher level shall undertake administrative disciplinary measures. If the act constitutes a crime, criminal liability will be pursued.

Compulsory licensing

If the invention patents of state-owned enterprises, institutions, collectively owned enterprises, and individuals are of great significance in terms of national or public interests, the relevant departments-in-charge under the State Council and the people's governments of provinces, autonomous regions, and municipalities directly under the central government may, after obtaining the approval of the State Council, diffuse the use of the patents within the scope of approval by allowing designated entities to exploit the patents. The entities exploiting such patents shall pay royalties in accordance with state regulations.

More specifically, the SIPO may grant a compulsory license to exploit the patent on an invention or a utility model where:

1 any entity possessing the conditions for exploiting the invention or utility model has requested permission from the patent holder to exploit the patent on reasonable terms, but has been unable to obtain such permission within a reasonable period of time;
2 the country faces an emergency or extraordinary circumstances, or public interest so necessitates; or
3 a patented invention or utility model is an important technical improvement of considerable economic significance over a previously patented invention or utility model, and the exploitation of such invention or utility model depends on the exploitation of the previously patented invention or utility model.

In the first case, the applicant may apply for compulsory licensing three years after the grant of the patent. In the third case, either the patent holder of the later invention or utility model, or the patent holder of the previous invention or utility model, may apply for compulsory licensing.

To obtain compulsory licensing, the applicant must furnish proof that it has not been able to conclude a licensing contract on reasonable terms with the patent holder. If the SIPO grants a compulsory license, it must notify the patent holder promptly as well as register and publicly announce its decision. The term and scope of a compulsory license must be specified in accordance with the reason(s) on which the application is made. Where the reason(s) has (have) disappeared and will cease to occur, the SIPO shall, upon the application of the patent holder, terminate the compulsory license. The licensee has a nonexclusive right to exploit the patent, cannot permit others to exploit the patent, and must pay the patent holder a reasonable royalty, the amount of which is to be determined by both parties through consultation. If the parties fail to reach an agreement on the amount of royalty, the SIPO will make a judgment. If the patent holder is dissatisfied with the decision of the SIPO granting the compulsory license, or the patent holder or the licensee is dissatisfied with the decision of the SIPO on the amount of royalty, it may file a lawsuit in the people's court within three months of the receipt of the notification.

3 Trademarks

Apart from the Trademark Law, the Chinese regulatory scheme of trademarks includes administrative regulations and government rules. For example, there are the Regulations for the Implementation of the Trademark Law,[11] the Rules on the Recognition and Protection of Well-Known Marks,[12] and the Measures on the Registration and Administration of Collective Marks and Certification Marks.[13] Since the Trademark Law and the Regulations for the Implementation of the Trademark Law constitute the core of the regulatory scheme, the following discussion will highlight the important provisions in those two pieces of legislation.

Requirements

According to the Trademark Law, registered trademarks are those that have been approved and registered by the Trademark Bureau (TMB) under the State Administration for Industry and Commerce, including trademarks, service marks, collective marks, and certification marks. A collective mark is a mark registered in the name of a group, association, or other organization for use by its members in commercial activities in order to indicate the membership. A certification mark is a mark controlled by an organization capable of supervising certain goods or services for use by other entities or individuals on goods and services to certify their origin, raw materials, manufacturing processes, quality, or other special characteristics. The trade-mark registrant enjoys the right to the exclusive use of its trademark.

Any sign that is visually perceptible and capable of distinguishing the goods or services of a natural person, legal person, or other organization from those of others, including words, design, letters of the alphabet, numerals, three-dimensional signs (except for those that merely result from the nature of the goods or are necessary to obtain a technical result or give the goods substantial value), combination of colors, or any combination of these, may be used for trademark registration. Moreover, the sign must have distinctive characteristics so as to facilitate identification and must not conflict with the prior legal rights obtained by others. Nonetheless, the following signs may not be registered as trademarks:

1   a sign consisting only of the generic name, design, or type of the goods (generic mark);
2   a sign merely indicating directly the quality, main ingredients, func-tions, weight, quantity, or other characteristics of the goods (descriptive mark); and
3   a sign lacking distinctiveness.

Even so, these signs may be registered as trademarks if they have acquired distinctiveness through their use and facilitate identification (secondary meaning).

Furthermore, the following signs may not be used as trademarks:

1   a sign identical or similar to the national name, national flag, national emblem, military flag or medal of China, or identical to the name of a specific site or the name or design of a symbolic building where any central state organ is located;
2   a sign identical or similar to the national name, national flag, national emblem, or military flag of any foreign country, except for those other-wise permitted by the government of such foreign country;
3   a sign identical or similar to the name, flag, or emblem of any inter-governmental international organization, except for those otherwise permitted by such organization or not easily misleading for the public;
4   a sign identical or similar to the official mark or inspection stamp that indicates the execution of control or grant of guaranty, except for those otherwise authorized;
5   a sign identical or similar to the name or mark of the Red Cross or the Red Crescent;
6   a sign which is discriminatory against any ethnic group;
7   a sign which exaggeratedly advertises the goods or services and is deceptive;
8   a sign detrimental to social morality or customs or having other bad influences; and

9   the geographical name of an administrative division at or above the county level or foreign geographical name known to the public, except for those having other meanings or used as part of a collective or certification mark, or those that have already been registered.

If the mark for registration on identical or similar goods or services is the duplication, imitation, or translation of others' well-known marks that are not registered in China and will easily cause confusion, such a mark will not be registered and will be forbidden from use. If the mark for registration on dissimilar goods or services is the duplication, imitation, or translation of others' well-known marks that are registered in China and will mislead the public, which may cause damage to the registrants of such well-known marks, such marks will not be registered and will be forbidden from use. In determining whether a mark is well known, the following factors should be considered:

1   the extent of knowledge of the trademark in the relevant sector of the public;
2   the duration of the use of the trademark;
3   the duration, extent, and geographical scope of any promotion of the trademark;
4   the record of the trademark being protected as a well-known mark; and
5   any other factors contributing to reputation of the trademark.

Similarly, if the trademark contains a geographical indication of the goods, but the goods do not originate from the place identified by such indication, thus misleading the public, such trademark will not be registered and will be forbidden from use. However, if such a trademark has been registered in good faith, it will continue to be effective. The geographical indication refers to any thing that identifies the goods as originating from a certain place whose natural and humanistic factors principally contribute to the specific quality, reputation, or other characteristics of the goods. Likewise, if an agent or representative, without authorization, applies in its name for registration of the trademark of the principal and the principal has objected to the registration, such a trademark will not be registered and will be forbidden from use.

Registration procedure

The TMB is in charge of trademark registration and administration throughout the country. Any natural person, legal person, or other organization that needs to acquire the right to the exclusive use of a mark for the goods that it produces, manufactures, processes, selects or sells on commission, or of a service mark for the services it provides, must file an application for the registration of the mark with the TMB. Two or more applicants may jointly file an application for the registration of an identical trademark. In such a case, the applicants jointly own and exercise the right to the exclusive use of the trademark. With respect to goods about which the state has prescribed the use of a registered trademark, an application for trademark registration must be filed, and the goods may not be sold on the market prior to registration. In any event, the application for trademark registration must not prejudice any existing rights of others obtained by priority, and any registration by improper means of trademarks that have been used by others and have become influential shall be prohibited.

To apply for trademark registration, the applicant must state the class and the name of the goods on which the trademark is to be used in accordance with the prescribed list of classifications of goods. If the applicant wants to apply for the registration of the same trademark on goods in different classes, it must follow the list of classifications of goods to submit applications. If a registered trademark needs to be used on other goods in the same class, a separate application for registration must be filed. If the sign of a registered trademark needs to be changed, a new registration application must be filed.

Where the applicant files in China an application for the registration of the same trademark on the same goods or services within six months of the date on which it first filed trademark registration in a foreign country, it may enjoy the right of priority pursuant to any agreement concluded between China and the foreign country, any international treaty to which China and the foreign country are signatories, or the principle of mutual recognition of the right of priority. In such a case, the applicant must submit a written declaration together with its application, and must, within three months, submit a copy of the documents relating to the first trademark registration. If the applicant fails to do so, the claim to the right of priority will be deemed to have not been made. Likewise, where a trademark was first used on goods displayed at an international exhibition sponsored or recognized by the Chinese government, the trademark applicant may enjoy the right of priority within six months of the date on which the goods were exhibited. In such a case, the applicant shall submit a written declaration together with its application, and must, within three months, submit documents proving the name of the exhibition at which the goods were exhibited, the use of the trademark on the goods exhibited, the date of exhibition, etc. If the applicant fails to do so, the claim to the right of priority will be deemed to have not been made.

If the application is in conformity with the Trademark Law, the TMB will conduct a preliminary examination and approval of the trademark and make a public announcement. If the application is made to register a trademark that does not meet the requirements of the Trademark Law, or that is identical or similar to another's trademark that has already been registered or given preliminary examination and approval for use on the same or similar kind of goods, the TMB will reject the application and not make a public announcement. Where a trademark application has been rejected, the TMB shall notify the applicant in writing. If the applicant does not agree with the rejection, it may apply to the Trademark Review and Adjudication Board for a re-examination within 15 days of the receipt of the notification. The Trademark Review and Adjudication Board shall make a decision, and if the applicant does not agree with the decision, it may file a lawsuit in the people's court within 30 days of the receipt of the notification.

When two or more applicants apply for the registration of identical or similar trademarks on the same or similar kind of goods, the trademark for which registration was first applied is to be given preliminary examination and approval and, thus, be publicly announced. In other words, China has the first-to-file system. If the applications are filed on the same day, the trademark that was used first will be given preliminary examination and approval, while the other applications will be rejected without public announcement. If two or more applicants started using the same or similar trademarks on the same day or have not yet used the trademarks, they should decide on the choice of applicant through consultation. If they are unwilling or unable to reach a settlement, the TMB will draw lots to determine which applicant may apply for trademark registration.

Any foreigner or foreign enterprise intending to apply for the registration of a trademark in China must file an application in accordance with any agreement concluded between China and the applicant's home country, any international treaty to which both countries are signatories, or the principle of reciprocity. As mentioned above, China has acceded to the Paris Convention for the Protection of Industrial Property and the Madrid Agreement on the Registration of International Trademarks. Furthermore, a foreign trademark owner must entrust a trademark agency officially recognized by the Chinese government with the task of registration and other trademark matters.

Opposition

Any party may file an opposition to a trademark that has been preliminarily examined and approved within three months of the public announcement. If no opposition is filed when the period of public announcement expires, registration will be granted, a certificate of trademark registration will be issued, and the trademark will be publicly announced. If an opposition is filed, the TMB will hear the statements of facts and reasons made by the opponent and the applicant, and will make a decision after investigation and verification. If the opposition is upheld, registration of the trademark will be denied. If it is ruled that the opposition cannot be supported, registration of the trademark will be granted, a certificate of trademark registration will be issued, and the trademark will be publicly announced. In that case, the time for the applicant to obtain the exclusive right to the use of the trademark shall be counted from the date on which the three-month period of public announcement expires. A decision upholding the approval for registration of a trademark will have no retroactive effect on any use of an identical or similar mark on the same or similar kind of goods during the period after the opposition period expires but before the decision takes effect. However, if any damage is sustained as a result of the user's bad faith, the user will have to pay compensation.

If any party is dissatisfied with TMB's decision, it may apply to the Trademark Review and Adjudication Board for a re-examination within 15 days of the receipt of the notification. The Trademark Review and Adjudication Board shall make a decision, and if any party does not agree with the decision, it may file a lawsuit in the people's court within 30 days of the receipt of the notification. In that case, the people's court shall notify the other party of the re-examination proceedings so that it can participate as a third party. If neither party applies for re-examination of the decision made by the TMB or institutes court proceedings against the decision of the Trademark Review and Adjudication Board, such a decision will become effective.

Revocation

Under any of the following circumstances, the TMB shall order rectification of the situation within a fixed period of time,[14] and if the registrant refuses to rectify, the TMB shall revoke the registered trademark:

1   the registered trademark is altered without authorization;
2   the registrant's name, address, or any other registered matter is modified without authorization; or
3   the registered trademark is assigned without authorization.

Where a registered trademark has not been used for three consecutive years, any party may apply to the TMB to have the registered trademark revoked. In such a case, the TMB shall notify the trademark registrant and order the registrant to submit evidence of use or to provide reasons for nonuse within two months of the notification. If the registrant fails to produce evidence, or the evidence is not valid and the registrant fails to provide proper reasons, the TMB shall revoke the trademark. Likewise, where a registered trademark is used on poorly manufactured goods that are passed off as high-quality goods, thus deceiving consumers, the TMB may revoke the registered trademark. If any party disagrees with the decision of the TMB to revoke its registered trademark, it may apply to the Trademark Review and Adjudication Board for a re-examination within 15 days of the receipt of the notification. If the party also disagrees with the decision of the Trademark Review and Adjudication Board, it may file a lawsuit within 30 days of the receipt of the notification.

Furthermore, if a registered trademark is a sign that may not be used as a trademark, may not be registered as a trademark, or has a three-dimensional shape resulting from the nature of the goods or due to technical result or substantial value; or if its registration is obtained by fraudulent or unfair means, the TMB shall, or any party may request that the Trademark Review and Adjudication Board make a decision to, revoke such a registered trademark. Similarly, if a registered trademark contravenes the provisions relating to well-known marks, unauthorized registration of a trademark, misleading geographical indication, or prior rights, the owner of the trademark or any interested party may, within five years of the registration, request that the Trademark Review and Adjudication Board revoke such a registered trademark. Nonetheless, the owner of a well-known mark will not be subject to the five-year time limit if the registration was made in bad faith. Apart from these circumstances, if a prior trademark registrant believes that the trademark of a later registrant used on the same or similar kind of goods is identical or similar to its trademark, it may apply for revocation with the Trademark Review and Adjudication Board within five years of the approval for registration. Nevertheless, if an opposition had been filed and a decision had been made prior to the approval for registration of the trademark, the same facts and reasons may not be used in another application for a decision.

After the Trademark Review and Adjudication Board has made a decision upholding or revoking a registered trademark, it shall notify the parties in writing. If any party does not agree with the decision of the Trademark Review and Adjudication Board, it may file a lawsuit within 30 days of the receipt of the notification. In such a case, the court shall notify the other party of the trademark-ruling proceedings so that it can participate as a third party. If a registered trademark is revoked under any of the circumstances discussed in the paragraph above, it will be deemed nonexistent from the beginning. The decision revoking such a trademark has no retroactive effect on any previous: judgments or rulings regarding trademark infringement that have been made and enforced by the people's courts; decisions on trademark infringement disputes that have been made and enforced by the AIC; or contracts assigning the trademark or licensing the use of the trademark that have been performed. Nonetheless, if any party sustains damages as a result of the registrant's bad faith, the registrant will have to pay compensation.

Renewal, assignment, and licensing

The duration of a registered trademark is 10 years, starting from the date when the registration was approved. If the registrant needs to continue the use of the trademark after the expiration of its term, an application for renewal must be made within six months prior to the expiration. If the registrant fails to make such an application, a grace period of six months may be granted. If no application has been filed prior to the expiration of the grace period, the registered trademark will be cancelled. In this connection, it is noteworthy that if a registered trademark is revoked or is not renewed after the expiration of its term, the TMB will not approve any application for the registration of a trademark identical or similar to such trademark within one year of the date of revocation or cancellation.

Where a registered trademark is to be assigned, the assignor and the assignee shall enter into an agreement and jointly file an application with the TMB. The assignee must also guarantee the quality of the goods on which the registered trademark is to be used. Having approved the assignment of the registered trademark, the TMB shall make a public announcement. The assignee enjoys the exclusive right to the use of the trademark from the date of the public announcement.

A trademark registrant may also authorize another party to use its registered trademark by concluding a licensing contract. On one hand, the licensor shall supervise the quality of the goods on which the licensee uses the trademark. On the other hand, the licensee shall guarantee the quality of the goods on which the registered trademark is used. In addition, the name of the licensee and the origin of the goods must be indicated on the goods on which the registered trademark is used. The licensing contract must also be submitted to the TMB for the record.

Infringement and remedies

The right to the exclusive use of a registered trademark is limited to the trademark that has been approved for registration and the goods on which the use of such trademark has been approved. Accordingly, the following acts constitute trademark infringement:

1   using a trademark that is identical or similar to a registered trademark on the same or similar kind of goods without a license from the trademark registrant;
2   selling goods that infringe upon the exclusive right to the use of a registered trademark;
3   counterfeiting or the making without authorization of a registered trademark of another, or selling a mark that is a counterfeit registered trademark or is made without the trademark registrant's authorization;
4   altering a registered trademark and marketing goods with the altered trademark without authorization from the trademark registrant; and
5   causing other damage to another's right to the exclusive use of a registered trademark.

Currently, the last type of infringement includes naming a product or putting on its packaging a mark identical or similar to the registered trademark of another on the same or similar kind of goods to mislead the public;

and intentionally facilitating the infringing acts of others by providing storage, transportation, mailing, hiding, etc. If any acts of infringement arise, the parties should first resolve their dispute through consultation. If the parties are unwilling or unable to resolve their dispute through consultation, the trademark registrant or any interested party may request that the AIC handle the case or file a lawsuit in the people's court.

With respect to administrative remedies, the AIC has the power to investigate and punish trademark infringement, and if the infringement may constitute a crime, promptly transfer the case to the judicial department in accordance with the law. In investigating and disposing of suspected cases of infringement, the AIC at the county level or above, based on evidence of suspected illegal conduct or report, may:

1   interrogate the parties and investigate the circumstances pertinent to the infringement;
2   inspect and copy the contracts, invoices, account books, and other relevant materials of the parties in relation to the infringement;
3   conduct an onsite inspection of the premises where the party is suspected of having committed the infringement; and
4   examine articles relating to the infringement, and based on probative evidence, seal up and seize those articles.

If the AIC finds infringement, it may order the infringer to stop the infringing act immediately, confiscate and destroy the infringing goods and instruments used especially for manufacturing the infringing goods or counterfeiting the registered trademark, and impose a fine of up to three times the illegal turnover or, if the amount of turnover cannot be determined, up to RMB 100,000. If any party does not agree with the decision of the AIC, it may file a lawsuit in the people's court within 15 days of the receipt of the notification in accordance with the Administrative Procedure Law. If the party has neither filed a lawsuit nor complied with the decision upon the expiration of the 15-day period, the AIC may apply to the people's court for enforcement. Upon the request of the parties, the AIC may conduct mediation on the amount of compensation for the infringement. If mediation fails, any party may file a lawsuit in accordance with the Civil Procedure Law.

Furthermore, where the state has prescribed the use of a registered trademark on certain goods, but an application for trademark registration has not been filed, the local AIC may order the violator to apply for trademark registration within a fixed period of time and may, at the same time, impose a fine of up to 10 percent of the illegal turnover. Indeed, under any of the following circumstances relating to the use of an unregistered trademark, the local AIC shall stop the use of the trademark, order rectification of the situation within a fixed period of time, and may, at the same time, circulate a notice on the illegal conduct or impose a fine of up to 20 percent of the illegal turnover or twice the illegal profits:

1   the trademark is passed off as a registered trademark;
2   a sign is used that may not be used as a trademark; and
3   the trademark is used on poorly manufactured goods that are passed
    off as high-quality goods, thereby deceiving consumers.

If any party disagrees with the decision of the AIC to impose a fine, it may
file a lawsuit within 15 days of the receipt of the notification. If neither party
has filed a lawsuit or complied with the decision, the AIC shall apply to the
people's court for enforcement.

Since administrative procedure is not mandatory, the trademark owner
may directly file a lawsuit against infringement. If the court finds infringement, the amount of compensation is to be the profits obtained by the
infringer or the losses sustained by the infringed as a result of the infringement, including reasonable expenses paid by the infringed to stop the
infringement. If it is difficult to determine the amount of profit or loss, the
people's court may order the infringer to pay damages in the amount of
RMB 500,000 or less. Even so, if the alleged infringer did not know that the
goods it sold were infringing upon another's right to the exclusive use of a
registered trademark and can prove that the goods have been obtained
legally from a specific supplier, it will not be liable for damages. Where the
trademark registrant or any interested party has evidence to prove that
another is infringing or is going to infringe upon its trademark right, and
that failure to stop the infringement will cause irreparable injury to its
rights and interests, it may petition to the people's court for preliminary
injunction and property preservation prior to the filing of the lawsuit. Likewise, where the evidence may be destroyed or will be difficult to obtain at a
later time, the trademark registrant or any interested party may apply to the
people's court for evidence preservation prior to the filing of the lawsuit.
The court may order the registrant to provide a guarantee and shall make a
ruling in 48 hours. If the applicant fails to institute a lawsuit in 15 days, the
court shall cease the preservation measures.

If the use of a trademark that is identical to a registered trademark on the
same kind of goods without authorization from the trademark registrant
constitutes a crime, criminal liability will be pursued, in addition to compensatory damages. Similarly, if the counterfeiting or unauthorized making of a
registered trademark of another, or the sale of a mark that is a counterfeit
registered trademark or is made without the trademark registrant's authorization, constitutes a crime, criminal liability will be pursued, in addition to
compensatory damages. Furthermore, if the infringer knowingly sells goods
on which a counterfeit registered trademark is used constitutes a crime,
criminal liability will be pursued, in addition to compensatory damages.
According to articles 213–15 of the Criminal Law, if any of these three
infringing acts is serious, the court may impose a fine and/or up to three
years' imprisonment. If the infringement is very serous, the court may
impose a fine and three to seven years' imprisonment.

4 Copyright

With respect to copyright, the Copyright Law, the Regulations for the Implementation of the Copyright Law,[15] the Regulations on the Protection of Computer Software, the Regulations for the Implementation of International Copyright Treaties,[16] the Measures on the Implementation of Administrative Punishment Regarding Copyright, and the Measures on the Registration of Computer-Software Copyright[17] comprise the core of the Chinese regulatory framework. The Copyright Law contains general provisions on copyrightable works and provisions specifically applicable to publication of books, periodicals and newspapers, performance, audio and video recording, and broadcast. The specific provisions expound the rights and obligations of the copyright owner and the publisher, performer, producer of audio and video recording, or broadcaster. For instance, a radio or television station must obtain permission from and pay remuneration to the copyright owner of an unpublished work; however, it needs to pay remuneration to, but needs not obtain permission from, the copyright owner of a published work. To provide an overview of copyright protection in China, this section first discusses important general provisions in the Copyright Law and the Regulations for the Implementation of the Copyright Law and then highlights provisions in the Regulations on the Protection of Computer Software.

Copyrightable subject matter

According to the Copyright Law, Chinese citizens, legal persons, or other organizations enjoy the copyright in their works, whether the works are published or not. Foreigners and stateless persons enjoy the copyright in their works pursuant to any agreement concluded between China and their home countries or countries in which they regularly reside, or any treaty to which both China and their home countries or countries of regular residence are signatories. Nonetheless, foreigners and stateless persons whose works are first published in China shall enjoy copyright in accordance with the Copyright Law. Indeed, if the work of a foreigner or stateless person is published in China within 30 days of its first publication outside China, it will be deemed to have been published simultaneously in China. Similarly, the work of an author of a country that has not concluded any agreement with China or is not a member of any international treaty to which China is a signatory, and the work of a stateless person that is first published in a member country of an international treaty to which China is a signatory, or is simultaneously published in a member country of the treaty and a non-member country, shall be protected by the Copyright Law.

"Works" refers to original intellectual creations that are capable of being reproduced in a tangible medium, including works of literature, art, natural sciences, social sciences, engineering, and technology created in any of the following forms:

1   written works;
2   oral works;[18]
3   musical, dramatic, *quyi* (曲艺),[19] choreographic, and acrobatic works;
4   works of fine arts (including calligraphy) and architecture;
5   photographic works;
6   cinematographic works and works created by a process similar to cinematography;
7   graphic works and models, such as engineering designs, product designs, maps, and sketch maps;
8   computer software; and
9   other works stipulated by laws and administrative regulations.

However, the Copyright Law does not apply to:

1   laws and regulations, resolutions, decisions and decrees of state organs, and other legislative, administrative or judicial documents and their official translations;
2   news on current affairs; and
3   calendars, numerical tables, general forms, and formulae.

Ownership of copyright

Generally, the copyright in a work belongs to its author. The author is the citizen who creates the work. However, if a work is created according to the intention and under the direction of a legal person or other organization, and the legal person or organization is responsible for the work, then the legal person or organization will be deemed its author. Absent any proof to the contrary, the citizen, legal person, or other organization whose name appears on a work shall be deemed the author. The ownership of the copyright in a commissioned work shall be stipulated in the contract between the commissioning and the commissioned parties. In the absence of such a clear stipulation or a contract, the copyright in the work shall belong to the commissioned party.

If a work is created by adaptation, translation, annotation, or arrangement of a pre-existing work, the copyright in the work is to be enjoyed by the adapter, translator, annotator, or arranger, provided that the exercise of such copyright does not infringe upon the copyright in the pre-existing work. For a work created jointly by two or more authors, the copyright in the work will be enjoyed jointly by the co-authors. If a work of joint authorship can be separated into parts and used alone, each co-author may independently enjoy the copyright in the part that he or she creates, provided that the exercise of such copyright does not infringe upon the overall copyright in the joint work.

The collection of pre-existing works, excerpts, or data or other material that does not constitute a work is a compilation work if originality exists in the selection or arrangement of its contents. The compiler is to enjoy the copyright in a compilation work, provided that the exercise of such copyright does not infringe upon the copyright in the pre-existing works. The copyright in a cinematographic work or a work created by a process similar to cinematography is to be enjoyed by the producer of the work; however, the scriptwriter, director, camera operator, lyricist, composer, etc. shall enjoy the right of attribution and shall be entitled to receive remuneration in accordance with the terms of the contracts concluded between them and the producer. Even so, the authors of works that can be used alone, such as the script and musical scores, are entitled to exercise their copyright independently. Furthermore, the transfer of ownership of the original copy of an artistic work shall not be deemed the transfer of the copyright in such work; however, the right to exhibit the original copy of the work shall be enjoyed by the owner of the original copy.

Types of rights

The copyright in a work includes the following personal (人身权) and property (财产权) rights:

1 the right of publication (the right to decide whether to make a work available to the public);
2 the right of authorship (attribution) (the right of the author to indicate identity and have his or her name appear on a work);
3 the right of revision (the right to revise or authorize others to revise a work);
4 the right of integrity (the right to protect a work against distortion and alteration);
5 the right of reproduction (the right to produce one or multiple copies of a work by such means as printing, photocopying, lithographing, sound recording, video recording, re-recording, and re-filming);
6 the right of distribution (the right to provide the public with the original copy or reproductions of a work by sale or donation);
7 the right of rental (the right to allows others to use for a fee and temporarily a cinematographic work, a work created by a process similar to cinematography, or computer software, except where the software is not the principal object of the rental);
8 the right of exhibition (the right to publicly display the original copy or reproductions of an artistic work or a photographic work);
9 the right of performance (the right to publicly perform a work and publicly broadcast the performance of a work by various means);
10 the right of presentation (the right to publicly present an artistic work, a photographic work, a cinematographic work, a work created by a process similar to cinematography, etc. by such technology and equipment as projector and slide projector);

11 the right of broadcast (the right to publicly broadcast or transmit a work by wireless means, publicly transmit the broadcast of a work by wire or re-broadcasting, and publicly transmit the broadcast of a work by loud speakers or any other similar instruments transmitting signs, sounds, or images);

12 the right of transmission through an information network (the right to provide a work to the public by wire or wireless means so that the public may have access to the work from a place and at a time they choose);

13 the right of cinematography (the right to fix a work in a medium by cinematography or a process similar to cinematography);

14 the right of adaptation (the right to convert a work into a new one with originality);

15 the right of translation (the right to convert the language in which a work is written into another language);

16 the right of compilation (the right to compile by selection or arrangement pre-existing works or its excerpts as a new work); and

17 the other rights to be enjoyed by the copyright owner.

Accordingly, in China, the author of a copyrightable work enjoys moral rights (rights of attribution, revision, integrity, and publication) and such economic rights as the rights of reproduction, distribution, exhibition, performance, and making derivative works. With respect to the rights of attribution, revision, and integrity, no time limit is set on the term of protection. If the author is a natural person, the term of protection for economic rights is the lifetime of the author plus 50 years after death (ending on 31 December of the 50th year). In the case of a work of joint authorship, the term of protection expires on 31 December of the 50th year after the death of the last surviving author. If the author is a legal person or other organization, the term of protection for the right of publication and economic rights is 50 years after the first publication. Likewise, in the case of a cinematographic work, a work created by a process similar to cinematography, or a photographic work, the term of protection for the right of publication and economic rights is 50 years after the first publication.

Limitations on rights

Under the following circumstances, a work may be used without the permission of the copyright owner and without the need to pay remuneration, provided that the name of the author and the title of the work are indicated and the other rights enjoyed by the copyright owner are not infringed:

1 the use of another person's published work for the purposes of personal study, research, or appreciation;

2 apposite quotation from another person's published work in one's own work for the purpose of introducing or commenting on a certain work or explaining a certain issue;

3 inevitable inclusion or quotation of a published work in such media as newspapers, periodicals, radio, and television for the purpose of reporting current affairs;

4 publication or broadcast by such media as newspapers, periodicals, radio, and television of an article published by another newspaper, periodical, radio station, or television station regarding current political, economic, or religious issues, except where the author states that such publication or broadcast is not permitted;

5 publication or broadcast by such media as newspapers, periodicals, radio, and television of a speech delivered at a public gathering, except where the author states that such publication or broadcast is not permitted;

6 translation or reproduction in a small quantity of a published work by teachers or scientific researchers for use in classroom teaching or scientific research, provided that the translation or reproduction is not published for distribution;

7 reasonable use of a published work by a state organ for the purpose of executing its official duties;

8 reproduction of a work in its collection by a library, archives depository, memorial hall, museum, art gallery, etc. for the purpose of display or preservation of the work;

9 performance of a published work for which no admission fee is charged to the public and no remuneration is made to the performer;

10 copying, drawing, photographing, or video recording of a work of art put up or displayed in an outdoor public place;

11 translation of a published work of a Chinese citizen, legal entity, or other organization from the Han language into the languages of ethnic minorities for publication and distribution in China; and

12 conversion of a published work into Braille for publication.

Furthermore, unless the author declares in advance that the use of his or her work is not permitted, excerpts from works, short written works, musical works, or single-width artistic or photographic works that have been published may, without the permission of the copyright owners, be compiled in textbooks for the nine-year compulsory education and the national education planning, provided that remuneration is paid, the name of the authors and the titles of the works are indicated, and the other rights enjoyed by the copyright owners are not infringed. All these limitations are also applicable to the rights of publishers, performers, producers of audio and video recordings, radio stations, and television stations.

Licensing and assignment

The copyright owner may authorize others to exercise economic rights and receive remuneration in accordance with contractual stipulations or the Copyright Law. In addition, the copyright owner may transfer, in whole or in part, economic rights to others. Any party who uses another's work must conclude a copyright licensing contract with the copyright owner, unless permission is not required under the Copyright Law. A copyright licensing contract must include:

1   the type of right to be licensed;
2   whether the license is exclusive or nonexclusive;[20]
3   the territory covered by the license and the duration of use;
4   the remuneration standards and means of payment;
5   liability for breach; and
6   any other matters that the parties deem it necessary to include.

Likewise, to assign economic rights, the copyright owner and the assignee must conclude a written contract. A contract for copyright transfer must include:

1   the title of the work;
2   the type of right to be transferred and the territory covered by the transfer;
3   the transfer price;
4   the date and means of payment for the transfer price;
5   liability for breach; and
6   any other matters that the parties deem it necessary to include.

   The remuneration for the use of a work may be stipulated by the parties or may be paid in accordance with the rates set by the National Copyright Administration in conjunction with the other relevant departments. Moreover, the copyright owner or the owner of copyright-related rights may authorize a collective copyright-administration organization (著作权集体管理组织) to exercise its rights. The "copyright-related rights" refer to the right enjoyed by the publisher regarding the typographical design of its books and periodicals, the right enjoyed by the performer with respect to his or her performance, the right enjoyed by the producer of an audio or video recording as to its product, and the rights enjoyed by radio and television stations in respect to their broadcast programs. In some countries, the last three types of copyright-related rights are the so-called "neighboring rights." After obtaining authorization, the collective copyright-administration organization may assert claims in its own name for the copyright owner and the owners of copyright-related rights, and participate as a party in legal or arbitration proceedings relating to the copyright or copyright-related rights.

Infringement and remedies

According to the Copyright Law, the following acts constitute copyright infringement:

1 publishing a work without the permission of the copyright owner;
2 publishing a work of joint authorship as a work created solely by oneself without the permission of the other co-authors;
3 having one's name stated in another's work without having been involved in the creation of the work in order to seek personal fame and profit;
4 distorting or altering another's work;
5 plagiarizing another's work;
6 using a work in an exhibition, film-making or a process similar to film-making, or to creating adaptation, translation, annotation, etc., without the permission of the copyright owner, unless otherwise prescribed by the Copyright Law;
7 using another's work without paying the required remuneration;
8 renting and audio- or video-recording a cinematographic work or a work created by a process similar to cinematography, computer software, or audio or video recordings without the permission of the copyright owner or the owners of copyright-related rights, unless otherwise prescribed by the Copyright Law;
9 using the typographical design of a published book or periodical without the permission of the publisher;
10 broadcasting or transmitting to the public a live performance, or recording a performance, without the permission of the performer; and
11 committing any other acts infringing upon the copyright and copyright-related rights.

Depending on the circumstances, anyone who has committed any of these infringing acts shall bear civil liability, including cessation of the infringement, elimination of bad effects, making a public apology, and paying compensatory damages.

Apart from the aforementioned acts of infringement, the Copyright Law also prohibits:

1 the reproduction, distribution, performance, presentation, broadcast, compilation, or transmittion to the public through an information network of a work without the permission of the copyright owner, unless otherwise prescribed by the Copyright Law;
2 publication of a book whose exclusive right of publication is enjoyed by another;
3 reproduction or distribution of an audio or video recording of a performance, or transmittion of the performance to the public through an

information network, without the permission of the performer, unless otherwise prescribed by the Copyright Law;

4 the reproduction, distribution, or transmittion to the public through an information network of an audio or video recording without the permission of the producer, unless otherwise prescribed by the Copyright Law;

5 the broadcast or reproduction of a radio or television program without the permission of the radio station or television station, unless otherwise prescribed by the Copyright Law;

6 the intentional circumvention or sabotage, without permission, of technological measures used by a copyright owner or a owner of a copyright-related right to protect the copyright or the copyright-related right in its work, audio or video recording, etc., unless otherwise provided by laws or administrative regulations;

7 the intentional deletion or alteration of any electronic information regarding the management of rights in a work, an audio or video recording, etc. without the permission of the copyright owner or the owner of a copyright-related right, unless otherwise prescribed by the Copyright Law; and

8 the manufacture or sale of a work whose authorship is forged.

Depending on the circumstances, the infringer in the preceding cases of infringement shall bear civil liabilities, such as cessation of the infringement, elimination of bad effects, making a public apology, and paying compensatory damages. Where public interests are also impaired, the copyright-administration department, that is, the National Copyright Administration or local copyright administrations, may order the infringer to stop the infringement, confiscate its unlawful profits, confiscate or destroy the pirated copies, and impose a fine of up to three times the illegal turnover or, if it is difficult to determine the turnover, up to RMB 100,000. Where the circumstances are serious, the copyright-administration department may confiscate the materials, tools, and equipment used to manufacture the pirated copies. If the infringer objects to an administrative penalty, it may file a lawsuit within three months of the receipt of the administrative decision. If the infringer neither files a lawsuit within the time limit nor complies with the decision, the copyright-administration department may apply to the people's court for enforcement. If the act constitutes a crime, criminal liability shall be pursued.

As a matter of fact, articles 217–18 of the Criminal Law prohibit:

1 the reproduction and distribution of another's written, musical or cinematographic work, video recording, computer software, etc. without the permission of the copyright owner;

2 publication of a book whose exclusive right of publication is enjoyed by another;

3   the reproduction and distribution of audio and video recordings without the permission of the producer; and
4   the manufacture and sale of works of fine arts whose authorship is forged.

If any of these crimes is committed for profit and the amount of illegal income is relatively large or other circumstances are serious, the court may impose a fine and/or up to three years' imprisonment. If the amount of illegal income is enormous or there are other exceptionally serious circumstances, the court may impose a fine and three to seven years' imprisonment. Moreover, anyone who knowingly sells pirated copies made from the aforementioned infringing activities for profit and the amount of illegal income is enormous, the court may impose up to three years' imprisonment and/or impose a fine.

When a copyright dispute arises, the parties may resolve it through mediation. They may also submit the dispute to an arbitration commission for arbitration in accordance with a written arbitration agreement or an arbitration clause in the copyright contract. Absent an arbitration agreement or arbitration clause, any party may institute a lawsuit directly in a people's court. If the people's court finds infringement, it shall order the infringer to pay compensatory damages. The amount of compensatory damages is the actual losses of the copyright owner or the owner of a copyright-related right. If it is difficult to determine the losses, the infringer shall pay the infringed its illegal income. The amount of compensation shall also include reasonable expenses that the infringed has spent to stop the infringement. Where the actual losses of the infringed or the illegal income of the infringer cannot be determined, the people's court shall decide a compensatory amount of not more than RMB 500,000. Moreover, if the copyright owner or the owner of a copyright-related right can produce evidence to prove that another is infringing or is going to infringe its right(s), and that irreparable injury will result if the infringement is not stopped promptly, it may apply to the people's court for preliminary injunction and property preservation prior to the filing of a lawsuit. Indeed, the copyright owner or the owner of a copyright-related right may also apply for evidence preservation if it is likely that the evidence will be lost or difficult to obtain later. In such a case, the people's court may ask the applicant to provide a guarantee and shall make a ruling in 48 hours. If the applicant fails to institute proceedings within 15 days of the adoption of the measures, the court shall cease the preservation measures. In trying an infringement case, the people's court may also confiscate the unlawful income, pirated copies, and any property used for the infringing activities.

Finally, it is noteworthy that a publisher or producer of reproductions who fails to prove that its publication or production is legally authorized, or a distributor of reproductions or anyone renting reproductions of a cinematographic work or a work created by a process similar to cinematography, computer software, or audio or video recording who fails to prove the legal source of the reproductions, shall bear legal liability.

Computer software

According to the Regulations on the Protection of Computer Software, "computer software" refers to computer programs and related documentation. "Computer programs" refers to coded instructional sequences, or symbolic instructional sequences or numerical language sequences that can be converted automatically into coded instructional sequences, and that are designed to obtain a certain result and can be operated on such information processing equipment as computers. The source code and object code of a computer program is deemed as one work. Documentation refers to written materials and diagrams that are used to describe the contents, organization, design, functions and specifications, development situation, testing results, and method of use of the computer program, such as program design manuals, flow charts, user manuals, etc.

To be eligible for copyright protection, the computer software must be developed independently by the software developer and must be fixed in a tangible form. Chinese citizens, legal persons, and other organizations enjoy the copyright in the software they develop, regardless of whether the software has been published. Foreigners whose software is first released in China enjoy copyright protection pursuant to the Regulations on the Protection of Computer Software. Computer software published outside of China by foreigners enjoys copyright protection in China pursuant to any agreement concluded between China and their home countries or countries in which they regularly reside, or any international treaties to which China is a signatory.

The copyright in a piece of computer software belongs to its developer, unless otherwise provided by law. Absent contradictory evidence, the natural person, legal person, or other organization named on the software is the developer. If two or more persons or entities jointly develop the software, its copyright shall be governed in accordance with the stipulations in a written contract. If there is no written agreement, or if the stipulations are not clear, but the jointly developed software can be used in separate parts, the co-developers may independently enjoy the copyright in the parts they respectively developed. However, the exercise of their independent copyright cannot extend to the overall copyright in the jointly developed software. If the jointly developed software cannot be used in separate parts, its copyright will be jointly enjoyed by the co-developers and will be exercised through consensus. If consensus cannot be reached, and absent any proper reason(s), no party may prevent the others from exercising rights other than the right of transfer. In such a case, any profits earned must be distributed fairly among all the co-developers. Where the software is developed under commission, its copyright shall be governed by a written contract concluded between the commissioning party and the commissioned party. If there is no written agreement, or if the stipulations are not clear, the copyright shall be enjoyed by the commissioned party.

As regards rights in computer software, the copyright owner enjoys:

1   the right of publication (the right to decide whether the software should be released to the public);
2   the right of authorship (attribution) (the right to indicate the developer's identity and to put its name on the software);
3   the right of revision (the right to add, supplement, delete, change instructions, or alter the order of sentences);
4   the right of reproduction (the right to make one or more copies);
5   the right of distribution (the right to provide the public with the original or copies of the software by sale or gift);
6   the right of rental (the right to allow others to use the software temporarily and for a fee, unless the software is not the principal object of the rental);
7   the right of transmission through an information network (the right to provide the public with the software by wire or wireless means, and the public may choose the time and place to acquire the software);
8   the right of translation (the right to convert the software from one natural language to another natural language); and
9   any other rights that should be enjoyed by the software developer.

If the developer is a natural person, the term of protection will be 50 years after his or her death (ending on 31 December). If the software is jointly developed, the term of protection is 50 years after the death of the last surviving developer. If the developer is a legal person or other organization, the term of protection is 50 years after the first publication of the software.

In respect to infringement, the following acts are prohibited:

1   publishing or registering the software without the permission of the copyright owner;
2   publishing or registering another's software as one's own;
3   publishing or registering the software of joint authorship as the software created solely by oneself without the permission of the other co-developers;
4   having one's name indicated on another's software or changing the name of the developer on the software;
5   revising or translating another's software without the permission of the copyright owner; and
6   any other acts of infringement.

In these cases of infringement, the infringer must bear such civil liability as ceasing the infringement, eliminating any bad effects, making an apology, and paying compensatory damages.

Similarly, the following acts constitute infringement:

1   the reproduction of the entire software or part of the software owned by another;
2   the distribution to the public, rental, or transmittion through an information network of the software;
3   the deliberate circumvention or sabotage of technological measures used by a copyright owner to protect the copyright in the software;
4   the intentional deletion or alteration of any electronic information regarding management of rights in the software; and
5   transferring or allowing others to use the software of another.

Depending on the circumstances, the infringer in these cases of infringement shall bear civil liability, such as cessation of the infringement, elimination of bad effects, making a public apology, and paying compensatory damages. Where public interest is also impaired, the copyright-administration department may order the infringer to stop the infringement, confiscate its unlawful profits, confiscate or destroy the pirated copies, and impose a fine. For points 1 and 2, the infringer may have a fine imposed of RBM 100 per copy or up to five times the price. For points 3, 4, and 5, the fine can be up to RBM 50,000. Where the circumstances are serious, the copyright-administration department may also confiscate the materials, tools, and equipment used to manufacture the pirated copies. Where the act constitutes a crime, criminal liability shall be pursued in accordance with the provisions on copyright infringement in the Criminal Law.

In judicial proceedings, the amount of compensatory damages is to be determined in accordance with the Copyright Law. Moreover, the infringed may seek preliminary injunction, property preservation, and evidence preservation prior to the filing of a lawsuit. A publisher or producer of software reproductions that fails to prove that its publication or production is legally authorized, or a distributor of software reproductions or anyone renting software reproductions who fails to prove the legal source of the reproductions, shall bear legal liabilities. Nonetheless, if the reproducer of the software does not know or has no reason to know that the software is a pirated copy, it will not be liable for compensation. Even so, the reproducer must stop using and destroy the pirated copy. If the cessation of use or destruction causes serious losses, the reproducer may pay reasonable royalty to the copyright owner and continue to use the software.

5 Trade secrets

In China, various laws, administrative regulations, or government rules provide for the protection of trade secrets. Most importantly, article 10 of the Law against Unfair Competition[21] protects trade secrets pursuant to article 39 of the TRIPS Agreement.[22] According to article 10, a trade secret refers to technical or business information that is not known to the public but has utility and can generate economic benefits for its owner, who has adopted measures to maintain its confidentiality. Moreover, a business may not commit any of the following trade secret infringements:

1   obtain a trade secret by means of theft, inducement, coercion, or any other improper means;
2   disclose, use, or allow others to use a trade secret that has been obtained by means of theft, inducement, coercion, or any other improper means; or
3   disclose, use, or permit others to use a trade secret held by it in violation of an agreement or the request of the trade secret owner.

Likewise, if a third party who knew or should have known of the aforementioned illegal conduct obtains, uses, or discloses the trade secret, it will be deemed an infringer of the trade secret. In the case of trade secret infringement, article 219 of the Criminal Law provides that if the infringement causes serious losses to the trade secret holder, a fine and/or up to three years' imprisonment may be imposed; and if the infringement causes serious consequences, a fine and imprisonment of three to seven years may be imposed.

6 Selected cases

Xu Ximing *v.* Shenzhen City Longgangqu Bujizhen Gangtou Telulian Zippers Factory and Hong Kong Telu Trading Co. *(2002)* 深中法知产初字第111号, *Guangdong Province Shenzhen City Intermediate People's Court, 12 March 2003*

Facts

On 18 August 2000, Xu Ximing (hereinafter XX) applied to the State Intellectual Property Office for a utility-model patent on his "Zipper Cutting Without Thread Coming Off Lace Machine." The No. ZL00237965.1 patent was granted on 9 June 2001 and announced on 8 July 2001. The invention of this patented product successfully solved the decade-long technical problems in the cutting of zippers, such as the thread coming off, the knife breaking, and the knife sticking.

According to XX, this patented product had generated economic benefits for him since its launch into the market. However, Shenzhen City Longgangqu Bujizhen Gangtou Telulian Zippers Factory (hereinafter TZF) and Hong Kong Telu Trading Co. (hereinafter TTC) produced and sold the same product without his permission. Since TZF and TTC acted in violation of the Patent Law, they should bear the corresponding liability. Thus, XX requested that the court instruct TZF and TTC to:

1   stop the act of infringing his patent right immediately, and to destroy
     all the blueprint and propaganda information in relation to the
     infringement;
2   make a public apology to him in a newspaper;
3   compensate him for economic loss of RMB 500,000;
4   compensate him for such reasonable expenses as the investigation fee
     and lawyer's fee in the amount of RMB 86,500; and
5   bear joint and several liability for the infringement.

TZF was a *sanlaiyibu* enterprise[23] established and registered on 18 April
1994. TTC was the investor of TZF. Neither TZF nor TTC objected to the
fact that XX was the holder of the patent No. ZL00237965.1 "Zipper
Cutting Without Thread Coming Off Lace Machine," and that on 22 September 2001 the Fushan City notarized XX's purchase of their "Lace Cutting
Without Edge Becoming Loose Machine." The parties did not dispute these
facts, so the court affirmed them. However, TZF and TTC claimed that
their machine was a product of their design, having a technology different
from XX's patented technology; therefore, they did not infringe upon XX's
patent right. Moreover, based on the report on patent search submitted by
XX, TZF and TTC asserted that part of XX's patent claims did not have
inventiveness, and thus, should not be protected by law.

Reasoning

With respect to the argument that the product sold by TZF and TTC
was different from XX's patent technology, the court found that the independent claim of the No. ZL00237965.1 patent was as follows: "A zipper
cutting lace machine." It was composed of a stand, a mold, etc. The stand
was firmly connected with a control panel, a vertical pillar, and a supporting
board. The supporting board was firmly connected with a cylinder and a
piston rod linked to a flange through a locknut. A gland makes the flange
and the mold connected. The lower part of the adjustable board of the mold
was firmly connected to a knife stand and a punching knife. On the side of
the adjustable board was a firmly connected safety protective cover. The
board at the bottom of the mold was connected to the control panel, while
its upper part was connected to a pressure-board stand. On the side of the
pressure-board stand was a touching switch and a conductive device, and
the top of the pressure-board stand was fixed with a punching board. The
inventive features of XX's patent included that the cylinder was the source
of motive power, the mold was a rotating device, and the punching knife
and the punching board below were the cutting device. This utility model
did not need to add heat. After the zipper was cut, its thread would not
come off, and the lace was neat and looked good. During production, knife-
sticking and knife-breaking would not occur. Productivity was high, and the
equipment was long-lasting.

Compared with XX's patent claims, the alleged infringing "Lace Cutting Without Edge Becoming Loose Machine" consisted of a control panel, a vertical pillar, and a supporting board. The supporting board was connected with a cylinder, which was connected to a flange through a piston rod. The flange and the mold were connected. The lower part of the adjustable board of the mold was connected to a knife stand and a punching knife. The board at the bottom of the mold was connected to the control panel, while its upper part was connected to a pressure-board stand. In addition, there were such parts as a touching switch, conductive device, and punching board. As regards the structural components of the product of TZF and TTC, except for "on the side of the adjustable board was a firmly connected safety protective cover," the remainder was the same as those stated in XX's patent claims. In the product of TZF and TTC, the cylinder was the source of motive power; the mold was a rotating device; and the punching knife and the punching board below were the cutting device. The product of TZF and TTC lacked the feature of "safety protective cover" and did not solve the problem of safety when using the machine.

The scope of protection of a utility-model patent was the contents of the claims. Where an individual technical feature is deliberately omitted from a patent claim, thus making the technical design inferior than the patented technical design in terms of function and effect, and it is obvious that the inferior technical design results from the omission of the necessary technical feature, the doctrine of equivalents should be applied to find patent infringement. The structural components of the product of TZF and TTC are the same as those of XX's patent, except for the absence of an external protective cover. Moreover, the technical features found in the product of TZF and TTC are the same as those of XX's patent. Although the product of TZF and TTC, unlike XX's patent, did not resolve the safety problem by having "a firmly connected safety protective cover on the side of the adjustable board," thereby making the overall technology inferior, it fell within the protective scope of XX's patent because its structure and technical features were equivalent to those of XX's patent. Since TZF and TTC, without the permission of XX, unilaterally used the same technology on their products, which infringed upon XX's patent rights, they should be held liable.

Since TZF and TTC infringed upon XX's patent, the court granted XX's request to stop the infringement, compensate for economic loss, and pay the costs of litigation. However, the court denied XX's request that TZF and TTC make a public apology because there was not sufficient evidence. In respect of compensation, since XX had not submitted evidence to prove direct losses, the court could not determine his losses. According to TZF and TTC, they had produced only 20 infringing products. The cost of each machine was RMB 5,500, and the sales price was RMB 6,600. Nonetheless, TZF and TTC could not produce evidence to prove that only 20 machines had been produced, and XX did not agree with their assertion. Thus, the court did not accept the claim of TZF and TTC concerning the quantity of the infringing product and the proceeds derived. Instead, the court applied the "principle of discretion" to decide the amount of compensation for infringement. In determining the amount of compensation, the court took into consideration such factors as the type of patent at issue, the duration of the infringement, the price of the infringing product, and the amount of expenditure on protecting the patent. Furthermore, since TZF was a *sanlaiyibu* enterprise, it did not have the status of a legal person. Being the investor of TZF, TTC should be jointly and severally liable for the patent infringement.

As to litigation costs, XX claimed that the total cost was RMB 86,500, of which the lawyer's fee was RMB 80,000 (RMB 10,000 had been paid in advance), the cost for purchasing the product of TZF and TTC for notarization was RMB 6,000, and the notary fee was RMB 500. Since TZF and TTC did not agree with such an amount and it was obvious that the lawyer's fee submitted was higher than the relevant standards on lawyer's fees, the court did not support XX's claim that the cost for protecting his right was RMB 86,500.

Regarding the validity of the patent No. ZL00237965.1, the court found that after the submission of the report on the patent search, the Patent Re-examination Board of the State Intellectual Property Office, in response to a request for invalidating the patent, made a ruling on 21 May 2002 that the No. ZL00237965.1 patent was valid. Thus, the court held that XX's patent rights should be protected in accordance with the law.

Judgment

According to articles 11 and 56(1) of the Patent Law,[24] article 21 of the Supreme People's Court's Several Regulations Regarding Questions on the Application of Law in Trying Patent Infringement Cases[25] and article 2 of the Supreme People's Court's Several Regulations on Evidence in Civil Litigation,[26] the court held that:

1   TZF should immediately stop all acts of infringing XX's patent rights in the No. ZL00237965.1 patent.
2   TZF must compensate XX RMB 200,000 within 10 days from the date on which this judgment became effective (TTC is to be jointly and severally liable for damages).
3   XX's other claims were dismissed.

If any party was not satisfied with this judgment, it might, within 15 days of the delivery of the judgment, submit an application for appeal to this court for the purpose of appealing to the Guangdong Province People's High Court.

Guangdong Province Light Industrial Products Import-Export (Group) Co. *v.* Hong Kong TMT Trading Ltd. *(1998)* 知终字第8号, *Supreme People's Court, 15 May 2000*

Facts

In 1979, at the Spring Chinese Export Commodities Fairground, Guangdong Province Light Industrial Products Import-Export (Group) Co. (hereinafter LIP) negotiated with Wang Shaoming of Hong Kong Tung Ming Trading Ltd. about the production and export of ceiling fans. The parties reached a consensus that the TMT trademark provided by Tung Ming Trading Ltd. would be used on the ceiling fans, and that other foreign companies could not order TMT-brand ceiling fans from LIP. At that time, Wang Shaoming was the sole shareholder of Tung Ming Trading Ltd. Subsequently, in November of the same year, Tung Ming Co. was established. Wang Shaoming became the general manager and a shareholder of the newly formed Tung Ming Co.

On 15 September 1979 and 1 November 1980, respectively, Tung Ming Trading Ltd., or Tung Ming Co., and LIP signed two separate exclusive sales agreements, stipulating that Tung Ming would establish and exclusively sell the TMT-brand and TMC-brand ceiling fans, as well as provide free-of-charge enamel-insulated wires, bearings, condensers, UL outlet lines, trademarks, etc. that were needed for production, while LIP would engage in the manufacture of ceiling fans. In addition, the parties agreed that Tung Ming would finance and adopt various effective propaganda and advertising measures, but would consult LIP in advance regarding the design and wording.

On 24 February 1981, LIP and Tung Ming Co. jointly announced in the *People's Daily* that Tung Ming Co. was the exclusive wholesaler of TMT-brand ceiling fans. Similarly, on 20 June 1981, Tung Ming Co. published the following statement in the *Hong Kong Economic Journal*: "Since 1 January 1980, Guangdong Province Light Industrial Products Import-Export (Group) Co. had entrusted Tung Ming Co. with the exclusive distributorship of TMT-brand ceiling fans."

Moreover, in the two agreements submitted by LIP, which were signed on 11 July 1980 and 23 January 1981 and concerned the ownership of the right to use TMT, TMC, SMT, and SMC trademarks, the parties indicated that the right to use these trademarks belonged to LIP, and that Wang Shaoming had complete authority to represent LIP in applying for the registration of these trademarks in Hong Kong and other major home appliances markets in the world. However, these two agreements did not bear the official seals of the companies.

In March 1982, Tung Ming Co. closed down due to disputes among shareholders. Wang Shaoming and Lin Guiquan, another shareholder, formed TMT Trading Co. (hereinafter TMT), which took over Tung Ming's business in TMT, TMC, and SMT ceiling fans, assumed the debt that Tung Ming owed to LIP, and succeeded to the three trademarks.

Over the years, TMT and its predecessor Tung Ming Co. had signed various exclusive sales agreements and sales confirmations with LIP, including the agreements signed on 15 September 1979; 1 November 1980; 21 November 1981; 5 January 1983; 3 November 1984; 13 January 1986; and the confirmations signed on 27 November 1979; 8 December 1980; and subsequent dates). These documents clearly stated that TMT was to provide the trademarks in dispute. Both sides acknowledged the authenticity of these agreements and confirmations.

With respect to trademark registration, LIP registered the TMT mark with the State Administration for Industry and Commerce in 1980. To prevent other companies from copying or insinuating the TMT trademark, LIP also had the TMC and SMT marks registered in 1981. Meanwhile, Tung Ming Co. registered the TMT trademark in Hong Kong and some countries in the Middle East. Moreover, over several years, TMT had the TMT, SMT, and TMC trademarks registered in those countries and regions where TMT-brand ceiling fans were mainly sold. It spent huge amounts of money in advertising and promoting products of the aforementioned brands, thus making TMT-brand products famous overseas while, at the same time, attracting quite a number of companies to pass off their products as TMT-brand goods. In 1983, both TMT and LIP were the plaintiffs of a lawsuit against a Hong Kong company for trademark infringement. On 11 October 1990, the Hong Kong High Court ruled in favor of TMT and LIP.

According to TMT, on 23 October 1987 and 16 December 1987 LIP sent out two certificates, indicating that its registered "No. 142201 TMT trademark of 1980," "No. 151390 SMT trademark of 1981," and "No. 151392 TMC trademark of 1981" were owned and benefited by TMT, and that LIP held these trademarks only as an trustee of TMT. Nevertheless, LIP suspected that these two certificates were false and thus applied for judicial appraisal on 20 May 1998.

On 6 October 1994, LIP signed an agreement with TMT, stipulating as follows. First, in mainland China, the trademark TMT was to be registered by LIP, and LIP had absolute power of management. If any companies or manufacturers passed off or infringed upon the TMT trademark, LIP must, effectively or through legal means, stop the counterfeiting or infringing activities, and the relevant costs would be borne by LIP. Second, outside mainland China (including Hong Kong), the TMT trademark was to be registered by TMT, which had absolute power of management. If any companies or manufacturers passed off or infringed upon the TMT trademark, TMT must, effectively or through legal means, stop the infringing activities, and the relevant costs would be borne by TMT. Third, all the TMT-brand electric fans and spare parts produced in China by TMT for export must be completely exported by LIP. If LIP could not provide export services for any other reasons, TMT, after obtaining the consent of LIP, might allow other companies or manufacturers to engage in exporting. In such a case, TMT must pay 2 percent of the factory price as a trademark licensing fee and sign a trademark licensing agreement.

After the agreement was signed, disputes arose between the parties in performing the contract. TMT claimed that it had sustained huge economic losses because LIP had not cracked down on infringement activities in China. Thus, it requested that the TMT, TMC, and SMT trademarks be returned to it, or that these trademarks be assigned to it together with the change of the registration for HK$300,000. On the other hand, LIP claimed that TMT had not paid licensing fees in accordance with the trademark licensing agreement, and that the unpaid balance was US$19,232. Moreover, TMT had arranged, without its consent, the production and sale of TMT products in China. For many years, both parties held consultations in order to resolve the trademark dispute. Nonetheless, they failed to reach a consensus. LIP then sought intellectual property protection from the General Office of the Customs. As a result, TMT could not export its products manufactured in China, resulting in overstocking of products by the manufacturers.

On 25 December 1997, He Yaosong and Wu E, the original managers of LIP, in a written report to the leadership of the company, stated the following with respect to the TMT trademark dispute. At the beginning of 1980, Wang Shaoming, the general manager of Tung Ming Co., brought the company's self-designed TMT trademark to LIP and requested that it be used on the ceiling fans. According to Wang Shaoming, the TMT trademark was derived from the first letter of the first three words of Tung Ming Trading Ltd. After consultation with him, our leadership agreed to use the trademark. In 1980, Wang Shaoming raised the issue of applying for trademark registration. As the Trademark Law had not been promulgated at that time, the state had not allowed foreign investors to register their trademarks in China. Thus, both sides agreed that the TMT mark would be registered by LIP in China, but would be registered by Tung Ming Co. overseas. Subsequently, upon Wang's suggestion, LIP also registered the TMC and SMT trademarks. Prior to 1985, all TMT-brand ceiling fans had their labels printed in Hong Kong and provided free of charge by Tung Ming Co. The three designated manufacturers of TMT-brand ceiling fans confirmed that TMT continuously provided them with market information and technology, and sent personnel, over a period of time, to their factories to spot check the quality of the products.

TMT filed a lawsuit with the Guangdong Province High People's Court, claiming that LIP had breached the trust agreement, intending to embezzle the trademarks registered under its mandate and preventing it from exporting products made with designated brands, which had caused it to incur economic losses. It sought termination of the trust relationship with respect to the registration and management of the TMT, TMC, and SMT trademarks; the return of any property acquired under the mandate and compensation in the amount of RMB 100 million; litigation costs and attorney's fees; and punishment of LIP in accordance with the law. On the other hand, LIP argued that the people's court had no jurisdiction because a dispute over the ownership of a trademark should be resolved by the administrative department that handled trademarks. Thus, it asked the court to dismiss the appeal.

The Guangdong Province High People's Court reasoned that the TMT, TMC, and SMT trademarks were designed and first used by Tung Ming Co., and that LIP temporarily registered and managed these trademarks in China on its behalf. As TMT succeeded to the business and debts of Tung Ming Co., it should receive the trademark rights. Based on the exclusive sale agreements, the testimonies of He Yaosong and Wu E, etc., the court held that TMT's claim for ownership of these trademarks had legal basis. In addition, since TMT could not continue to manufacture and export products with these brands in China and LIP could not sell products with the same brand names overseas, TMT's requests that the trademarks be returned to it and its authorization be terminated should be granted. Nevertheless, because LIP had registered and effectively managed the trademarks in China, TMT should provide an appropriate amount of economic compensation. With respect to the jurisdiction issue, the court ruled that it had jurisdiction because this case concerned the ownership of trademarks where the trademarks were registered under authorization, but not the improper registration of trademarks.

In ruling for TMT, the court concluded that:

1 TMT owned the TMT, TMC, SMT trademarks that had been registered by LIP.
2 TMT, after the judgment became effective, must register the change of ownership of these trademarks with the TMB within the State Administration for Industry and Commerce.
3 TMT was to pay LIP RMB 500,000 as compensation within one month from the effective day of the judgment.
4 Other requests of TMT were denied.

LIP appealed to the Supreme People's Court on the grounds that:

1 It obtained the exclusive right to use the trademarks in dispute by means of registration.
2 TMT and Tung Ming Co. had never registered the trademarks in dispute with the TMB of the State Administration for Industry and Commerce, and could not produce any written documents to prove that they authorized LIP to register the trademarks.
3 The agreement signed on 6 October 1994 clearly stated that the trademarks were owned by it.

4   TMT had no right to succeed to Tung Ming's rights.
5   It had never produced any documents indicating that the TMT trademark belonged to TMT.

Thus, LIP maintained that the court of first instance lacked the factual support to grant ownership of the trademarks to TMT. In addition, LIP argued that the court of first instance was mistaken in applying the law, that is, the Trademark Law and its implementation rules as well as article 96 of the General Principles of the Civil Code[27] were not used, and that the court of first instance, being a people's court, did not have jurisdiction over the case. Furthermore, LIP argued that the judgment of the court of first instance in granting a Hong Kong company a huge amount of state property resulted in serious depletion of state assets, which was incompatible with state interests.

TMT responded that:

1   Since trademark right is a civil right, a dispute over its ownership falls within the scope of civil litigation of the people's courts.
2   The TMT, TMC, and SMT trademarks were designed by Wang Shaogming, and in accordance with the agreement between Tung Ming Co. and LIP on designated-brand production, and Wang let LIP use the trademarks and entrusted with it the task of registering the marks in mainland China.
3   After Tung Ming Co. closed down, Wang Shaoming established TMT to succeed to Tung Ming Co.'s business and the trademark-related rights; thus, LIP and TMT had a trust relationship.
4   TMT had never agreed to be authorized by LIP to register the trademarks overseas.

TMT claimed that it had the right to request that LIP return the trademarks because the latter had breached the contract. Hence, TMT sought affirmation of the judgment of the court of first instance on the basis of clear facts and proper application of law.

Reasoning

The Supreme Court found that the "TMT" mark provided by Tung Ming Co. was designed by Wang Shaoming, who adopted the first letter of the English name of Tung Ming Trading Ltd. and Tung Ming Co. and combined them with the rhombus figure of the entry stamp of the Saudi Arabian Customs. It also found that the SMT mark, similar to the TMT mark, has derived from the initials of the words SHAO and MING (Wang's given name in Chinese Pinyin). As the No. 142201 TMT trademark of 1980 did not contain the rhombus figure, LIP, upon the request of Wang Shaoming, registered the combined word-figure TMT trademark (No. 200833) with the state TMB in April 1983. This word-figure TMT trademark was the same as the one actually used on designated-brand products manufactured in mainland China and as the one registered and propagated by TMT overseas. In mainland China, LIP had registered the TMT trademark for five categories of goods, the TMC trademark for two categories of goods, and SMT trademark for two categories of goods. In addition, it had registered these three trademarks in some countries. By 21 August 1999, TMT had filed 78 registrations for TMT, *et al.* trademarks in mainland China, Hong Kong Special Administrative Region, and other countries and regions in the world.

To succeed to the relevant rights of Tung Ming Co., TMT repaid LIP, on behalf of Tung Ming Co., a debt of more than HK$3,170,000 on 5 June 1982 and 15 April 1983. In its report to the Guangdong Foreign Trade Bureau on 3 September 1982, LIP acknowledged that after the debt was offset by the raw and supplemental materials provided free by Tung Ming Co., Wang Shaoming and Lin Guiquan had paid the remainder of HK$3,113, 667. Thus, the amount actually paid by TMT on behalf of Tung Ming Co. exceeded the amount of debt as confirmed by LIP in the aforementioned document.

LIP denied that it had issued two certifying documents on 23 October 1987 and 16 December 1987 and suspected that the two documents submitted by TMT were false. Thus, at the court of first instance, LIP applied for judicial appraisal of the authenticity of the seals affixed on the documents. However, on appeal, LIP changed its request to an appraisal of the production time of these two documents, as well as the sequence of the tying and the affixation of official seals. The court commissioned the Beijing Huaxia Documentary Evidence Appraisal Center to do the appraisal. The Center concluded that these two documents were first typed and then sealed in the second half of 1987. To prove the authenticity of these two documents, TMT also submitted a certificate by a Hong Kong law firm, which proved that the 23 October 1987 document had been used by the law firm in another case on 19 April 1988, and that the date of affixing the official seals was accurate.

On 7 December 1994, LIP sent TMT a notice on strengthening the management of the TMT trademark, which stated: "The TMT trademark was a well-known mark created by both of us through years of joint operations. To treasure this intangible property, we, after many consultation sessions, signed an agreement on October 6 of this year in order to strengthen and perfect management, more effectively crack down counterfeits, stop infringing activities in a timely manner, and safeguard our legal rights and interests." Furthermore, over the years, TMT had signed various exclusive sales agreements and sales confirmations with LIP (including the agreements signed on 5 January 1983, 3 November 1984, and 13 January 1986) and confirmations signed on 27 November 1979, 8 December 1980; etc.), which clearly stated that labels and trademarks were to be provided by TMT and Tung Ming Co.

According to the Supreme Court, trademark right was a property right under civil law. Although special legal provisions existed with respect to the acquisition, duration, and assignment of a trademark, the law had not given the administrative organ the right to affirm its ownership. Based on the nature of trademark, lawsuits over its ownership were civil proceedings for affirmation and should fall within the scope of civil litigation of the people's courts. Thus, LIP's argument for appeal that disputes over trademark ownership were not within the jurisdiction of the people's courts could not be sustained.

The combination of the word TMT and a rhombus figure was the core of all the trademarks disputed in this case. This trademark was the same as the one used on goods for export and the one that TMT used for external promotion. This trademark was designed by Wang Shaoming when he was legal representative of Tung Ming Trading Co. and the general manager of Tung Ming Co. Wang was the first and principal person who handled the signing of the trading agreements between Tung Ming Co. and LIP. Based on witness testimonies and the agreements relating to the manufacture of products with designated brands, it could be firmly established that Wang, in representing Tung Ming Co., proposed the use of trademarks provided by his company, and that LIP was to organize the production of ceiling fans with the TMT, TMC, etc. brands. LIP agreed to such an arrangement, and Wang was the first person who suggested that these trademarks be registered in mainland China. Misled by LIP, Tung Ming Co. mistakenly believed that companies based in Hong Kong could not have their trademarks registered in the mainland, and thus, agreed with LIP that the latter register the trademarks in China.

After Tung Ming Co. closed down, LIP, upon the request of Wang Shaoming, the legal representative of TMT, registered the word-figure combination mark as No. 200833 trademark in China. Moreover, in accordance with the agreement on brand-designated production, LIP was responsible for organizing the production of TMT brand ceiling fans, as well as applying for the export of those goods, while Tung Ming Co. was responsible for providing labels and trademarks, advertising products, soliciting orders, and exclusively selling products to countries and regions overseas. In the course of performing the contract, TMT succeeded to Tung Ming Co. TMT then provided technology, supervised production, engaged in advertising and exclusive sale of the products, as well as assuming Tung Ming Co.'s debt owed to LIP.

Wang Shaoming designed and, on behalf of Tung Ming Co., provided the TMT trademarks to LIP, the purpose of which was to have LIP produce goods with brands designated by Tung Ming Co. Since both sides had actually performed the contract to produce goods with designated brands, they had formed a *de facto* legal relationship of trust with respect to the trademark rights. In addition, Wang Shaoming, as the legal representative of TMT, directly requested LIP to register the No. 200833 trademark. The legal relationship between the parties could be proven not only by the request to register and the design, delivery and use of the trademarks, but also by the stipulations in the trading contract on designated-brand production, and the fact that only Tung Ming Co. (subsequently TMT) could engage in the sale of the goods, as well as the advertising and promotion of the goods and trademarks, gradually making the trademarks in dispute gain fame and added value.

The two certifying documents issued by LIP on 23 October 1987 and 16 December 1987, while proving that LIP and TMT had a trust relationship with respect to the registration and management of the trademarks, confirmed that Tung Ming Co., before its closing down, also had a trust relationship with LIP. These two documents were authenticated by appraisal. In addition, the Hong Kong law firm verified that the 23 October 1987 document had been used in 1988. Thus, these two pieces of documentary evidence should be admitted.

The trademarks in question were registered in China by LIP based on the mandate and request of Tung Ming Co. LIP was the nominal holder of the trademarks, while TMT was the holder in substance. When LIP requested to have the case investigated and TMT's exports seized, TMT, in the capacity of trustor, demanded the return of these trademarks. Since this demand had sufficient factual basis, the court of first instance had correctly held that the trademarks must be returned to TMT. Although the court of first instance recognized that TMT had authorized LIP to register the trademarks, it failed to consider the fact that the trademarks were registered in the name of the trustee and did not recognize the existence of a trust relationship.[28] This holding was not proper.

The agreement signed in 1994 again provided for the ownership of the trademarks. Based on the declaration of TMT and the notice sent by LIP in July 1994, it could be established that the purpose of reaching the agreement was to strengthen the management of the trademarks and to crack down on counterfeit goods. As the dispute had not yet arisen, TMT did not raise the issue of returning the trademark rights, and LIP was still the registrant of the trademarks. Hence, what this agreement stipulated with respect to the trademarks should be treated as a confirmation of the then-existing condition of the trademark rights, which did not affect TMT's post-dispute claim of returning the trademarks.

As LIP had applied and obtained intellectual property protection measures from the Customs, TMT could not export products for two years. As a result, TMT had sustained huge losses, for which LIP should bear responsibility. In view of the fact that TMT did not appeal the lower court's rejection of its compensation claim, the Supreme Court affirmed that holding. The markets for TMT-brand products were located overseas. Moreover, TMT had registered the TMT trademarks in major markets overseas, enjoying the exclusive right to use the trademarks. Thus, it was difficult for LIP to export products with TMT brands, which made LIP lose the ability to earn profits. At the same time, TMT could not order goods for export from manufacturers in China. The manufacturers in China also incurred huge losses and could not supply the goods for overseas markets, which resulted in market shrinkage. Thus, LIP's request that the court protect its trademarks based on the argument that state property would be washed away was unconvincing and lacked factual basis. On appeal, TMT agreed to increase the amount of compensation, which the Supreme Court approved.

In sum, the Supreme Court maintained that the appeal of LIP lacked both factual and legal bases, and thus, should not be supported. In addition, the judgment of the court of first instance was based on clear facts and correct application of law, which should be affirmed, except that the award of a relatively small amount of compensation was not fair. However, since the statement of the court of first instance regarding the reasons for its judgment and its expression in the principal text were improper, its judgment should be amended.

Judgment

According to article 4 of the General Principles of the Civil Law[29] and article 153(1)(i) and (ii) of the Civil Procedure Law,[30] the court held as follows:

1   Provision 4 of the judgment of the Guangdong Province High People's Court was affirmed.
2   Provisions 1 and 2 of the judgment of the Guangdong Province High People's Court were revised as follows. The ownership of the TMT, TMC, and SMT trademarks, both in word alone and in word-figure combination, registered by LIP inside China belonged to TMT, and LIP should assist TMT in applying for the change of registrant of these trademarks within one month of the effective date of this judgment.
3   Provision 3 of the judgment of the Guangdong Province High People's Court was revised as follows. TMT was to compensate LIP RMB 2.5 million, the payment of which must be made within one month of the effective day of this judgment.

This judgment was final.

Twentieth Century Fox Film Corp. *v*. Beijing Xianke Laser Market
(1996) 一中知初字第62号, *Beijing City No. 1 Intermediate People's Court, 26 November 1996*

Facts

Twentieth Century Fox Film Corporation (hereinafter FFC), a company registered in the U.S.A., produced "Commando," "Die Hard," and "Die Hard 2" in 1985, 1988, and 1990, respectively. FFC registered these films with the U.S. Copyright Office and owned the copyright in these cinemato-graphic works. On 18 February 1994, FFC's lawyer purchased the laser discs of "Die Hard 1" and "Die Hard 2" published and distributed by Shenzhen City Laser Program Publishing and Distributing Co. (hereinafter SLC) from Beijing Xianke Laser Market (hereinafter XLM). On 7 June 1994, FFC's lawyer purchased the laser disc of "Commando" published and distributed by SLC from XLM. FFC had the Beijing City Notary Office notarized these laser discs for the purpose of evidence preservation.

FFC maintained that prior to the lawsuit, it had never authorized XLM to distribute or sell its cinematographic works, nor had it authorized a third party to give XLM permission to engage in such conduct. Thus, XLM distributed and sold laser discs of its films without permission. Based on the Memorandum of Understanding on the Protection of Intellectual Property concluded between China and the U.S.A. on 17 January 1992 and the Berne Convention, which became effective in China on 15 October 1992, FFC's cinematographic works were to be protected by the Copyright Law of China. Since the Copyright Law prohibited the use of another's work in the form of video-recording, distribution, etc. without the permission of the copy-right owner, XLM should bear legal liability. Accordingly, FFC requested that the court:

1 Order XLM to provide the quantity of sales and inventory of the infringing products.
2 Seal up and confiscate all the infringing products that had not been sold.
3 Order XLM to guarantee in writing that infringement would not occur again in the future.
4 Order XLM to pay at least RMB 50,000 as compensation.
5 Order XLM to bear the expenses on investigating the infringement and ascertaining responsibility.

XLM submitted an explanation from SLC, indicating that the Ministry of Culture had approved the publication of the aforementioned films as evidenced by the relevant approval numbers. XLM provided certificates that permitted the import and publication of overseas entertainment audio and video products as well as receipts. In addition, XLM defended that the open sale of these laser discs was based on its legal relationship – selling on commission – with the publisher SLC.

Upon the application of FFC, in November 1995, the court adopted evidence preservation and entrusted an auditing firm to audit XLM's sales of the laser discs. On 10 February 1996, the Beijing Tianzheng Auditing Firm submitted a report with the following conclusions. During the period from 6 October 1993 to 31 October 1995, 22 laser discs of "Commando" were sold at the price of RMB 5,764 (with a profit of RMB 929.50) and 55 "Die Hard 1 and 2" were sold at the price of RMB 16,920.20 (with a profit of RMB 4,165.70).

FFC did not raise an objection to the auditing report during the statutory time limit. However, in its explanation regarding compensatory damages, FFC pointed out how the auditing firm had calculated XLM's profits: using the total amount of sale revenues during the period of investigation and examination, the cost of sale, the average tax rate, and the average expenditure rate to reckon the profits derived from the sale of the laser discs. FFC maintained that it was indisputable to use such auditing method to examine the profits of only one entity. In addition, FFC did not object to the use of an average expenditure rate during a certain period to appraise and determine the expenses for selling the pirated copies. Nonetheless, since the operating cost of selling the pirated copies was related to the acts of infringement, the operating cost should not be deducted from the sale revenues. Instead, FFC argued that the gross profit from the sale of the pirated copies should be used as XLM's illegal income, that is, the balance obtained after subtracting the cost of sale and tax from the sale revenues.

On 29 May 1996, XLM also submitted a written objection to the auditing report. It stated that after FFC filed a lawsuit in September 1994, XLM immediately stopped selling the laser discs at issue, and until September 1994, the cost of each laser disc was higher than RMB 150, so the average cost of RMB 150 as used in the auditing report lacked any basis. In addition, it claimed that appendix 5 of the auditing report had nothing to do with XLM because Beijing City Xianke Laser Company mentioned in the shipping list and XLM were independent individual legal persons. Moreover, since XLM and the Yinxiang Dashijie did not have business dealings with respect to the laser discs at issue, the data relating to the latter in the auditing report should be adjusted.

In response, the auditing firm submitted an explanation. It stated that, during the auditing, it found that the accounting information provided by XLM was exceedingly incomplete, even the furnished information was remarkably incomplete, and the information on sales and purchases was also incomplete. After September 1994, XLM still sold the laser discs at issue, and there were sale vouchers as proof. Since the accounting information provided by XLM was incomplete, the furnished information was also incomplete, and the recording and handling of the accounts and receipts was too perfunctory, the auditing work was difficult to conduct, and the cost of goods was based on XLM's estimated subsidiary ledgers on inventory and sales. As to appendix 5, after checking and ratifying that Beijing City Xianke Laser Company was a separate entity not related to XLM, the mistake committed during collection of information should be rectified, appendix 5 should be removed, and the corresponding record should be adjusted.

During the trial, FFC indicated that since it did not know whether the production of the laser discs at issue occurred prior to the effectiveness of the Memorandum of Understanding on the Protection of Intellectual Property, it did not sue the producer and the publisher for the time being, and sued only the seller instead. Moreover, FFC claimed that it had incurred the following litigation expenses:

1   the cost of purchasing laser discs so as to secure evidence was RMB 1,490 (RMB 298 for "Commando," RMB 596 for "Die Hard 1" and RMB 596 for "Die Hard 2");
2   the notary fee for evidence preservation was RMB 562.50;
3   the notary fee for confirming that the Chinese version of the documents submitted in this lawsuit conformed to their English version was RMB 600;
4   the translation fee for documents required for the lawsuit was RMB 638.75; and
5   the lawyer's fee was RMB 4,662.41.

The total amount was RMB 7,953.66. Furthermore, FFC sought to be compensated for:

1   the prepaid court cost of RMB 2,010;
2   the purchase price of RMB 7,350 of a laser disc player for the court to examine the evidence;
3   the expenses of RMB 125 on auditing and evidence preservation; and
4   the estimated auditing fee of RMB 10,000.

XLM pleaded that it had never infringed upon the copyright of FFC because:

1   XLM was a legal-person enterprise established with the approval of the relevant government department and permitted to engage in such commercial activities as the retail of audio and video recordings.
2   XLM had never published and distributed in excess of the legally permitted scope of business, namely, the use and reproduction of works, and had never used the works of FFC for publication, reproduction, and distribution.
3   Pursuant to the Copyright Law, Berne Convention, etc., only reproduction and distribution may involve copyright infringement without permission.
4   The alleged pirated laser discs sold by XLM were audio- and video-recordings delivered by publishers and distributors who had been lawfully licensed to sell on a commission basis, and such audio- and video-recordings are official publications in accordance with relevant publishing management.

Being the seller of audio- and video-recordings, XLM had no right or obligation to request publishers and distributors to provide documentary proof of their copyright, nor had it the right or obligation to judge the legality the use of the works by publishers or distributors. The obligations of a seller included to refrain from selling unofficial copies and be jointly and severally liable with the publisher and distributor to consumers for damages in the case of poor product quality. In sum, FFC's lawsuit had no legal and factual bases; thus, the court should dismiss its claims. Besides, FFC had abused its right to file a lawsuit, so XLM reserved the right to file a counterclaim or file a lawsuit separately.

Reasoning

The court reasoned that the principal facts of the case were clear. That is, XLM had sold the laser discs of FFC's copyrighted films "Commando," "Die Hard 1," and "Die Hard 2." As the reproductions were made without the permission of the copyright owner, the laser discs sold by XLM were infringing products. The contested issue, however, was whether XLM's selling of these pirated copies constituted copyright infringement. To answer this question, the court analyzed XLM's conduct in accordance with copyright laws, including international treaties, and the main elements comprising the infringing act.

First, it was necessary to examine whether XLM was subjectively at fault to sell pirated laser discs. This led to the question of whether XLM was obliged to examine the legality of the laser discs in terms of copyright. XLM insisted that the main reason for its non-infringement was that it did not have such an obligation. In this case, to determine the subjective fault of the act of infringement, it is necessary to analyze XLM's subjective state of mind during the act and the pertinent obligations as required by law. Being a professional seller of audio and video products, XLM should heed copyright laws and the regulations on the sale of audio and video products promulgated by the relevant state departments. In particular, after China had acceded to the relevant international copyright conventions and treaties, the sellers of audio and video products must not only comply with regulations on the administration of their industry, but also pay attention to whether the audio and video products they sold might infringe upon others' intellectual property rights. With respect to foreign works protected by Chinese law, sellers should pay even more attention. Thus, the determination of whether XLM was obliged to pay attention might be based on the relevant notice promulgated by the National Copyright Administration. According to the Notice Regarding the Use of Specially Designated Reproductions of Foreign Works for Specially Designated Purposes promulgated by the National Copyright Administration, specially designated reproductions of foreign works owned and used by Chinese citizens or legal persons for specially designated purposes prior to the effectiveness of international copyright treaties in China could be sold after 15 October 1993 only with the permission of the original copyright owners; otherwise, the sale would be treated as infringement. As a result, although the laser discs sold by

XLM were official copies furnished by a third party, XLM could not be exempt from liability based on such a reason. XLM was subjectively at fault for selling pirated laser discs of foreign works.

Objectively, the copyright in FFC's cinematographic works of "Commando," "Die Hard 1" and "Die Hard 2," after the conclusion of the Memorandum of Understanding on the Protection of Intellectual Property and China's participation in the Berne Convention, should be protected by Chinese law. In Beijing, XLM had sold pirated laser discs published by others, which objectively infringed upon FFC's lawful rights and interests. According to the Copyright Law, selling falls within the scope of distribution, and selling pirated copies may constitute an independent act of infringement. Hence, XLM's emphasized that it had not engaged in reproduction and thus distribution could not be supported. Since XLM's conduct violated article 45(5) of the Copyright Law,[31] it should bear the corresponding legal liability. Pursuant to FFC's requests, XLM should stop the infringement and compensate FFC for losses. Of course, after the seller had born the liability, it could seek indemnity from the distributor and publisher in accordance with relevant regulations or contractual provisions.

Although SLC's explanation indicated that the aforementioned laser discs had been published with the approval numbers of the relevant government organ, XLM had not produced evidence to prove that its sale of these laser discs had been granted permission. Since the preceding approval numbers were given prior to the effectiveness of the Memorandum of Understanding on the Protection of Intellectual Property and the Berne Convention, and the relevant government organ did not examine whether there was permission from the copyright owner in granting approval, the explanation from SLC could not be used as evidence for defense. XLM maintained that the open sale of the laser discs was based on its legal relationship – selling on commission – with the publisher SLC. However, XLM did not provide evidence to support its claim. Legally, whether the relationship of XLM and SLC was that of selling on commission or buying and selling did not affect XLM's legal liability for infringing the copyright of a third party.

Concerning the amount of compensation, FFC believed that since XLM infringed upon its copyright even after China had given protection to works of nationals of member countries of international copyright treaties for more than two years, XLM seriously hindered and delayed the lawful entry of its works into the Chinese market, thereby causing it to lose competitive advantage for a long time. FFC claimed that this type of loss was real, and that the loss or reduction of competitive advantage directly signified the loss or reduction of its profits. Because this type of loss could not be compensated by XLM's illegal profits, FFC pleaded that the court order XLM to pay at least RMB 50,000 as compensation. Moreover, FFC requested that the losing party be responsible for the total expenses in pursuing liability for the infringement. The court reasoned that the amount of compensation should be determined in light of the circumstances of XLM's infringement, taking into consideration such factors as the duration of infringement, the quantity of pirated copies sold, the detrimental consequences of selling pirated copies, and the effects of infringement on society. In addition, since FFC's request that the operating cost of XLM not be deducted from the revenues derived from the sale of pirated laser discs was reasonable, the court supported FFC. Furthermore, the court believed that FFC's losses might be determined by considering the reasonable profit that FFC should obtain from the sale of each laser disc and the quantity of laser discs sold by XLM. The reasonable fee of RMB 7,953.66 paid by FFC to protect its legal rights by seeking judicial assistance should be borne by the losing party. However, the court did not order XLM to guarantee in writing that it would not commit infringement again and to confiscate the pirated laser discs because these requests were not to be resolved by a civil judgment.[32]

In conclusion, the court made the following judgment in accordance with article 45(5) of the Copyright Law:

1   XLM should immediately stop selling laser discs that infringe upon the copyright of FFC from the date on which this judgment became effective.
2   XLM should pay RMB 31,053.66 to FFC as compensatory damages within 30 days of the effectiveness of this judgment.
3   The other claims of FFC were denied.

XLM was also required to pay the court cost, auditing fee, etc. If FFC was not satisfied with this judgment, it might, within 30 days of the delivery of the judgment, or if XLM was not satisfied with this judgment, within 15 days of the delivery of the judgment, submit an application for appeal to this court for the purpose of appealing to the Beijing City High People's Court.

Further reading

Lehman, Edward Eugene, Ojansivu, Camilla, and Abrams, Stan, "Well-Known Trademark Protection in the People's Republic of China," *Fordham International Law Journal* 26, 2003, 257–73.

Newberry, Warren, "Copyright Reform in China: A 'Trips' Much Shorter and Less Strange Than Imaged?" *Connective Law Review* 35, 2003, 1425–462.

Sorell, Louis S., "A Comparative Analysis of Selected Aspects of Patent Law in China and the United States," *Pacific Rim Law and Policy Journal* 11, 2002, 319–39.

Notes

1 The Trademark Law of the People's Republic of China, adopted at the 24th Session of the Standing Committee of the 5th National People's Congress on 23

August 1982 and amended at the 30th Session of the Standing Committee of the 7th National People's Congress on 22 February 1993 and at the 24th Session of the Standing Committee of the 9th National People's Congress on 27 October 2001.

2 The Patent Law of the People's Republic of China, adopted at the 4th Session of the Standing Committee of the 6th National People's Congress on 12 March 1984 and amended at the 27th Session of the Standing Committee of the 7th National People's Congress on 4 September 1992 and at the 17th Session of the Standing Committee of the 9th National People's Congress on 25 August 2000.

3 The Copyright Law of the People's Republic of China, adopted at the 15th Session of the Standing Committee of the 7th National People's Congress on 7 September 1990 and amended at the 24th Session of the Standing Committee of the 9th National People's Congress on 27 October 2001.

4 During his tour, Deng Xiaoping visited a high-technology company. When the chairman of the board of directors talked about the annual production of foreign-film laser discs, Deng inquired how the copyrights were handled. The chairman answered that the company obtained licenses from foreign-film producers pursuant to international standards. Deng expressed satisfaction and said: "It should be like that. [You] should observe relevant international regulations on intellectual property rights." See Propaganda Department of China Shenzhen City Committee, ed., *1992 Spring: Deng Xiapeng and Shenzhen* [in Chinese], Shenzhen, China: Haitian Publishing, 1992, p. 25.

5 The Criminal Law of the People's Republic of China, adopted at the 2nd Session of the 5th National People's Congress on 1 July 1979 and amended by the 5th Session of the Standing Committee of the 8th National People's Congress on 14 March 1997, the 13th Session of the Standing Committee of the 9th National People's Congress on 25 December 1999, the 23th Session of the Standing Committee of the 9th National People's Congress on 31 August 2001, the 25th Session of the Standing Committee of the 9th National People's Congress on 29 December 2001, and the 31st Session of the Standing Committee of the 9th National People's Congress on 28 December 2002. Articles 213–20 of the Criminal Law deal with intellectual property infringement.

6 The Regulations on the Protection of Computer Software, promulgated by the State Council on 20 December 2001.

7 The Measures on the Implementation of Administrative Punishment Regarding Copyright, promulgated by the National Copyright Administration on 24 July 2003.

8 The Regulations of the People's Republic of China on the Protection of Intellectual Property by the Customs, promulgated by the State Council on 2 December 2003.

9 The Detailed Regulations for the Implementation of the Patent Law of the People's Republic of China, promulgated by the State Council on 15 June 2001.

10 The Measures on the Administration of Patent Agencies, promulgated by the State Intellectual Property Office on 6 June 2003.

11 The Regulations for the Implementation of the Trademark Law of the People's Republic of China, promulgated by the State Council on 3 August 2002.

12 The Rules on the Recognition and Protection of Well-Known Marks, promulgated by the State Administration for Industry and Commerce on 17 April 2003.

13   The Measures on the Registration and Administration of Collective Marks and Certification Marks, promulgated by the State Administration for Industry and Commerce on 17 April 2003.

14   Article 44 of the Trademark Law provides that the TMB is to order the rectification of the situation, but art. 39 of the Regulations for the Implementation of the Trademark Law states that the AIC is to order the rectification.

15   The Regulations for the Implementation of the Copyright Law of the People's Republic of China, promulgated by the State Council on 2 August 2002.

16   The Regulations for the Implementation of International Copyright Treaties, promulgated by the State Council on 25 September 1992.

17   The Measures on the Registration of Computer-Software Copyright, promulgated by the National Copyright Administration on 20 February 2002.

18   Examples of oral works include impromptu speeches, lectures, and court debates.

19   *Quyi*, which consist of recitation, singing, or both, are works created mainly for performance, such as *xiangsheng* (cross-talk), *kuaishu* (clapper-talk), *dagu* (story singing with the accompaniment of a drum), and *pingshu* (story telling).

20   The parties should stipulate the terms of the exclusive license. If the terms are not clearly stipulated, the licensee will be deemed to have the right to exclude anyone, including the copyright owner, from using the work in the same way. In addition, the licensee must obtain permission from the copyright owner before allowing any third party to exercise the same right, unless otherwise stipulated in the licensing contract.

21   The Law against Unfair Competition of the People's Republic of China, adopted at the 3rd Session of the Standing Committee of the 8th National People's Congress on 2 September 1993.

22   Article 39 of the TRIPS Agreement provides that members shall protect undisclosed information and data submitted to governmental agencies, and that natural and legal persons shall have the right of preventing information lawfully within their control from being disclosed to, acquired by, or used by others without their consent in a manner contrary to honest commercial practises so long as such information is secret, has commercial value, and has been subject to reasonable steps to keep it secret.

23   A *sanlaiyibu* enterprise is an enterprise that is engaged in *lailiaojiagong* (来料加工), *laiyangjiagong* (来样加工), *laijianjiagong* (来件加工), and *buchangmaoyi* (补偿贸易). In the case of *lailiaojiagong*, the foreign investor furnishes raw materials, packaging materials, etc., and the Chinese enterprise produces and delivers the finished products in accordance with the foreign investor's requirements on quality, specifications, etc. for a processing fee. In the case of *laiyangjiagong*, the foreign investor provides samples and specifications, while the Chinese enterprise produces and delivers the finished products and is paid for the cost of raw materials and processing. In the case of *laijianjiagong*, the foreign investor furnishes spare parts, components, etc., and if necessary, technology and equipment, and the Chinese enterprise assembles and delivers the finished products for a processing fee. As to *buchangmaoi*, the importer buys machines, equipment, materials, or labor services from an exporter on credit, and the importer compensates the exporter with merchandise or labor services one time or by installment within a fixed period of time.

24   Article 11 of the Patent Law provides that after a patent is granted on an invention or a utility model, no entity or individual may, without the permission of

the patent holder and for production and business purposes, manufacture, use, promise to sell, sell, or import a patented product; use a patented process; or use, promise to sell, sell or import products directly obtained by the patented process. Article 56(1) of the Patent Law provides that the scope of protection for an invention or utility-model patent is to be determined by the contents of the patent claim(s), and the specification and appended drawings may be used to interpret the patent claims.

25 Article 21 of the Supreme People's Court's Several Regulations Regarding Questions on the Application of Law in Trying Patent Infringement Cases provides that where it is difficult to determine the losses of the infringed or the profits of the infringer, and if there is licensing fee to refer to, the people's court may, based on the type of patent right; the nature and circumstances of the infringement; the amount of licensing fee; the nature, scope, and duration of the licensing; etc., set the compensatory amount as one to three times the licensing fee. If there is no licensing fee to refer to, or if the licensing fee is obviously unreasonable, the people's court may, based on the type of patent right, the nature and circumstances of the infringement, etc., set the compensatory amount as RMB 5,000 to 300,000, not exceeding RMB 500,000.

26 Article 2 of the Supreme People's Court's Several Regulations on Evidence in Civil Litigation provides that the parties have the responsibility to submit evidence to prove the facts on which their claims are based or disprove the facts on which the other party's claims are based.

27 Article 96 of the General Principles of the Civil Law concerns the exclusive right to use a trademark that a legal person, an individual industrial or commercial household, or a partnership has legally acquired and will receive legal protection.

28 If the relationship was that of trust, LIP, as the trustee, could apply for registration of the trademarks in its own name. Thus, LIP should apply for change of registrant of the trademarks. If LIP was an agent rather than trustee, it could not apply for registration of the trademarks in its own name. In such a case, TMT should apply to the Trademark Review and Appraisal Board to have the trademarks revoked.

29 Article 4 of the General Principles of the Civil Law states that civil activities should follow the principles of voluntariness, impartiality, compensation for equal value, and honesty and good faith.

30 Article 153(1)(i) and (ii) of the Civil Procedure Law provides that the court of second instance should dismiss the appeal and affirm the judgment of the court of first instance if the original judgment is based on clearly established facts and correct application of law; and amend the judgment if the original judgment is based on incorrect application of law.

31 Article 45(5) of the 1990 revision of the Copyright Law provides that the use of another's work in the form of performance, broadcast, exhibition, distribution, filming, video-recording, adaptation, translation, annotation, compilation, etc. without the permission of the copyright owner constitutes copyright infringement, and the infringer must bear such civil liabilities as cessation of infringement, elimination of bad effects, making an apology, and paying compensatory damages.

32 The revised Copyright Law (2001) provides that the court may confiscate pirated copies as well as tools and equipment for making pirated copies.

6   Labor and employment

For decades, Chinese workers in state-owned enterprises were served with an "iron rice bowl," that is, they enjoyed virtually lifetime employment, lived in enterprise housing, received medical care at little or no cost, and were provided with pensions and various fringe benefits. However, with the intensification of economic reform and the restructuring of state-owned enterprises, the "iron rice bowl" has been smashed. Nowadays, employment security is no longer guaranteed, a social security system has been introduced to replace the old enterprise-based welfare system, and labor mobility has greatly increased. During the course of labor reform, FIEs have played an important role because labor surpluses from the state and collective sectors have been absorbed considerably by the foreign sector. Moreover, with China's accession to the WTO, further growth of foreign trade and foreign direct investment is expected. Through whatever investment vehicles foreign investors choose to do business in China, they must staff their establishments. As a result, it is imperative for foreign investors to understand the basics of Chinese labor laws.

Since the embarkation of economic reform, the Chinese regulatory scheme for labor and employment can be divided into two periods. In the first period (1980–93), the Chinese regulatory framework was piecemeal because except for the Trade Union Law,[1] there existed only administrative regulations and a large number of government rules and decrees dealing with sundry labor and employment issues. As regards labor management in FIEs, major legal provisions were contained in a series of administrative regulations and government rules enacted to implement the laws on FIEs, such as the Regulations on Labor Management in Sino-Foreign Equity Joint Ventures, Regulations for the Implementation of the Law on Sino-Foreign Equity Joint Ventures, and Rules on the Right of Autonomy of Foreign Investment Enterprises in the Hiring of Personnel and on Employees' Wages, Insurance and Welfare Expenses. In the second period (1994–Present), however, the passage of the Labor Law[2] and the subsequent enactment of a series of implementation rules have rendered the Chinese regulatory framework more systematic. Specifically, the Rules on Labor Management in

Foreign Investment Enterprises³ are meant to provide foreign investors with more guidance on labor management in China.

To present an overview of Chinese labor laws pertinent to FIEs, this chapter is composed of two sections. The first section provides the necessary background for understanding the current regulatory framework, while the second section highlights important legal provisions relating to labor management in FIEs. Since only national legal norms are discussed here, foreign investors should also consult provincial and municipal regulations on labor and employment when they make personnel decisions.

1 During the 1980s and early 1990s

After China opened its doors to the outside world in 1979, many multinational corporations, foreign firms, and overseas Chinese established offices and/or factories in China either in preparation for its potentially huge market or to benefit from its relatively cheap labor cost. To acquire foreign capital, technology, and management expertise, the Chinese government gradually gave FIEs a certain amount of autonomy in dealing with personnel matters. Nonetheless, with the increased incidence of labor unrest resulting from layoffs and arrears of wages or pensions in the domestic sector or labor abuses in the foreign sector, the Chinese government also stepped up its efforts to enact a comprehensive labor law. Accordingly, the following discussion will first provide an overview of the regulatory framework during the 1980s and early 1990s and then mention the problems relating to labor management in FIEs.

Overview

At the beginning, joint ventures were allowed to recruit staff and workers (职工) only within the areas stipulated by the labor-and-personnel department. Even so, they were allowed to hire outside their localities engineering, technical, and managerial employees who were not available in their areas, subject to the approval of the labor-and-personnel departments of the provincial, autonomous-regional, or municipal government and of the relevant district. Subsequently, geographical restrictions were lifted, and FIEs might recruit staff and workers outside their localities.

To hire employees, FIEs must conclude collective labor contracts with trade unions or individual labor contracts with staff and workers. In a labor contract, the parties must stipulate the terms of employment, including hiring, dismissal, or resignation; tasks of production or work; wages, awards, and punishment; labor insurance and welfare; labor protection; labor discipline; duration of the contract; conditions for modifying and terminating the contract; and the rights and obligations to be executed by both parties. After its conclusion, a labor contract or its subsequent revision must be submitted to the labor-and-personnel department of the provincial, autonomous-regional, or municipal government for approval.

With respect to remuneration, the wages of staff and workers of joint ventures initially were to be set at 120 to 150 percent of the actual wages of staff and workers of state-owned enterprises of the same trade in the locality. Nonetheless, since wage increases were to be determined by the board of directors based on the production and operations conditions and in accordance with the joint-venture contract, joint ventures did not have to synchronize their wage increases with those of state-owned enterprises. Thereafter, the wage levels of staff and workers in FIEs were to be determined by the board of directors, but could not be less than 120 percent of the average wage of employees of similar state-owned enterprises of the same trade in the locality. In addition, wages were to be adjusted gradually in accordance with the economic performance of the enterprise.

Apart from wages, FIEs must pay for their workers' old-age pensions, unemployment insurance, welfare benefits, and the amount which the government subsidized for housing, basic living necessities, culture, education, and hygiene and health of workers, pursuant to the standards existing in state-owned enterprises. Nonetheless, export-oriented and technologically advanced enterprises were exempt from paying subsidies. Moreover, FIEs must observe the relevant regulations and rules on occupational safety. In particular, they must provide labor protection articles to staff and workers with reference to the standards used in state-owned enterprises and report work-related injuries or deaths to the government.

At the same time, the staff and workers of FIEs had the right to form trade unions and conduct union activities. As representatives of staff and workers, trade unions could conclude collective labor contracts with their enterprises and supervise the execution of those contracts. Even so, trade unions were supposed not only to represent the interests of workers, but also to assist in utilizing welfare and bonus funds and to reduce the disruption of economic tasks. In fact, although union representatives could attend board meetings concerning the interests of workers, they did not have power because the law required the board only to listen to their views and obtain their cooperation. On their part, FIEs must provide housing and facilities for unions to conduct office work; meetings; and welfare, cultural, and sports activities. Every month FIEs must pay an amount equal to 2 percent of the total actual wages of their staff and workers as trade union funds.

Last of all, FIEs might dismiss surplus staff and workers resulting from changes in production and technical conditions. A notice of dismissal must be given to the trade union and the worker one month in advance and be filed with the enterprise's department-in-charge and the local labor-and-personnel department. Moreover, punishment by discharge was allowed. At the outset, joint ventures must secure the approval of their departments in-charge and the labor and personnel department. Subsequently, FIEs were required only to report the dismissal to the local labor-and-personnel department. On the other hand, a staff or worker could obtain an early termination of the labor contract, but was required to reimburse the enterprise an appropriate amount of training expenses.

Problems

During this period, legal provisions were enacted to provide some structure for labor management in FIEs. Notwithstanding these provisions, many FIEs encountered obstacles, while at the same time, failed to observe the law.

Among the obstacles commonly encountered by FIEs, the shortage of qualified people for managerial and technical positions was the most acute. Consequently, many FIEs dispatched highly paid expatriates to China and/ or spent large amounts of money on training local employees. Moreover, since unemployment would cause social instability, many joint ventures experienced pressure from their Chinese partners to maintain unqualified employees or to hire more employees than was necessary. In fact, as labor discipline was quite lax during the Cultural Revolution, managers in FIEs had to deal with workers who were not used to administration of disciplinary measures.

On the other hand, many FIEs had not abided by the law. For instance, although the law required FIEs and their workers or the trade unions to sign labor contracts, this mandate had been disregarded.[4] Besides, many FIEs did not provide workers with safe working conditions.[5] Similarly, the majority of FIEs were not unionized, as, for example, by the end of 1993, only about 10,000 of China's more than 40,000 FIEs had any forms of union organization.[6] Indeed, the innovative and strict disciplinary measures[7] imposed by some FIEs raised the question of their legitimacy and reasonableness.

2 Since 1994

In July 1994, China enacted its Labor Law, which is the first comprehensive legislation dealing with labor and employment and applies to all enterprises located in China. One month later, the Ministry of Labor (now the Ministry of Labor and Social Security) and the MOFTEC (now the Ministry of Commerce) promulgated the Rules on Labor Management in Foreign Investment Enterprises, which explicitly provided that contradictory provisions in previous regulations would be superseded. Accordingly, these two statutes provide the governing rules for labor management in FIEs. Nevertheless, in January 2002, the Ministry of Labor and Social Security published a list of government rules that might be repealed or amended or would be maintained in light of WTO regulations.[8] The Rules on Labor Management in Foreign Investment Enterprises were listed as "repeal recommended" on the grounds that the Labor Law and its accompanying rules had replaced them. As of March 2004, this set of rules had not yet been repealed. As a result, the highlights below are based primarily on the relevant provisions of the Labor Law, but relevant provisions taken from the Rules on Labor Management in Foreign Investment Enterprises and other legislative sources will be so noted.

Recruitment

The Labor Law does not contain any specific provisions on recruitment, except for the fact that it prohibits discrimination based on ethnicity, race, gender, and religious belief as well as employment of anyone who is under 16. The Rules on Labor Management in Foreign Investment Enterprises provide that, in recruiting staff and workers, FIEs have autonomy in deciding the time, conditions, format, and quantity. Moreover, FIEs may recruit through employment services endorsed by the local labor-administration department or, if the local labor-administration department approves, recruit directly or outside their localities. Consequently, the Rules on Labor Management in Foreign Investment Enterprises appear to be more restrictive because under the Labor Law, FIEs are not required to secure prior approval for direct recruitment or recruitment from other regions. However, if the rules are repealed as recommended, FIEs will be treated equally with domestic enterprises in terms of recruitment. In any case, it is noteworthy that the employment of staff by the representative office of a foreign enterprise should go through the foreign affairs services or other units as designated by the Chinese government.[9]

Furthermore, the Labor Law provides that if a hiring unit (用人单位), namely, the employer, hires someone whose labor contract with another employer has not yet been terminated, thereby causing economic losses to the original employer, it will be jointly and severally liable for compensation. Similarly, the Rules on Labor Management in Foreign Investment Enterprises provide that FIEs cannot hire workers whose labor contracts with other employers have not been terminated. Thus, it will be prudent for an FIE to find out whether a prospective worker has any ongoing employment relationship before it offers him or her the job.

Labor contract

According to the Labor Law, an employment relationship is to be established by a labor contract. However, a labor contract will be void if it violates any laws or administrative regulations, or if it is concluded by means of fraud or duress. Individual workers may sign labor contracts, but the trade union, or the elected representatives of staff and workers, may conclude a collective contract on behalf of the entire workforce. A collective labor contract must be submitted to the labor-administration department; if the labor-administration department raises no objection within 15 days of its receipt, the collective contract will become effective. As regards an individual contract, the Rules on Labor Management in Foreign Investment

Enterprises require that it be submitted for examination by the local labor-administration department within one month of its conclusion. At any rate, the working conditions and remuneration stipulated in the contracts signed by individual workers must not be inferior to those provided in the collective contract.

Specifically, a labor contract must be concluded in writing and contain:

1   the term of the contract;
2   the job requirements;
3   labor protection and working conditions;
4   remuneration;
5   labor discipline;
6   conditions for termination; and
7   liability for breach.

Apart from these mandatory provisions, the parties may agree to include in the labor contract any other provisions. The term of a labor contract may be fixed, not fixed, or limited to a certain amount of work. If a worker has been with the same employer for 10 years or more without any interruption, he or she may ask to enter into a labor contract without a definite term. Besides, a labor contract may stipulate a probationary period, which cannot exceed six months, and the parties may agree on provisions relating to the protection of trade secrets.

Remuneration

The Labor Law provides that a hiring unit can autonomously determine its methods of wage distribution and wage levels with reference to its production and operations characteristics as well as economic performance. However, the minimum wage of staff and workers cannot be lower than the local minimum wage. In addition, wages are to be paid to the worker in cash and on a monthly basis, and no deduction or delay of payment without cause is allowed. Apart from the Labor Law, the Rules on Labor Management in Foreign Investment Enterprises also provide guidance on remuneration. In particular, the Ministry of Labor has issued the Provisional Measures on the Administration of Wage Incomes in Foreign Investment Enterprises and the Several Opinions on the "Collective Consultation" of Wages in Foreign Investment Enterprises to further explain the management of wage incomes and collective bargaining of wages in FIEs.[10] This section summarizes the major provisions of these three pieces of legislation.

First and foremost, FIEs are to implement the principles of distribution according to work and equal pay for equal work. They must pay wages in full, on time, and at least once a month, as well as withhold and pay income taxes for their staff and workers. In addition, the average wage level of an FIE at the time of establishment is to be determined by the board of directors and must not be lower than the average wage level of staff and workers in the same trade or industry in its locality. The increase of the average wage level of an FIE should be determined by its board of directors or through "collective consultation" (集体协商) in accordance with the enterprise's economic efficiency and labor productivity, and with reference to local consumer price index and wage guidelines.

As mentioned in Chapter 3, the remuneration of senior managerial personnel, including the general manager, deputy general manager, chief engineer, deputy engineer, and financial officers, are to be determined by the board of directors. In an equity or cooperative joint venture, if the wages of senior management from the foreign side are not paid by the joint venture, the wages of senior management from the Chinese side should be determined by the "actual wages" system. "Actual wages" (实得工资) refers to basic wages, allowances, subsidies, etc. However, if the joint venture pays the wages of senior managers appointed by the foreign party, the wages of senior management from the Chinese side will be paid in accordance with the "actual wages and nominal wages" system. The "nominal wages" (名义工资) of senior management from the Chinese side are to be determined by the board of directors in accordance with the principle of equal pay for equal work and with reference to the wages of senior management from the foreign side. The "actual wages" of the senior management from the Chinese side are to be determined by the Chinese partner in consultation with its department-in-charge in accordance with the joint venture's internal wage system, wage standards, labor productivity, realized profits, other economic performance indicators, the average wage of staff and workers, and relevant state regulations. The difference between the "actual wages" and "nominal wages" is to be used for the supplemental social security, welfare benefits, and housing funds for the staff and workers from the Chinese side. In any event, directors appointed by the Chinese party who do not hold any real posts should not be paid wages. Besides, FIEs must report the total amount of wages, the average wage, and the incomes of senior management and directors to the Chinese partner's department-in-charge and the local labor-administration department for the record.

Additionally, FIEs and trade unions established therein or representatives of half of its workforce may negotiate over and sign collective contracts on such matters as the system of wage distribution, form of wage distribution, wage level and its rate of increase, insurance, welfare benefits, awards, overtime work, and overtime pay. In conducting collective bargaining, both parties should abide by the following principles:

1 Wage distribution should be based on the principles of distribution according to work and equal pay for equal work.
2 Wage level should be appropriately increased in accordance with the economic developments of the enterprise and of the locality.
3 The interests of both parties should be considered.
4 Neither party must adopt drastic measures during negotiation.

Social security and welfare benefits

The Labor Law provides that workers enjoy social security under the following situations: retirement; illness or injury; work-related disabilities or occupational diseases; unemployment; and childbirth. Likewise, the Rules on Labor Management in Foreign Investment Enterprises mandate that FIEs participate in old-age, unemployment, medical, work-related injury, maternity, and other insurance schemes in accordance with the relevant state regulations. Accordingly, FIEs must make social security payments in full and on time to social-security agencies in conformity with the standards prescribed by the state and local people's governments, and must establish the systems of "labor manuals" and "old-age insurance manuals" in which to record employees' length of service; wages; payment of premiums; and expenditures on old-age, unemployment, work-related-injury, and medical insurance.

Furthermore, if an FIE is dissolved pursuant to the relevant regulations, or the parties agree after consultation to terminate the labor contract, it must, in accordance with the relevant regulations of the local people's government, make a lump-sum payment to the social-security agency as living expenses and social security premiums on behalf of:

1   workers who have suffered work-related injuries or occupational diseases and have been certified by hospitals that they are undergoing medical treatment or convalescing;
2   post-treatment workers who are confirmed by the labor-appraisal committee to have fully or partially lost ability to work;
3   the pension-receiving dependents of workers who have died as a result of work-related injuries;
4   female workers who are pregnant, on maternity leave, or nursing babies; and
5   workers who are not covered by any type of social insurance.

The relevant regulations and rules on social security are the Regulations on Unemployment Insurance,[11] the Decision Regarding the Establishment of a Uniform System of Basic Old-Age Pensions for Enterprise Staff and Workers,[12] the Decision Concerning the Establishment of a Basic Medical Insurance System for Urban Staff and Workers,[13] the Regulations on Work-Related Injury Insurance,[14] and the Trial Measures on Maternity Insurance for Enterprise Staff and Workers.[15] In addition, the Circular on the Strengthening and Improvement of the Management of Foreign Investment Enterprises over the Drawing, Remittance, and Use of Funds Relating to Chinese Employees' Rights and Interests[16] further explains how FIEs should comply with the statutory provisions on social security and welfare benefits. Accordingly, the following highlights the respective premiums to be paid by the employer and the employee.

With respect to unemployment insurance, the premium paid by the employer is to be 2 percent of the total wages, while the premium paid by the employee is to be 1 percent of his or her wages. Nonetheless, subject to the approval of the State Council, the governments of provinces, autonomous regions, and municipalities directly under the central government may adjust these premiums in accordance with the number of unemployed workers and the balance in the unemployment insurance fund. As regards the old-age pension, the premium paid by the employer generally cannot exceed 20 percent of the total wages, but the specific rates are to be determined by the governments of provinces, autonomous regions, and municipalities directly under the central government. In 1997, the premium paid by the employee must be at least 4 percent of his or her wages. Starting from 1998, the contribution rate of the employee must be increased by at least 1 percent every two years. The ultimate rate is to be 8 percent.

With regard to medical insurance, the premium paid by the employer is to be about 6 percent of the total wages, while the premium paid by the employee is to be 2 percent of his or her wages. Nevertheless, these rates can be adjusted in accordance with economic development. As to worker compensation, the employee is not required to pay any insurance premium. The contribution rate of the employer is to be determined with reference to two factors: the "differential rate based on the risks of injury in a particular industry" (行业差别费率) and the "rate scale based on insurance claims and incidence of injuries within the industry" (行业内费率档次). Thus, the premium paid by the employer is equal to the contribution rate times the total wages. In respect of maternity insurance, the employee is not required to pay any premium, but the employer is to pay no more than 1 percent of the total wages. Since many FIEs have both Chinese and foreign employees, the "total wages" for social security purposes should be based on the total wages of Chinese employees.

Apart from social security, the staff and workers of FIEs are also entitled to receive welfare benefits pursuant to the relevant state regulations. Generally, FIEs are to draw an amount equal to 14 percent of the total wages as employee-welfare funds (职工福利费). These funds should be used for basic medical insurance, living allowance, child-care, transport, etc. Moreover, FIEs should draw an amount equal to 1.5 percent of the total wages for education and training. In the case of welfare benefits, the "total wages" should be the total wages of the entire body of staff and workers. Furthermore, FIEs are required to contribute to the housing accumulation fund (住房公积金) for their Chinese workers.

Maximum hours and overtime work

The Labor Law provides that workers must not work more than eight hours a day or 44 hours a week and must be guaranteed at least one day's rest per week. However, in 1995, the State Council adopted a five-day workweek.[17] Accordingly, workers generally may not work more than 40 hours a week and must be guaranteed at least two days' rest per week. Nonetheless, if an

FIE cannot implement this schedule due to production characteristics, it may adopt other measures for work and rest with the approval of the labor-administration department.

If an FIE has production and operations needs, it may consult the trade union and workers to extend the working hours. Generally, overtime work must not exceed one hour per day. However, when special circumstances render it necessary to do more overtime work, the FIE may request over-time work for a maximum of three hours per day or 36 hours per month. With respect to recompense, overtime work should be paid as follows: at least 150 percent of the normal-hour wages for work done after regular hours; at least 200 percent of the normal-hour wages for work done on rest days if the rest days cannot be rescheduled; and at least 300 percent of the normal-hour wages for work done during legal holidays. Nevertheless, the FIE may not arrange overtime work for female workers who are seven-months or more pregnant or who are nursing babies that are less than one year old.

Union representation

Although various statutes contain provisions on union representation, the Trade Union Law and the Labor Law together comprise the basic regulatory framework. That is, the Labor Law provides general guidance, while the Trade Union Law supplies the details. In particular, to meet the changing needs of a market economy, the Trade Union Law was revised in 2001. Therefore, this section highlights the important provisions of these two pieces of legislation.

The Labor Law provides that staff and workers have the right to organize and participate in trade unions. In addition, trade unions at various levels should protect the legal rights and interests of staff and workers and supervise employers in complying with labor laws and regulations. Furthermore, if any organization or individual has acted in violation of labor laws and regulations, the trade union has the right to report and file a charge against such illegal conduct.

Likewise, the Trade Union Law provides that while safeguarding the overall interests of all citizens, trade unions represent and protect the legal rights and interests of staff and workers. In an enterprise, institution, or government organ, a grassroots trade union should be established if there are 25 or more members. If there are fewer than 25 members, the members may elect an organizer to launch union activities, establish a grassroots trade union alone, or form a grassroots trade union jointly with the members of another work unit. A work unit (工作单位) is the enterprise, institution, or government organ to which an employee belongs. If the trade union of an enterprise or institution has 200 people or more, a full-time union chairperson may be appointed. Moreover, the number of full-time union personnel is to be determined by the trade union and the enterprise or institution through consultation. Indeed, the hiring unit must contribute an amount equal to 2 percent of its monthly total wages as union funds and provide the necessary material conditions, such as facilities and sites, for union work and activities.

Other than grassroots trade unions in individual enterprises, federations of grassroots trade unions may be formed in villages, townships, or urban streets where there are many enterprise staff and workers. Moreover, regional federations of trade unions are to be formed at the county level or above, while national or regional industrial trade unions may be formed for the same industry or similar industries. The establishment of a grassroots trade union, a regional federation of trade unions, or an industrial union must be approved by a trade union at the next higher level. All trade unions in China are under the unified leadership of the All China Federation of Trade Unions.

In terms of rights and responsibilities, the trade union represents staff and workers to conclude a collective labor contract with the enterprise or institution. The draft of a collective labor contract should be submitted to the congress of staff and workers (in a state-owned enterprise or collectively owned enterprise) or the entire body of staff and workers for adoption. If the enterprise or institution does not distribute wages, does not provide safe working conditions, extends working hours at will, infringes upon the special rights and interests of workers who are women or minors, etc., the trade union should represent staff and workers to negotiate with the enterprise or institution and request it to adopt measures to rectify the situation. Where there are incidents of stop-work or slow-down, the trade union should reflect the views and requests of staff and workers and suggest solutions such that production can quickly be resumed.

Furthermore, when the trade union discovers any working conditions that jeopardize the life and safety of staff and workers, it has the right to propose that staff and workers be evacuated from the dangerous site, and the enterprise must make a prompt decision. Indeed, when the enterprise or institution considers such important issues as operations, management, and development, it should solicit the views of the trade union. Similarly, when the enterprise or institution holds meetings to discuss issues relating to the immediate interests of staff and workers, such as wages, welfare, labor protection, and social security, it must invite union representatives to attend.

Where the enterprise unilaterally terminates a labor contract, it should inform the trade union of the reason(s) in advance. If the trade union thinks that the termination has violated the law or breached the labor contract, it has the right to request treatment of the case anew. If the trade union thinks that a disciplinary action is improper, it has the right to voice its opinions. When a staff or worker thinks that the enterprise infringes upon his or her labor rights and thus applies for arbitration or files a lawsuit, the trade union should provide support and assistance. In fact, if a worker's contract is terminated due to his or her participation in union activities, or union personnel has his or her contract terminated because of fulfilling union duties, the labor-administration department can order the enterprise to reinstate the worker and pay either the wages that the worker would have earned or a compensatory amount equal to twice the annual wages of the worker.

Occupational safety

An FIE must establish and strengthen a system of labor safety and health; strictly implement state regulations and standards on labor safety and health; educate workers on labor safety and health; prevent accidents at work; and reduce occupational hazards. Moreover, an FIE must provide its workers with safe and hygienic conditions as prescribed by the state and the necessary protective articles, as well as regularly check the health of workers who are engaged in work involving occupational hazards. Furthermore, workers have the right to refuse to carry out orders that violate safety rules and put them at risk, and to criticize, report, and file charges against conduct which jeopardizes their lives and safety.

Dispute resolution

Generally, when a labor dispute arises, the parties may request mediation by the labor-dispute mediation committee (劳动争议调解委员会), which is an organization established within the FIE and is composed of representatives of staff and workers, representatives of the enterprise, and trade unionists. If mediation fails, one party may seek arbitration from the labor-dispute arbitration committee (劳动争议仲裁委员会), which is composed of representatives of the labor-administration department, trade unionists at the same administrative level, and representatives of the FIE. Moreover, one party may directly request arbitration from the labor-dispute arbitration committee without going through mediation. In any case, the party seeking arbitration must submit a written application to the labor-dispute arbitration committee within 60 days of the occurrence of the dispute. If the arbitration award is not acceptable, the parties may file a lawsuit in the people's court within 15 days of its receipt.

With respect to a collective labor contract, if the dispute arises out of its formation, the parties may resolve it through mutual consultation. If consultation fails, the local labor-administration department may coordinate the discussions between the relevant parties to resolve the dispute. Similarly, if the labor dispute arises out of the performance of a collective labor contract, the parties may resolve it through consultation. If consultation fails, the parties may submit the dispute to arbitration. If the arbitration award is not acceptable, the parties may file a lawsuit within 15 days of its receipt.

Termination

A labor contract will be terminated upon the expiration of its term or when one of the conditions for termination has arisen. Alternatively, the parties may agree after consultation to terminate the labor contract.

As the employer, an FIE may terminate a labor contract if:

1   the worker is found to be unqualified during the probationary period;
2   the worker has seriously violated labor discipline or the work rules;
3   the worker has committed a serious dereliction of duty or has engaged in misconduct for personal gains, thereby gravely impairing the interests of the enterprise; or
4   the worker has been pursued with criminal liability.

Moreover, the Labor Law provides that a hiring unit may terminate a labor contract if it has sent a written notice to the staff or worker 30 days in advance and under one of the following circumstances:

1   the worker has been ill or has suffered non-work-related injury and cannot resume his or her original duty or perform other work arranged by the hiring unit;
2   the worker is not qualified after receiving training or despite a change of post; or
3   significant changes in objective circumstances have rendered the performance of the labor contract impossible and the parties cannot reach an agreement to modify the contract.

Under the same circumstances, the Rules on Labor Management in Foreign Investment Enterprises require the FIE to solicit the opinion of the trade union in addition to the 30-day notice. Thus, if the rules are repealed as recommended, prior consultation with the trade union will not be required.

Aside from these circumstances, an FIE may lay off workers during the period of reorganization pending bankruptcy or when serious difficulties arise in production and operations. In that case, the FIE must give a 30-day advance notice to the trade union or the entire workforce, listen to the views of the trade union or workers, and report to the labor-administration department. If the FIE wants to hire workers in the following six months, it must first employ those who have been laid off.

Nonetheless, an FIE may not terminate a labor contract under the aforementioned circumstances by giving a 30-day advance notice, during the reorganization period, or when facing production or operations difficulties if:

1   a worker has been confirmed to have lost entirely or partly the ability to work due to occupational disease or work injury;

2   a worker is being treated for illness or injury;
3   a worker is pregnant, on maternity leave, or is nursing baby; or
4   other circumstances as prescribed by law or administrative regulations
    have arisen.

On the other hand, a worker may terminate the labor contract by giving the FIE a 30-day advance notice. Moreover, a worker may terminate the labor contract at any time during the probationary period; if the enterprise uses violence, threats, or illegal restraint of freedom to force labor; or the enterprise does not pay remuneration or provide working conditions in accordance with the contract. Indeed, the Rules on Labor Management in Foreign Investment Enterprises also contain a catchall provision, that is, a worker may terminate the labor contract if the enterprise has violated laws or administrative regulations, thus infringing the worker's legal rights and interests.

Severance pay

The Labor Law provides that if the hiring unit terminates a labor contract by mutual agreement; due to inability to resume duty, disqualification after training or change of post, or significant changes in objective circumstances; during the reorganization period; or when experiencing production or operations difficulties, it is required to pay the employee economic compensation. Likewise, the Rules on Labor Management in Foreign Investment Enterprises provide that an FIE must pay a lump-sum living allowance to a worker whose labor contract is terminated by mutual agreement; because he or she cannot resume duties after an illness or non-work-related injury; because he or she is unqualified for the job after training or change of post; or because changes in objective circumstances have rendered the performance of the labor contract impossible. In the case of inability to resume duties after an illness or non-work-related injury, the FIE must also pay a medical allowance.

According to the Measures on Economic Compensation for Breach and Termination of Labor Contracts,[18] if a labor contract is terminated by mutual agreement, the hiring unit should pay the worker one month's wages for each year of service, but not exceeding 12 months. In most instances, "one month's wages" refers to the average monthly wage of the worker during the 12 months prior to termination. Moreover, if a labor contract is terminated due to the worker's inability to resume duties or perform other work after an illness or non-work-related injury, the hiring unit should pay one month's wages for each year of service and a minimum of six months' wages as medical allowance. If the worker is seriously ill or has a terminal disease, the hiring unit should pay an additional amount of allowance, that is, at least 50 percent (for serious illness) or at least 100 percent (for terminal disease) of the medical allowance. These provisions are slightly different from those of the Rules on Labor Management in Foreign Investment Enterprises, because the latter provides that a medical allowance equivalent to three months' actual wages will be paid if the employee has served for less than five years, but six months' wages will be paid if the employee has served for five years or more. In addition, the average monthly actual wage for the six months prior to the termination of the labor contract is to be used as the basis for calculating living and medical allowances.

Furthermore, the Measures on Economic Compensation for Breach and Termination of Labor Contracts provide that if a labor contract is terminated due to disqualification, the hiring unit should pay the worker one month's wages for each year of service, but not exceeding 12 months. Similarly, if a labor contract is terminated due to significant changes in objective circumstances, during the reorganization period, or when the hiring unit experiences serious difficulties in production and operations, the hiring unit should pay the worker one month's wages for each year of service. In any event, if the hiring unit fails to pay economic compensation after a labor contract is terminated, it will have to pay an additional amount of 50 percent of the required compensation.

Foreign experts

As stated in the Measures on the Administration of Foreign Experts in Foreign Investment Enterprises,[19] foreign experts are foreign professionals, technical staff, and managerial personnel who are hired by FIEs to engage in production, operations, and administration. To qualify as a foreign expert, the foreigner must engage in the kind of job that is commensurate with his or her specialty and skills and meet the following requirements:

1   To possess at least a bachelor degree or the professional title of engineer, or have an equivalent degree or title.
2   To have five or more years of work experience in his or her specialty, being able to give technical guidance, and being qualified for the job.
3   To possess the expertise or special skills urgently needed by China or any other vocational specialties.
4   To have five or more years of managerial experience overseas and hold the position of a departmental manager or its equivalent in a large or medium-sized FIE or in a high-technology or new-technology enterprise.

If an FIE wants to employ a foreign technical or managerial employee, it should first have the prospective employee certified as a foreign expert because the Document Affirming the Employment of a Foreign Expert (聘请外国专家确认件) is necessary for obtaining a work visa. To obtain such certification, the FIE must submit to the foreign-expert-certifying organ the notice of appointment, documentation of medical check-up, certificate(s) of no criminal record, and proof of having met the four requirements above.

Having obtained the Document Affirming the Employment of a Foreign Expert, the FIE must then ask an authorized unit inside China to send an invitation letter (or telegram) to the prospective employee. With the Document Affirming the Employment of a Foreign Expert, the invitation letter (or telegram), and a valid passport or travel document, the prospective employee may then go to a Chinese diplomatic mission or consulate office abroad to apply for a work visa.

In applying for the Document Affirming the Employment of a Foreign Expert, the FIE may simultaneously apply for a Foreign Expert Certificate (外国专家证明书) for the prospective employee. The Foreign Expert Certificate entitles the prospective employee to preferential treatment by the Chinese Customs. Within 15 days of entering China, the foreign expert must, with the notice of appointment and a valid passport or travel document, obtain a Foreign Expert Card (外国专家证) from the foreign-expert-certifying organ. With the Foreign Expert Card and relevant documentation, the foreign expert must, within 30 days of arrival in China, go to the local public-security department to obtain a Foreigner-Resident Card (外国人居留证) or a temporary Foreigner-Resident Card. Since the validity of the Foreign Expert Card cannot exceed one year, the foreign expert must apply for an extension upon the completion of one year's service. Failure to do so will result in the automatic invalidation of the Foreign Expert Card.

Foreign workers

According to the Rules on the Administration of the Employment of Foreigners in China,[20] when an FIE wants to employ a foreigner, it must apply for a Foreigner Employment Permit (外国人就业许可证) and show that no qualified candidates in China can fill the post. However, foreigners who are hired to engage in cooperative or exchange projects in accordance with China's agreements with foreign governments or international organizations, or the chief representatives and representatives of the resident offices of foreign enterprises, are exempt from these requirements. In addition, a foreigner who wants to work in China must be at least 18 years old and healthy; possess the professional skills required by the job as well as relevant work experience; have no criminal record; have a definite employer; and hold a valid passport or travel document. To apply for a Foreigner Employment Permit, the FIE must go through the examination-and-approval formalities with the labor-administration department located in the province, autonomous region, or municipality directly under the central government or any authorized local labor-administration department. A designated permit-issuing organ will then decide whether or not to issue a Foreigner Employment Permit.

Having obtained the approval, the FIE should ask an authorized unit to send to the foreigner who is to be employed a notice of securing a visa and the Foreigner Employment Permit. Thereafter, the foreigner should submit the notice, Foreigner Employment Permit, and a valid travel document to a Chinese embassy or consulate to obtain a work visa. In the case of a representative of the resident office of a foreign enterprise, the foreigner needs to submit only the notice of securing a visa and the certificate of registration issued by the AIC. When entering China, the foreigner must hold a work visa, unless there is an agreement between China and his or her home country on mutual exemption of visas. After entry into China, the foreigner must obtain a Foreigner Employment Certificate (外国人就业证) and a Foreigner-Resident Card before he or she can work. That is, within 15 days of the foreigner's entry into China, the FIE must submit the Foreigner Employment Permit, the labor contract, and the foreigner's travel document to the original permit-issuing organ to obtain a Foreigner Employment Certificate and complete a Foreigner Employment Registration Form. The foreigner to whom a Foreigner Employment Certificate has been issued should, within 30 days of entering China, present the Foreigner Employment Certificate to the public-security department to apply for a Foreigner-Resident Card.

An FIE can sign a labor contract with a foreigner for a maximum term of five years. Within the 30 days prior to each full year of employment, the FIE must go to the permit-issuing organ to complete the annual check on behalf of the foreigner. Failure to do so will result in the automatic invalidation of the Foreigner Employment Certificate. To renew a labor contract, the FIE must apply to the labor-administration department for an extension within the 30 days prior to the expiration of the original labor contract. Upon termination of the labor contract, the FIE should report promptly to the labor-administration and public-security departments, return the Foreigner Employment Certificate and Foreigner-Resident Card, and go through the formalities for the departure of the foreigner worker.

Employee inventions

The governing rules on employee inventions are set forth in the Patent Law and the Detailed Regulations for the Implementation of the Patent Law. If an invention-creation is made in the execution of the tasks of the work unit to which the inventor belongs, or is completed mainly by using the material and technical conditions of the work unit, it will be deemed a service invention-creation (职务发明创作). The phrase "in the execution of the tasks of the work unit" refers to:

1   in the course of performing one's duties;
2   in the execution of any entrusted tasks other than one's own duties; or
3   within one year of one's resignation, retirement, or change of job, and relating to one's own duties and any other entrusted tasks.

In addition, the term "material and technical conditions" refers to the work unit's funds, facilities and equipment, spare parts, raw materials, or technical data not disclosed to the public.

If an invention-creation is a service invention-creation, the right to apply for a patent will belong to the work unit. However, if an invention-creation is made as a result of using the material and technical conditions of the work unit, the agreement between the work unit and the inventor or designer governing the right to apply for a patent or the patent right will be decisive. In other words, the employer and the employee may agree that an invention-creation made by using the material or technical conditions of the employer belongs to the employee. On the other hand, if an invention-creation is not a service invention-creation, the right to apply for a patent belongs to the inventor or designer.

The work unit that has been granted the patent right should compensate or reward the inventor or designer of a service invention-creation. Upon the exploitation of a patented invention-creation, the work unit should provide the inventor or designer with reasonable compensation in accordance with the extent of the patent's diffusion and application as well as the economic benefits derived. Specifically, within three months of the issue of a patent, the state-owned enterprise or institution should give the employee a monetary award, the amount of which cannot be less than RMB 2,000 (for an invention) or RMB 500 (for a utility model or design). If the invention-creation is made based on the proposal of the inventor or designer that has been adopted by the work unit, the state-owned enterprise or institution holding the patent should provide the employee with a monetary award in accordance with merit. After the patent has been put into practice and during the patent term, the state-owned enterprise or institution holding the patent right should pay the inventor or designer an annual sum of at least 2 percent (in the case of an invention or utility model) or 0.2 percent (in the case of a design) of any after-tax profits earned as a result of exploiting the invention-creation. Alternatively, the state-owned enterprise or institution may make a lump-sum payment calculated pursuant to the aforementioned percentage. If the state-owned enterprise or institution holding the patent authorizes others to exploit the patent, it should pay at least 10 percent of any after-tax licensing fees to the inventor or designer. Accordingly, remuneration is required when a patent is issued, when the employer exploits the patent, and when the patent is licensed out. Although the preceding guidelines are addressed to state-owned enterprises or institutions, the Detailed Regulations for the Implementation of the Patent Law state that other types of work units may refer to them in providing monetary awards or compensation.

Works for hire

The governing rules on works for hire are set forth in the Copyright Law and the Regulations for the Implementation of the Copyright Law. Generally, the author of a copyrightable work is the individual who creates it. However, if a work is created according to the intention and under the direction of a legal person or other organization, and the legal person or organization is responsible for the work, then the legal person or organization will be deemed its author. In addition, a work created in fulfillment of the work assignments given by a legal person or an organization is a service work (职务作品). The author of a service work enjoys the copyright, but the legal person or organization has the right of priority to use the work within its scope of business. Within two years of the submission of a service work, the employee cannot, without the consent of the work unit, allow a third party to use the service work in the same way as the work unit does. If the employee, with the consent of the work unit, permits a third party to use the service work in the same way as the work unit does, the remuneration received shall be divided between the employee and the work unit in accordance with an agreed-upon ratio.

With respect to two types of service works, however, the employee has only the right of attribution, while the other rights provided by the Copyright Law belong to the legal person or organization. The first type includes engineering designs, product designs, maps, computer software, etc. that are created mainly by using the material and technical conditions of the legal person or organization which bears responsibility for the works. The term "material and technical conditions" refers to funds, equipment, or data specially provided by the legal person or organization for the employee to complete the work. The second type consists of works, the copyright of which is to be owned by the legal person or organization pursuant to law, administrative regulation, or contractual stipulations. In either case, the legal person or organization may reward the employee for creating the work.

As to computer software developed by an employee during the employment period, the Regulations on the Protection of Computer Software provide that the copyright of the software belongs to the legal person or organization if the software is the outcome of a clearly defined development target in the course of work; a foreseen or natural outcome of engaging in work activities; or a product that is developed mainly by using the material and technical conditions of the legal person or organization, such as funds, special equipment, and specialized information not disclosed to the public, and for which the legal person or organization bears responsibility. In these cases, the legal person or organization may give the employee a reward.

3 Selected cases

Bao Zhenmin *v*. Thomson Golf (Shanghai) Ltd. *(1999)*
沪一中民终字第2469号, *Shanghai City No. 1 Intermediate People's Court, 28 December 1999*

Facts

On 12 May 1994, Bao Zhenmin (hereinafter BZ) and Thomson Group Jiadi (Shanghai) Real Estates Ltd. signed a labor contract for the period from then to 31 December 1996. BZ and Thomson Golf (Shanghai) Ltd. (hereinafter TGL) signed two labor contracts for the respective periods from 1 January 1997 to 31 December 1997 and from 1 January 1998 to 31 December 1998 as a driver for the general office. The wages stipulated in the two respective contracts were RMB 2,020 and 2,220. Article 5(5) of the second contract provided that the old-age pension, medical insurance, housing accumulation fund, and unemployment insurance for BZ would be handled by TGL in accordance with the relevant regulations of Shanghai. Moreover, article 8(2) relating to liability for breach of contract stated that if either party terminated the contract without informing the other in advance according to the relevant statutory provision, the breaching party would have to compensate the non-breaching party, and that the amount of damages would be equal to BZ's actual wages for the last two months.

On 27 August 1998, TGL orally dismissed BZ, who filled out a termination form on the same day. TGL signed the form and processed the case as if the termination were based on mutual agreement after consultation. From the next day, BZ stopped going to work. TGL paid BZ full wages on 5 September and 5 October 1998. On 5 November and 5 December 1998, TGL paid BZ RMB 325 of wages, after a total deduction of RMB 317 for contributions to old-age pension, housing accumulation fund, and medical insurance. From May 1994 to December 1998, TGL had paid, on behalf of BZ, RMB 20,922.58 short of the required old-age pension premiums, while BZ himself had also paid RMB 1,176 less than it should be. On 21 January 1999, BZ received a termination notice from TGL. During this time, both parties negotiated several times over the amount of compensation without avail. BZ applied for arbitration, but his stance was not supported. Thus, BZ filed a lawsuit with the Shanghai City Pudong New District People's Court.

At the court of first instance, BZ alleged that:

1 TGL should pay him one month's wages because TGL did not inform him in advance of the termination of the contract.
2 Since TGL breached the contract, it should give him two months' wages as damages for the breach and five months' wages as compensation as stipulated in the labor contract.
3 TGL should compensate him for his economic losses plus 25 percent for the delay in issuing the termination notice.
4 TGL had to make up for the deficient amount of old-age pension premium and contribution to housing accumulation fund.

TGL responded that on 1 September 1998, BZ resigned, and that when it accepted his resignation, the employment relationship was terminated. In fact, BZ had stopped going to work since then. In December 1998, TGL issued an employment termination notice, so the termination formalities were duly completed. Based on its annual wages review in April, TGL had paid BZ's old-age pension premiums. Hence, there was no deficiency in the amount of contribution.

The court of first instance found that TGL orally terminated the labor contract in advance and, on the same day, BZ completed all the necessary hand-over formalities. TGL wrote down the termination as a voluntary termination. TGL should provide BZ with compensation, promptly comply with the termination formalities, and issue a termination notice in conformity with the law. Legally, if TGL did not give BZ a 30-day advance termination notice, it should pay BZ one month's wages in lieu of notice. However, since the contract provided that two months' wages should be used as compensation, BZ's claim that TGL should give him another month's wages after the latter had paid him two months' wages was not supported. The law required that if both parties agreed to terminate the contract, the employer should pay the employee one month's wages for every full year of service, and, in the case of service for less than one year, pay the employee based on one year's service. BZ worked for TGL from 1 January 1997 to 27 August 1998, which was less than two years. Therefore, TGL should pay BZ two months' wages as compensation. Furthermore, since BZ received the termination notice on 21 January 1999, which made BZ unemployable before that date, TGL should pay BZ for his economic losses during that period, plus 25 percent as economic compensation. Nonetheless, TGL should also deduct any payments made to BZ during that period. In addition, both parties should pay BZ's old-age pension premiums according to the law. Any insufficient portion should be replenished. Since BZ could not substantiate his claim that TGL should also contribute to the housing accumulation fund, the court would not support it. According to articles 24, 26, 28, 73(3) and (4) of the Labor Law,[21] the court of first instance held that:

1   The labor contract between BZ and TGL was terminated as of 1 September 1998.
2   TGL should compensate BZ two months' wages in the amount of RMB 4,440 pursuant to the contract because TGL did not give BZ a 30-day advance termination notice.
3   TGL should give BZ RMB 4,440 as economic compensation for the termination of the contract.
4   TGL should compensate BZ a total amount of RMB 8,600, including RMB 6,880 for his economic losses resulting from the delay of the issue of the termination notice and RMB 1,720 (25 percent of RMB 6,880) as economic compensation.
5   Both parties had to make up for the unpaid pension premiums for the period of 1 January 1997 to 31 August 1998 according to state law.
6   TGL should compensate BZ the arbitration fee of RMB 200.

On appeal, TGL pleaded to affirm item 1 and annul items 2, 3, 4, 5 and 6 of the judgment for the following reasons:

1 Items 2, 3 and 4 had never been arbitrated. However, the court of first instance also tried and judged them, which violated procedural law.
2 The labor contract between BZ and TGL was terminated as of 1 September 1998, but TGL had already paid BZ one month's wages on 5 October 1998 in lieu of notice. Since there was no breach of contract, TGL should not be liable for any compensation.
3 The court of first instance incorrectly applied the law to order TGL to pay BZ economic compensation. Under the law, TGL should pay BZ only one month's wages as economic compensation.
4 The court of first instance held that the employment period between TGL and BZ was from 1 January 1997 to 27 August 1998, but the period for the deficiency in old-age pension premium ran from May 1994 to December 1998. In addition, TGL did not fail to pay in full the pension premiums during the employment period.

BZ responded that TGL's breach of contract resulted in the termination of the contract. Therefore, the ruling of the court of first instance was correct and pleaded that the court of second instance affirm the ruling.

Reasoning

The court of second instance found that the facts established at the court of first instance were correct. However, the term of the labor contract and the date when BZ filled out the termination form were incorrect. With respect to the former issue, the correct finding should be two separate labor contracts, running from 1 January 1997 to 31 December 1997 and from 1 January 1998 to 31 December 1998. Regarding the latter issue, the court found that BZ filled out the termination form on 1 September 1998. The labor contracts, the termination form, and the oral testimonies of the parties in court comprised the evidence for these facts. In addition, the court of second instance found that from January 1997 to August 1998, TGL and BZ had failed to pay old-age pension premiums in the amount of RMB 1,238.30 and RMB 552.90, which was verified by the Pudong New District Social Security Administration Center.

Moreover, the court found that on 27 August 1998, TGL orally dismissed BZ, who raised no objection. On 1 September 1998, BZ filled out a termination form, on which he specifically wrote down "the contract immediately terminated by the general manager." TGL did not request BZ to correct the statement, which confirmed TGL's acquiescence to such fact. Subsequently, TGL indicated on the termination notice "the contract terminated after consultation," which BZ did not affirm. Thus, TGL was deemed to have unilaterally terminated the labor contract, making the employment relationship end on 1 September 1998. Accordingly, the court of first instance correctly determined the termination date of the labor contract. However, the court did not think that the contract was terminated by mutual agreement and decided to rectify it. Because TGL terminated the labor contract without notifying BZ in advance, it should pay him one month's wages in lieu of notice. Moreover, the labor contract stipulated that if either party failed to give advance notice, the damages for the breach would be two months' actual wages. This agreement reflected the true intention of both parties and was not contrary to the law. The court of the first instance was correct in ordering TGL to compensate BZ two months' wages of RMB 4,440.

According to the Regulations of the Shanghai City on Labor and Personnel Administration in Foreign Investment Enterprises and the Measures on Economic Compensation for Breach and Termination of Labor Contracts,[22] TGL should provide BZ with a living allowance plus 50 percent. Since the employer should pay the employee one month's wages for every full year of service, and BZ had worked for less than two years, TGL should pay BZ one month's wages plus 50 percent, totaling RMB 3,330. As to the living allowance, employees who had worked for less than one year and those who had worked for one year were subject to two different standards of calculation. The standard adopted by the court of first instance was not applicable in this case; thus, its judgment was based on an erroneous standard. After terminating the contract, TGL failed to process the available-for-employment application for BZ in a timely manner, thus making it difficult for BZ to be employed, as well as negatively affecting his livelihood. Hence, TGL was responsible for BZ's economic loss, which should be calculated on the basis of BZ's monthly wages, but with the deduction of wages received by BZ on 5 November 1998 and 5 December 1998. Having made such a judgment, the court of first instance ordered TGL to pay an additional 25 percent as economic compensation, which had no legal basis and should be reversed. Nevertheless, it was not improper for the court of first instance to hold that TGL should make up for BZ's old-age pension premiums from 1 January 1997 to 31 August 1998 and be responsible for the arbitration fee. Furthermore, TGL alleged that items 2, 3 and 4 of the original judgment had never been arbitrated; thus the court of first instance had violated procedural law in judging them. The court rejected this argument because the court of first instance may try claims raised in the arbitration proceedings and claims raised before the court together if they are related.

Judgment

According to article 153(1) of the Civil Procedure Law,[23] the court held that:

1   Items 1, 2, 5, and 6 of the original judgment were affirmed.
2   Items 3 and 4 of the original judgment were amended.
3   TGL should pay BZ RMB 3,300 as living allowance.
4   TGL should pay BZ RMB 7,596 as economic compensation.

This judgment was final.

Beijing Wannianqing Diary Products Ltd. *v.* Lu Surui *(2001)* 一中民终字第3934号, *Beijing City No. 1 Intermediate People's Court, 21 November 2001*

Facts

In December 1994, Beijing Nanjiao Dairy Products Factory (hereinafter NJF) and Hong Kong Pacific Dairy Ltd. jointly established Beijing Wannianqing Dairy Products Ltd. (hereinafter WDL), an equity joint venture. Lu Surui (hereinafter LS) had worked for NJF since January 1982. On 1 June 1995, LS, together with all the workers of NJF, was transferred to work at WDL and signed a labor contract without a fixed term. On 1 April 2000, WDL, due to difficulties in business operations, could not maintain normal production and thus completely ceased production. On 22 December 2000, WDL, as a result of serious difficulties in production and operations, sent LS a termination notice, which was to be effective from 1 January 2001. On 29 December 2000, WDL issued a notice bearing the title of "The Compensation Standard with Respect to Termination of Labor Contracts" to the entire workforce and requested LS to discuss and confirm the amount of economic compensation. Subsequently, disputes arose between WDL and LS when they discussed economic compensation for termination of the labor contract. The parties could not reach an agreement. On 16 January 2001, WDL announced to all the workers its plan on economic compensation as a result of the termination of the labor contracts. LS disagreed with the plan and requested arbitration from the Labor-Dispute Arbitration Committee of the Beijing City Daxing County Labor Bureau (hereinafter DAC).

In March 2001, WDL filed a lawsuit with the Beijing City Daxing District People's Court, alleging that there was no legal basis for DAC to decide on the standard for calculating economic compensation, and to order WDL to pay LS her living expenses, three kinds of social security premiums, and additional compensation for the period from January to March 2001, that is, after the termination of the labor contract. Instead, WDL requested the court of first instance to use the average monthly wage in 2000, namely, RMB 530.16, as the standard to calculate economic compensation. Besides, WDL had already announced to LS the compensation plan, but since LS requested arbitration, the plan could not be realized. Thus, WDL had not violated the relevant provisions on economic compensation and objected to paying LS an additional amount of economic compensation. Furthermore, the contract between WDL and LS had already been terminated; therefore, WDL was not obligated to pay LS living expenses and the three kinds of social security premiums. In fact, since WDL had already paid LS one month's wages for its failure to notify her of the termination of the labor contract 30 days in advance, one month's living expenses should be deducted. To safeguard the interests of LS, WDL had already paid, on behalf of LS, the three kinds of social security premiums for January to June 2001 to the Beijing Daxing District Social Security Fund Administration Center (hereinafter FAC). Hence, LS should reimburse WDL.

On the other hand, LS pleaded that she originally was the employee of NJF, but that on 1 June 1995, she and all other workers of NJF were transferred to WDL and signed labor contracts without a fixed term. WDL ceased production in April 2000, but prior to then, WDL had engaged in normal production. On 22 December 2000, WDL suddenly announced the terminatation of the labor contract, but did not pay economic compensation. LS maintained that she was satisfied with the arbitration award rendered by DAC, and requested that WDL continuously pay her living expenses and social security premiums, compensate her RMB 60,000 for the loss of employment and RMB 20,000 for mental distress, and make contributions to the housing accumulation fund.

The court of first instance held that the labor contract signed between WDL and LS was legally valid. After the contract was signed, both parties should have performed their respective obligations in according with its terms. Having experienced difficulties in production and operations, WDL unilaterally terminated the labor contract with LS. To comply with relevant regulations, WDL should use the average monthly wages for the 12 months prior to the cessation of production to pay LS economic compensation. Since WDL did not compensate LS upon the termination of the labor contract, WDL violated the Measures on Economic Compensation for Breach and Termination of Labor Contracts. Accordingly, WDL should bear civil liability and pay LS an additional 50 percent of economic compensation for the termination of the labor contract.

Moreover, after the contract was terminated, the parties could not reach an agreement. As a result, the dossier of LS could not be transferred on time, and LS could not receive unemployment compensation. Both parties should bear their respective civil liabilities. WDL should pay, on behalf of LS, old-age pension premiums, unemployment insurance, and contributions to the socially pooled fund for serious-illness, as well as providing her with the basic living expenses for the period of January to March 2001. LS should also pay her required portions of the three kinds of social security premiums. However, LS should pay WDL back the premiums paid for the three kinds of social security for the period of April to June 2001. The reasons for WDL's request to have LS pay back all of its expenditure on the three kinds of social security and its refusal to pay LS the basic living expenses were insufficient and untenable. Similarly, the claim of LS that WDL should contribute to the housing accumulation fund was beyond the scope of labor-dispute resolution and thus should be handled separately. Furthermore, the request of LS that WDL compensate her RMB 60,000 for economic losses and RMB 20,000 for mental distress had no legal basis. Accordingly, the court of first instance held as follows:

1 Within 10 days of the effective date of this judgment, WDL had to pay LS RMB 20,554.20 as economic compensation for the termination of the labor contract, RMB 10,277.10 as additional economic compensation, and RMB 888 as living expenses for the period from January to March 2001.

2 Within 10 days of the effective date of this judgment, WDL had to pay LS the annual vacation pay of RMB 1,075.53 and the single-child fee of RMB 20 for the period from September to December 2000.

3 Within 10 days of the effective date of this judgment, LS had to pay back WDL RMB 748.65 for her individual portions of old-age pension premium, unemployment insurance, and contribution to the socially pooled fund for serious-illness that WDL had already paid on her behalf for the period from January to March 2001 and for the total amount of premiums paid for the period from April to June 2001.

4 LS's requests that WDL compensate her RMB 60,000 for economic losses and RMB 20,000 for mental distress as well as make contributions to the housing accumulation fund were dismissed.

WDL and LS were not satisfied with the judgment. WDL alleged that the facts established by the court of first instance were erroneous, that there was no legal basis for the court to use the average monthly wage as the standard for calculating economic compensation, and that it should not pay any additional compensation. WDL appealed to have the original judgment dismissed. LS claimed that it was illegal for WDL to unilaterally amend the labor contract by canceling the provisions regarding the housing accumulation fund. LS requested that WDL, based on the average monthly wage of the members of staff and workers of WDL, compensate her RMB 20,000 for economic losses. In addition, LS demanded that WDL pay her RMB 60,000 for her losses due to her diminished capacity to seek employment, social security premiums until she retired, a settlement allowance of RMB 60,000, and RMB 20,000 for the housing accumulation fund, and make up for her living expenses, the single-child fee, and social security premiums for the period of January 2001 until the conclusion of this case.

On appeal, the court found that during the arbitration, WDL paid LS RMB 296 as living expenses for December 2000, when LS waited for assignment, and RMB 412 for its failure to give LS a 30-day advance notice of the termination of the labor contract. In addition, the average monthly wage of WDL for April 1999 to March 2000 was RMB 1,081.80. LS had worked at WDL for 19 years, and her average monthly wage for the 12 months prior to the termination of the labor contract was RMB 545.29. WDL had already paid the three kinds of social security premiums for LS until June 2001. Furthermore, since disputes arose between the parties over the labor contract, WDL had not yet been able to transfer the dossier of LS. These facts were supported by such evidence as the statements of both parties; the labor contract; the articles of association of WDL; the wage ledgers of WDL; the name list of staff and workers and the table regarding their length of service; the detailed reports on old-age pension premium, unemployment insurance and contribution to the socially pooled fund for serous-illness; the receipt issued by the collecting bank entrusted by FAC; the resolutions of the board of directors of WDL; the notices regarding the termination of the labor contracts; and the relevant materials on which the arbitration award was based. Meanwhile, LS indicated her willingness to accept the original judgment and requested that her appeal be withdrawn.

Reasoning

The court reasoned that the termination of a labor contract should conform with the law. Since WDL unilaterally terminated labor contracts due to difficulties in production and operations, it should notify the workers 30 days in advance, as required by the Labor Law. In addition, WDL should use the average monthly wage for the 12 months prior to the cessation of production as the standard to calculate economic compensation. After the termination of the labor contract, WDL did not pay LS economic compensation in accordance with the prescribed standard. Thus, WDL had violated the Measures on Economic Compensation for Breach and Termination of Labor Contracts, and should pay an additional 50 percent in addition to the required economic compensation. Moreover, WDL terminated the labor contract, but did not notify LS 30 days in advance. After the termination, the parties could not reach an agreement. Consequently, the dossier of LS could not be transferred on time, and LS could not receive unemployment compensation. It was correct for the court of first instance to conclude that both parties were responsible.

WDL claimed that after its establishment, it could not maintain normal production; thus, the court of first instance erred in affirming that WDL should use the average monthly wage as the standard to calculate economic compensation. WDL asserted that the standard for calculation should also include the living expenses of the workers who were waiting to be given assignments. Nonetheless, the court maintained that WDL's argument lacked both factual and legal grounds. With respect to WDL's claim that since the labor contract was terminated in January 2001, there was no legal basis for the court of first instance to order it to contribute, on behalf of LS, to old-age pension, unemployment insurance, and the socially pooled fund for serious-illness, and to pay LS basic living expenses, the court reasoned that it was not improper for the court of first instance to give such a judgment, considering the facts that WDL had already paid, on behalf of LS, part of her social security premiums, and that the parties did not agree about the termination of the labor contract.

Judgment

In conclusion, the reasons submitted by WDL for amending the original judgment were untenable; thus, WDL's requests were not granted. During the trial, LS indicated her willingness to accept the original judgment and requested that her appeal be withdrawn. The court granted her request because it conformed with the law. Based on the aforementioned and article 153(1)(i) of the Civil Procedure Law,[24] the court held that the appeal was dismissed and the original judgment was affirmed.

This judgment was final.

Further reading

Lo, Vai Io, "Employee Inventions and Works for Hire in Japan: A Comparative Study against the U.S., Chinese, and German Systems," *Temple International and Comparative Law Journal* 16, 2002, 279–323.

Lo, Vai Io, "Labor and Employment in the People's Republic of China: From a Nonmarket-Driven to a Market-Driven Economy," *Indiana International and Comparative Law Review* 6, 1996, 337–410.

Notes

1 The Trade Union Law of the People's Republic of China, adopted at the 5th Session of the 7th National People's Congress on 3 April 1992 and amended at the 24th Session of the Standing Committee of the 9th National People's Congress on 27 October 2001.

2 The Labor Law of the People's Republic of China, adopted at the 8th Session of the Standing Committee of the 8th National People's Congress on 5 July 1994.

3 The Rules on Labor Management in Foreign Investment Enterprises, promulgated by the Ministry of Labor and the Ministry of Foreign Trade and Economic Cooperation on 11 August 1994.

4 It has been reported that 70 percent of all FIEs in Shantou and 90 percent of all FIEs in Zhuhai had not concluded labor contracts with their workers. See "'Massive Survey' Accuses Foreign Firms of 'Wantonly' Abusing Workers," BBC Summary of World Broadcasts, 2 March 1994, Part 3: Asia-Pacific. Available on LexisNexis: News and Business, News, All (accessed 18 October 2003).

5 For example, in Qinhuangdao, 12 workers in a Sino-foreign equity joint venture were poisoned the first day the plant started operations. In Tianjin, 30 female workers of an FIE lived in a room of 20m^2 in which there were no beds. All the windows in the workshop were sealed, and the window glass was painted over. "'Massive Survey' Accuses Foreign Firms of 'Wantonly' Abusing Workers," BBC Summary of World Broadcasts, 2 March 1994, Part 3: Asia-Pacific. Available on LexisNexis: News and Business, News, All (accessed 18 October 2003).

6 Crothall, Geoffrey "Strikes Prompt Call to Unionize; Call to Unionize Strike-Plagued Foreign Enterprises," South China Morning Post, 22 February 1994, News, p. 1. Available on LexisNexis: News and Business, News, All (accessed 18 October 2003).

 7 For example, workers were beaten for producing poor-quality goods, fired for dozing on the job during long working hours, fined for chewing gum, and locked up in a doghouse for stealing. Tefft, Sheila, "Growing Labor Unrest Roils Foreign Businesses in China," Christian Science Monitor, 22 December 1993, World, p. 1. Available on LexisNexis: News and Business, News, All (accessed 18 October 2003).
 8 See the Notice Regarding the Further Enhancement of the Clean-Up Work of Local Regulations, Local Government Rules and Other Policies and Measures on Labor Protection so as to Meet the Needs Arising from the WTO Accession, promulgated by the Ministry of Labor and Social Security on 4 January 2002.
 9 See art. 11 of the Provisional Regulations on the Administration of Resident Representative Offices of Foreign Enterprises.
10 The Provisional Measures on the Administration of Wage Incomes in Foreign Investment Enterprises, promulgated by the Ministry of Labor on 14 February 1997; the Several Opinions on the "Collective Consultation" of Wages in Foreign Investment Enterprises, promulgated by the Ministry of Labor on 14 February 1997.
11 The Regulations on Unemployment Insurance, promulgated by the State Council on 22 January 1999.
12 The Decision Regarding the Establishment of a Uniform System of Basic Old-Age Pensions for Enterprise Staff and Workers, promulgated by the State Council on 16 July 1997.
13 The Decision Concerning the Establishment of a Basic Medical Insurance System for Urban Staff and Workers, promulgated by the State Council on 14 December 1998.
14 The Regulations on Work-Related Injury Insurance, promulgated by the State Council on 27 April 2003.
15 The Trial Measures on Maternity Insurance for Enterprise Staff and Workers, promulgated by the Ministry of Labor on 14 December 1994.
16 The Circular on the Strengthening and Improvement of the Management of Foreign Investment Enterprises over the Drawing, Remittance, and Use of Funds Relating to Chinese Employees' Rights and Interests, promulgated by the Ministry of Finance and the Ministry of Labor and Social Security on 28 December 1999.
17 See the Regulations on Working Hours for Workers, promulgated by the State Council on 25 March 1995.
18 The Measures on Economic Compensation for Breach and Termination of Labor Contracts, promulgated by the Ministry of Labor on 3 December 1994.
19 The Measures on the Administration of Foreign Experts in Foreign Investment Enterprises, promulgated by the State Bureau of Foreign Experts Affairs on 1 September 1996.
20 The Rules on the Administration of the Employment of Foreigners in China, promulgated by the Ministry of Labor, Ministry of Public Security, Ministry of Foreign Affairs, and Ministry of Foreign Trade and Economic Cooperation on 22 January 1996. This set of rules does not apply to the employment of residents from Taiwan, Hong Kong, and Macao.
21 Article 24 of the Labor Law provides that the parties may agree to terminate the labor contract after consultation. Article 26 provides that a hiring unit may terminate a labor contract if it has sent a written notice to the worker 30 days in

advance; and if the worker who has been ill or has suffered a non-work-related injury cannot resume his or her original duty or perform other work arranged by the hiring unit; if the worker is not qualified after receiving training or despite a change of post; or if significant changes in objective circumstances have rendered the performance of the labor contract impossible and the parties cannot reach an agreement to modify the contract. Article 28 provides that if the hiring unit terminates a labor contract by mutual agreement; due to inability to resume duty, disqualification after training or change of post, or significant changes in objective circumstances; during the re-organization period; or when experiencing production or operations difficulties, it is required to pay the employee economic compensation. Article 73(3) and (4) provides that the worker is entitled to enjoy social security in the case of work-related injury or occupational disease as well as unemployment.

22 Article 5 of the Measures on Economic Compensation for Breach and Termination of Labor Contracts provides that if the hiring unit terminates a labor contract, it will have to pay one month's wages for every full year of service as economic compensation, but not exceeding 12 months. If the employee has worked for less than one year, the hiring unit should pay economic compensation based on one year's service. In addition, art. 10 of the Measures on Economic Compensation for Breach and Termination of Labor Contracts provides that if the hiring unit does not pay economic compensation after a labor contract is terminated, it will have to pay an additional amount of 50 percent of the required compensation. On the other hand, art. 18 of the Regulations of the Shanghai City on Labor and Personnel Administration in Foreign Investment Enterprises provides that if the employee has worked for less than one year, he or she should be given half a month's actual wages as living allowance, and that if the employee has worked for one year or more, the FIE should give one month's actual wages for every full year of service, but not exceeding 12 months. The Standing Committee of the Shanghai City People's Congress repealed this set of regulations on 24 September 2002.

23 Article 153(1) of the Civil Procedure Law provides that the court of second instance should: (i) dismiss the appeal and affirm the judgment of the court of first instance if the original judgment is based on clearly established facts and correct application of law; (ii) amend the judgment if the original judgment is based on incorrect application of law; (iii) remand the case for retrial or amend the original judgment if the original judgment is based on erroneous or unclear facts or insufficient evidence; and (iv) remand the case for retrial if the original judgment is made in violation of procedural rules, which may affect the court in rendering a correct judgment.

24 Article 153(1)(i) of the Civil Procedure Law provides that the court of second instance should dismiss the appeal and affirm the judgment of the court of first instance if the original judgment is based on clearly established facts and correct application of law.

7 Consumer protection

Consumers, the ultimate buyers and users of products and services, make purchase decisions based on whatever information is available. If manufacturers, wholesalers, or retailers commit fraud or misrepresentation, consumers will not be able to make rational choices, which will affect the normal functioning of market forces. Similarly, if unscrupulous manufacturers distribute defective or unsafe products, consumers may sustain financial losses and/or physical injuries a result of using such products. Hence, consumer protection is of paramount importance in market-driven economies.

To protect Chinese consumers and to ensure the normal functioning of market forces, China has enacted various statutes to shield consumers from dishonest and unscrupulous business practices. With China's accession to the WTO, an increasing number of products and services will be at the disposal of Chinese consumers, who, in turn, will be exposed to more financial and health risks. To safeguard product quality, China has recently implemented a compulsory system of certification for such types of products as home appliances, automobiles, and medical equipment, and local AICs periodically conduct random inspection of products. To facilitate the reporting of violation of consumer rights, the State Administration for Industry and Commerce has set up the hotline 12315 for consumers to file complaints nationwide. Considering the importance of consumer protection, this chapter aims to provide a basic legal framework of product liability, advertising, direct/pyramid selling, and Internet sales in China.

1 Product liability

In China, a number of statutes contain provisions on product liability. For instance, article 122 of the General Principles of Civil Law provides that if a substandard-quality product causes property damage or physical injury to a person, the manufacturer or seller will be civilly liable, but that if a carrier or warehouse operator causes the defect, the manufacturer or seller may seek indemnification. The two major laws on product liability are the Product Quality Law[1] and the Law on the Protection of the Rights and

Interests of Consumers.² Accordingly, the following discussion will highlight the important provisions of these two laws.

The Product Quality Law

The Product Quality Law is applicable to manufacturers or sellers of products within the Chinese territory. "Products" refers to goods processed or manufactured for the purpose of sale. In general, industrial products that may jeopardize human health or life or the safety of property must conform to the relevant state or trade standards, or in the absence of such standards, meet the requirements for safeguarding human health or life and the security of property. Moreover, it is illegal for manufacturers or sellers to counterfeit quality marks (such as certification marks), misrepresent the place of production, falsely use the names and addresses of other factories, sell products that have been eliminated by the state, adulterate products by mixing impure or false ingredients, pass off fake products as genuine ones, or pass off inferior or substandard products as quality or standard ones. Furthermore, consumers have the right to make inquiries to manufacturers and sellers concerning the quality of their products and to file complaints with the government department supervising product quality, the AIC, or other relevant departments. Social organizations that are responsible for consumer protection may, based on consumer reports about product-quality problems, suggest to the relevant departments that they handle the cases, as well as support consumers in lawsuits for damages caused by product-quality problems.

More specifically, manufacturers must ensure that their products:

1   are free from unreasonable dangers jeopardizing the safety of human life or property as well as conforming to the relevant state or trade standards safeguarding human health or life and the safety of property;
2   possess the functions that they ought to possess, except for those with explanations regarding functional defects; and
3   conform to the adopted quality standards as shown on the products or their packaging or as indicated through product descriptions, samples, etc.

Apart from the requirement that all indications on a product or its packaging must be true, the following items must be included:

1   certification that the product has passed quality inspection;
2   the name of the product as well as the name and address of the manufacturing plant written in Chinese;
3   the specifications, grade, main ingredients and their quantities of the product written in Chinese in conformity with the characteristics and

usage of the product; and if consumers must be notified beforehand, such information must be indicated on the outer package or otherwise provided to consumers in advance;

4   the production date and the safe-use period or expiration date of the product clearly indicated at a conspicuous place if the product must be used within a certain period of time; and

5   warning signs or warning explanations in Chinese for the product which, if is misused, may easily cause damage to itself or endanger the safety of human life or property.

Even so, unpackaged food products or other unpackaged goods that are difficult to contain indications due to their characteristics are exempt from these requirements.

Where products are dangerous (namely, fragile, combustible, explosive, poisonous, corrosive, or radioactive), must be kept upright during storage or transportation, or require special handling procedures, manufacturers must provide warning signs or warning explanations written in Chinese in accordance with state regulations on storage and transportation. Furthermore, manufacturers are liable for defective products that cause personal injury or property damage other than the product sold. A "defect" refers to any unreasonable danger existing in a product that jeopardizes the safety of human life or the property of another, or, where there are state or trade standards safeguarding human health or life or the safety of property, failure to conform to such standards. Nonetheless, the manufacturer of a defective product will not be liable if it can prove the existence of one of the following circumstances:

1   the product has not been put in circulation;
2   the defect in the product did not exist when the product was put in circulation; or
3   the state of science and technology at the time when the product was put in circulation was incapable of detecting the defect.

Likewise, sellers should establish an inspection system when replenishing their stock and adopt measures to maintain the quality of the products they sell. Sellers must not sell products that the state has ordered be discontinued, products that have lost their effect, or deteriorated products. Under any of the following circumstances, the seller is liable to repair, replace, or refund the price of the product, or pay damages if the product has caused loss to the consumer:

1   the product does not function as it ought to function, and no prior explanation has been given;
2   the product does not conform to the quality standards as indicated on the product or its packaging; or

3 the product does not conform to the standards as indicated through the product literature, samples, etc.

Having borne liability, the seller may seek indemnity from its supplier (the seller from whom it has bought the product) or the manufacturer if the supplier or the manufacturer is responsible, unless otherwise provided by the parties through agreement. Where a product defect is the seller's fault, the seller will be liable for personal injury or property damage. Where the seller does not cause the defect but cannot identify the manufacturer or the supplier of the product, it will still be liable for compensation.

If a defective product causes personal injury or property damage, the victim may claim compensation from the manufacturer or the seller. If the manufacturer is responsible and the seller has provided compensation, the seller will have the right to seek indemnity from the manufacturer. If the seller is responsible for the defect and the manufacturer has paid compensation, the manufacturer will have the right to seek indemnity from the seller. In the case of personal injury, the infringer is liable for medical expenses, nursing expenses during the treatment period, reduced earnings due to loss of work, etc. If the victim is disabled, the manufacturer or seller will be liable for expenses on self-help apparatus, a subsistence allowance, compensation for deformity, the necessary living expenses for his or her dependents, etc. In the case of death, the infringer is liable for funeral expenses, compensation for death, the necessary living expenses of the victim's surviving dependents, etc. In the case of property damage, the infringer is liable for restoring the damaged property to its original state or paying compensation at market value. Where the victim sustains other serious losses, the infringer will also be liable for compensation.

When a civil dispute over product quality arises, the parties may seek a settlement through consultation or mediation. If the parties are unwilling to resort to consultation or mediation, or if consultation or mediation proves unsuccessful, they should apply for arbitration provided that they have an arbitration agreement. If the parties fail to reach an arbitration agreement, or the arbitration agreement is invalid, they may directly file a lawsuit. The time limit for filing a lawsuit based on product defect is two years, starting from the date when the party concerned knew or should have known of the infringement of its rights and interests. The right to seek compensation arising from the use of defective product is forfeited 10 years from the date when the defective product was delivered to the first consumer, unless the clearly indicated safe-use period has not yet expired.

The Law on the Protection of the Rights and Interests of Consumers

The Law on the Protection of the Rights and Interests of Consumers is a basic law specifically designed to protect the legitimate rights and interests of consumers. Consumers are defined as those who buy or use commodities for the purpose of consumption or those who receive services. This law applies to business operators (经营者), who are defined as those who manufacture or sell commodities to consumers or those who provide services. Moreover, this law provides for the establishment of the Consumers Association, which is to furnish information and consultation, assist administrative agencies in their supervision and inspection of commodities and services, handle consumer complaints and conduct investigations into and mediation of such complaints, assist consumers in litigation, reveal and criticize behavior impairing the rights and interests of consumers through mass media, etc. Compared with the Product Quality Law, this law provides a broader scope of protection in two respects: first, service providers, not only manufacturers or sellers of merchandise, are covered; and, second, the rights and interests of consumers in general, not just protection against defective products, are taken into account. Accordingly, the following discussion will not only focus on product (service) liability, but also touch upon other types of consumer protection.

As a rule, consumers are entitled to request business operators to provide commodities and services that safeguard personal safety and the safety of property. Thus, consumers have the right to receive compensation for personal injury or property damage sustained as a result of the use of commodities or the reception of services. Moreover, consumers are entitled to have accurate information about the merchandise they buy or the services they receive. In particular, consumers have the right to request that business operators provide such information as the price, place of origin, manufacturer, usage, functions, specifications, grade, main ingredients, date of production, date of expiration, certificate of inspection, user's manual, and after-sale services of a commodity, or the contents, specifications, and fees of a service. Furthermore, consumers have the right to report or file charges against conduct that infringes upon their rights and interests and the unlawful or derelict acts of government organs or officials in the course of protecting their rights and interests.

Specifically, business operators have various obligations. First of all, the merchandise or services must comply with the requirements of the Product Quality Law and other relevant laws and regulations, unless otherwise agreed between the consumer and business operator. Moreover, business operators should guarantee that the merchandise or services furnished meet the standards safeguarding the person and property of consumers, and in the case of merchandise or services that may jeopardize human life or the safety of property, provide true explanations or clear warnings, as well as indicating the proper ways to use the merchandise or services and the methods to prevent the occurrence of risks. If a business operator discovers that its commodity or service has a serious defect, which, despite being used properly, may still jeopardize human life or the safety of property, it should promptly report to the relevant authorities, notify consumers, and adopt preventive measures.

With respect to inquiries from consumers regarding the quality and operating instructions of commodities and services, business operators must provide true and clear answers. Business operators, including those who lease counters and sites, must indicate clearly their true names and marks, and must not engage in false advertising to mislead consumers. Indeed, business operators are to issue purchase receipts or service bills to consumers in accordance with relevant state regulations or commercial practices and upon the request of consumers. Furthermore, business operators must guarantee that the commodities or services they provide possess the quality, functions, usage, and effective period that they should have for normal use, except where the consumer is aware of the existence of the defect prior to purchase or acceptance of service. Likewise, business operators who indicate the quality of their commodities or services by means of advertisement, product description, sample, etc. must ensure that the actual quality of the commodities or services is consistent with the stipulations.

In providing merchandise or services, business operators should repair, replace, refund the price, or bear other liabilities in accordance with state regulations or agreements with consumers, and must not deliberately delay or refuse to do so without reason. More importantly, business operators must not set unfair or unreasonable terms for consumers or mitigate or exempt themselves from civil liability for impairing the legal rights and interests of consumers by means of form contracts, circulars, announcements, shop bulletins, etc. Apart from not insulting or slandering consumers, business operators must not search the bodies of consumers or articles carried by them and cannot infringe upon the personal freedom of consumers. When disputes arise between consumers and business operators, the following dispute-resolution mechanisms are recommended:

1 consultation and settlement between the parties;
2 mediation by the Consumers Association;
3 filing a complaint with the relevant administrative agencies;
4 arbitration pursuant to an arbitration agreement between the parties; and
5 litigation in court.

If the rights and interests of a consumer are impaired through the purchase or use of a commodity, the consumer may request that the seller provide compensation. Having borne liability, the seller may seek indemnity from its supplier or the manufacturer if the responsibility lies with the supplier or the manufacturer. When a defect in a commodity causes personal injury or property damage to a consumer or other victim, the injured party may claim compensation from the seller or the manufacturer. If the manufacturer is responsible for the defect and the seller has paid compensation, the seller will have the right to seek indemnity from the manufacturer. If the seller is responsible for the defect and the manufacturer has paid compensation, the manufacturer will have the right to seek indemnity from the seller. In other words, the manufacturer and the seller of merchandise bear joint and several liability. Nonetheless, if the rights and interests of a consumer are impaired while receiving service, the recipient of the service may seek compensation from the service provider.

Furthermore, where a business operator illegally conducts business by using the business license of another and harms the rights and interests of a consumer, the consumer may seek compensation from either the business operator or the holder of the business license. Similarly, a consumer whose rights and interests are impaired through the purchase of a commodity or reception of a service at a trade exhibition or at a leased counter may request compensation from the seller of the commodity or the service provider. If the trade exhibition has ended or the lease of the counter has expired, the consumer may demand compensation from the organizer of the trade exhibition or the lessor of the counter. Having borne liability, the organizer or the lessor has the right to seek indemnity from the seller or the service provider.

In terms of remedy, if the consumer or other victim sustains personal injury, the injured party may claim the cost of medical treatment, nursing expenses during the treatment period, reduced earnings due to loss of work, etc. from the business operator. If the victim is disabled, the business operator will be liable for expenses on self-help apparatus, a subsistence allowance, compensation for deformity, the necessary living expenses for his or her dependents, etc. If death results from the use of a commodity or service, the business operator will be liable for funeral expenses, compensation for death, the necessary living expenses of the victim's surviving dependents, etc. In either case, if a crime is involved, criminal liability will also be pursued. Where property damage results from the use of a commodity or service, the consumer may request the business operator to repair, remake, replace, refund the price, supply the deficient quantity, compensate for losses, etc., unless otherwise agreed between the parties. If state regulations require repair, replacement and return, or the business operator and the consumer have reached an agreement upon it, the business operator must comply or perform. For any repair, replacement, or return of bulky merchandise, the business operator must also bear such reasonable expenses as freight. If a commodity cannot be used normally after being repaired twice within the warranty period, the business operator must replace the commodity or accept its return. If any commodity has been appraised as substandard by the relevant administrative authorities, the business operator must, upon the request of the consumer, accept its return. Finally, a business operator who has committed fraud in providing a merchandise or service must, upon the request of the consumer, compensate to the amount of twice the price paid.

The Contract Law

As discussed in Chapter 4, the Contract Law requires the party providing standard terms to direct the other party's attention to exclusions or restrictions on liability and to provide an explanation if so requested. Moreover, if the party providing standard terms exempts itself from liabilities, enhances the liabilities of the other party, or eliminates the major rights of the other party, the standard terms will be null and void. Hence, the Contract Law also restricts the use of exclusionary clauses on product liability.

2 Advertising

Apart from product liability, foreign investment enterprises must know what they can or cannot do in promoting their products or services. Article 9 of the Law against Unfair Competition forbids businesses from using advertisements or other methods to make misleading and false propaganda about the quality, composition, function, usage, manufacturer, effective period, and place of production of their merchandise. Moreover, there are separate regulations or rules governing advertising based on the industry (such as real estate) and the type of advertising tools (such as radio and television broadcasts). The principal legislation on advertising in China is the Advertising Law[3], and its important provisions are highlighted below.

The Advertising Law applies to advertisers, advertising agents, and publishers of advertisements. "Advertisers" refers to legal persons, other economic organizations, or individuals that design, produce, and publish advertisements on their own or through entrustment in order to promote the sale of their goods or the provision of their services. Advertising agents are legal persons, other economic organizations, or individuals that are entrusted with the tasks of designing and producing advertisements. "Publishers of advertisements" refers to legal persons or other economic organizations that publish advertisements on behalf of advertisers or advertising agents.

As a general rule, an advertisement must not contain false contents to deceive or mislead consumers. Moreover, an advertisement must not contain anything that may impair the physical and mental health of minors or disabled persons. Furthermore, an advertisement must not disparage the goods or services of other businesses. More specifically, an advertisement must not contain:

1   the national flag, national emblem, or national anthem;
2   the names of government organs or government officials;
3   words such as "state-level", "highest grade", or "best";
4   anything that is detrimental to social stability, personal and property safety, and public interests;
5   contents that jeopardize public order or violate fine social conventions;

6   contents that are obscene, superstitious, terrifying, violent, or hideous;
7   contents that are discriminatory based on ethnicity, race, religion, or gender;
8   contents that impede the protection of the environment or natural resources; or
9   anything else that is forbidden by laws or administrative regulations.

Additionally, an advertisement should indicate clearly the function, place of origin, usage, quality, price, producer, and effective period of the merchandise, or the content, format, quality, and price of the service, as well as promises if there are any. When a gift is attached to the goods or service, the advertisement should specify the kind and quantity of the gift. Any data, statistics, survey results, abstracts, or quotations used in an advertisement must be true and accurate, and the sources of these materials must be identified. If an advertisement involves a patented product or patented process, the patent number and the type of patent should also be indicated. However, it is forbidden to use a patent application or a patent that has been terminated, revoked, or become invalid in an advertisement. In any event, an advertisement must be clearly recognizable to the consumer as an advertisement.

With respect to medicines and medical equipment, an advertisement must not contain:

1   unscientific assertions or assurances in terms of effectiveness;
2   a cure rate or efficacy rate;
3   comparisons with other medicines or medical equipment regarding effectiveness and safety;
4   the use of the names or images of medical research institutes, academic institutions, medical organizations, experts, doctors, or patients as evidence; or
5   any other contents proscribed by laws or administrative regulations.

Similarly, the contents of food, alcohol, and cosmetics advertisements must not contain medical terms or terms confusingly similar to medical terms. In the same vein, advertising tobacco by means of broadcast, film, television, newspapers, or periodicals is prohibited. An advertisement of tobacco must contain the indication that "smoking is harmful to health." Indeed, it is unlawful to post tobacco advertisements in such public places as waiting rooms, cinemas and theaters, conference halls, and sports facilities.

Aside from content, advertisers should entrust the design, production, and publication of advertisements to advertising agents and publishers that are legally qualified. Advertisements for drugs, medical apparatus, pesticides and veterinary medicines through broadcast, film, television, newspapers, periodicals and other media, as well as advertisements that must be examined in accordance with law and administrative regulation, must be examined by the relevant department(s) before they are published. If the names or images of others are used for advertising, the advertiser or advertising agent should obtain their written approval in advance. If the names or images of persons having no or limited capacity to engage in civil acts are used, the advertiser must obtain prior written approval from their guardians.

Furthermore, the posting of outdoor advertisements is prohibited if the posting:

1   is on traffic safety facilities or traffic signs;
2   will affect the use of public facilities, traffic safety facilities, or traffic signs;
3   will interrupt production or people's lives or impair the appearance of the city;
4   is within the controlled zone of the buildings of government organs, units preserving cultural relics and scenic spots; or
5   is in an area prohibited for outdoor advertising by people's government at and above the county level.

When the lawful rights and interests of consumers are harmed by false advertisements that are meant to deceive and mislead, the advertisers shall bear civil liability. The advertising agents and publishers will have to bear joint and several liability if they design, produce, and publish the advertisements even though they knew or should have known the falsity of the advertisements. Nevertheless, if the advertising agents and publishers are unable to provide the true names and addresses of the advertisers, they will have to bear civil liability entirely. In addition, social or other organizations will bear joint and several liability if they recommend goods or services through false advertisements, thus damaging the lawful rights and interests of consumers.

3 Direct/pyramid selling

Generally, "direct selling" refers to the direct, person-to-person sale of goods or services to consumers without the involvement of wholesalers and retailers who have a fixed place of business. A direct-selling business may take various forms. For instance, the direct salesperson may obtain income mainly through commissions from product sales, which is a well-accepted and lawful practice in many countries. Alternatively, the direct salesperson may frequently recruit new salespersons and obtain income primarily through the initiation fees of, and sales made by, the new recruits, which is usually referred to as pyramid scheme or pyramid selling. In a pyramid scheme, new recruits usually must invest large amounts of money to sign up as members, and members who join earlier earn considerable amounts of commissions due to multi-layered recruitment, while the latecomers may receive little return. Since income in a pyramid scheme is generated principally through the recruitment of salespersons rather than the sale of goods or services, pyramid selling is outlawed in a number of countries.

Direct selling, including pyramid selling, was introduced to China in the late 1980s and early 1990s. The terms "direct selling" (直销) and "pyramid selling" (传销) have been used interchangeably, although the latter generally refers to a pyramid scheme. Prior to 1998, there were many direct sellers in China, including the U.S. direct-selling firms Amway and Avon. Nonetheless, lawless individuals used pyramid selling to engage in smuggling, the sale of counterfeit and low-quality products, and other illegal activities. As a result, the State Administration for Industry and Commerce launched re-certification campaigns to close down many illegal operations. Even so, its efforts did not prove to be very effective. In 1998, the State Council promulgated the Circular on the Prohibition of Business Activities by Pyramid Selling,[4] forbidding all businesses from engaging in pyramid selling activities or pyramid selling in disguise. Two months later, the MOFTEC, the State Administration for Industry and Commerce, and the State Domestic Trading Bureau issued the Notice on the Relevant Issues Concerning the Conversion of Sales Methods by Foreign-Funded Pyramid-Selling Enterprises,[5] urging foreign enterprises and FIEs engaging in pyramid selling to change their sales methods. In 2002, the State Administration for Industry and Commerce, the MOFTEC, and the State Economic and Trade Commission promulgated the Rules on Relevant Questions Regarding the Execution of the "Notice on the Relevant Issues Concerning the Conversion of Sales Methods by Foreign-Funded Pyramid-Selling Enterprises."[6] Accordingly, this section summarizes the major provisions on the ban of direct/pyramid selling in China.

To protect the lawful rights and interests of consumers and to maintain market order and social stability, pyramid sales are completely forbidden. Pyramid selling, with its organizational closeness, concealed transactions, and dispersed sales personnel, is not appropriate for China in its current state of affairs. While the degree of its market development has been low, managerial means have lagged behind, and consumer maturity has yet to come, lawless individuals have used pyramid selling to promote cults, gangs, superstition, and hooliganism, thus gravely deviating from China's drive for spiritual and cultural construction as well as affecting social stability. Moreover, party cadres, government officials, soldiers, and even full-time students have been recruited to engage in pyramid selling, which seriously disrupts the normal order of work and education. Indeed, some individuals have used pyramid selling to commit fraud, promote the sale of counterfeit and low-quality products and smuggled goods, and engage in profiteering and tax evasion, which significantly impairs the interests of consumers and disrupts the normal economic order.

Specifically, people's governments at all levels, the AIC, the Public Security, and all relevant departments must adopt effective measures to resolutely ban and/or seriously handle:

1   pyramid selling from becoming an underground activity;
2   pyramid selling disguised in the form of a win-win system, computer-generated net, or frame selling;
3   pyramid selling disguised in the name of exclusive sales, agency, special permission to join as an ally, direct sales, franchise sales, and network sales;
4   the use of membership cards, saving cards, lotteries, and vocational training to defraud membership fees, alliance fees, permission fees, and training fees; and
5   any other acts of pyramid selling or pyramid selling in disguise.

In enforcing the ban of pyramid selling, foreign-funded direct-selling firms are urged to adopt measures to convert their businesses into legal operations. That is, they may choose to convert their firms into either those with hired salespersons, who are not regular employees and receive wages through product sales, or those without hired salespersons. To convert to the latter, the enterprise must be established after approval in accordance with the law; be a production enterprise and only sell its own products; and have not violated the law during production and operations and passed the 1998 annual review. To convert to the former, the enterprise must satisfy the preceding three requirements plus its total amount of capital must be US$10 million or more, not including the investment in establishing sales branches; and the principal business of the enterprise's foreign party must be direct selling.

Moreover, a transformed enterprise must first establish a shop in the place where its branch is located before hiring salespersons, provided that the branch has been granted approval to hire salespersons. This is because each salesperson is allowed to conduct sales activities only in the area where his or her shop is located. In addition, a transformed enterprise must ensure that consumers can purchase all of its products at the shop and must not state that certain products can be bought only through its salespersons. Furthermore, a transformed enterprise must submit a biannual report on the number of its salespersons in each province and relevant matters to the State Administration for Industry and Commerce, the MOFTEC (now the Ministry of Commerce), and the State Economic and Trade Commission.

Considering its WTO commitments, China has begun drafting legislation on "wholesale and retail trade services away from a fixed location," such as mail order, vending machines, and door-to-door sales.[7] Since pyramid scheme has been used to commit crimes, has disrupted the normal order of work and education, etc., it is doubtful that China will remove the ban on direct selling in the pyramid form in the forthcoming legislation.

4 Internet sales

In recent years, online business-to-business (B2B) and business-to-consumer (B2C) transactions have been growing dramatically in various parts of the world. Nowadays, many firms believe that going online is an important component of their overall business strategy. According to the China Internet Network Information Center, at the end of June 2003, China had about 68 million Internet users who accessed through leased lines, dial-up, ISDN, and broadband, and 341,753 Web sites with the top-level domain name of .com (.cn).[8] Given the rapidly growing population of Internet users, foreign investors may consider operating a Web site to sell merchandise or services to Chinese consumers. Thus, apart from consumer protection in general, foreign investors should find out whether there are any legal provisions specifically applicable to Internet sales and purchases.

According to the Decision on Safeguarding Internet Security,[9] businesses cannot use the Internet to sell fake or shoddy products or to advertise products or services falsely. Moreover, article 46 of the Law on the Protection of the Rights and Interests of Consumers provides that if business operators who sell commodities by mail order fail to deliver, they must, upon the request of consumers, refund the payment and bear any reasonable expenses paid by the consumers. Similarly, article 47 provides that if business operators who provide commodities or services based on advance payment fail to deliver, they must, upon the request of consumers, refund the advance payment, pay interest, and bear any reasonable expenses paid by the consumers. Since Internet sales and purchases may involve the use of e-mail and/or advance payment, these two provisions are likely to be used to protect online consumers.

Apart from the fact that government agencies have issued industry-specific rules regulating various activities online, such as banking; news reporting; trading of cigarette materials; production, reproduction, import, sale, rental, or transmission of audiovisual products; etc., national laws or regulations on online consumer protection have not yet been passed, even though the enactment of an anti-spam regulation (prohibiting unsolicited e-mail advertisements to consumers without their consent) may be forthcoming. Nevertheless, local AICs have enacted government rules to regulate e-commerce within their respective jurisdictions. For instance, the Beijing City Administration for Industry and Commerce has promulgated the Notice Regarding the Protection of the Lawful Rights and Interests of Consumers in Internet Economic Activities[10] and the Notice on Standardizing the Behavior of Using E-mail to Send Commercial Information,[11] while the Guizhou Province Administration for Industry and Commerce has promulgated the Provisional Measures on the Administration of Business Behavior over the Internet.[12] Of various provisions, it is noteworthy that both Beijing and Guizhou require Internet business operators to register and display the registration marks on their home pages, and that the use of spam is subject to administrative punishment. For illustrative purposes, this section discusses Beijing's regulatory framework in more detail.

The Beijing Notice applies to online, profit-seeking activities of selling commodities or providing services within the municipality's jurisdiction.

Consumers who buy merchandise or receive services via the Internet are entitled to the rights as provided by the Law on the Protection of the Rights and Interests of Consumers. Web site owners and others using the Internet to engage in business activities bear the obligations required by the Law on the Protection of the Rights and Interests of Consumers. If business operators sign online contracts to sell merchandise or provide services, they must keep those contracts for at least two years. On their Internet sites, business operators must not engage in such unfair competition measures as passing off others' registered trademarks, unilaterally using the names of other enterprises or of their merchandise, falsifying or counterfeiting certification marks, etc. to mislead consumers. Likewise, business operators must not use advertisements or other methods to mislead consumers with respect to the type, specifications, quality, constituents, price, functions, usage, producer, effective period, place of origin, etc. of their merchandise.

Moreover, business operators who sell merchandise or provide services via the Internet should inform consumers of their true place of registration, contact information, or place of transaction, and must indicate clearly the true price. Business operators who sell merchandise via the Internet must clearly indicate the place of origin, manufacturer, specifications, grade, and quality of their merchandise. When consumers raise questions regarding the quality, functions, main ingredients, production date, effective period, certification of inspection, operations manuals, after-sale services, etc. of their merchandise, they must provide true answers or explain why they cannot answer. Furthermore, business operators who sell merchandise or provide services via the Internet should guarantee that the merchandise or services furnished meet the standards safeguarding the person and property of consumers, and in the case of merchandise or services that may jeopardize human life or the safety of property, provide true explanations or clear warnings, as well as indicating the proper ways to use the merchandise or services and the methods to prevent the occurrence of risks. Finally, business operators are to issue purchase receipts or service bills to consumers in accordance with relevant state regulations or commercial practices and upon the request of consumers.

Since information technology is being developed at a much faster rate than the evolution of Cyber law, the issues of confidentiality, authenticity and integrity are common among many countries. In China, other factors also exist that may prevent the rapid development of e-commerce. The first obstacle is related to China's current financial infrastructure. As credit cards are still not commonly used in China, many online purchasers pay cash on delivery. Moreover, since many unscrupulous merchants in China produce and/or sell counterfeit or shoddy products, most consumers are hesitant to order merchandise online because they cannot examine carefully the products prior to purchase. In addition, unlike brick-and-mortar businesses, Web-based businesses do not have a fixed place of operations. Hence, consumers who are concerned about after-sale services feel more secure making purchases in retail shops. Furthermore, unless the Web-based merchants are reputable businesses, consumers who are required to make advance payment often worry that the sellers may go bankrupt or run away with their money.

5 Selected cases

Shi Wufa v. Shanghai Donghai Beer Ltd. and Shanghai Nanhui County Tanzhi Supply and Marketing Cooperative (2000) 沪一中民终字第1289号, Shanghai City No. 1 Intermediate People's Court, 18 July 2000

Facts

During the evening of 10 August 1998, Shi Wufa (hereinafter SW) was invited by his landlord, Ni Weiqing, to the latter's home for a drink. A bottle of beer on the ground suddenly exploded and hurt his right leg. He was immediately sent to Xin Chang Hospital at Nanhui County for the wound to be cleaned and stitched. On 17 August 1998, when SW went back to have the stitches removed, the wound burst and bled seriously. He was again sent to Xin Chang Hospital for treatment until 31 August 1998. The total cost of treatment was RMB 3,500.70. In September 1998, SW wrote to the Shanghai Donghai Beer Ltd. (hereinafter DBL), demanding a resolution. However, DBL refused to compensate SW because there was no clear explanation for the accident. In November 1998, SW complained to the Consumers Association at Nanhui County, Shanghai. In the same month, SW entrusted the Shanghai City Glass Product Quality Supervision and Examination Station with appraising the exploded beer bottle. The appraisal fee was RMB 200. Since the exploded beer bottle was broken into numerous pieces that were impossible to collect, its original condition could not be recovered. As a result, it was impossible to ascertain the reason for the explosion. In April 1999, the Consumers Association notified SW by letter of the termination of mediation.

In May 1999, SW filed a lawsuit with the court of first instance and requested that DBL and Shanghai Nanhui County Tanzhi Supply and Marketing Cooperative (hereinafter NTS) pay compensation for his bodily jury in the amount of RMB 14,007.70. To prove that the self-exploded beer bottle was one of the Donghai Beers manufactured by DBL, SW submitted the purchase invoice dated 10 August 1998 for the Donghai Beer issued by Renyi Shuangdai Store, which was a subordinate of NTS. He also submitted written testimonies by Gu Mingguan, the responsible person of Renyi Shuangdai Store, Ni Weiqing, and Xi Bin, the sales manager of DBL. A witness, Jin Limin, took the stand. To prove his injury condition and the treatment cost, SW submitted his outpatient medical report card from Xin Chang Hospital, the invoices of hospital charges and medication fees, etc.

In its defense, NTS argued that SW had requested its subordinate Renyi Shuangdai Store to reissue an invoice for the 10 August 1998 purchase of the Donghai Beer. However, since the exploded beer bottle was not actually sold by Renyi Shuangdai Store, NTS refused to make compensation. To substantiate its argument, NTS submitted written testimonies from Gu Mingguan; Huang Shunming and Hu Yuerong, employees of Renyi Shuangdai Store; and Qu Rongsheng, a villager of Renyi Village. Similarly, DBL claimed that it could not be confirmed whether the exploded beer bottle was one of its products. Moreover, the hospital should be responsible for SW's second surgery. In fact, the medical charges were unreasonable. Therefore, DBL refused to compensate SW.

Based on DBL's application, the court of first instance appointed the Judicial Appraisal Center of the Shanghai City High People's Court and the Shanghai City Bodily-Injury Judicial-Appraisal-Specialist Committee to appraise the conditions of injury and treatment of SW. Their conclusion was as follows. SW's right ankle was injured. The wound was cleaned and stitched as an emergency condition. Seven days later, SW went back to the hospital to have the stitches removed, but the wound burst and bled seriously. The treatment measures adopted by the hospital were necessary and reasonable. In general, a patient could recover after resting for four to five months, with two to three months of good nutrition and two weeks of nursing.

The court of first instance held that if defective products caused property damage and bodily injury, the manufacturers and sellers should bear civil liability. Based on the facts of the case, the exploded beer bottle was one of the Donghai Beers that Jin Limin had purchased at Renyi Shuangdai Store. As the exploded beer bottle caused injury to SW, DBL and NTS, the manufacturer and the seller, should be liable for compensation. On 20 March 2000, the court of first instance held that NTS and DBL should compensate SW a total amount of RMB 7,912.65 (including RMB 3,500.70 as medical expenses, RMB 3,164.25 for loss of wages, RMB 900 as nutrition fees, RMB 147.70 for nursing, and RMB 200 as appraisal fees) and SW's other requests were denied.

Dissatisfied with the judgment, DBL appealed to have the original judgment reversed and to have SW's lawsuit dismissed on the following grounds:

1   There was insufficient evidence to prove that the beer bottle injuring SW was its product. According to Hu Yuerong, a salesperson of Yenyi Shuangdai Store, Jin Limin, the witness for SW and the alleged buyer of the beer, did not purchase the beer from Renyi Shuangdai Store on the day of the injury. Rather, several days after the incident, she asked the store to give her a broken Donghai Beer bottle. Seeing that broken beer bottle, the sales manager simply mistook that the beer bottle causing SW's injury belonged to DBL.
2   SW claimed that the beer bottle exploded on its own, but he could not provide any concrete evidence. Thus, the court should investigate the

cause for the explosion and ascertain who should be liable. DBL maintained that the injury of SW was not related to its beer bottle, and that the determination of the court of first instance regarding the scope and amount of SW's loss on the basis of relevant judicial appraisals and medical treatment expenses was not realistic, scientific, fair, or reasonable.

Furthermore, DBL submitted a written testimony by Xi Bin, its sales manager, indicating that he had not visited the site of accident, that the bottle he saw in SW's home in the broken pieces was provided by SW, and that he was surprised to note that there was no manufacturing date on the bottle cap because starting from February 1998, the caps of all the beer bottles manufactured by DBL were sprayed with production dates. Hence, DBL argued that technical appraisal should be used.

Likewise, NTS was dissatisfied with the original judgment and appealed to have it reversed and remanded for retrial or to have the case dismissed. NTS claimed that the original judgment affirmed that the exploded beer bottle was purchased at Yenyi Shuangdai Store based on the testimony of Jin Limin and the purchase invoice. First, Jin Limin was one of the hosts who invited SW to her home for a drink on the day of the explosion. Because she was an interested party, her testimony could not be accepted and trusted. Second, the invoice was reissued after the accident and under SW's claim that he and Renyi Shuangdai Store had no connection. Jin Limin claimed that Hu Yuerong, the salesperson at the store, sold her the Donghai Beer on that day. However, an investigation revealed that Hu Yuerong did not go to work on that day. Third, according to the relevant laws and regulations, consumers, whose legal rights and interests have been impaired through the use of products, might seek compensation from the manufacturers or sellers. Thus, either the manufacturer or the seller, but not both, should assume liability. Because SW had already located the manufacturer of the exploded beer bottle, he should not seek compensation from NTS.

SW responded that the exploded beer bottle was a bottle filled with Donghai Beer, which had been affirmed by Xi Bin, the sales manager of DBL. It was further evidenced by the appraisal of the Shanghai City Glass Product Quality and Examination Station. The said beer bottle was not a "B" bottle, but a reused one that had a defect. The exploded beer bottle was purchased at NTS's subordinate, Yenyi Shuangdai Store, which could be evidenced by an invoice. Since the explosion of the beer bottle injured him, he, as a consumer, could sue DBL, the manufacturer, and NTS, the seller, for joint liability. Moreover, the original judgment was based on sufficient evidence. Thus, SW disagreed with the appeals of DBL and NTS and pleaded to have the original judgment affirmed.

The court found that a contradiction existed between Xi Bin's written testimony submitted by DBL and his last one, which was made after the original judgment had been entered. Because Xi Bin's testimony lacked the conditions necessary for establishing proof, the court did not accept it. In addition, the court found that there were no errors in the facts found by the court of first instance. Similarly, the court found that on 13 October 1998, when questioned by SW's lawyer as to whether the beer bottle causing the injury was produced by his unit, Xi Bin responded as follows. He had personally examined the bottle. His unit should admit that it had produced the bottle. He had asked his colleagues why there was no production date on the cap. The reason might be that his unit could not spray the production date on the bubble plastic material. His unit did not doubt that it had produced the bottle; however, the final answer should be determined by technical appraisal. Furthermore, the report submitted by the Shanghai City Glass Product Quality Supervision and Examination Station on 12 November 1998 indicated that:

1   the said beer bottle was a bottle used by DBL to fill with Donghai Beer;
2   there was no "B" mark or manufacturing date on the beer bottle – it was a reused bottle;
3   since the beer bottle submitted for examination was seriously broken and the collection of its pieces was incomplete, it could not be restored to the original condition; and
4   the cause of the explosion could not be determined.

Reasoning

The court held that a consumer who suffered bodily injury from a defective product could sue either the seller or the manufacturer for compensation. If the manufacturer was responsible for the injury, the seller might, after paying compensation, seek indemnity from the manufacturer. If the seller was responsible for the injury, the manufacturer might, after paying compensation, seek indemnity from the seller. In this case, SW purchased the bottle of beer at Yenyi Shuangdai Store, a subordinate of NTS, which could be sufficiently evidenced by the store invoice. The personnel of the store stated at the court of first instance that normally the store would not issue invoices to individual customers. Hence, the store's reissue of the invoice after the incident affirmed in writing its selling conduct on the day of the injury. Since NTS was the seller of a defective product that injured a consumer, it should be civilly liable.

Likewise, the fact that the beer bottle that injured SW was manufactured by DBL was affirmed after examination by both the staff of DBL and the relevant professional examination organs. With respect to the issue of whether the beer bottle had exploded on its own or by external force, since the parties did not disagree on the fact that the beer bottle had exploded, and the relevant professional examination station had clearly established that the beer bottle was a reused one, the defective quality of the beer bottle was an undisputed fact. As the conditions for ascertaining the cause of the explosion did not exist, there was no need to investigate further. DBL, being the manufacturer of beer, should assume civil liability for damages sustained by an injured consumer as a result of the defective beer bottle.

Given that the parties were in dispute over the scope and amount of loss, the judgment of the court of first instance, based on SW's invoices of actual expenses and the judicial appraisals of the relevant professional organs, was proper and feasible. Although DBL did not agree to SW's stipulated amount of loss, it could not produce evidence to refute the judicial appraisals and objective evidence of expense invoices. As such, the court would not accept the assertion of DBL regarding the scope and amount of loss. Accordingly, there were no errors in the original judgment and the appeals of DBL and NTS were not supported.

Judgment

Based on article 153(1)(i) of the Civil Procedure Law,[13] the court held that the appeal was dismissed and the original judgment was affirmed.

This judgment was final.

Sun Xiangyong *v.* Hainan Zhongnan Telecommunications Market *(2002)* 海中法民终字第17号, *Hainan Province Haikou City Intermediate People's Court, 18 January 2002*

Facts

Fu Chan (hereinafter FC), a *getihu* (个体户) operating the Haikou Xinhua Hongfa Communications Equipment, rented Counter 83 from the Hainan Zhongnan Telecommunications Market (hereinafter HZT) from 1 August 1999 to 30 July 2001. They had a counter-leasing relationship. Sun Xiangyong (hereinafter SX) purchased a mobile phone from Counter 83, but a problem of quality arose. The court of first instance held that the quality problem should be handled by FC, and that SX had no legal basis to sue HZT and hold HZT jointly and severally liable for compensation. Since SX's lawsuit did not meet the statutory requirements, the court of first instance dismissed the case. SX appealed on the following grounds:

1 If the party against whom the lawsuit was filed was the wrong one, the court of first instance should inform him when it put the case on file for investigation and examination.

2 HZT had written the wording "Hainan Zhongnan Telecommunications Market" on the two sides of the building in which it was located. Inside the market, the counters were all linked together; the business licenses and certificates of tax registration of the operators were not displayed; and the names of the operators and the counter numbers were not

indicated. There was only "HZT" written in large characters at the center of the market. The receipt given to SX was stamped with the seal of Counter 83 of HZT. HZT had no objection in respect of the said receipt and proof of quality appraisal provided by SX. The afore-mentioned facts were sufficient to prove that HZT acquiesced in and subsequently confirmed Counter 83's conducting business in its name.

3   According to article 38 of the Law on the Protection of the Rights and Interests of Consumers[14] and article 10 of the Measures on the Admin-istration of Counter-Leasing Business Activities,[15] since HZT received rents for Counter 83, in effect, it shared profits with the operator of Counter 83. Thus, HZT had the duty to guarantee that Counter 83 conduct business lawfully and should compensate any losses caused by the illegal operations of Counter 83.

4   The liability clause stipulated in the lease agreement between HZT and the operator of Counter 83 was to evade statutory provisions and thus impaired the rights and interests of consumers. Accordingly, such stipulation was null and void.

SX pleaded that the court should annul or amend the original judgment.

HZT responded that it was FC who had sold the mobile phone to SX. According to the Law on the Protection of the Rights and Interests of Consumers, when a problem of quality arose, the consumer could sue the manufacturer or the seller for damages. After the lease had expired, FC's home address and contact phone number were both available. Thus, SX should sue FC for damages. As there was no direct relationship of rights and obligations between SX and HZT, HZT should not bear joint and several liability. HZT pleaded to have the appeal dismissed and the original judgment affirmed.

Reasoning

The court found that the available evidence indicated that FC did conduct business in the name of HZT, which was legally established and registered. Thus, SX had a clear case against HZT. Whether SX had a legal relation-ship with FC or with HZT, whether HZT should be liable, and the kind of liability HZT should bear were all issues within the scope of substantive examination. Moreover, according to article 38 of the Law on the Protection of the Rights and Interests of Consumers, when a consumer's legal rights and interests are impaired through the purchase of a commodity at a leased counter, it might, after the lease had expired, sue the lessor for damages. SX's appeal fulfilled the requirements of article 108 of the Civil Procedure Law.[16] The court of first instance did not conduct a substantive examina-tion, but dismissed the lawsuit on the grounds that FC, the lessee, should be responsible, which deprived SX's right to litigation and violated procedural law.

Ruling

Based on article 154 of the Civil Procedure Law,[17] the court ruled that the civil ruling of the court of first instance was reversed and the case was remanded to the court of first instance for trial.

This ruling was final.

Further reading

Fort, Timothy L. and Liu, Junhai, "Chinese Business and the Internet: The Infrastructure for Trust," *Vanderbilt Journal of Transactional Law* 35, 2002, 1545–99.
Williams, Mark, "Foreign Business and Consumer Rights: A Survey of Consumer Protection Law in China," *UCLA Pacific Basin Law Journal* 18, 2001, 252–72.

Notes

1 The Product Quality Law of the People's Republic of China, adopted at the 30th Session of the Standing Committee of the 7th National People's Congress on 22 February 1993 and amended by the 16th Session of the Standing Committee of the 9th National People's Congress on 8 July 2000.
2 The Law of the People's Republic of China on the Protection of the Rights and Interests of Consumers, adopted at the 4th Session of the Standing Committee of the 8th National People Congress on 31 October 1993.
3 The Advertising Law of the People's Republic of China, adopted at the 10th Session of the Standing Committee of the 8th National People's Congress on 27 October 1994.
4 The Circular on the Prohibition of Business Activities by Pyramid Selling, promulgated by the State Council on 18 April 1998.
5 The Notice on the Relevant Issues Concerning the Conversion of Sales Methods by Foreign-Funded Pyramid-Selling Enterprises, promulgated by the Ministry of Foreign Trade and Economic Cooperation, the State Administration for Industry and Commerce, and the State Domestic Trading Bureau on 18 June 1998.
6 The Rules on Relevant Questions Regarding the Execution of the "Notice on the Relevant Issues Concerning the Conversion of Sales Methods by Foreign-Funded Pyramid-Selling Enterprises," promulgated by the State Administration for Industry and Commerce, the Ministry of Foreign Trade and Economic Cooperation, and the State Economic and Trade Commission on 4 February 2002.
7 See "Expediting the Drafting of Legislation on Direct Sales by Foreign Investors," Mingpao, 14 December 2001, § China.
8 See China Internet Network Information Center, "The Macro Situation of the Internet Development in China," *Twelfth Statistical Survey Report on the Internet Development of China*, July 2003, pp. 4–6. The figure of 68 million is higher than the actual number of Internet users because Internet users who use multiple methods to access are recounted.
9 The Decision on Safeguarding Internet Security, adopted at the 19th Session of the Standing Committee of the 9th National People's Congress on 28 December 2000.

10 The Notice Regarding the Protection of the Lawful Rights and Interests of Consumers in Internet Economic Activities, promulgated by Beijing City Administration for Industry and Commerce on 7 July 2000.

11 The Notice on Standardizing the Behavior of Using E-Mail to Send Commercial Information, promulgated by the Beijing City Administration for Industry and Commerce on 15 May 2000.

12 The Provisional Measures on the Administration of Business Behavior over the Internet, promulgated by the Guizhou Province Administration for Industry and Commerce on 9 February 2001.

13 According to art. 153(1)(i) of the Civil Procedure Law, the court of second instance should dismiss the appeal and affirm the judgment of the court of first instance if the original judgment is based on clearly established facts and correct application of law.

14 Article 38 of the Law on the Protection of the Rights and Interests of Consumers provides that a consumer whose rights and interests are impaired through the purchase of a commodity or reception of a service at a trade exhibition or at a leased counter may request compensation from the seller of the commodity or the service provider. Moreover, after the trade exhibition has ended or the lease of the counter has expired, the consumer may demand compensation from the organizer of the trade exhibition or the lessor of the counter. The organizer or the lessor, however, has the right to seek indemnity from the seller or the service provider.

15 Article 10 of the Measures on the Administration of Counter-Leasing Business Activities provides that if the business conduct of the lessee impairs the lawful rights and interests of a consumer, the consumer may seek compensation from the lessee, and, after the lease of the counter has expired, seek compensation from the lessor.

16 Article 108 of the Civil Procedure Law lists four requirements for filing a lawsuit: the plaintiff should be a citizen, legal person, or other organization that has a direct interest in the case; there should be a definite defendant; there should be concrete claims with supporting facts and reasons; and the case should be within the scope of civil litigation of a people's court and within the jurisdiction of the people's court with which the lawsuit is filed.

17 Article 154 of the Civil Procedure Law provides that the court of second instance shall use ruling in all cases of appeal against the rulings of the courts of first instance.

8 Taxation, banking, and securities

To do business in China, foreign investors must also consider tax, the banking system, and securities. The first section of this chapter discusses the taxation system in China, focusing on those taxes that are most relevant to foreign investors. The second section briefly introduces China's banking system, the foreign banking institutions operating in China, and China's administration of foreign exchange related to foreign investors. The final section analyzes China's security market, focusing on the administration system, security offering and trading, the B-share and the qualified foreign institutional investors (QFII) scheme that are most relevant to foreign investors.

1 Taxation

Foreign investors should pay, as investors in other parts of the world, a variety of taxes in China. Along with the economic reform, the Chinese taxation system has become more and more complicated, with a total of 29 categories of taxes being levied to date, of which 17 are applicable to foreign investors. Foreign investors should study carefully both China's taxation law and regulations, consider the taxes they have to pay, work out what preferential tax treatments they may enjoy, and analyze the relative costs and benefits before they make a decision to invest in China.

Overview

In the pre-reform period, China's economic structure was simplified with the abolition of foreign-owned enterprises and the rapid decline of domestic private enterprises. By the late 1970s, state-owned enterprises and collective-owned enterprises had become the predominant components of the economy, accounting for about 99 percent of the output of the Chinese economy. Accordingly, China's taxation system was also simplified over the pre-reform period. Until 1978, China levied only 13 categories of taxes, including industrial and commerce tax, industrial and commerce income tax, agriculture tax and tariff. As the Chinese people earned little income, they did not pay any income tax. Chinese government's revenue came mainly from the profits earned by state-owned enterprises, not from these taxes.[1]

After 1979, China began to reform its taxation system to cope with changes in its economic structure brought about by the rapid economic reform and opening up. The reforms focused on:

1 imposing income tax on state-owned enterprise to separate the taxes from the profits;
2 imposing income tax on foreign-related enterprises;
3 adding new tax categories such as the individual income tax, the value-added tax, the resource tax, and the urban construction tax; and
4 revising existing tax categories, such as the land property tax, which used to be part of the urban real estate tax and now became part of the urban land use tax.

China's current taxation system is the result of these reforms since 1979.

Currently, China's taxes include value-added tax, consumption tax, business tax, customs duties, enterprise income tax, income tax on FIEs and foreign enterprises, individual income tax, resource tax, urban and township land use tax, urban maintenance and construction tax, tax on farmland occupation, fixed assets investment orientation regulation tax (now suspended), land appreciation tax, vehicle acquisition tax, fuel tax (not being levied yet), social security tax (not being levied yet), property tax, urban real estate tax, inheritance tax (not being levied yet), vehicle and vessel usage tax, vehicle and vessel usage license tax, vessel tonnage tax, stamp tax, contract tax, security transaction tax (not being levied yet), slaughter tax, banquet tax, agriculture tax, and animal husbandry tax. These taxes have become the main components of the Chinese government's revenue, accounting for 94 percent of the government's revenue.

Value-added tax is by far the most important part of the taxation system, accounting for more than 40 percent of the total taxes. The second largest contributor to the taxation system is business tax, accounting for 14 percent of the total taxes. The third largest contributor to the taxation system is enterprise income tax, accounting for 11 percent of the total taxes. All the remaining categories of taxes each accounted for less than 10 percent of the total taxes, for example consumption tax (6 percent), customs duties (5.7 percent), individual income tax (5 percent), stamp tax (4 percent), urban maintenance and construction tax (2.7 percent), income tax on FIEs and foreign enterprises (2.5 percent), and agriculture tax (2.3 percent).

These taxes are collected and shared by the central government and local government. Following the tax separation reform in 1994, all the taxes were divided into three groups:

1 Taxes as central government fixed revenue, including consumption tax, vehicle acquisition tax, customs duties, vessel tonnage tax, the value-added tax collected by the Customs Bureau.
2 Taxes as local government fixed revenue, including urban and township land use tax, farmland occupation tax, fixed assets investment orientation

regulation tax, land appreciation tax, house property tax, urban real estate tax, inheritance tax, vehicle and vessel usage tax, vehicle and vessel usage license tax, contract tax, slaughter tax, banquet tax, agriculture tax, and animal husbandry tax.

3   Taxes as revenue shared by central and local governments, including value-added tax (excluding those collected by the Customs Bureau), business tax, enterprise income tax, income tax on FIEs and foreign enterprises, individual income tax, resource tax, urban maintenance and construction tax, stamp tax, fuel tax, and security transaction tax.[2]

Tax categories for foreign investors

According to the current legal regulations of China, 17 categories of taxes are applicable to the enterprises with foreign investment, foreign enterprises and foreigners, including overseas Chinese from Hong Kong, Macao, Taiwan and other places and the enterprises they invested within China. These taxes are value-added tax, consumption tax, business tax, customs duties, income tax on enterprises with foreign investment and foreign enterprises, individual income tax, resource tax, land appreciation tax, vehicle acquisition tax, fuel tax, urban real estate tax, vehicle and vessel usage license tax, vessel tonnage tax, stamp tax, contract tax, slaughter tax and agriculture tax. Here we illustrate only those that are most relevant to foreign investors.

Value-added tax (增值税)

Taxpayers of the value-added tax include all enterprises, administrative units, military units, social organizations, other institutions and individuals that are engaged in the sales of goods, the importation of goods, and the provision of taxable services (including processing, repairs and replacement services). The basic regulations and rules on the value-added tax are stipulated in the Provisional Regulations on Value-Added Tax and the Detailed Rules for Implementation of the Provisional Regulations on Value-Added Tax.[3]

Currently there are three tax rates for normal value-added taxpayers: 0 percent, 13 percent and 17 percent. The 0 percent rate applies to exported goods, except for gold, materials given as aid to foreign countries and the goods prohibited by the central government for export (presently including natural bezoar, musk, copper, copper alloy, and platinum). The 13 percent rate applies to:

1   agricultural products, including grains, vegetables, tobacco (excluding re-cured tobacco), tea, horticulture plants, oil plants, fiber plants, sugar plants, forestry products, other plants, aquatic products, animal husbandry products, animal skins, animal hairs, and other animal tissues;

2   edible vegetable oil and food grains;

3   tap water, heating, air conditioning, hot water, coal gas, liquefied petroleum gas, natural gas, methane gas, and coal/charcoal products for household use;
4   books, newspapers and magazines (excluding newspapers and magazines issued by post and tele-communication departments);
5   feeds, chemical fertilizers, agricultural chemicals, agricultural machinery and covering plastic film for farming;
6   dressing metal mineral products, dressing non-metal mineral products, and coal.

The 17 percent rate applies to crude oil, mine salt, goods other than those mentioned above, and taxable services.

Value-added taxpayers are classified as normal taxpayers or small-scale taxpayers. They pay the value-added tax in different ways.

"Normal taxpayers" refers to those who engage in goods production or taxable labor services and those who mainly engage in goods production or taxable labor services and concurrently engage in wholesale or retail goods with taxable sales value over RMB 1 million. It also refers to those engaged in wholesale or retail goods, with an annual taxable sales value over RMB 1.8 million. The formula for computing the tax payable for normal taxpayers is:

tax payable = output tax for the period − input tax for the period

That is, the output tax for the period and the input tax for the same period are calculated separately first. The balance of output tax for the period after deducting the input tax for the period shall be the actual amount of value-added tax payable.

"Small-scale taxpayers" refers to those who engage in goods production or taxable labor services and those who mainly engage in goods production or taxable labor services and concurrently engage in wholesale or retail goods with taxable sales value below RMB 1 million. It also refers to those engaged in wholesale or retail goods (excluding gas stations selling oil products) with an annual taxable sales value below RMB 1.8 million. The small-scale taxpayers are taxed in a simplified manner: the value-added tax payable is computed on the basis of the sales value of goods and/or services and the prescribed applicable value-added tax rate. Currently, the tax rate is 4 percent for small-scale taxpayers engaged in wholesale or retail goods; small-scale taxpayers engaged mainly in wholesale or retail goods and concurrently engaged in goods production or provision of taxable services; and small-scale taxpayers engaged in commission shops, mortgage businesses, the sale of second-hand commodities, approved duty-free shops, and auction firms. All other small-scale taxpayers are liable to a 6 percent tax rate. The formula for calculating the tax payable for small-scale taxpayers is:

tax payable = sales value × applicable tax rate

Consumption tax (消费税)

Taxpayers of the consumption tax include all enterprises, administrative units, military units, social organizations, other institutions and individuals that are engaged in the production or import of taxable consumer goods in China, or that are subcontractors for processing taxable consumer goods in China. The basic regulations and rules on the consumption tax are stipulated in the Provisional Regulations on Consumption Tax and the Detailed Rules for Implementation of the Provisional Regulations on Consumption Tax.[4]

Consumption tax is computed in three ways: flat rate, fixed amount of tax per unit, and compound rate. Currently, 11 taxable items are subject to consumption tax. Seven items are levied by the flat rate approach, two items are levied by the fixed amount of tax per unit approach, and two items are levied by the compound rate approach.

The flat rate approach is based on the sales value of the taxable consumer goods and the applicable tax rate. The formula for computing the tax payable is:

tax payable = sales value of taxable consumer goods

× applicable tax rate

The following items are currently levied by the flat rate approach:

1 cosmetics, including perfumes, essence of perfumes, perfume powder, lipsticks, finger oil, rouge, eyebrow pencil, blue eye oil, mascara, complete set of cosmetics (30 percent tax rate);
2 skin-care and hair-care products, including vanishing cream, facial oil, toilet water, hair oil, hair paste, perm liquid, hair dye liquid, face washing milk, frosted paste, hair nutrition paste, face film, massage paste, shampoo, hair conditioning liquid, bath lotion, and hair spray (30 percent tax rate);
3 precious jewelry, including precious jade and stone (5 percent tax rate for gold and silver jewelry, diamond and diamond decoration, and 10 percent tax rate for other precious jade and stones);
4 firecrackers and fireworks (15 percent tax rate);
5 motor vehicle tires, excluding meridian line tires and renovated tires, used on various automobiles, trailers, special vehicles and other mothers (10 percent tax rate);
6 motorcycles (10 percent tax rate);
7 motor cars (3 percent tax rate for small cars with cylinder capacity of less than 1,000 ml, four-wheel drives with cylinder capacity of less than 2,400 ml, and small buses and vans with fewer than 22 seats and cylinder

capacity of less than 2,000 ml, 5 percent tax rate for small cars with cylinder capacity between 1,000 ml and 2,200 ml, 4-wheel forward cross-country motors with cylinder capacity of more than 2,400 ml and small buses and vans with fewer than 22 seats and cylinder capacity of more than 2,000 ml, and 8 percent tax rate for small cars with cylinder capacity of over 2,200 ml).

The fixed amount of tax per unit approach is based on the sales volume of the taxable consumer goods and the applicable tax amount per unit. The formula for computing the tax payable is:

tax payable = sales volume of taxable consumer goods

$\qquad$ × applicable tax amount per unit

The following items are currently levied by the fixed amount of tax per unit approach:

1 diesel oil, including light diesel oil, heavy diesel oil, farm-use diesel oil and army-use diesel oil (RMB 0.1 per liter);
2 gasoline, including gasoline for vehicles and aviation (RMB 0.2 per liter for unleaded gasoline and RMB 0.28 per liter for lead gasoline).

The compound rate approach is a combination of the above two approaches. The formula for computing the tax payable is:

tax payable = sales volume of taxable consumer goods

$\qquad$ × applicable tax amount per unit

$\qquad$ + sales value of taxable consumer goods

$\qquad$ × applicable tax rate

Currently tobacco, alcohol and alcoholic drinks are levied by the compound rate approach. For tobacco, the tax is first based on quantity, namely, RMB 150 tax for each standard box containing 50,000 cigarettes. Then the tax is levied on an *ad valorem* basis. That is, the 45 percent rate is applied to cigarettes with price more than RMB 50 (excluding value-added tax, the same hereinafter) for each standard package of 200 cigarettes, imported cigarettes and other cigarettes specified by the state; the 30 percent rate is applicable to cigarettes with a price of less than RMB 50 for each standard package of 200 cigarettes; the 25 percent rate is applicable to cigars; and the 30 percent rate is applicable to cut tobacco (including pipe tobacco, Mohe tobacco, fine tobacco, shredded tobacco for water pipes, and yellow and red cut tobacco). For alcohol and alcoholic drinks, the tax is first based on quantity, and is then imposed on an *ad valorem* basis. RMB 0.5 is imposed, for instance, on each 500 gram white wine first, and then a 25 percent rate is applicable to white spirits made from cereal and 15 percent rate is applicable to white spirits made from potatoes.

Business tax (营业税)

Taxpayers of the business tax include all enterprises, administrative units, military units, social organizations, other institutions and individuals that are engaged in the provision of taxable services, transfer of intangible assets and/or sale of immovable properties in China. The basic regulations and rules on the business tax are stipulated in the Provisional Regulations on Business Tax and the Detailed Rules for Implementation of the Provisional Regulations on Business Tax.[5]

The business tax payable is levied by a flat rate approach, and is computed on the basis of the turnover and the applicable tax rate. The formula for computing the business tax payable is:

tax payable = turnover × applicable tax rate

Currently, the following nine taxable items are subject to business tax:

1   the 3 percent rate for communications and transportation, including transportation by land, water, air and pipeline, loading and unloading, and delivery;
2   the 3 percent rate for the construction industry, including construction, installation, repair, decoration and other engineering work;
3   the 5 percent rate for finance and insurance, including making loans, financial leasing, transfer of financial products, the financial brokerage industry, and other financial and insurance businesses;
4   the 3 percent rate for post and telecommunications;
5   the 3 percent rate for culture and sports;
6   the 5 percent to 20 percent rate for entertainment (except for night clubs, sing halls, dance halls, shooting, hunting, race, games, golf, bowling and billiards, which are subject to the 20 percent rate nationwide, the tax rate for all kinds of entertainment is determined within the range specified by the tax law of the government of individual provinces and autonomous regions in light of the practical local conditions);
7   the 5 percent rate for the transfer of intangible assets, including transfer of land-use rights, patent rights, non-patent technologies, trademarks, copyrights and goodwill;
8   the 5 percent rate for sales of immovable properties, including sales of buildings and other attachments to land;
9   the 5 percent rate for other service industries, including agencies, hotels, catering, tourism, warehousing, leasing, and advertising.

Foreign investment enterprise income tax (外商投资企业和外国企业
所得税)[6]

Taxpayers of the FIE income tax are enterprises with foreign investment
in China, including Chinese-foreign equity joint ventures, Chinese-foreign
cooperative joint ventures, and wholly foreign funded enterprise; and foreign
enterprise, including foreign companies, enterprises, and other economic
organizations having establishments or places in China and being engaged
in production or business operations and those having no establishment or
place in China but having income from sources within China.[7] The basic
regulations and rules on the FIE income tax are stipulated in the Income
Tax Law on Foreign Investment Enterprises and Foreign Enterprises and
the Detailed Regulations for Implementation of the Income Tax Law on
Foreign Investment Enterprises and Foreign Enterprises.[8]

The formulas for computing the taxable income vary from industry to
industry. For the manufacturing industry, the formulae are:

taxable income = sales profit + other business profit

+ non-business income − non-business expenses

sale profit = net sales of the products − sales cost of the products

− tax on sales of the products − sales expenses

− administrative expenses − financial expenses

For commerce, the formulae are:

taxable income = sales profit + other business profit

+ non-business income − non-business expenses

sale profit = net sales − cost of sales − tax on sales − sales expenses

− administrative expenses − financial expenses

For the service industry, the formulae are:

taxable income = net business income + non-business income

− non-business expenses

net business income = gross business income − tax on business income

− business expenses − administrative expenses

− financial expenses

The taxes mentioned in these formulae do not include the price-exclusive value-added tax. The taxable income for other industries shall be computed with reference to the above formulae.

In general, the flat rate for FIE income tax is 30 percent plus 3 percent of local enterprise income tax. Thus the aggregate FIE income tax rate is 33 percent of the total taxable income.

Land appreciation tax (土地增值税)

China's land appreciation tax is levied on the appreciation from the transfer of real estate, and it is levied for the purpose of regulating the real estate market and reasonably adjusting the benefit from land appreciation. The basic regulations and rules on the land appreciation tax are stipulated in the Provisional Regulations on the Land Appreciation Tax and the Detailed Rules for Implementation of the Provisional Regulations on the Land Appreciation Tax.[9]

Taxpayers of the land appreciation tax include all enterprises, administrative units, military units, social organizations, other institutions and individuals that receive income from the transfer of state-owned land use rights, buildings (including auxiliary facilities on and under ground) and their attached facilities within China. The land appreciation tax is levied by a progressive tax rate approach. There are currently four progressive tax rates:

1   for the part of appreciation not exceeding 50 percent of the total appreciation, the tax rate is 30 percent;
2   for the part of appreciation from 50 percent to 100 percent of the total appreciation, the tax rate is 40 percent;
3   for the part of appreciation from 100 percent to 200 percent of the total appreciation, the tax rate is 50 percent;
4   for the part of appreciation exceeding 200 percent of the total appreciation, the tax rate is 60 percent.

The formula for calculating the tax payable is:

$$\text{tax payable} = \Sigma \text{ (appreciation} \times \text{applicable tax rate)}$$

Vehicle acquisition tax (车辆购置税)

China's vehicle acquisition tax is levied on the purchase of vehicles. The basic regulations and rules on the vehicle acquisition tax are stipulated in the Provisional Regulations on the Vehicle Acquisition Tax.[10] The taxpayers of the vehicle acquisition tax include enterprises, organizations and individuals who acquire the specified vehicles such as motor vehicles, motorcycles, trams, trailers and transportation vehicles for farm use.

The vehicle acquisition tax is levied on the basis of the taxable price, which is determined according to the following rules:

1   For vehicles purchased for self-use, the taxable price is the total payment of price and non-price expenses (including commissions, contribution to funds, indemnity for breaking contracts, package charges, transportation charges, storage charges and other charges by the selling party in addition to the price of the vehicle, except for value-added tax).
2   For vehicles imported for self-use, the taxable price is the custom dutiable price plus customs duty and consumption tax.
3   For vehicles obtained for self-use by means of self-production, gift, prize, etc., the taxable price is determined by the tax authorities in reference to the lowest taxable price specified by the State Tax Bureau.

The current rate of vehicle acquisition tax is 10 percent. The formula for computing the vehicle acquisition tax is:

tax payable = taxable price × applicable tax rate

Customs duties (关税)

Taxpayers of customs duties include the consignees importing goods, the consignors exporting the goods, and the owners of imported and exported goods in China. The customs duties include import tariff rates and export tariff rates. The basic regulations and rules on customs duties are stipulated in the Regulations on the Import and Export Duties.[11]

Import tariff rates fall into four categories:

1   Most favorable nations' tariff rates for goods imported from WTO member nations or other countries or regions with which China has concluded trade treaties or agreements with reciprocal favorable tariff clauses therein.
2   Conventional tariff rates for goods imported from countries or regions with which China has participated in the regional trade conventions with relevant customs duty preferential clauses.
3   Special treatment tariff rates for goods imported from countries or regions with which China has concluded a special preferential customs duty agreement.
4   General tariff rates for goods imported from countries or regions other than the above.

According to the Customs Import and Export Tariff Classifications of the People's Republic of China, there are currently 7,316 tariff items for all imported goods, most of which are subject to the most favourable nation tariff rates, ranging from 0 to 65 percent. Currently, there are 36 tariff items for exported goods in China, which are mainly the raw materials domestically in shortage and restricted from exports. The tariff rates for these exported goods range from 20 percent to 50 percent.

The customs duties are levied on the basis of either the price or the quantity of the imported or exported goods, or a combination of both. The formula for calculating the amount of customs duties payable on the basis of price is:

duties payable = quantity of dutiable imports or exports

$\times$ dutiable price per unit $\times$ applicable rate

The formula for calculating the amount of customs duties payable on the basis of quantity is:

duties payable = quantity of dutiable imports or exports

$\times$ applicable duty per unit

The formula for calculating the amount of customs duties payable on the basis of both price and quantity is:

duties payable = quantity of dutiable imports or exports

$\times$ customs completion price per unit $\times$ applicable rate

+ quantity of dutiable imports or exports

$\times$ applicable duty per unit

Along with the accession to the WTO, China's tariff rates for both imported and exported goods are expected to fall in the coming years.[12]

Preferential tax treatment

In a bid to attract foreign investment, the Chinese government has introduced a range of tax concessions to FIEs and foreign enterprises. These preferential tax treatments are granted either by the central government or by the local governments, and they are very complex, involving almost all the tax categories applicable to FIEs and foreign enterprises. Preferential tax treatments granted by the central government mainly involve corporate (enterprise) income tax, business tax, value-added tax and custom duty, and some examples are given here.

Concessions on foreign investment enterprise income tax

FIEs engaged in a production industry (such as machine-building, electronics, and textiles) for a period of no less than ten years are exempt from income tax in the first and the second years, and are granted 15 percent of income tax rate in the third to fifth years. Some FIEs in such areas as energy, transportation and port construction, and integrated circuit manufacturing may also enjoy 15 percent of the income tax rate.[13]

Export-oriented FIEs and FIEs with advanced technology are eligible for 15 percent or 10 percent (for those in SEZs) of income tax rate if the value of export of the current year amounts to more than 70 percent of the total annual production and the international payment for business is in balance or in surplus.

FIEs or foreign enterprises in SEZs, Economic and Technological Development Zones, Coastal Economic Open Zones, State New and High Tech Industry Development Zones and/or Bonded Zones enjoy a flat income tax rate ranging from 10 to 24 percent depending on where they are and in what industry they are engaged. Recently, FIEs in the western region began to enjoy preferential tax treatment as well.[14]

Concessions on business tax, value-added tax, and customs duties

Incomes derived by R&D centres established by FIEs and incomes derived by foreign enterprises and foreign individuals from technology transfer, technology development and related consultancy and technical services are exempt from business tax.

The raw materials, auxiliary materials, parts, components, accessories and packaging materials imported by FIEs for the outward processing or assembly of products and for the production of goods for export are exempt from import tariffs based on the quantity of finished products actually processed and exported. Alternatively, import tariffs are levied on the imported materials and parts first and rebates are made later based on the quantity of finished products actually processed and exported.

FIEs are entitled to the full value-added tax rebate on the purchase of domestically produced equipment within their investment amount if such equipment is listed in the catalogue of duty-free imports. The import by FIEs of equipment and supporting technologies, accessories and parts for their own use under the "encouraged category" or "restricted category II," foreign-invested R&D centers, FIEs with advanced technologies and export-oriented FIEs are exempt from import tariffs and import-related taxes in accordance with the Circular of the State Council on the Adjustment of Tax Policy on Equipment Imports.

2 Banking

Foreign investors need to deal with many issues related to corporate finance and, therefore, should understand the Chinese banking system and the banking services available to them. For those who plan to invest in the Chinese banking sector, it is necessary to know the development and the current status of foreign banks and financial institutions operating in China. As

China still exercises a certain degree of foreign exchange control and Chinese currency is not convertible under capital account, foreign investors should also pay attention to the Chinese foreign exchange system.

Overview

Before the economic reform and the opening up in 1978, China had a mono-banking system strictly controlled by the central government. The People's Bank of China, virtually the only bank in China, performed the mixed functions of a central bank and a commercial bank. Under the mono-banking system, interest rates, money supply, and the financial needs of the government and enterprise were all subject to central planning, and there was little room for financial intermediation. The PBOC was very much like the government cashier, exercising very limited functions such as issuing currency, taking deposits and leading on behalf of the government. It provided a large amount of loans to state-owned enterprises and bailed out loss-making enterprises.

From 1979, with the economic reform and opening up, the Chinese government began the reform of its banking system. First, the Agricultural Bank of China, the Bank of China and the Construction Bank of China were established in 1979, and the Industrial and Commercial Bank of China was established in 1984. The four new banks began to take up the role of an independent state commercial bank, while the People's Bank of China retained its central bank function. Throughout the 1980s, however, the four newly established banks were still not really commercialized, and were subject to the central government's policy instructions.

Then in 1994, three policy banks – the State Development Bank of China, the Agricultural Development Bank of China, and the Import and Export Bank of China – were established to separate policy banking and commercial banking in China's financial system. The three newly established policy banks began to take up the unprofitable "policy lending," while the four aforementioned state commercial banks began to operate on a commercial basis. With the Central Banking Law and the Commercial Bank Law promulgated and enacted in 1995, China began to have a rudimentary legal framework for the supervision and functioning of its banking system.

Meanwhile, other commercial banks and financial institutions – state-owned and non-state owned, as well as national and regional – were also established, such as the China International Trust and Investment Corporation, the Industrial Bank, the Bank of Communications, the Everbright Bank, the Huaxia Bank, the Minsheng Bank, the Guangdong Development Bank, the Shenzhen Development Bank, the Merchants Bank, the Fujian Industrial Bank, the Shanghai Pudong Development Bank, the Yantai Housing Savings Bank, the Bengbu Housing Savings Bank, and the Hainan Development Bank. Currently, China's banking system has become quite diversified in structure, and increasingly consumer-oriented in function offering almost all the financial services that are available in a market-based economy. To date, China has four state commercial banks, three policy banks, ten joint-equity commercial banks, 109 city commercial banks, and numerous urban credit cooperatives, rural credit cooperatives, trust and investment corporations, finance companies and leasing companies. These banks mainly engage in Chinese currency business, and only a few of them are authorized to engage in foreign currency business. At present, the regulations and rules on China's banking industry are mainly stipulated in the Law on the People's Bank of China[15] and the Commercial Bank Law.[16]

Foreign banks and financial institutions

As early as the 1980s, some foreign financial institutions were allowed to set up regional branches or representative offices in China's SEZs. In 1990, Shanghai was opened up to foreign banks. In 1996, the Administrative Measures on Representative Offices of Foreign Financial Institutions in China were adopted by the People's Bank of China, and more cities in China were opened up to foreign banks and financial institutions thereafter. Currently, there are 190 foreign banking institutions operating in China, mainly in big cities.

Foreign banking institutions are allowed to engage mainly in foreign exchange business activities, including foreign exchange deposits, loans, bill discounting, investment, remittance, guarantees, import and export settlement, investigation of creditworthiness, consultancy and foreign exchange trusts. In principle, they are not allowed to engage in Chinese currency business unless they receive special approval from the People's Bank of China. In 1996, for instance, several foreign banks in Shanghai were granted licenses to engage in Chinese currency business on a limited basis. Later on, more foreign banks were granted such preferential treatment. Currently, the number of foreign banks allowed to engage in Chinese currency business on a limited basis has reached 25 (19 in Shanghai and 6 in Shenzhen).

With the limitation on Chinese currency business, foreign banks and financial institutions cannot function fully as a local financial institutions, but they do provide a great deal of supplementation to the local financial institutions in the fields of foreign exchange business and services to the FIEs and foreign enterprises. As such, foreign bank and financial institutions play a very limited role in China today. Currently, their assets account for only about 2 percent of China's total financial assets, and their foreign currency loans account for only about 13 percent of China's total foreign exchange loans. Their Chinese currency assets amount to only about RMB 12 billion, their Chinese currency loans amount to only about RMB 8 billion, and their Chinese currency deposits amount to only about RMB 6 billion.

With China's accession to the WTO, the limitations on Chinese currency business will be eliminated gradually, and foreign banks and financial institutions will play an increasingly important role in the Chinese banking system.[17]

Foreign exchange

The current regulations and rules on foreign exchange are stipulated mainly in the Administrative Measures on the Movement of State Currency Into and Out of Chinese Territory, the Regulations on the Administration of the Foreign Exchange Adjustment Market, the Announcement of the People's Bank of China Concerning Further Reform of the Foreign Exchange Control System, the Regulations on Foreign Exchange Control, the Provisional Measures on the Administration of Foreign Exchange Registration for Foreign Investment Enterprises, the Announcement of the People's Bank of China on the Implementation of Foreign Exchange Settlements and Sales at Banks by Foreign Investment Enterprises, the Administrative Rules on Foreign Exchange Settlements, Sales and Payments, the Administrative Rules on Domestic Foreign Exchange Accounts, and the Administrative Measures on the Settlement of Foreign Exchange under Current Accounts.[18]

In China, "foreign exchange" refers to the assets or instruments of payment expressed in a foreign currency that can be used to make international payments, that is, foreign currencies including banknotes and coins; foreign currency payment instruments including negotiable instruments, bank deposit certificates and postal savings certificates, etc.; foreign currency marketable securities including government bonds, corporate bonds and shares, etc.; Special Drawing Rights and European Currency Units; and other foreign exchange assets.[19] Currently, although foreign exchange can be fully converted to renminbi under the current account, it is still tightly controlled under capital account in China. Therefore, foreign investors have to concern themselves with various aspects of the foreign exchange systems including whether they can keep their foreign currency investment in a foreign currency account with local banks, whether their local currency profits can be converted into foreign currency, and whether they can remit their profits back to their home country in foreign currency.

The foreign exchange authority in China is the State Administration of Foreign Exchange. The Foreign Exchange Adjustment Center is the official authority responsible for exchange adjustment transactions under the leadership and administration of the State Administration of Foreign Exchange, and it:

1   organizes market trade;
2   hears applications for buying and selling foreign exchange;
3   conducts transactions;
4   supervises the settlement and clearing of transactions undertaken by both buyer and seller;

5   provides information and services;
6   compiles foreign exchange adjustment statistical statements and market analysis; and
7   undertakes other business operations as authorized by the State Administration of Foreign Exchange.

However, more banks are now allowed to handle foreign exchange transactions, and the role of the Foreign Exchange Adjustment Center is diminishing.

FIEs can open foreign exchange settlement accounts for current account receipts and payments of foreign exchange and specialized accounts for capital account receipts and payments at designated foreign exchange banks in China. To open a foreign exchange account, an FIE must apply to register its foreign exchange and, upon approval, obtain the Foreign Exchange Registration Certificate and Notice to Open a Foreign Exchange Account from the State Administration of Foreign Exchange. With regard to current account, the State Administration of Foreign Exchange will determine the maximum amount of foreign exchange income under current account items that an FIE can retain, based on the FIE's paid-in capital and its current account foreign exchange circulation requirements. Where the foreign exchange exceeds this amount, it must be sold to a foreign exchange designated bank or sold through a Foreign Exchange Adjustment Center.

The legitimate Chinese currency earnings of foreign personnel or foreign organizations, including after-tax profits or wages, dividends and other legitimate income, can be converted into foreign currency upon presentation of the relevant certificates and valid documentation to designated foreign exchange banks, and the converted amount can be remitted out of China. Foreign exchange owned by individuals can be held personally, deposited in banks, or sold to designated foreign exchange banks. In some areas, such as Shanghai, individuals can engage in foreign exchange trading. The exchange rates between Chinese currency and other major foreign currencies are determined according to the prevailing rate on the inter-bank foreign exchange market and are announced by the People's Bank of China. The exchange rates are subject to a single and managed floating exchange rate system based on market supply and demand.

The following forms of behavior in relation to foreign exchange are considered illegal in China:

1   depositing foreign exchange earnings abroad without authorization in violation of state regulations;
2   failing to sell foreign exchange to a designated foreign exchange bank pursuant to state regulations;
3   remitting or taking foreign exchange out of China in violation of state regulations;

4   unauthorized carrying or posting of foreign currency deposit certificates or foreign currency marketable securities overseas, without the approval of the foreign exchange control authorities;
5   other acts related to foreign exchange evasion.

The foreign exchange control authority will order a party who has committed any of the above acts to repatriate the foreign exchange within a certain period and will compulsorily purchase the foreign exchange. Furthermore, it will impose a fine of between 30 percent and 500 percent of the amount of foreign exchange evaded.

According to the Regulations for the Implementation of the Law on Sino-Foreign Equity Joint Ventures, a joint venture must obtain approval from the State Administration of Foreign Exchange or one of its branches in order to open a foreign exchange account with an overseas bank or a bank in Hong Kong or Macao. In addition, a joint venture may apply to a financial institution inside China for foreign exchange or RMB loans. When a joint venture borrows funds in foreign exchange from banks abroad, it must go through the formalities for registration, or filing for record, with the State Administration of Foreign Exchange or one of its branches.

3 Securities

Foreign investors may want to raise funds through the securities market and, therefore, need to understand the operation of the Chinese security market, which is the second largest security market in Asia after the Tokyo security market. For those who want to invest in the Chinese security market, it is necessary to know the investment channels and services available to them, for example, the B shares and the QFII scheme.

Overview

The current regulations and rules on China's securities market are stipulated mainly in the Measures of the Shanghai Municipality on the Administration of Securities Trading, the Interim Measures of the Shenzhen Municipality on the Issue and Trading of Shares, the Company Law, and the Securities Law.[20]

China's securities market took shape formally along with the establishment of the Shanghai Stock Exchange and the Shenzhen Stock Exchange in 1990. The highest body in charge of supervision and administration of the securities market is the China Securities Regulatory Commission (CSRC), which was established in 1992. According to the Securities Law, the CSRC:

1   formulates rules and regulations related to the supervision and administration of the securities market;
2   exercises examination and approval powers;

3   supervises and administers the issuance, transaction, registration, trusteeship, and settlement of securities;
4   supervises and administers the securities-related activities of securities issuers, listed companies, stock exchanges, securities firms, securities registration and settlement institutions, securities investment fund management institutions, securities investment consultation institutions, and credit institutions involved in the securities business;
5   formulates standards of qualification and codes of conduct for securities professionals and supervises the implementation of such standards and codes;
6   supervises and inspects the public disclosure of information on securities issuance and transactions;
7   guides and supervises the activities of the stock brokers' association;
8   investigates and handles any conduct that violates the law and administrative regulations; and
9   conducts any other duties stipulated by the law and administrative regulations.[21]

Thus, the CSRC has vast power in regulating the securities market and in investigating potential violations. To ensure transparency, however, the Securities Law requires the CSRC to publish all its rules and regulations as well as its mechanisms in relation to supervision and administration, and publicize its decisions punishing violations. Other securities supervision and administration authorities include the Stock Brokers' Association and the Stock Exchanges.

Currently, there are only two stock exchanges in China: the Shanghai Stock Exchange and the Shenzhen Stock Exchange. A stock exchange is a non-profit legal person that provides a venue in which securities are collectively traded by bidding, and:

1   provides a guarantee of organized and fair collective trading;
2   handles issues regarding suspension, resumption, and termination of listing of stocks and corporate bonds; and
3   monitors and supervises securities trading.

A stock exchange must formulate detailed rules and regulations on competitive trading, its members and employees.

Investors are not allowed to purchase or sell securities on stock exchanges themselves. They have to conduct securities transactions through securities companies that are members of the stock exchange. Investors have to open an account with a securities company, give it a transaction order in the form of written notes, a recording of a telephone conversation. A security company may be established as a limited liability company or a stock company, and it may be a comprehensive securities company or a brokerage securities company. A comprehensive securities company may conduct the business of brokerage, investment and underwriting, while a brokerage securities company may only conduct brokerage business. A comprehensive securities company must have a minimum registered capital of RMB 500 million, while a brokerage securities company must have a minimum registered capital of RMB 50 million.

There are currently four types of securities in China's securities market: state bonds, financial bonds, corporate bonds, and stocks. State bonds are issued by the Ministry of Finance for the purpose of balancing the market and supporting construction projects. Financial bonds are issued by the specialized banks and other financial institutions as a method of raising money. Corporate bonds and stocks are issued by companies, including joint stock companies, and are the focus of our discussion.

Securities offerings

As discussed in Chapter 2, a company limited by shares may want to raise capital by offering its shares to the public. Similarly, an existing company may want to increase capital or raise operating funds by offering new shares or issuing corporate bonds. Shares of the same class must have the same rights and benefits. For shares issued at the same time, each share must have the same price on the same terms. The issue price of a share may be equal to or greater than, but not less than, the par value. If the issue price is above the par value, the company must obtain approval from the CSRC. Moreover, shares issued to promoters, investment organs authorized by the state, and legal persons shall be in the form of registered (inscribed) shares, bearing the names of such promoters, investment organs, or legal person. Shares issued to the general public may be in the form of registered or bearer shares. In the case of corporate bonds, the company covenants to repay the principal and interest within a given period of time. Corporate bonds may be in the form of bearer or registered bond.

Any company that wishes to issue either shares or corporate bonds must first satisfy the requirements of the Company Law. Then the issuer needs to submit all required documents and provide all relevant information to the Securities Regulatory Authority for approval. If a company issues securities without approval, it must return all the funds raised plus interests and pay a fine of an amount between 1 percent and 5 percent of the funds so raised. Persons in charge or directly responsible may pay a fine of an amount between RMB 30,000 and RMB 300,000, and are even subject to criminal liabilities.

In addition, the issuer needs to retain one or more securities company as underwriters, which must first sell the securities to investors and not retain or purchase such securities in advance of purchase by investors. An agreement should be reached between the issuer and underwriter of an underwriting arrangement on the rights and obligations of each party, which should include:

1 the names, addresses, and legal representatives of all the parties;
2 the types, quantity, monetary value, and issue price of the stocks underwritten;
3 the duration, including the commencement date and deadline, of the securities underwritten;
4 the payment method and date;
5 the fees and method of settlement;
6 liability for breach of contract;
7 any other matters that may be required to be stated by the authority.

Normally, the term of underwriting may not exceed 90 days.[22]

Securities offered by a new company

When a company limited by shares is to be established by means of subscription, it must obtain approval from the CSRC before offering its shares to the public. In making a public offer, the promoters shall publish a prospectus and prepare a subscription form. The prospectus should contain the company's articles of association and clearly state:

1 the number of shares subscribed by the promoters;
2 the par value and issue price of each share;
3 the total number of bearer shares;
4 the rights and obligations of the subscribers; and
5 the duration of the offer and an explanation that subscribers may revoke their subscriptions if the shares are under-subscribed at the close of the offer.

Likewise, the subscription form should provide the same information.

On the subscription form, subscribers should fill in the number of shares to be subscribed, the amount of payment, and their domiciles. A subscriber should first sign and seal the subscription form, and then make payment for the shares subscribed. A public offer should be underwritten by securities organs established in accordance with the law, and underwriting agreements must be concluded. The promoters shall also conclude agreements with banks that are to accept payments on behalf of the company. The banks shall issue receipts to subscribers who have made payments, and be obliged to produce evidence of the receipt of payments to the relevant government departments. Once a company limited by shares is established and registered, it must immediately deliver share certificates to its shareholders.

Securities offered by an existing company

To issue new shares, an existing company must satisfy the following requirements:

1   The previous issue of shares must have been fully subscribed, and one or more year must have elapsed since the last issue.
2   The company must have been profitable during the last three years and have been able to distribute dividends to its shareholders.
3   There should have been no false statements in the company's financial and accounting documents for the last three years.
4   The projected profit margin of the company should amount to the interest rate on bank deposits for the corresponding period.

However, if a company distributes a given year's profits in the form of stock dividend, it will not be subject to the requirement in point 2.

At the same time, shareholders must decide on the class and quantity of the new shares; the issue price of the new shares; the commencement and closing dates of the issue; and the class and quantity of shares to be issued to the existing shareholders. After the shareholders have passed a resolution on these matters, the board of directors shall apply to the department authorized by the State Council or to the provincial-level people's government for approval. If the company wants to issue new shares to the public, it must also secure the approval of the CSRC. Once approval is granted for the public offer of new shares, the company shall publish a prospectus for the new shares and the financial and accounting reports with detailed appendices, as well as preparing a subscription form. The company must also sign an underwriting agreement with a lawfully established securities organ. After the company has received payment from all the subscribers, it shall change its registration with the AIC and issue a public notice.

Apart from stock, a company limited by shares, a wholly state-owned limited liability company, and a limited liability company invested by two or more state-owned enterprises or by two or more state-owned investment entities may issue corporate bonds to raise funds for production and operations. To issue corporate bonds, the following requirements must be met:

1   the net assets of a company limited by shares must be no less than RMB 30 million, and the net assets of a limited liability company must be no less than RMB 60 million;
2   the aggregate amount of corporate bonds must not exceed 40 percent of the net assets of the company;
3   the average amount of profit to be distributed over the previous three years must be sufficient to pay for one year's interest on the corporate bonds;
4   the funds raised must be used in a way that is consistent with the state's industrial policies;
5   the interest rate payable on the corporate bonds must not exceed the levels set by the State Council; and
6   any other conditions as prescribed by the State Council.

The funds raised by corporate bonds must be used for the approved purposes and not be used to cover losses or defray non-production expenditures. Nonetheless, a company cannot re-issue corporate bonds if the previous issue of corporate bonds has not been fully subscribed or if the company has defaulted on previously issued corporate bonds or other debts or has been, and is still being, late in the payment of principal or interest.

When a company limited by shares or a limited liability company wants to issue corporate bonds, its board of directors shall draft a plan, and its shareholders shall pass a resolution. Once a resolution has been made, the company shall submit an application for approval to the CSRC. Upon approval, the company shall publicly announce any measures for the subscription of the corporate bonds. Specifically, the company should clearly state:

1 the company's name;
2 the total amount and par value of the bonds;
3 the interest rate of the bond;
4 the time limit and means for the payment of principal or interest;
5 the commencement and closing dates of the issue;
6 the net assets of the company;
7 the total amount of bonds issued but not yet due; and
8 the underwriter for the bonds.

Furthermore, subject to the resolution of its shareholders, a listed company may issue corporate bonds that are convertible into shares. To issue convertible corporate bonds, the company must first obtain approval from the CSRC. In addition, convertible corporate bonds must satisfy not only the requirements for the issue of the bonds but also the requirements for the issue of shares.

Securities trading

A shareholder may transfer its shares through a lawfully established stock exchange. Registered shares are transferred by means of endorsement or any other means as prescribed by law or administrative regulations. However, no changes in the register of shareholders can be made in the 30 days immediately before the shareholders' general meeting or within the five days immediately before the record date for the distribution of dividends. The transfer of bearer shares is effective upon delivery of the share certificates to the transferee through a lawfully established stock exchange. In any event, a company limited by shares may not repurchase its own shares except in the case of a merger or for the purpose of reducing capital through cancellation of shares. Within ten days of the repurchase, the company must cancel that portion of its shares, change its registration, and issue a public notice.

If a company limited by shares wants its shares to be traded on a stock exchange, it must obtain approval from the CSRC. To apply for approval, the company must meet the following requirements:

1   its shares must have been issued to the public with the approval of the CSRC;
2   the company's total stock capital must be no less than RMB 50 million;
3   the company must have been profitable in the last consecutive three years if it has been in operation for three or more years;
4   the number of shareholders each holding shares with a par value of RMB 1,000 or more should be no less than 1,000;
5   the company's shares already issued to the public should account for no less than 25 percent of the company's total shares (if the company's total stock capital exceeds RMB 400 million, the company's shares already issued to the public should account for no less than 15 percent of the company's total shares);
6   for the last three years, the company should not have committed any serious unlawful acts, and its financial statements should not have contained any false information; and
7   any other requirements as prescribed by the State Council.

Having obtained the permission to list its shares on a stock exchange, the company should present the approval documents and other documents to a stock exchange that is obliged to arrange the listing within six months. Before actually listing, the issuer must display all the relevant documents for public review and examination, including the approved listing date, the names of the top ten shareholders and the number of shares held by each, and the names of directors, supervisors, managers and other high-ranking administrators as well as their stock and bond holdings in the issuer. The listing of corporate bonds requires similar procedures, but the issuer must meet such additional requirements as the maturity of the corporate bonds should be no less than one year and the total value of the corporate bonds to be issued should be no less than RMB 50 million.

Once listed in the stock market, the company must regularly make pubic its financial and operating conditions as well as publish its financial statements on a regular basis according to the rules set by the CSRC. The CSRC will temporarily suspend the listing of a company's shares if:

1   changes in the company's total stock capital, stock distribution, etc. have occurred such that the company no longer meets the listing requirements;
2   the company does not make public its financial conditions as required by the regulations or its financial statements contain false information;
3   the company has committed a serious unlawful act; or
4   the company has continuously sustained losses for the last three years.

The principle governing securities trading is price and time preference. The person who offers higher prices has priority over the other purchaser in trading. When more than one purchaser offers the same price, the person who makes the offer first has priority over the others. There are a number of rules and restrictions in respect of securities trading:

1   Only the actual lawful holder is allowed to trade securities; thus, people cannot borrow securities for the purposes of trading, and the transaction on securities that are not held by the parties is forbidden.
2   Securities that are subject to restrictions by law may not be traded within the restricted period, the shares owned by the promoters may not be transferred within three years after the establishment of the issuer, and the shares held by the directors, supervisors and managers may not be transferred during their term of office.
3   Those working in stock exchanges, securities companies and securities registration and settlement institutions, and securities supervision and administration organizations may not own, purchase, sell, or receive as a gift securities on their own behalf during their term of office.
4   Those working in the institutions that are involved in preparing audit reports, asset evaluation reports and legal opinions in relation to a stock issue by an issuer may not purchase or see the stocks of the issuer during the underwriting period and six months thereafter.
5   Any shareholder owning 5 percent or more shares of an issuer may not conduct a sale and purchase within any six-month period.
6   Legal persons are prohibited from using natural persons' names to open accounts or transact securities; public funds cannot be used to conduct securities transactions; state enterprises or enterprises with state-controlling ownership are not allowed to engage in securities transactions.
7   Insiders and those who illegally acquire inside information are forbidden from trading in securities.

Violation of these rules and restrictions may result in the confiscation of illegal earnings or a fine of up to five times the illegal earnings, or even criminal liability.

According to current Chinese law and regulations, FIEs are allowed to be listed on the securities market. In reality, however, the application requirements are tough and the Chinese government has followed an internal policy to limit the approval of applications for listing FIEs. Nevertheless, a number of FIEs have managed to become listed companies by an acquisition of equity interest or indirect holding of shares of a joint stock company that is listed on the securities market. This is possible because securities trading has been increasingly open to foreign investors in China through the B shares and the QFII scheme.

The B shares

When the two stock exchanges were established, 'Shanghai Stock Exchange in December 1990 and Shenzhen Stock Exchange in July 1991', shares were first made available only to Chinese investors and were traded only in Chinese currency. In February 1992, a special class of shares began to be listed and traded on both the Shanghai Stock Exchange and the Shenzhen Stock Exchange. This special class of shares refers to registered shares that are denominated in Chinese currency and offered to foreign investors and investors from Hong Kong, Macao and Taiwan for purchase and sale using foreign exchange. These shares are commonly referred to as the B shares, as distinguished from the A shares that are available only to Chinese investors and are traded only in Chinese currency. Not until 2001, could Chinese investors trade the B shares using a foreign exchange.

The issuers of the B shares must be companies limited by shares. A company seeking to issue and list the B shares has to satisfy a number of requirements on the stock exchange. The Shanghai Stock Exchange, for instance, has the following requirements:

1   An existing company limited by shares must have continuously achieved profits for at least the preceding two years and the preceding quarter of the current year, and must have received shareholders' approval to increase capital by issuing the B shares.
2   A state-owned enterprise restructured as a company limited by shares must have obtained a confirmation of asset valuation and a report on the conclusions from the asset valuation issued by the relevant asset valuation organization, and the percentage of the B shares among the total shares must fall within the limit set by the Chinese authorities.
3   The issuer must have a stable, adequate source of foreign exchange revenue, must submit an application form for share issue to relevant administrative authorities for approval, etc.

The Shenzhen Stock Exchange has similar requirements for the issuance and listing of the B shares. For both stock exchanges, the issuer needs to retain one or more securities companies as underwriters, and the subscription for the B shares is carried out through authorized securities institutions.

Although all the B shares are denominated in Chinese currency, the B shares transactions must be settled in foreign currencies, U.S. dollars for the Shanghai Stock Exchange and Hong Kong dollars for the Shenzhen Stock Exchange. The price of conversion between Chinese currency and foreign currency carried out in the course of the B share transactions are calculated at the official weighted average exchange rate for the preceding week.

To trade the B shares, foreign investors must first open settlement accounts at the Shanghai Securities Central Clearing and Registration Corporation and Shenzhen Securities Clearing Company. The accounts may be opened on behalf of the investors by its broker or custodian bank in the local market. Foreign investors may invest in B shares during the initial offering period, or on the secondary market through exchange trading. In the primary market, investments can be made through the issuer's underwriters. For secondary market trade, orders must be placed through foreign or local brokers. Foreign brokers may establish links with local brokers for trade execution and settlement, and share commissions with them. Alternatively, foreign brokers may apply to have their own "special" trading seats on the exchanges, and thus put trade orders directly into the trading system without going through local brokers.

Owners of B shares enjoy the same rights and bear the same obligations as holders of A shares. They must not break the rules that govern B shares trading. For instance, foreign investors are strictly prohibited from engaging in borrowing and lending activities, including short-selling, margining and securities lending. If an investor holds more than 5 percent of the total issued share capital of a stock of a listed company, the investor must inform the relevant regulatory authorities.

Currently, there are 52 B shares companies listed on the Shanghai Stock Exchange, and 56 B shares companies listed on the Shenzhen Stock Exchange. The emergence of the B shares has served as a means of attracting foreign direct investment in Chinese enterprises as well as in FIEs, and has generated the valuable foreign capital necessary for China's continued productivity improvement and economic growth.

The QFII scheme

The A shares, traded only in Chinese currency, were not open to foreigners until the end of 2002 when the QFII scheme was initiated by the Chinese government. Under this scheme, foreign institutional investors can invest in the A shares market if they meet certain requirements and are granted approval from the Chinese government. The regulations and rules on the QFII scheme are stipulated mainly in the Provisional Rules on Administration of Domestic Securities Investment by Qualified Foreign Institutional Investors (QFII).[23]

Under the QFII scheme, qualified foreign institutional investors refer to overseas fund management institutions, insurance companies, securities companies and other assets management institutions that have been approved by the CSRC to invest in China's securities market and have been granted an investment quota by the State Administration of Foreign Exchange. QFII should mandate domestic commercial banks as custodians and domestic securities companies as brokers for their domestic securities trading. QFII should comply with laws, regulations and other relevant rules in China.

Both Chinese banks and foreign banks can apply to the People's Bank of China for a license to deal with custodian business for QFII in trading of domestic securities if they:

1 have a specific fund custody department;
2 have no less than RMB 8 billion paid-in capital;
3 have sufficient professionals who are familiar with custody business;
4 have the ability to manage the entire assets of the fund safely;
5 have the qualifications to conduct foreign exchange and RMB business; and
6 have not committed any material breach of foreign exchange regulations for the last three years.

To date, nine banks have been granted such custodianship, namely, the Industrial and Commercial Bank of China, the Bank of China, the Agricultural Bank of China, the Bank of Communications, the China Construction Bank, the China Merchants Bank and the branches of the Standard Chartered Bank, HSBC, and Citibank in Shanghai.

To apply for a QFII license, the foreign institutional investors must meet the following basic requirements:

1 Fund management institutions must have been in fund business for five years and have managed US$10 billion in assets in the last financial year.
2 Insurance companies must have been in the insurance business for more than 30 years and have managed US$10 billion in securities assets, with no less than US$1 billion in paid-in capital, in the last financial year.
3 Securities companies must have been in the securities business for more than 30 years and have managed US$10 billion in securities assets, with no less than US$1 billion in paid-in capital, in the last financial year.
4 Commercial banks must be in the world's top 100 in terms of total assets and have managed US$10 billion in securities assets in the last financial year.
5 Trust firms and government-invested institutions can also apply, but the requirements will be determined by the Chinese government individually.

Upon approval, a qualified foreign institutional investor should open a RMB special account with its custodian bank, and apply to the State Administration of Foreign Exchange through its custodian bank for investment quotas. Then, it needs to mandate a domestically registered securities company to manage its investment. Under the QFII scheme, a qualified foreign institutional investor can invest in the following financial instruments:

1 all shares listed on China's Stock Exchanges;
2 treasury bonds listed on China's Stock Exchanges;
3 convertible bonds and corporate bonds listed on China's Stock Exchanges; and
4 other products approved by the CSRC.

Apart from the basic legal regulations governing China's securities market, some specific rules have to be followed in the securities trading under the QFII scheme:

1 A qualified foreign institutional investor must remit principals from outside into China and directly transfer them into its RMB special accounts after full settlement of foreign exchange within three months of the license being approved.
2 If the QFII is a closed-end China fund management company, it cannot withdraw its money from the country for three years after its remittance of the principals.
3 Other qualified foreign institutional investors cannot withdraw their money from china for one year after its remittance of the principals.
4 Shares held by each QFII in one listed company should not exceed 10 percent of the total outstanding shares of the company.
5 Total shares held by all QFIIs in one listed company should not exceed 20 percent of the total outstanding shares of the company.

Up to September 2003, Morgan Stanley, Citigroup Inc., Swiss Bank UBS AG, Japan's Nomura Securities, a Unit of Nomura Holdings Inc., Britain's HSBC Holdings Plc, Deutsche Bank AG, U.S.A.'s Goldman Sachs have been granted the QFII status, with the total investment quotas amounting to US$875 million. In July 2003, the Swiss bank UBS AG made the first trade with a purchase of shares in four companies listed in China's A shares market.

4 Selected cases

The Tianjin City Nankai Branch of the China Construction Bank *v.* Tianjin Development Zone Maikeheng Industrial and Trading Ltd. *(2001)* 民二终字第126号, *Supreme People's Court, 21 February 2002*

Facts

On 28 August 1998, Tianjin Development Zone Maikeheng Industrial and Trading Ltd. (hereinafter MIL) opened account No. 512-273036189 with RMB 5,000,000 at the Tianjin City Nankai Branch of the China Construction Bank (hereinafter CBC). On 28 September 1998, MIL deposited RMB 7,000,000. On 9 October 1998, MIL made two deposits totaling RMB 8,000,000. On 9 December 1998, MIL went to CBC to withdraw funds, but discovered that RMB 19,998,000 had already been taken out by ten withdrawals from its account on MIL's behalf. MIL filed a lawsuit with the Tianjin High People's Court on 11 December 1998, requesting CBC to pay RMB 20,000,000 of principal and interest, overdue fines, and litigation fees.

On 11 December 1998, CBC reported the case to the Tianjin Public Security Bureau. The preliminary investigation of the Tianjin Public Security Bureau on 14 December 1998 revealed that its criminal division verified that the impression of the seal on the withdrawal slips was fabricated, and that the criminal suspect used forged withdrawal slips to swindle funds out of the bank accounts. Subsequently, the Tianjin Public Security Bureau started to investigate a suspect, Cheng Jing. On 6 June 2000, Cheng Jing was arrested by the Tianjin Public Security Bureau and was prosecuted at the Tianjin High People's Court for financial fraud. Having been interrogated, Cheng Jing confessed that he used high-interest yield as a bait to lure MIL to deposit RMB 25,000,000 with CBC. He then used high technology, including computer scanners and ink-jet printers, to fabricate bank draft authorization letters and transfer slips. He made several withdrawals totaling more than RMB 249,000,000 and absconded until he was arrested. After interrogating Cheng Jing, the Tianjin Public Security Bureau again interrogated the two main staff members of MIL, Li Feng and Zhao Jianfeng, about the details of the deposits. Both Li Feng and Zhao Jianfeng denied Cheng Jing's allegation of the high-interest yield, and until now there was no evidence to support such allegation.

The Tianjin High People's Court found that MIL's opening of an account at CBC constituted a deposit relationship between the two parties. After MIL deposited the funds with CBC, CBC had the duty to safeguard the funds. According to article 57 of the Negotiable Instruments Law, when payers or their agents made payments, they should examine the continuity of the series of endorsements as well as the legal or other valid identification documents of the persons presenting the negotiable instruments; and if payers and their agents made payments in bad faith or due to gross negligence, they should be liable. According to article 69 of the Rules on Several Issues Regarding the Trial of Disputes over Negotiable Instruments promulgated by the Supreme People's Court, the making of payments by payers or their agents due to their failure to identify forged negotiable instruments or fraudulent identification constitutes gross negligence under article 57 of the Negotiable Instruments Law, and if such payment causes loss to the bearers, the payers or their agents should bear civil liability. Nonetheless, after payers or their agents have assumed liability, they have the right to seek indemnity from the forgers. If the bearers make mistakes, they should also assume corresponding civil liability. CBC should carry out its duty to verify the payee's legal or other valid identification documents. In this case, MIL was not involved in the fraudulent withdrawals, and CBC could not prove that MIL had made mistakes in its deposit procedures; therefore, CBC still had the duty to pay MIL. The Tianjin High People's Court granted the requests of MIL.

Based on article 57 of the Negotiable Instruments Law and article 69 of the Rules on Several Issues Regarding the Trial of Disputes over Negotiable Instruments by the Supreme People's Court, the Tianjin City High People's Court held as follows:

1 Within ten days of the effective date of this judgment, CBC had to return to MIL RMB 20,000,000 with interest calculated from the deposit dates to 9 December 1998 in accordance with the current deposit rates set by the People's Bank of China.

2 Within ten days of the effective date of this judgment, CBC had to pay MIL overdue interest calculated from 10 December 1998 to the effective date of this judgment according to the rates for overdue bank loans set by the People's Bank of China for the corresponding period.

3 If CBC failed to make the aforementioned payments, the judgment would be enforced in accordance with article 232 of the Civil Procedure Law.[24]

CBC did not agree to the judgment and appealed to the Supreme People's Court to have the original judgment reversed and amended on the following grounds:

1 MIL's deposit of RMB 20,000,000 with CBC was not for the purpose of normal deposit, but was for the purpose of earning the high interest given by Cheng Jing.

2 Cheng Jing provided details of the time, place, amounts, the source of funds, and the means of payment when interrogated at the Tianjin Public Security Bureau.

3 The high interest involved in this case amounted to RMB 2,700,000, consisting of cash borrowed by Cheng Jing from other people and cash converted from postal savings deposit, which had already been given to MIL. This amount should be deducted from the principal of RMB 20,000,000.

4 Cheng Jing testified that MIL had furnished him with a written promise stamped with the "official seal of the unit," "financial seal," and "legal-person seal." Objectively, MIL assisted Cheng Jing in his scam. According to article 69 of the Rules on Several Issues Regarding the Trial of Disputes over Negotiable Instruments promulgated by the Supreme People's Court, if bearers make mistakes, they should assume corresponding civil liability. Therefore, MIL should bear civil liability for its own fault. According to article 17 of the Measures on the Settlement of Payments,[25] CBC had already fulfilled its duty in examining the documents and, thus, should not be held responsible for the swindled funds.

5 The Tianjin High People's Court did not investigate and collect evidence on its own initiative and, thus, violated trial procedure.

6 The "judicial interpretation of deposit receipt" should be applied to this case, and the interest should be calculated according to the deposit interest rates.

MIL responded that there was no evidence to verify Cheng Jing's testimony. MIL had never received such a great amount of interest from

Cheng Jing. The original judgment was based on clearly established facts, correct application of law, and compliance with legal procedure. Thus, MIL pleaded to have the appeal dismissed and the original judgment affirmed.

Reasoning

The court found that when CBC received the funds from MIL, the former had the duty to safeguard the deposit. However, Cheng Jing, the criminal suspect, defrauded MIL of its RMB 20,000,000 deposit by using forged bank drafts. Article 57 of the Negotiable Instruments Law provides that if payers or their agents pay out funds in bad faith or due to gross negligence, they should be liable. In addition, article 69 of the Rules on Several Issues Regarding the Trial of Disputes over Negotiable Instruments promulgated by the Supreme People's Court provides that if payers or their agents mistakenly pay out funds because of their inability to identify forged negotiable instruments or fraudulent identification documents, such mistake constitutes gross negligence under article 57 of the Negotiable Instruments Law, and they should be civilly liable if they cause the bearer to suffer serious losses. After discharging their civil liabilities, the payers or their agents can sue the forgers for indemnification. If the bearers make mistakes, they should also assume corresponding civil liability. Since MIL suffered economic losses due to CBC's inability to identify the forged seals on the bank draft authorization letters and transfer slips, CBC had to assume civil liability. As to whether MIL had issued a written promise to Cheng Jing, the court could not affirm because there was no evidence other than Cheng Jing's own testimony. In any event, a written promise from MIL could not justify Cheng Jing's illegal and fraudulent behavior, nor prove that MIL was an accomplice in the scam. Given that there was no solid proof with respect to MIL's fault in the swindle, the judgment of the Tianjin High People's Court that CBC had to bear full responsibility for MIL's defrauded deposit was not erroneous. The court did not support CBC's claim to hold MIL partially liable because there were no factual and legal grounds.

MIL denied CBC's allegation, based on Cheng Jing's testimony, that MIL had received RMB 2,700,000 of interest from Cheng Jing. Since Cheng Jing's testimony was not substantiated by additional evidence and thus lacked credibility, the court could not confirm whether it was a fact that MIL had received a large amount of interest from Cheng Jing. Hence, the court denied CBC's appeal to have the RMB 2,700,000 of interest received by MIL deducted from the principal of RMB 20,000,000.

The original judgment was based on clearly established facts and proper application of the law. However, the judgment that interest should be calculated in accordance with the rates for overdue bank loans set by the People's Bank of China for the corresponding period should be rectified because such a calculation would be repetitive.

Judgment

According to article 153(1)(i) and (ii) of the Civil Procedure Law,[26] the court held that within ten days of the effective date of this judgment, CBC had to pay back MIL the principal of RMB 20,000,000 with interest. The interest for the period from the date of deposit to 9 December 1998 should be calculated in accordance with the current deposit rates set by the People's Bank of China for the corresponding period, and the interest for the period from 10 December 1998 to the payment date specified by this judgment should be calculated pursuant to the rates for overdue bank loans set by the People's Bank of China for the corresponding period. If the principal and the interest were not paid by the due date, the case would be enforced according to article 232 of the Civil Procedure Law.

This judgment was final.

Sun Yanzhen *v.* Changning Office of Shanghai Pudong Lianhe Trust Investment Ltd. *(2000)* 沪一中经终字第1518号, *Shanghai City No. 1 Intermediate People's Court, 6 November 2000*

Facts

Sun Yanzhen (hereinafter SY) had been trading stocks at the Changning Office of the Shanghai Pudong Lianhe Trust Investment Ltd. (hereinafter LTI) since 25 December 1992. As of June 1997, SY held 400 tradable public shares[27] of Oriental Pearl. On 4 September 1997, SY requested that LTI purchase 607 transfer right shares[28] of Oriental Pearl at RMB 5.20 per share by filling out a purchase order No. 092329. On the same day, SY also applied to purchase rights issues[29] of Oriental Pearl. The following day, when SY settled the trading, she received only a settlement statement regarding the rights issues of Oriental Pearl, which showed a balance of RMB 5,852.06, but did not obtain a settlement statement for the transfer right shares of Oriental Pearl. On 8 August 1997, the prospectus of Shanghai Oriental Pearl Ltd. regarding rights issues stipulated that when the holders of tradable public shares wanted to purchase transfer right shares of legal-person shares, they had to write down on the purchase order "Oriental Pearl Right Shares Transfer." Moreover, when the holders of transfer right shares of legal-person shares wanted to subscribe to rights issues this time, they had to write down on the purchase order "Oriental Pearl Rights Issues Transfer." The last day to pay for the subscription was 5 September 1997. On 9 October 1997, SY withdrew RMB 9,600 from her investment account, which showed a balance of RMB 70.32. On 3 April 2000, SY inquired about her purchase of the transfer right shares of Oriental Pearl.

The court of first instance found that according to the prospectus of shanghai Oriental Pearl Ltd. regarding rights issues, since SY held tradable public shares of Oriental Pearl, she could apply to purchase "Oriental Pearl rights issues" and "Oriental Pearl transfer right shares." SY mistakenly wrote down "Oriental Pearl Rights Issues Transfer" on her purchase order, thus causing the intended transaction not to be made. SY was responsible for all the legal consequences. Investment account holders should have the common knowledge to infer from the changes of their account balance whether a trading transaction had been done. On 5 September 1997, when SY settled the trading of Oriental Pearl rights issues, she knew or should have known that her "Oriental Pearl Rights Issues Transfer" transaction had not been completed. Besides, SY did withdraw RMB 9,600 from her account on 9 October 1997. The argument of SY that she had no way of knowing whether her transaction had been made because the transfer right shares could not be publicly traded was not tenable. SY's request to protect her civil rights was denied because the two-year time limit for her to file a lawsuit, starting from 9 October 1997, had expired. According to article 135 of the General Principles of the Civil Law,[30] SY's lawsuit was dismissed.

On appeal, SY requested that court reverse the original judgment on the following grounds:

1   She could not distinguish the difference between "Oriental Pearl Right Shares Transfer" and "Oriental Pearl Rights Issues Transfer," and believed that the only way to tell the difference between transfer right shares and rights issues was the subscription price. LTI should be liable because the failure of subscription was caused by LTI's negligence.
2   When she settled the trading, she could not obtain a settlement statement. However, she did not pay attention because she trusted the employees of LTI. She did not even know that the transaction had not gone through until she tried to sell her transfer right shares on 3 April 2000.
3   The court of first instance stated that investment account holders should have the common knowledge to infer from the changes of their account balance whether a trading transaction had been done. The determination of the court of first instance was erroneous. Although she did withdraw funds from her account on 9 October 1997, since the account balance of stockholders always fluctuated, she had no way to remember the details clearly.

In response, LTI set forth the following:

1   Since the time limit for filing the lawsuit should run from 9 October 1997, SY's argument that she discovered the failure of subscription only when the transfer right shares of Oriental Pearl were publicly traded was untenable.
2   SY's entrustment failed because she incorrectly wrote down the instructions. In the past, SY had successfully purchased shares by writing down "Ya Tong Right Shares Transfer" and "Ya Tong Rights Issues

Transfer." Therefore, SY's claim that she was unable to distinguish the difference between "Oriental Pearl Right Shares Transfer" and "Oriental Pearl Rights Issues Transfer" was sophistry.

3   SY should notify LTI of any discrepancies the day after her entrustment; otherwise, the settlement statement was deemed as her confirmation. Moreover, when she received the settlement statement, the payment deadline of 5 September 1997 had not expired. Thus, SY could resubmit her purchase order for the transfer right shares, but her failure to do so implied that she had given up her right.

Reasoning

The court found that the failure to purchase the transfer right shares was due to SY's mistake on her purchase order. LTI simply followed SY's instructions on her purchase order, so it had not committed any mistake. Therefore, SY had no legal basis to shift her own fault to LTI. SY could not evade responsibilities by claiming lack of professional knowledge. SY should have promptly found out whether her purchase had been successful. Her idleness to exercise her right and misunderstanding of the success of her purchase were due to her own negligence, which could not be a reason for suspending the running of the time limit for instituting litigation. Furthermore, the court rejected SY's argument that since she discovered the failure of her purchase on 3 April 2000, when she tried to sell her transfer right shares, the time limit of filing the lawsuit should run from that time.

Judgment

The judgment of the court of first instance was not erroneous. Based on article 153(1)(i) of the Civil Procedure Law,[31] the court dismissed the appeal and affirmed the original judgment.

This judgment was final.

Further reading

Hutchens, Walter, "Private Securities Litigation in China: Material Disclosure about China's Legal System," *University of Pennsylvania Journal of International Economic Law* 24, 2003, 599–689.
Jiang, Zhaodong, "China's Tax Preference to Foreign Investment: Policy, Culture and Modern Concepts," *Northwestern Journal of International Law and Business* 18, 1998, 549–654.

Notes

1 Taxes accounted for less than half of the Chinese government's revenue in the pre-reform period.

2 It has not been decided how the social security tax will be levied and shared.
3 The Provisional Regulations of the People's Republic of China on Value-Added Tax, promulgated by the State Council on 13 December 1993; the Detailed Rules for Implementation of the Provisional Regulations of the People's Republic of China on Value-Added Tax, promulgated by the Ministry of Finance on 25 December 1993.
4 The Provisional Regulations of the People's Republic of China on Consumption Tax, promulgated by the State Council on 13 December 1993; the Detailed Rules for Implementation of the Provisional Regulations of the People's Republic of China on Consumption Tax, promulgated by the Ministry of Finance on 25 December 1993.
5 The Provisional Regulations of the People's Republic of China on Business Tax, promulgated by the State Council on 13 December 1993; the Detailed Rules for Implementation of the Provisional Regulations of the People's Republic of China on Business Tax, promulgated by the Ministry of Finance on 25 December 1993.
6 This is a short title for income tax on FIEs and foreign enterprises.
7 The establishments and places mentioned here refer to the establishments of management, business operation, representative offices and factories, and the places for natural resource exploitation, for engineer work of contracted construction, installation and assembly, and for labor services and business agents (i.e., the companies, enterprises and other economic organizations or individuals entrusted by foreign enterprises for business operation).
8 The Income Tax Law of the People's Republic of China on Foreign Investment Enterprises and Foreign Enterprises, adopted at the 4th Session of the 7th National People's Congress on 9 April 1991; the Detailed Regulations for Implementation of the Income Tax Law of the People's Republic of China on Foreign Investment Enterprises and Foreign Enterprises, promulgated by the State Council on 30 June 1991.
9 The Provisional Regulations of the People's Republic of China on the Land Appreciation Tax, promulgated by the State Council on 13 December 1993; the Detailed Rules for Implementation of the Provisional Regulations of the People's Republic of China on the Land Appreciation Tax, promulgated by the Ministry of Finance on 27 January 1995.
10 The Provisional Regulations of the People's Republic of China on the Vehicle Acquisition Tax, promulgated by the State Council on 22 October 2000.
11 The Regulations of the People's Republic of China on the Import and Export Duties, promulgated by the State Council on 7 March 1985 and amended by the State Council on 12 September 1987 and 18 March 1992.
12 See Chapter 10 for details of China's commitments to the WTO on tariff cuts.
13 See Chapter 11 for examples of preferential tax treatments granted by local governments.
14 See Chapter 11 for details of these preferential tax treatments.
15 The Law of the People's Republic of China on the People's Bank of China, adopted at the 3rd Session of the 8th National People's Congress on 18 March 1995 and amended at the 6th Session of the Standing Committee of the 10th National People's Congress on 27 December 2003.
16 The Commercial Bank Law of the People's Republic of China, adopted at the 13th Session of the Standing Committee of the 8th National People's Congress on 10 May 1995 and amended at the 6th Session of the Standing Committee of the 10th National People's Congress on 27 December 2003.

17 See Chapter 10 for details of China's commitments to the WTO on banking services.
18 The Administrative Measures of the People's Republic of China on the Movement of State Currency Into and Out of Chinese Territory, promulgated by the State Council on 20 January 1993; the Rules on the Administration of the Foreign Exchange Adjustment Market, promulgated by the State Administration of Foreign Exchange on 14 April 1993; the Announcement of the People's Bank of China Concerning Further Reform of the Foreign Exchange Control System, promulgated by the People's Bank of China on 28 December 1993; the Regulations of the People's Republic of China on Foreign Exchange Control, promulgated by the State Council on 29 January 1996 and amended by the State Council on 14 January 1997; the Provisional Measures on the Administration of Foreign Exchange Registration for Foreign Investment Enterprises, promulgated by the State Administration of Foreign Exchange on 28 June 1996; the Announcement of the People's Bank of China on the Implementation of Foreign Exchange Settlements and Sales at Banks by Foreign Investment Enterprises, promulgated by the People's Bank of China on 20 June 1996; the Administrative Rules on Foreign Exchange Settlements, Sales and Payments, promulgated by the People's Bank of China on 20 June 1996; the Administrative Rules on Domestic Foreign Exchange Accounts, promulgated by the People's Bank of China on 7 December 1997; and the Administrative Measures on the Settlement of Foreign Exchange under Current Accounts, promulgated by the State Administration of Foreign Exchange on 25 July 1997.
19 See art. 3 of the Regulations of the People's Republic of China on Foreign Exchange Control.
20 The Measures of the Shanghai Municipality on the Administration of Securities Trading, promulgated by the Shanghai Municipal People's Government on 27 November 1990; the Interim Measures of the Shenzhen Municipality on the Issue and Trading of Shares, promulgated by the Shenzhen Municipal People's Government on 15 May 1991; the Company Law of the People's Republic of China, adopted at the 5th Session of the Standing Committee of the 8th National People's Congress on 29 December 1993 and amended at the 13th Session of the Standing Committee of the 9th National People's Congress on 25 December 1999; the Securities Law of the People's Republic of China, adopted at the 6th Session of the Standing Committee of the 9th National People's Congress on 29 December 1998.
21 Securities Law, art. 167.
22 Securities Law, arts. 23 and 26.
23 The Provisional Rules on Administration of Domestic Securities Investment by Qualified Foreign Institutional Investors (QFII), promulgated jointly by the China Securities Regulatory Commission and the People's Bank of China on 5 November 2002.
24 Article 232 of the Civil Procedure Law provides that where a party fails to make payment within the period specified by a court judgment, ruling, or legal document, it shall pay twice the interest earned during the period of delay; and where a party fails to perform other obligations within the period specified by a judgment, ruling, or legal document, it shall pay compensation for the delay.
25 Article 17 of the Measures on the Settlement of Payments provides that where a bank pays out funds on a forged negotiable instrument, or based on a fraudulent signature, seal, or identification document, after it has examined such items in

good faith, in conformity with regulations and in compliance with the normal operation sequence, but has not discerned any abnormalities, it shall not be liable to the drawer or payer, and shall not be responsible for making payment to the bearer or payee.

26 Article 153(1)(i) and (ii) of the Civil Procedure Law provides that the court of second instance should dismiss the appeal and affirm the judgment of the court of first instance if the original judgment is based on clearly established facts and correct application of law; and amend the judgment if the original judgment is based on incorrect application of law.

27 Tradable public shares (可流通社会公众股) are shares held by individuals or entities that can be traded in stock exchanges.

28 Transfer right shares (转配股) refer to special kinds of securities in China. The holders of state shares (国有股) or legal-person shares (法人股) may transfer their rights issues to other legal persons or the general public for compensation. When the latter exercise their rights to subscribe to new issues, the new shares are referred to as "transfer right shares".

29 Rights issues (配股) refer to those shares offered by listed companies to the existing shareholders for subscription in order to raise capital for further expansion.

30 Article 135 of the General Principles of the Civil Law provides that the time limit for filing an action with the people's court for the protection of civil rights is two years, unless otherwise provided by law.

31 Article 153(1)(i) of the Civil Procedure Law provides that the court of second instance should dismiss the appeal and affirm the judgment of the court of first instance if the original judgment is based on clearly established facts and correct application of law.

9 Dispute resolution

By and large, disputes arising from doing business are civil disputes. In China, the predominant means for resolving civil disputes are mediation, arbitration, and litigation. Depending on the nature of a dispute, the disputants may resort to one, two, or even all of these mechanisms. For instance, when a dispute arises between joint-venture partners, the disputants may first seek mediation, then request arbitration, and finally file a lawsuit. In fact, the same dispute-resolution institution may also try to resolve a dispute through more than one of these modes. For example, to resolve a dispute over the performance of a contract, the court may first undertake mediation and, if mediation fails, conduct adjudication. At times, businesses may disagree with government agencies on denial of licenses, imposition of fines, or dispensation of orders. To challenge administrative actions, complainants may either seek administrative reconsideration or file a suit against the government in court. Accordingly, foreign investors should familiarize themselves with the basic means of resolving civil disputes and the avenues to contest administrative decisions.

To provide an overview of dispute-resolution mechanisms in China, this chapter discusses conciliation/mediation, administrative proceedings, litigation, and arbitration. The sections on conciliation/mediation, administrative proceedings, and litigation are succinct, while the discussion on arbitration of commercial disputes is more elaborate. The main reason for such an approach is that although litigation has increased in recent years and will continue to increase as a result of further improvement of China's legal infrastructure, arbitration has been a very popular dispute-resolution means for foreign investors in China and many commercial disputes in the world have been resolved by arbitration rather than litigation. With a basic understanding of dispute-resolution modes, foreign investors can be better prepared to undertake commercial endeavors in China.

1 Conciliation/mediation

"Alternative dispute resolution" refers to the resolution of disputes by means other than litigation. In recent years, alternative dispute resolution has increasingly been employed to resolve various kinds of disputes around the world. Its common forms are conciliation, mediation, and arbitration. Conciliation is a dispute resolution procedure in which a neutral third party helps the disputants to communicate and reach an amicable settlement. Mediation is a dispute resolution procedure in which a neutral third party facilitates communication between the disputants, clarifies important facts, and recommends non-binding solutions satisfactory to both sides. Hence, conciliation differs from mediation in that the conciliator is not to recommend solutions, even though in practice he or she often does.

In China, *tiaojie* (调解) – whether it is translated as conciliation or mediation – has been an important means of resolving civil disputes since the 1950s. Prior to the economic reform, people's mediation (人民调解) was used primarily to mobilize the masses for the revolutionary cause. Since the early 1980s, mediation based on persuasion and education has been used to resolve minor civil disputes and to promote social cohesion, and, thus, economic construction and modernization. Over the years, people's mediation committees (人民调解委员会), which have the status of mass organizations, have mediated numerous civil disputes, such as those on domestic relations and conflicts between neighbors.

Apart from people's mediation, judicial mediation (法院调解) has also been used extensively to resolve civil disputes in China. According to the Civil Procedure Law,[1] the court, relying upon the willingness of the parties, should mediate based on clear facts and distinguish right from wrong. If mediation is successful, a mediated agreement (调解书) should be made, which becomes legally binding once it has been delivered to and signed by the parties. Hence, if one party refuses to carry out its obligations under the mediated agreement, the other party may apply to the court for enforcement. Nevertheless, if mediation does not result in a mediated agreement or one party retracts before the delivery of the agreement, the court should adjudicate promptly. Judicial mediation can be conducted before trial or at any stage prior to judgment. Indeed, the court of second instance can also conduct mediation, and the judgment of the court of first instance will be deemed reversed once the mediated agreement is delivered.

Conciliation/mediation has also been used frequently in commercial disputes, particularly because the parties do not want a confrontation in court and risk the loss of an ongoing business relationship. The Mediation (Conciliation) Center of the China Chamber of International Commerce (formerly the China Council for the Promotion of International Trade) has been established to assist disputants in settling disputes relating to economics, trade, finance, securities, investment, intellectual property, technology transfer, real estate, transportation, insurance, maritime business, etc. by means of conciliation/mediation. Currently, the Mediation (Conciliation) Center has more than 30 local centers, which conduct conciliation/mediation by using a set of uniform rules – the China Chamber of International Commerce Mediation (Conciliation) Rules.[2] Moreover, the Mediation (Conciliation) Center

Table 9.1 Mediation (conciliation) fee schedule

Amount in dispute (RMB)	Fee (% of the amount in dispute)
100,000 or less	6–4 (no less than RMB 1,500)
100,000 to 500,000	4–2.5
500,000 to 1 million	2.5–1.75
1 million to 5 million	1.75–1
5 million to 10 million	1–0.75
10 million to 50 million	0.75–0.5
50 million or more	0.5

Source: China Chamber of International Commerce Mediation (Conciliation) Center (2003).

Visit: www.cietac.org.cn/BBC/a22.html.

has signed cooperation agreements with such institutions as the Beijing-Hamburg Conciliation Center, the Argentine-China Conciliation Center, the New York Conciliation Center, and the London Court of International Arbitration.

The Mediation (Conciliation) Center accepts a case based on the mediation (conciliation) agreement between the parties, or in the absence of such agreement, upon one party's application with the consent of the other party. Each party may either appoint or authorize the Mediation (Conciliation) Center to designate a mediator (conciliator). The two mediators (conciliators) will jointly mediate the dispute, unless the parties agree to have only one mediator (conciliator). Generally, mediation (conciliation) is conducted in the place where the Mediation (Conciliation) Center is located. However, mediation (conciliation) may be conducted in another place if the parties so agree with the approval of the Mediation (Conciliation) Center, or if the Mediation (Conciliation) Center so proposes with the consent of the parties. If the parties reach a settlement agreement, they should affix their signatures on it. Based on the contents of the settlement agreement, the mediator (conciliator) will make a mediated agreement, sign on it, and affix it with the seal of the Mediation (Conciliation) Center. If mediation (conciliation) fails, the parties may not, in subsequent arbitration or litigation proceedings, use any statements, viewpoints, opinions, or proposals that have been raised, suggested, admitted, or indicated as acceptable by the parties or the mediator (conciliator) in the course of mediation (conciliation) as the basis for a claim or defense.

2 Administrative proceedings

To provide more transparency, China has recently enacted the Administrative License Law.[3] This law sets forth the substantive rules for the establishment and implementation of administrative licenses as well as the procedural rules for the application of administrative licenses. In particular, article 7 of the Administrative License Law provides that as regards the implementation of administrative licenses by administrative agencies, citizens, legal persons, and other organizations are entitled to make statements, defend themselves, apply for administrative reconsideration, or institute administrative litigation in accordance with the law. Apart from the implementation or denial of various types of licenses, other acts of administrative agencies, such as a fine or an order to stop production, are subject to administrative reconsideration, administrative litigation, or both. There follows, an introduction to these two types of administrative proceedings.

Administrative reconsideration

According to the Administrative Reconsideration Law,[4] citizens, legal persons, or other organizations may apply for administrative reconsideration (行政复议) of certain "concrete administrative acts" (具体行政行为) that infringe upon their lawful rights and interests. Specifically, they may seek administrative reconsideration if they find the following "concrete administrative acts" unacceptable or unlawful:

1   administrative punishment, such as a warning, a fine, the confiscation of illegal income or property, an order to suspend production or business, the suspension or revocation of a license or permit, and administrative detainment;
2   coercive administrative measures, such as restriction of personal freedom and the sealing up, seizure, or freezing of property;
3   administrative decisions to change, suspend, or revoke such certificates as permits, licenses, and credentials;
4   infringement of autonomy in business operations;
5   collection of funds, expropriation of property, apportionment of expenses, or the request to perform other obligations;
6   failure, despite the fulfillment of legal requirements, to issue such certificates as permits, licenses, and credentials, or to examine and approve or register relevant items;
7   failure to carry out the statutory duties of protecting the person or property of the applicant, etc.

To seek administrative reconsideration, the citizen, legal person, or organization must file an application within 60 days of the time when it knows of the "concrete administrative act," unless otherwise prescribed by law. If the delay is due to *force majeure* or other valid reasons, the time limit will be continuously counted from the date when the obstacle is removed. The proper organ for administrative reconsideration depends on who the administrative actor is. For instance, if the applicant wants to seek administrative reconsideration of a "concrete administrative act" of a department under the local people's government at or above the county level, it may apply to the people's government at the same level or the department-in-charge at the next higher level. If the administrative actor practices vertical leadership, such as the Customs, state tax, financial, and foreign exchange authorities, or is a state security organ, the applicant should go to the department-in-charge at the next higher level. Similarly, if the applicant wants to seek administrative reconsideration of a "concrete administrative act" of a local people's government at various levels, it should apply to the local people's government at the next higher level. For a "concrete administrative act" of a department under the State Council or of the people's government of a province, autonomous region, or municipality directly under the central government, the applicant should go to the same department or people's government for administrative reconsideration. However, if the applicant does not accept the decision of the administrative-reconsideration organ, it may apply to the State Council for a final judgment or file a lawsuit in court.

The administrative-reconsideration organ should make a decision within 60 days of the acceptance of the application, unless otherwise stipulated by law. If the "concrete administrative act" is based on clear facts, conclusive evidence, proper grounds, and lawful procedure and consists of appropriate contents, the administrative-reconsideration organ shall affirm the validity of the act. If the administrative actor fails to perform its statutory duties, the administrative-reconsideration organ shall require performance within a fixed period of time. Furthermore, the administrative-reconsideration organ shall annul, amend, or outlaw the "concrete administrative act" if it finds ambiguity of crucial facts and insufficient evidence, erroneous grounds, violation of legal procedure, excess or abuse of power, or obvious inappropriateness. If the "concrete administrative act" is annulled or declared unlawful, the administrative actor may be ordered to act anew within a fixed period of time.

Generally, to challenge a "concrete administrative act," the citizen, legal person, or organization may either apply for administrative reconsideration or file an administrative lawsuit. If administrative reconsideration is sought and the decision of the administrative-reconsideration organ is not acceptable, the applicant may file a lawsuit in court pursuant to the Administrative Procedure Law, unless the decision is final as prescribed by law. Where the administrative-reconsideration organ has accepted the case, or if the law mandates administrative reconsideration prior to administrative litigation, but the applicant refuses to accept the decision of the administrative-reconsideration organ, no lawsuit may be filed within the statutory time limit for administrative reconsideration. However, if the administrative-reconsideration organ does not accept the case or fails to reach a decision upon the expiration of the time limit, the applicant may file a lawsuit from the date when it receives the refusal or within 15 days of the expiration of the time limit. On the other hand, if the citizen, legal person, or organization brings a lawsuit and the court has accepted the case, administrative reconsideration may not be pursued.

Administrative litigation

According to the Administrative Procedure Law,[5] citizens, legal persons, or other organizations have the right to file lawsuits against administrative organs for "concrete administrative acts" that infringe upon their lawful rights and interests. Specifically, they may undertake administrative litigation (行政诉讼) if they do not want to accept the following "concrete administrative acts":

1   administrative punishment, such as detention, a fine, the revocation of a permit or license, an order to stop production or business, or confiscation of property;
2   coercive administrative measures, such as the restriction of personal freedom and the sealing up, seizure, or freezing of property;
3   infringement of autonomy in business operations;
4   failure to issue permits or licenses or to respond to an application, despite the fulfillment of legal requirements;
5   failure to execute the statutory duties of protecting the person or property of the applicant or to respond accordingly;
6   infringement of personal or property rights, etc.

Nonetheless, the people's court will not accept a case if the subject matter concerns an administrative regulation or government rule, or an administrative decision or order that has a general binding force. The people's court will also not accept a case if the "concrete administrative act" is finally to be decided by an administrative organ as prescribed by law. Moreover, if the only claim is the amount of compensation, the administrative organ should first handle the case. If the claimant does not accept the disposition of the administrative organ, it may then file an administrative lawsuit.

Where a citizen, legal person, or organization refuses to accept the decision of the administrative-reconsideration organ, or if the administrative-reconsideration organ fails to reach a decision upon the expiration of the time limit, the applicant may bring a lawsuit within 15 days of the receipt of the decision or the expiration of the time limit, unless otherwise stipulated by law. However, if the citizen, legal person, or organization wants to file a lawsuit directly, it may do so within three months of the time when it knows of the "concrete administrative act," unless otherwise prescribed by law. Where the delay is due to *force majeure* or other valid reasons, the citizen, legal person, or organization may apply for an extension within 10 days of the removal of the obstacle, in which case, the court will decide on the extension request.

As a rule, the basic people's court has jurisdiction as the court of first instance over administrative cases. However, in the following types of cases, the intermediate people's court has jurisdiction as the court of first instance:

1   cases affirming patent rights and cases handled by the Customs;
2   suits against "concrete administrative acts" done by departments under the State Council or by the people's governments of provinces, autonomous regions, or municipalities directly under the central government; and
3   important and complicated cases within the area under its jurisdiction.

Similarly, the high people's court has jurisdiction as the court of first instance over important and complicated cases within the area under its jurisdiction, while the Supreme People's Court has jurisdiction as the court of first instance over important and complicated cases nationwide. Even so, a higher-level people's court may adjudicate administrative cases over which a lower-level people's court has jurisdiction as the court of first instance, or transfer its own administrative cases to a lower-level people's court. Likewise, if a lower-level people's court deems it necessary to have an administrative case adjudicated by a higher-level people's court, it may submit the case to the higher-level people's court for determination.

In the lawsuit, each party may entrust one or two persons to represent it. A lawyer, a social organization, a close relative of the plaintiff, a person recommended by the plaintiff's work unit, or any citizen approved by the court may be entrusted as an agent *ad litem*. However, foreigner nationals, stateless persons, or foreign organizations must appoint lawyers of Chinese law organizations as agents *ad litem*. If there is the likelihood that evidence will be destroyed, lost, or difficult to obtain later, the parties may apply for evidence preservation. Alternatively, the court may, on its own initiative, take measures to preserve evidence. In handling administrative cases, the court shall not conduct mediation, unless the claim concerns compensatory damages. If the "concrete administrative act" is based on conclusive evidence, correct application of law or regulation, and proper compliance with legal procedure, the court shall affirm the validity of the act. Moreover, under any one of the following circumstances, the court shall annul or partially annul the "concrete administrative act" and may order the defendant to act anew:

1   insufficiency of principal evidence;
2   incorrect application of law or regulation;
3   violation of legal procedure;
4   acts beyond the scope of power; and
5   abuse of power.

Furthermore, if the defendant fails to perform or delays the performance of its statutory duties, the court shall order performance within a fixed period of time. If the administrative punishment at issue is obviously unfair, the court may also modify the punishment. Generally, the court of first instance shall make a judgment within three months of the acceptance of the lawsuit. If a party refuses to accept the judgment, it may appeal to the court at the next higher level within 15 days of the delivery of the written judgment. If a party refuses to accept a ruling, it shall lodge an appeal with the court at the next higher level within 10 days of the delivery of the written ruling.

On appeal, the court is to make a final judgment within two months of the receipt of the appellate brief. If the original judgment is based on clearly established facts and correct application of law or regulation, the appellate court shall dismiss the appeal and affirm the lower court's judgment. If the original judgment is based on clearly established facts but incorrect application of law or regulation, the appellate court shall amend the lower court's judgment in accordance with the law. If the facts are not clearly established in the original judgment, the evidence is inadequate, or a violation of the legal procedure may affect the making of a correct judgment, the appellate court shall reverse and remand the case for retrial. Alternatively, the appellate court may amend the judgment after investigating and ascertaining the facts.

3 Litigation

For centuries, litigation has been used extensively to resolve disputes. With the intensification of economic reform in China, litigation has been used increasingly to resolve disputes arising from complex business transactions. The governing rule for civil litigation (民事诉讼) is the Civil Procedure Law. Apart from providing a general framework for conducting civil trials, the Civil Procedure Law contains special provisions on foreign-related civil litigation (涉外民事诉讼). Accordingly, this section first introduces civil litigation in China, then highlights special provisions on foreign-related civil litigation, and finally discusses issues relating to enforcement of judgments or rulings.

General framework

As mentioned in Chapter 1, China has a two-trial system: one trial at the court of first instance and one appeal at the court of second instance.[6] The civil jurisdiction of a court depends on two factors: level (级别) and territory (地域). Regarding jurisdiction based on the level of a court, the basic people's court is usually the court of first instance. However, the intermediate people's court is the court of first instance in major foreign-related cases,[7] cases that have great impact within its jurisdiction, and cases determined by the Supreme People's Court to come under its jurisdiction. Similarly, the high people's court is to be the court of first instance in cases that have great impact within its jurisdiction, and the Supreme People's Court is the court of first instance in cases that have great impact nationwide and in cases that it thinks it should try.

On the other hand, territorial jurisdiction covers both *in personam* jurisdiction and *in rem* jurisdiction. The domicile (住所地) or place of dwelling (经常居住地) of the defendant or plaintiff; location of an insured object;

place of performance of a contract; place of infringement; place of tort; agreement between the parties; etc. determines territorial jurisdiction. Nevertheless, some courts have exclusive jurisdiction over certain types of cases. For example, the court of the place where an immovable property is located has jurisdiction over a case involving the immovable property, and the court of the place where a harbor is located has jurisdiction over a dispute arising from harbor operations.

Furthermore, a higher-level court may order a lower-level court to exercise jurisdiction if the court having proper jurisdiction cannot try a case due to special reasons. If two courts try to assert jurisdiction over a case, a common higher-level court will designate one of them as the proper forum. In any event, a case is to be transferred from a court without jurisdiction to a court with proper jurisdiction. If the defendant wants to challenge a court's jurisdiction, it must do so within the prescribed period for filing a reply.

In conducting civil litigation, the court is to practice the systems of collegial bench, withdrawal, and open trial. In the court of first instance, a bench may be composed of judges or judges and assessors (陪审员); in the court of second instance, a bench is to be composed of judges. For summary procedure (简易程序), however, only one judge is required. A judge must withdraw if he or she is a close relative of a litigant or of its agent(s) *ad litem*, has a conflict of interest with the case, or has other relations with a litigant, which may affect the administration of justice. A civil trial is to be an open trial, unless the case involves state secrets, trade secrets, etc. In a trade-secret case, the litigant may apply for a closed trial. Each litigant has the right to entrust its agent(s) *ad litem* with the tasks of applying for withdrawal, collecting and presenting evidence, engaging in debate, requesting mediation, lodging an appeal, and seeking enforcement. The agents *ad litem* may be lawyers, close relatives, persons recommended by relevant social organizations or the litigants' work units, or any other citizens approved by the court. Moreover, a litigant may apply for evidence preservation if the evidence may be lost, destroyed, or difficult to obtain afterward. Where it will be impossible or difficult to enforce a judgment due to the conduct of one litigant or for other reasons, the other litigant may apply for property preservation, in which case, the court may order the applicant to provide a guarantee. Alternatively, the court may, on its own initiative, adopt measures to preserve evidence or property. Indeed, the court must conscientiously examine and verify litigation materials as well as investigate and collect necessary evidence.

Where there are two or more litigants with the same litigious objective(s), but the exact number of litigants cannot be determined at the time of litigation, the court may make a public announcement, explaining the circumstances of the case and the claims and informing those who have the right to join in the litigation to register with the court within a fixed period of time. The registered litigants may elect a representative to conduct litigation. The judgment or ruling of the court is binding on all registered litigants and those who have not registered but have instituted legal proceedings within the prescribed period for litigation. In other words, class action may be filed in China. Likewise, a third party who has an independent claim against the object in dispute also has the right to file a lawsuit. If the third party does not have an independent claim, but the outcome of the case will affect its legal interest(s), it may apply to join in the lawsuit, or the court may notify it to do so. A third party who is adjudged to bear civil liability has the rights and obligations of a litigant.

The court of first instance may render either a judgment (判决) or ruling (裁定). A written judgment should set forth the following:

1   the cause of action, the claim(s), and the facts of and reasons for the dispute;
2   the facts, reason(s), and legal provision(s) on the basis of which the judgment is made;
3   the outcome of the adjudication and how the litigation cost is to be borne; and
4   the time limit for appeal and the name of the appellate court.

On the other hand, a ruling should be given for:

1   refusal to accept a case;
2   a decision on jurisdictional objection;
3   dismissal of a lawsuit;
4   preservation of property and enforcement of alimony, child support, etc. in advance;
5   approval or disapproval of the withdrawal of a lawsuit;
6   suspension or termination of litigation;
7   correction of an error in a written judgment;
8   suspension or termination of enforcement;
9   denial of the enforcement of an arbitration award;
10   denial of the enforcement of a credit document that a notary organ has rendered effective for coercive execution; or
11   any other matters to be resolved by a ruling.

The litigants may appeal (上诉) a judgment or a ruling on refusal to accept a case, jurisdictional challenge, or dismissal of a lawsuit within a prescribed period of time. If no appeal is filed within the prescribed time limit, the judgment or ruling will become legally effective. After the judgment or ruling has become legally effective, the litigants may *shensu* (申诉) on the grounds of error(s) or new evidence.

On appeal, the court of second instance should:

1   dismiss the appeal and affirm the judgment of the court of first instance if the original judgment is based on clearly established facts and correct application of law;

2   amend the judgment if the original judgment is based on incorrect application of law;
3   reverse and remand the case for retrial, or amend the original judgment after ascertaining the facts, if the original judgment is based on erroneous or unclear facts or insufficient evidence; or
4   reverse and remand the case for retrial if the original judgment is made in violation of procedural rules, which may affect the making of a correct judgment.

To handle an appeal against the ruling of the court of first instance, the court of second instance should use a ruling. The judgment or ruling of the court of second instance is final.

To ensure the proper administration of justice, the Civil Procedure Law also provides a procedure for the supervision of adjudication (审判监督程序). That is, the Supreme People's Court or a higher-level court has the right to bring up a case to retry or instruct a lower-level court to conduct a retrial when a definite error is found in a legally effective judgment or ruling. Similarly, the Supreme People's Procuratorate or people's procuratorates at various levels shall lodge a protest against (抗诉) a legally effective judgment or ruling of a lower-level court if:

1   the crucial evidence in the original judgment or ruling was insufficient;
2   the application of law in the original judgment or ruling was erroneous;
3   the court violated a legal procedure, which might affect the making of a correct judgment or ruling; or
4   the judge(s) took bribes or bent the law for personal gains.

After a protest is lodged, the people's court should conduct a retrial.

Foreign-related civil litigation

Simply stated, a civil action is foreign-related if one of the litigants is a foreigner, stateless person, or foreign enterprise or organization; the object in dispute is located in a foreign country; or the facts creating or terminating the legal relationship between the litigants took place outside China. For foreign-related civil litigation, the Civil Procedure Law sets forth special provisions; however, other relevant provisions will apply whenever an issue is not addressed by any of the special provisions. First, the Civil Procedure Law provides that the provisions in an international treaty that China has concluded or to which China is a signatory will take precedence over domestic law, except for those provisions about which China has made reservations. If a foreigner, stateless person, or foreign enterprise or organization wants to entrust a lawyer with filing or defending a lawsuit, it must retain a lawyer who is licensed to practice law in China.

Where the defendant in a civil lawsuit involving contract or property dispute does not reside in China, but the contract is signed or is to be performed in China, the object of the litigation is located in China, the defendant has property in China that can be seized, or the defendant has a representative office in China, the court of the place where the contract is concluded or is to be performed, the place where the litigious object is located, the place where the defendant has property that can be impounded, the place where the infringement has occurred, or the place where the representative office of the defendant is located will have jurisdiction. Nonetheless, the parties to a foreign-related contract or property dispute may agree in writing to submit to the jurisdiction of a court in the place that has an actual connection with the dispute. Such a choice may not violate the provisions on jurisdiction based on the level of the court and exclusive jurisdiction. If the defendant files a reply without any objections, it will be deemed to have accepted the jurisdiction of the court. However, the people's courts have jurisdiction over disputes arising from the performance of contracts of Chinese-foreign equity joint ventures, Chinese-foreign cooperative joint ventures, or Chinese-foreign cooperative exploration and development of natural resources.

Furthermore, the Supreme People's Court mandates that five types of foreign-related civil and commercial cases be handled centrally by five groups of courts of first instance.[8] The five types of foreign-related civil and commercial cases are:

1   foreign-related contractual and infringement disputes;
2   letter-of-credit disputes;
3   application for the setting aside, recognition, or enforcement of international arbitration awards;
4   examination of the validity of arbitration provisions in foreign-related civil and commercial cases; and
5   application for the recognition and enforcement of civil- and commercial-case judgments and rulings rendered by foreign courts.

However, trade disputes at the Chinese borders, foreign-related real estate cases, and foreign-related intellectual property cases are not covered. The five groups of courts of first instance are:

1   people's courts approved by the State Council and established in Economic and Technological Development Zones;
2   intermediate people's courts located in provincial capitals, autonomous-regional capitals, and municipalities directly under the central government;
3   intermediate people's courts located in SEZs and Separately Planned Cities;[9]
4   other intermediate people's courts designated by the Supreme People's Court; and
5   high people's courts.

Table 9.2 Foreign-related civil and commercial cases to be handled centrally

---

Five types of foreign-related civil and commercial cases
1 Foreign-related contractual and infringement disputes
2 Letter-of-credit disputes
3 Application for the setting aside, recognition, or enforcement of international arbitration awards
4 Examination of the validity of arbitration provisions in foreign-related civil and commercial cases
5 Application for the recognition and enforcement of civil- and commercial-case judgments and rulings rendered by foreign courts

Exceptions
Trade disputes at the Chinese borders, foreign-related real estate cases, and foreign-related intellectual property cases

Five groups of courts of first instance
1 People's courts approved by the State Council and established in Economic and Technological Development Zones
2 Intermediate people's courts located in provincial capitals, autonomous-regional capitals, and municipalities directly under the central government
3 Intermediate people's courts located in SEZs and Separately Planned Cities
4 Other intermediate people's courts designated by the Supreme People's Court
5 High people's courts

Enforcement

Generally, if one litigant refuses to comply with a judgment or ruling, the other litigant may apply for enforcement with the court of first instance. The judge may then transfer the petition to the sheriff for execution. In enforcing a judgment or ruling, the court has the powers to freeze or transfer bank deposits; seize and draw income (other than necessary living expenses); and seal up, seize, freeze, auction, or sell property. Where a people's court has rendered a judgment or ruling, but the party against whom the judgment or ruling is enforced or its property is not within the territory of China, the applicant may apply directly to the foreign court having jurisdiction for recognition and enforcement. Alternatively, the people's court may request that the foreign court recognize and enforce its judgment or ruling pursuant to international treaties that China has concluded or to which China is a signatory or in accordance with the principle of reciprocity.

Until now, the enforcement of judgments or rulings has encountered various obstacles. For instance, local protectionism has made some courts refuse to enforce the judgments or rulings rendered by courts located in other parts of the country. Moreover, it has been difficult to enforce judgments against state-owned enterprises because enforcing a substantial judgment may drive the enterprise into bankruptcy, which will result in a massive layoff of workers and, thus, social instability. In fact, judicial corruption and insufficient funding of some courts have further compounded the difficulty of enforcing judgments or rulings.

4 Arbitration

Arbitration (仲裁) is a dispute-resolution procedure in which an arbitrator or a panel of arbitrators hears the dispute and renders an arbitration award, which, in most cases, is binding upon the parties. In the business world, arbitration has been a very popular means of dispute resolution because arbitration has advantages over litigation. Since China opened its door to foreign investors in the late 1970s, arbitration has been a major vehicle to resolve disputes arising from foreign direct investment and foreign trade. This section, therefore, aims to provide an overview of arbitration of commercial disputes in China.

Background

When China had a command economy, enterprises would refer an economic dispute to their common department-in-charge or a higher-ranking organization that had jurisdiction over them. Taking all relevant factors into account, the department-in-charge or higher authority would render a decision akin to an arbitration award. In the 1950s, when China's trade with Eastern European countries increased, the Foreign Trade Arbitration Commission was established within the China Council for the Promotion of International Trade. The Foreign Trade Arbitration Commission was to arbitrate disputes arising from foreign trade contracts; however, in the ensuing years, it arbitrated only a handful of cases.

Shortly after the implementation of economic reforms, arbitral organs established at various levels of the AIC conducted arbitration of disputes involving economic contracts. Moreover, in 1980, the Foreign Trade Arbitration Commission was re-named the Foreign Economic and Trade Arbitration Commission. Its jurisdiction was expanded to handle disputes arising from China's economic cooperation with foreign countries. As the number of commercial disputes involving foreign parties multiplied, the Foreign Economic and Trade Arbitration Commission established offices in Shenzhen and Shanghai.

In 1988, the State Council approved the conversion of the Foreign Economic and Trade Arbitration Commission into the China International Economic and Trade Arbitration Commission (CIETAC), expanded its jurisdiction to cover all disputes arising from international economic and trade transactions, and authorized it to revise arbitration rules thereafter. Accordingly, in 1994, the China Council for the Promotion of International Trade (now the China Chamber of International Commerce) revised the CIETAC Arbitration Rules. The jurisdiction of the CIETAC was further expanded to handle "disputes arising from international or foreign-related, contractual or non-contractual, economic and trade transactions, including disputes between foreign legal persons and/or natural persons and Chinese legal persons and/or natural persons, between foreign legal persons and/or natural persons, and between Chinese legal persons and/or natural persons." In the same year, China promulgated its Arbitration Law,[10] establishing a general framework for arbitration, standardizing arbitration commissions, and rendering arbitration commissions independent of local administration.

Specifically, the Arbitration Law provides for the establishment of the China Arbitration Association, which is empowered to superintend arbitration commissions and to formulate rules of arbitration to be applied by arbitration commissions. Arbitration commissions may be established in the cities where the governments of provinces, municipalities directly under the central government, and autonomous regions are located, and must be registered with the local judicial-administration departments. Since arbitration commissions do not have subordinate relationships with administrative organs or any subordinate relations of their own, they are independent dispute-resolution entities. In a nutshell, an arbitration commission must have its own name, domicile, and articles of association; the necessary assets; constituent personnel; and appointed arbitrators. It must have one chairperson, two to four vice-chairpersons, and seven to eleven members, of whom at least two-thirds must be experts in the fields of law, economics, and trade. It must maintain a speciality-based list of arbitrators, from which the disputants may choose their own arbitrators. To become an arbitrator, a person must have engaged in arbitration work, served as a judge, or worked as a lawyer for eight years; engaged in legal research or education work and held a senior position; or acquired legal knowledge, engaged in such professional work as economics and trade, and held a senior position or attained the equivalent professional level. To meet these requirements of the Arbitration Law, the then-existing arbitral organs were either closed down or reorganized.

On the international front, the Arbitration Law empowers the China Chamber of International Commerce to organize foreign-related arbitration commissions and to formulate rules for foreign-related arbitration. The China Chamber of International Commerce revised the CIETAC Arbitration Rules in 1995 and 1998. The 1995 CIETAC Arbitration Rules expanded the jurisdiction of the CIETAC by allowing it to accept cases pursuant to special provisions in or special authorization from Chinese laws or administrative regulations. Prior to the 1998 revision, the CIETAC did not arbitrate disputes arising between Sino-foreign equity joint ventures, between Sino-foreign equity joint ventures and domestic entities, or between Sino-foreign equity joint ventures and wholly foreign-owned enterprises, because equity joint ventures and wholly foreign-owned enterprises were Chinese legal persons and no foreign-related elements were involved. The 1998 CIETAC Arbitration Rules expanded the jurisdiction of the CIETAC to cover disputes arising between FIEs or between FIEs and Chinese legal persons, natural persons and/or economic organizations. Besides, the CIETAC was authorized to arbitrate disputes arising from project financing, invitation to tender, bidding, project construction, and other activities conducted by Chinese legal persons, natural persons or economic organizations using capital, technology, or services originating from foreign countries, international organizations, or Hong Kong, Macao, and Taiwan. Furthermore, the CIETAC might arbitrate disputes related to the Hong Kong Special Administration Region, Macao Special Administration Region, or the Taiwan Region.

In anticipation of China's entry into the WTO and to make arbitration services more readily accessible, the China Chamber of International Commerce revised the CIETAC Arbitration Rules in 2000.[11] Among various revisions, the 2000 CIETAC Arbitration Rules expand the jurisdiction of the CIETAC to other domestic disputes that the parties agree to submit to the CIETAC for arbitration. Moreover, a new set of special provisions applies to the arbitration of the following domestic disputes:

1   Disputes between FIEs or between an FIE and a Chinese legal person, natural person, and/or economic organization.
2   Disputes arising from activities using capital, technology, or services from foreign countries, international organizations, or Hong Kong, Macao, and Taiwan.
3   Disputes that may be arbitrated in accordance with special provisions in or upon special authorization from Chinese laws or administrative regulations.
4   Other domestic disputes that the parties agree to submit to the CIETAC.

Furthermore, under the 1998 CIEATC Arbitration Rules, when a party challenged the arbitration agreement or the jurisdiction of the CIETAC, the arbitration proceedings were stayed until a decision was made on the issue. To prevent a party from raising such objections to delay the arbitration proceedings, the 2000 CIETAC Arbitration Rules provide that such objections will not affect the progress of the arbitration proceedings.

General framework

The Arbitration Law provides the governing rules for arbitration in China. Although it has a chapter of special provisions on foreign-related arbitration, other relevant provisions are applicable whenever an issue is not addressed in that chapter. This section, therefore, discusses the general framework of arbitration, while the next section highlights the important provisions on foreign-related arbitration.

According to the Arbitration Law, contractual disputes and disputes involving the rights and interests of property between citizens, legal persons, and other organizations that are equal subjects may be resolved by arbitration. Disputes involving marriage, adoption, guardianship, support, and succession, as well as administrative disputes that must be handled by administrative organs, are not to be arbitrated. Moreover, separate regulations govern the arbitration of labor disputes and disputes in agricultural-collective-economic organizations over agricultural management contracts. In other words, except for the enumerated jurisdictional limitations, arbitration can be conducted pursuant to an arbitration agreement between the disputants.

An arbitration agreement (仲裁协议) can be evidenced by either an arbitration clause contained in a contract or a written agreement on arbitration that is concluded before or after the dispute arose. The revision, termination, or invalidity of a contract will not affect the validity of an arbitration agreement. Basically, an arbitration agreement must indicate the parties' intention to submit their disputes to arbitration, the matters to be arbitrated, and their choice of an arbitration commission. If an arbitration agreement contains no or unclear provisions regarding the matters to be arbitrated or the choice of an arbitration commission, it will be void unless the parties have reached a supplemental agreement. The parties may challenge the validity of an arbitration agreement either with the arbitration commission or in court. If one party requests that the arbitration commission determine the validity of an arbitration agreement while the other party applies to the court for a ruling on the same issue, the court shall make a ruling. On the other hand, if one party files a lawsuit in court despite the existence of a valid arbitration agreement, the court shall not accept the case. Indeed, if one party files a lawsuit without revealing the existence of an arbitration agreement and the other party fails to object by appearing before the court, the latter will be deemed to have discarded the arbitration agreement and the court will continue to try the case.

To institute an arbitration proceeding, one party must submit to the arbitration commission the arbitration agreement and an application. The application must clearly indicate:

1 the name, gender, age, occupation, employer, and domicile of the parties, or the name, domicile, and legal representative (or chief responsible person) of the legal person (or organization);
2 the claims with supporting facts and reasons; and
3 the evidence and its sources as well as the names and domiciles of the witnesses.

Upon receipt of the application, the arbitration commission must decide within five days whether or not to accept the case. If the application is accepted, the arbitration commission should notify the respondent; if the application is rejected, the written notification should also explain the reason(s). The respondent may then admit or deny the claim or make a counterclaim. Meanwhile, the applicant may apply for property preservation, in which case, the arbitration commission must submit the application to the people's court in accordance with the Civil Procedure Law.

Once the application is accepted, an arbitration tribunal consisting of either three arbitrators or a single arbitrator must be formed. Arbitrators are chosen from a list, which is delivered to the applicant and the respondent upon acceptance of the case. If the arbitration tribunal consists of three members, each party may appoint one arbitrator and the third one, the presiding arbitrator, is to be appointed by agreement between the parties or by the chairperson of the arbitration commission. If the arbitration tribunal consists of only one arbitrator, the parties may appoint the arbitrator by agreement or may entrust the chairperson of the arbitration commission to make the appointment. In either case, the parties may challenge an arbitrator. If an arbitrator is a close relative of a party or its agent, has a conflict of interest with the case, has a relationship with a party or its agent that may affect his or her impartiality, has *ex parte* communications with a party or its agent, or has accepted an invitation or a gift from a party or its agent, he or she must withdraw from the case.

Arbitration may be conducted by a hearing or on the basis of documents submitted if the parties so agree. The hearing itself is not open to the public, unless the parties otherwise agree. If the applicant does not appear before the hearing or leaves the hearing without permission, its application will be deemed withdrawn. If the respondent does not appear before the hearing or leaves the hearing without permission, the arbitration tribunal may render an award in its absence. To support their claims, the parties should produce evidence. Alternatively, the arbitration tribunal may, on its own initiative, collect the necessary evidence. If the evidence may be destroyed, lost, or be difficult to obtain later, the applicant may apply for evidence preservation, in which case, the arbitration commission should submit the application to the basic people's court of the place where the evidence is located. Furthermore, the parties may engage legal counsel or other agents, debate over the issues, and make a final submission before the closing of the hearing.

After the application for arbitration is submitted, the parties may try to settle their dispute. If a settlement is reached, the applicant may withdraw the application, or the arbitration tribunal may render an arbitration award based on the settlement agreement. Moreover, the arbitration tribunal may conduct mediation before rendering an arbitration award. If mediation is successful, the arbitration tribunal should either make a mediated agreement or render an arbitration award based on the outcome of the settlement. The mediated agreement and the arbitration award have the same legal effect. If mediation proves unsuccessful, the arbitration tribunal must render an award promptly. An arbitration award is made on the basis of a majority vote, but any dissenting arbitrator may file an opinion. If the arbitration tribunal fails to reach a majority vote, the arbitration award will be made pursuant to the view of the presiding arbitrator. Once an award is made pursuant to the Arbitration Law, it is final because another arbitration commission or the people's court will not hear the same dispute.

Notwithstanding the finality of an arbitration award, a party may request the court to set it aside within six months of its receipt. Under any one of the following circumstances, the intermediate people's court of the place where the arbitration commission is located shall set aside an arbitration award:

1 the parties did not have an arbitration agreement;
2 the matters decided in the arbitration exceeded the scope of the arbitration agreement or the authority of the arbitration commission;
3 the formation of the arbitration tribunal or the arbitration proceedings did not conform to the statutory requirements;
4 the evidence on which the award was based was fraudulent;
5 the other party withheld evidence which was sufficient to affect the impartiality of arbitration;
6 the arbitrator(s) committed bribery or bent the law out of personal considerations; or
7 the award violated a social or public interest.

If an arbitration award is set aside, the parties may enter into a new agreement to submit their dispute to arbitration again or file a lawsuit in court.

Where one party does not comply with the arbitration award, the other party may ask the people's court to enforce it. Nonetheless, the court may refuse to enforce an arbitration award. According to article 217 of the Civil Procedure Law, the people's court shall refuse to enforce an arbitration award if:

1 the parties had no arbitration clause in their contract or had not subsequently reached any written arbitration agreement;
2 the matters decided in the arbitration exceeded the scope of the arbitration agreement or the authority of the arbitration commission;
3 the formation of the arbitration tribunal or the arbitration proceedings did not conform to the statutory requirements;
4 the principal evidence for ascertaining the facts was insufficient;
5 there was an error in the application of law;
6 the arbitrator(s) committed bribery or bent the law out of personal considerations; or
7 the execution of the award would violate a social or public interest.

In other words, when a party asks the court to enforce an arbitration award, the court can review the evidence and legal reasoning upon which the award is based. If an arbitration award is denied enforcement, the parties may agree to submit the dispute to arbitration anew or bring a lawsuit in court.

Foreign-related arbitration

Apart from providing a general framework, the Arbitration Law contains special provisions on foreign-related arbitration (涉外仲裁). These provisions apply to the arbitration of disputes arising from foreign economic relations and trade, transportation, and maritime affairs. Specifically, foreign-related arbitration commissions may appoint foreign nationals who have professional knowledge in law, economics, trade, science, or technology as arbitrators. If one party wants to preserve evidence, the foreign-related arbitration commission should submit the application to the intermediate people's court of the place where the evidence is located. This procedure is different from that of domestic arbitration where the arbitration commission is to submit the application to the basic people's court of the place where the evidence is located.

Moreover, the Civil Procedure Law provides that if a party wants to apply for property preservation, the foreign-related arbitration commission should submit the application to the intermediate people's court of the place where the property is located or the respondent is domiciled. If one party does not comply with the arbitration award, the other party may apply to the intermediate people's court of the place where the property is located or the respondent is domiciled for enforcement. However, the court shall set aside or refuse to enforce a foreign-related arbitration award if:

1   the parties had no arbitration clause in their contract or had not subsequently reached any written arbitration agreement;
2   the respondent did not have its designated arbitrator appointed, was not duly notified of the arbitration proceedings, or was not able to state its views due to reasons for which it was not responsible;
3   the formation of the arbitration tribunal or the arbitration procedure did not conform to the arbitration rules;
4   the matters decided in the arbitration exceeded the scope of the arbitration agreement or the authority of the arbitration commission; or
5   the enforcement of the arbitration award would contravene social and public interests.

Thus, compared with domestic arbitration, the scope of judicial review of foreign-related arbitration is more limited.

As mentioned above, the Supreme People's Court mandates that five types of foreign-related civil and commercial cases be handled centrally by five groups of courts of first instance. One of these types of foreign-related civil and commercial cases is the examination of the validity of arbitration provisions in foreign-related civil and commercial cases. Hence, to challenge the validity of an arbitration agreement in court, a party in a foreign-related civil and commercial case should go to:

1   a people's court approved by the State Council and established in an Economic and Technological Development Zone;
2   an intermediate people's court located in the provincial capital, autonomous-regional capital, or municipality directly under the central government;
3   an intermediate people's court located in a SEZ or a Separately Planned City;

Table 9.3 Arbitration fee schedule for international cases

Amount in dispute (RMB)	Amount of fee
1 million or less	3.5% of the amount in dispute (no less than RMB 10,000)
1 million to 5 million	RMB 35,000 plus 2.5% of the amount above 1 million
5 million to 10 million	RMB 135,000 plus 1.5% of the amount above 5 million
10 million to 50 million	RMB 210,000 plus 1% of the amount above 10 million
50 million or more	RMB 610,000 plus 0.5% of the amount above 50 million

Source: China International Economic and Trade Arbitration Commission (2003).

Visit: www.cietac.org.cn/english/E_cd6/E_fr_9.htm.

4 an intermediate people's court designated by the Supreme People's Court; or

5 a high people's court.

Aside from the Arbitration Law, the CIETAC Arbitration Rules will also apply if the parties submit their dispute to the CIETAC for arbitration, unless otherwise agreed between the parties and approved by the CIETAC. Since the CIETAC Arbitration Rules are formulated with reference to the Arbitration Law, the provisions of the former are substantially similar to those of the latter. Even so, several provisions of the CIETAC Arbitration Rules are worth mentioning. First of all, the CIETAC also requires that the parties list their telephone numbers, fax numbers, and any other means of electronic communication. Moreover, the parties may authorize both Chinese and foreign citizens to act as agents in dealing with arbitration matters. Generally, a case is to be arbitrated in the place where the accepting arbitration commission, whether the CIETAC or one of its local offices, is located; however, if the parties have agreed on a particular place for arbitration, their dispute will be arbitrated in the agreed-upon location. Furthermore, if the amount in dispute is less than RMB 500,000, or if the amount in dispute is more than RMB 500,000 but one party applies and the other party agrees, the summary procedure conducted by a sole arbitrator will be applied to hear the dispute.

In applying for the enforcement of an arbitration award rendered by a foreign-related arbitration commission, the applicant may find that the respondent or its property is not in China. In such a case, the applicant should go directly to the foreign court having jurisdiction to obtain recognition and enforcement of the arbitration award. As a rule, CIETAC arbitration awards are enforceable outside China because China is a signatory to the New York Convention on the Recognition and Enforcement of Foreign Arbitral Awards. Furthermore, in 1999, the Supreme People's Court and the Hong Kong Special Administrative Region Government made arrangements to facilitate the reciprocal enforcement of arbitration awards. That is to say, the High Court of the Hong Kong Special Administrative Region will enforce arbitration awards rendered by mainland arbitration commissions, and the intermediate people's court of the place where the respondent resides or the property is located will enforce arbitration awards made in Hong Kong.

Arbitration v. litigation

Generally speaking, disputants choose arbitration to resolve disputes because of its flexibility (they can choose the place of arbitration, arbitrators, arbitration procedure, and substantive law), finality (arbitration awards may be challenged in annulment or enforcement lawsuits but are not subject to appeal), enforceability (arbitration awards are enforced in conformity with domestic law as well as international conventions or treaties), and confidentiality (arbitration proceedings are usually not open to the public). For foreign investors in China, two other major reasons exist for the popularity of arbitration in resolving commercial disputes. First, foreign investors tend to doubt the quality of Chinese judges. The arbitrators of the CIETAC are qualified professionals in whom they have much more confidence. Second, with many years of experience in handling foreign-related commercial disputes, the CIETAC appears to have more expertise than the majority of local courts. Indeed, the CIETAC often refers to international commercial practices in deciding cases when no domestic laws or international conventions apply. Nevertheless, arbitration in China does not function completely independently of the Chinese court system because a party who has obtained a favorable arbitration award must go to a people's court for enforcement if the other party refuses to perform. Hence, the enforcement of arbitration awards may encounter obstacles similar to those in the case of a court judgment.

Arbitration in practise

Over the years, the CIETAC has arbitrated two major types of disputes: foreign trade and foreign direct investment. The foreign trade cases covered a variety of topics, including disputes over the quality of goods, disputes over the place or time of delivery, and cases regarding the effect of trading with Chinese enterprises that were not authorized to engage in foreign trade. The foreign direct investment cases frequently concerned disputes between joint-venture partners over capital contributions and business operations, such as the failure of the Chinese party to contribute the required amount of capital within a certain period of time and conflicts over the management of a joint venture. With the latest expansion of its jurisdiction, the CIETAC now accepts other domestic cases that the disputants choose to submit to it for arbitration. To what extent this jurisdictional expansion will diversify the caseload of the CIETAC remains to be seen.

5 Selected cases

Nantong Development Zone Fudatehua Ltd. *v.* Head Office of the State Administration of Taxation *(2000)* 一中行初字第147号, *Beijing City No. 1 Intermediate People's Court, 19 December 2000*

Facts

Nantong Development Zone Fudatehua Ltd. (hereinafter FL) claimed that, during the period of 1997 to 1998, the relevant "concrete administrative acts" (acts) of the Nantong Office of the State Administration of Taxation (hereinafter NSAT) were illegal and infringed upon its legal rights and interest. Although it had filed administrative lawsuits against the NSAT with the relevant courts at Nantong City at various times, the courts either dismissed the lawsuits or affirmed the acts. On 30 December 1999, FL submitted three applications for administrative reconsideration to the Jiangsu Office of the State Administration of Taxation (hereinafter JSAT), alleging that the NSAT had infringed upon its legal rights. On 10 February 2000, FL applied for administrative reconsideration with the Head Office of the State Administration of Taxation (hereinafter HSAT), requesting the HSAT to order the JSAT to render administrative reconsideration within the statutory period or to accept its application for administrative reconsideration in respect of the illegal acts of the NSAT; confirming the legal status and effective period of the Measures on the Determination of General Taxpayer Application Regarding Value-Added Tax and the Measures of the Jiangsu Province on the Administration of the Determination of General Taxpayers Regarding Tax; and affirming the illegality of the acts of the NSAT. On 14 February 2000, the HSAT received FL's application for administrative reconsideration. Having investigated the case, the HSAT ruled that FL's request to have the JSAT render a decision through administrative reconsideration within the statutory period did not fall within the scope of administrative reconsideration, and that FL's other requests for reconsideration involved acts that were not made by the JSAT. On 18 February 2000, the HSAT denied FL's application according to article 17(1) of the Administrative Reconsideration Law.[12]

FHL alleged that the NSAT's various acts had seriously infringed upon its legal rights and interests. However, the JSAT did not sincerely perform its duty to reconsider the case, which might suggest the JSAT's covering up for the NSAT. Thus, FL's only alternative was to apply to the HSAT so that the latter would examine its case and conduct administrative reconsideration. Since there was no basis for the HSAT to reject FL's application, FHL appealed to the court to:

1   reverse the HSAT's decision to deny its application for administrative reconsideration;

2   order the HSAT to handle directly FL's case regarding the acts of its subordinate tax organs; and

3   order the HSAT to examine and explain its own documents that lacked binding effects.

The HSAT claimed that administrative reconsideration was a one-tiered system. Irrespective of whether the JSAT rendered a decision through administrative reconsideration within the statutory period, FL could not seek administrative reconsideration from the HSAT. In fact, none of FL's other matters for reconsideration were addressed by the JSAT. Hence, the HSAT's decision to reject FL's application was based on correct application of law and in conformity with legal procedure. Therefore, the HSAT requested that the court affirm its decision.

During this lawsuit, the HSAT submitted to the court FHL's written application for administrative reconsideration, demonstrating FL's application for administrative reconsideration and its requests; and 12 copies of administrative judgments made by the courts of first and second instance at the Nantong Chongchuan District People's Court and Jiangsu Nantong City Intermediate People's Court, proving that the people's courts had already adjudged the acts as raised in FL's application for administrative reconsideration. During the interrogation in court, FL did not object to the authenticity of the aforementioned evidence, but claimed that it simply knew the outcome of the trial at second instance and had not actually received the judgment.

On the other hand, FL submitted to the court:

1   a legal-person business license, proving its legal-person status;

2   a value-added tax return filled out by FL on 8 February 1999, proving that the NSAT did not deduct the initial progressive tax and the provisional tax from the tax payable;

3   a void value-added tax invoice of Jiangsu Province, proving the illegal act of the relevant department in the NSAT, which voided its value-added tax invoice by cutting its corner;

4   a value-added tax return, the annual review report on the general taxpayer of value-added tax, and a taxation registration certificate filled out by FL on 7 September 1998, proving that the relevant department in the NSAT had denied its applications for an annual review and for the change of taxation registration;

5   the approval document regarding the application for registration of the value-added-tax taxpayer and the application for being a general taxpayer, proving the NSAT's refusal to grant the general taxpayer status to its branch;

6   the notice to cancel the general taxpayer status in respect of value-added tax and the annual review report on the general taxpayer of

value-added tax, proving that the NSAT had disqualified it as a general taxpayer by using fictitious and false evidence;

7   an agreement to entrust someone with filing taxes for FL, proving that the NSAT had violated the regulations on the administration of invoices, shifted its administrative duties, forced entrustment, evaded responsibilities, etc.;

8   a taxation registration form, showing its request to examine whether the contents of the taxation registration certificate issued by the NSAT conformed to the taxation registration form prescribed by the HSAT; and

9   three written applications for administrative reconsideration, proving that it had requested administrative reconsideration from the JSAT.

During the interrogation in court, the NSAT raised no objections to the authenticity of the preceding evidence.

The court found that all the evidence submitted by the HSAT and evidence 1 and 9 submitted by FL could substantiate their respective claims. However, evidence 2 to 8 submitted by FL could merely prove that the acts mentioned therein were committed by the NSAT. Since the evidence had no bearing on the case, the court declined to investigate or affirm.

Reasoning

The court found that, according to article 2 of the Administrative Reconsideration Law, citizens, legal persons or other organizations might apply for administrative reconsideration when their legal rights and interests are infringed by concrete administrative acts. The HSAT alleged that since FL's request to have the JSAT render a decision through administrative reconsideration within the statutory period did not fall within the scope of administrative reconsideration, and FL's other requests for reconsideration involved acts that were not committed by the JSAT, the FL's application did not meet the requirements for accepting a case. The court affirmed the HSAT's decision because it was based on clearly established facts, correct application of law, and compliance with legal procedure.

According to the Administrative Reconsideration Law, a higher-level administrative department might order a lower-level administrative department to accept a case only if the case had been rejected without proper reasons. If necessary, the higher-level administration department might even hear the case directly. FL's application for administrative reconsideration with the HSAT was still within the statutory time limit during which the JSAT should make a decision. Thus, there was no reason to assume that the JSAT denied FL's application without proper reasons. As FL's request that the HSAT directly handle its case regarding the acts of its subordinate tax departments lacked factual and legal grounds, the court did not support it.

In respect of FL's request that the HSAT examine the documents pertaining to standardization, on which the NSAT based its acts, the court denied it because FL could not apply directly for reconsideration of such a matter.

Judgment

According to article 54(1) of the Administrative Procedure Law[13] and article 56(4) of the Explanations on Issues Regarding the Implementation of the Administrative Procedure Law,[14] the court held that the HSAT's decision on 18 February 2000 to reject FHL's application for administrative reconsideration was affirmed and FL'S other requests were dismissed.

If any party was not satisfied with this judgment, it might, within 15 days of the delivery of the judgment, submit an application for appeal to this court for the purpose of appealing to the Beijing City High People's Court.

**China International Iron and Steel Investment Co. *v*. Japan Daiichi Kangyo Bank K.K. *et al. (2001)* 民四终字第12号, *Supreme People's Court, 21 May 2001*

Facts

China International Iron and Steel Investment Co. (hereinafter CIC) and Japan Daiichi Kangyo Bank K.K. Shanghai Branch, Japan Kōgyō Bank Beijing Branch, Sanwa Bank K.K. Shanghai Branch, and Yamaguchi Bank K.K. Qingdao Branch (hereinafter collectively referred to as JDK) had a loan contract. Dissatisfied with the ruling of the Beijing City High People's Court, CIC appealed to the Supreme People's Court on the following grounds:

1   Although the loan agreement stipulated that jurisdiction was not exclusive, the contents of the agreement were governed by the laws of Hong Kong. CIC and JDK obviously had an understanding that all legal disputes should be resolved in the courts of Hong Kong.
2   Based on the principle of fairness, application of the laws of foreign lands by the courts at Beijing would complicate and lengthen the legal procedure, and thus, further burden the court and the parties.
3   There was no doubt about the status of JDK as the branch of a foreign bank in China. According to articles 21 and 22 of the Commercial Bank Law,[15] although JDK had already obtained a business license from the State Administration for Industry and Commerce, it did not have the status of a legal person.
4   Pursuant to article 13 of the Company Law[16] and article 2 of the General Principles of the Civil Law,[17] JDK was not legally qualified to be a principal (that is, a party) of a lawsuit. In fact, JDK acted as an agent for its foreign headquarters when it signed the loan contract with

CIC. Since JDK was not legally qualified to be a party in the lawsuit and its foreign headquarters had not agreed to amend the loan contract, making itself the party of a lawsuit, amending the loan contract, and filing the lawsuit were all illegal.
5   Based on article 153(2) of the Civil Procedure Law,[18] JDK sought to have original judgment reversed and CIC's lawsuit dismissed.

JDK responded as follows:

1   The courts in Hong Kong had only nonexclusive jurisdiction over this case. JDK had the right to file a lawsuit with a court in Hong Kong or in any place with jurisdiction over the case. Hence, CIC's grounds for appeal could not be sustained. In addition, the place of conclusion and performance of the loan contract and CIC's domicile were in China; therefore, adjudicating the case at the Beijing City High People's Court facilitated not only the timely handling of the case, but also the enforcement of the judgment.
2   It was absolutely unnecessary for CIC to worry that, under the principle of fairness, applying the laws of foreign lands by the courts at Beijing would complicate and lengthen the legal procedure, and thus, further burden the court and the parties. This was because it was not the first time that the Beijing City High People's Court had applied the laws of foreign lands. Moreover, CIC's concern could not be a legal reason for changing the jurisdiction of Beijing City High People's Court.
3   There were absolutely no factual and legal grounds for CIC's claim that according to articles 21 and 22 of the Commercial Bank Law, although JDK had already obtained a business license from the State Administration for Industry and Commerce, it did not have the status of a legal person; and that pursuant to article 13 of the Company Law and article 2 of the General Principles of the Civil Law, JDK was not legally qualified to be a party of the lawsuit. In addition, the Reply Regarding the Civil Liabilities of a Branch of a Commercial Bank provided that according to article 49 of the Civil Procedure Law and article 40 of the Supreme People's Court's Opinions on Several Issues Regarding the Application of the Civil Procedure Law, when the branch of a commercial bank conducting business within the scope of authorization from their headquarters was involved in civil disputes with other citizens, legal persons, or organizations, it, rather than the headquarters, should be the party of a lawsuit. Thus, JDK was legally qualified to be a party in this case, and CIC's appeal should be dismissed.

Reasoning

The court found that article 23(B) of the loan contract provided that the parties irrevocably agreed that the courts in Hong Kong had nonexclusive jurisdiction to hear, decide, and resolve disputes arising out of or related to the loan agreement in any lawsuit or litigation proceedings, and that to this end and for the benefit of all parties, the parties would submit themselves to the jurisdiction of such courts. Since CIC and JDK agreed that the courts in Hong Kong had nonexclusive jurisdiction over their disputes, courts in other places having jurisdiction in accordance with the law could not be excluded. Article 23(D) of the loan contract provided that the filing of a lawsuit by CIC or JDK in any of the jurisdictions listed in article 23(B) did not exclude either of them from suing in other courts having jurisdiction. Accordingly, JDK had the right to sue in courts having jurisdiction other than Hong Kong courts with respect to disputes arising from the loan contract. In this case, JDK filed the lawsuit with the Beijing City High People's Court, where CIC was domiciled. According to article 24 of the Civil Procedure Law,[19] the Beijing City High People's Court, being the court at CIC's place of domicile, had jurisdiction over the case. Hence, the argument that CIC and JDK obviously had an understanding that disputes should be resolved first in Hong Kong courts could not be sustained. Furthermore, CIC alleged that under the principles of fairness, the Beijing courts' application of the laws of foreign lands complicated and lengthened the legal procedure, which would further burden the court and the parties. Nonetheless, this was merely CIC's own subjective speculation and could not deprive Beijing City High People's Court of its jurisdiction over this case.

Ruling

According to article 49 of the Civil Procedure Law, other organizations may be parties of a civil lawsuit. Moreover, according to article 40 of the Supreme People's Court's Opinions on Several Issues Regarding the Application of the Civil Procedure Law, JDK was an organization that could be a party in a civil lawsuit. Furthermore, pursuant to the spirit of the Reply Regarding the Civil Liabilities of a Branch of a Commercial Bank, JDK might be a party of a lawsuit, but not the headquarters. Therefore, CIC's assertion that JDK lacked standing to sue was groundless. Based on articles 24, 38 and 158 of the Civil Procedure Law,[20] the court held that CIC's appeal was dismissed and the original judgment was affirmed.

This ruling was final.

Further reading

Lo, Vai Io, "Resolution of Civil Disputes in China," *UCLA Pacific Basin Law Journal* 18, 2001, 117–56.

Peerenboom, Randall, "Seek Truth from Facts: An Empirical Study of Enforcement of Arbitral Awards in the PRC," *American Journal of Comparative Law* 49, 2001, 249–328.

Zhang, Mo, "International Civil Litigation in China: A Practical Analysis of the Chinese Judicial System," *Boston College International and Comparative Law Review* 25, 2002, 59–96.

Notes

1 The Civil Procedure Law of the People's Republic of China, adopted at the 4th Session of the 7th National People's Congress on 9 April 1991.
2 The China Chamber of International Commerce Mediation (Conciliation) Rules, effective on 1 January 2000.
3 The Administrative License Law of the People's Republic of China, adopted at the 4th Session of the Standing Committee of the 10th National People's Congress on 27 August 2003 (effective 1 July 2004).
4 The Administrative Reconsideration Law of the People's Republic of China, adopted at the 9th Session of the Standing Committee of the 9th National People's Congress on 29 April 1999.
5 The Administrative Procedure Law of the People's Republic of China, adopted at the 2nd Session of the 7th National People's Congress on 4 April 1989.
6 Notwithstanding the two-trial system, certain types of cases are to be tried only once. These cases concern the qualifications of an elector, the death or disappearance of a person, the incapacity or limited capacity of a person to engage in civil conduct, and the absence of the owner of a piece of property.
7 In a major foreign-related case, the amount in dispute is great, the facts are complicated, or many of the litigants reside overseas.
8 The Rules Regarding Several Questions on Litigious Jurisdiction of Foreign-Related Civil and Commercial Cases, promulgated by the Supreme People's Court on 25 February 2002.
9 Separately Planned Cities, such as Dalian, Qingdao, and Ningbo, are cities that can make economic development plans independently and whose administrative level is below that of the province.
10 The Arbitration Law of the People's Republic of China, adopted at the 9th Session of the Standing Committee of the 8th National People's Congress on 31 August 1994.
11 The China International Economic and Trade Arbitration Commission (CIETAC) Arbitration Rules, revised and adopted by the China Chamber of International Commerce on 5 September 2000.
12 Article 17(1) of the Administrative Reconsideration Law provides that the administrative-reconsideration organ should examine an application for administrative reconsideration within five days of its receipt and notify the applicant in writing if it rejects the application according to the law. In addition, if the applicant meets the statutory requirements but is not an application to be accepted by the administrative-reconsideration organ, such organ should ask the applicant to file the application with the appropriate administrative-reconsideration organ.
13 Article 54(1) of the Administrative Procedure Law provides that the people's court should affirm the judgment if the "concrete administrative act" is based on solid evidence and correct application of law, as well conforming with legal procedure.

14 Article 56(4) of the Explanations on Several Questions Regarding the Enforcement of the Administrative Procedure Law provides that the people's court should dismiss the lawsuit if other circumstances necessitating dismissal arise.

15 Article 21 of the Commercial Bank Law provides that the People's Bank of China shall issue a banking permit to the branch of a commercial bank after the application of its establishment has been approved, and that the branch shall submit the permit to the AIC for registration and to obtain a business license. Article 22 of the Commercial Bank Law provides that a commercial bank shall adopt for its branches a financial system of unified accounting, unified allocation of funds, and level-by-level management. In addition, the branch of a commercial bank does not have the status of a legal person and may conduct business within the scope authorized by the headquarters, and the headquarters shall assume its civil liabilities.

16 Article 13 of the Company Law provides that the branch of a company does not have the status of a legal person, and its civil liabilities are to be assumed by the company; however, the subsidiary of a company has the status of a legal person and assumes civil liability independently.

17 Article 2 of the General Principles of the Civil Law provides that the civil law of China shall adjust property and personal relationships between civil subjects with equal status, namely, between citizens, between legal persons, and between citizens and legal persons.

18 Article 153(2) of the Civil Procedure Law provides that a party may appeal against a judgment or ruling after retrial.

19 Article 24 of the Civil Procedure Law provides that disputes over contracts come under the jurisdiction of the people's court at the place of the defendant's domicile or the place of performance.

20 Article 38 of the Civil Procedure Law provides that if a party wants to challenge the jurisdiction of a court, it must do so during the time when a reply is to be filed, and that if the objection is tenable, the court shall transfer the case to a court having jurisdiction over the case. Article 158 of the Civil Procedure Law provides that the judgment or ruling of the court of second instance is final.

10 Accession to the World Trade Organization

In the last quarter of the twentieth century, although China was becoming increasingly integrated into the world economy, it was not a member of the WTO (formerly known as the GATT), which is the only international organization that makes and enforces rules of trade between nations. Foreign investors were sometimes confused and frustrated by the Chinese rules and regulations that were not in conformity with the WTO, and Chinese enterprises were also constrained in conducting international business. On 11 November 2001, after lengthy and tough negotiations, China finally became a member of the WTO, and began to commit to the WTO rules. Today, therefore, foreign investors should know what commitments China has made to the WTO and the nature of the new business opportunities open to them since China's WTO accession. This chapter first introduces the WTO and the background of China's WTO accession. Then it highlights China's basic rights and obligations to the WTO, together with the key points of China's commitments to the WTO on freer trade in goods and services. Finally it briefly analyzes the new business opportunities for foreign investors after China's WTO accession.

1 Background

The WTO follows such principles as trade without discrimination, freer trade, predictability, fair competition, and more benefits for the less developed, and thus requires member countries to reach, through multilateral or bilateral negotiations, agreements on trade in goods and services, property rights protection, and dispute settlement so that trade can move smoothly and more freely within this multinational global trading system. In this way, the WTO has played an important role in promoting international trade and investment in the last 50 years. China was one of the 23 original signatories of the GATT in 1948. After China's revolution in 1949, however, the government in Taiwan announced that China would leave the GATT system. In 1986 China notified the GATT of its wish to resume its status as a GATT contracting party and was finally accepted as a member of the WTO in 2001.

The World Trade Organization and its principles

The WTO came into being in 1995. As the successor to the GATT established in 1948, the WTO has been the only international organization dealing with the global rules of trade between nations since the end of the Second World War. Its main function is to establish a multilateral trading system ensuring that trade flows as smoothly, predictably and freely as possible. At the heart of the multilateral trading system are the WTO's agreements, negotiated and signed by a large majority of the world's trading nations, and ratified in their parliaments. These agreements are the legal ground rules for international commerce. They guarantee member countries important trade rights and bind governments to keep their trade policies within agreed limits to everybody's benefit. Although the agreements are negotiated and signed by governments, their purpose is to help producers of goods and services, exporters, and importers conduct their business internationally. Currently, the WTO has 144 member countries. These member countries adhere to the following important principles in this multilateral trading system.

Trade without discrimination

This principle has two components. The first is the most-favored-nation treatment. In this multilateral trading system, countries cannot normally discriminate between their trading partners. If you grant someone a special favor (such as a lower customs duty rate for one of their products), you have to do the same for all other WTO members. The second component is national treatment (treating foreigners and locals equally). Imported and locally produced goods should be treated equally – at least after the foreign goods have entered the market. The same should apply to foreign and domestic services, and to foreign and local trademarks, copyrights and patents. The first component asks a member country to treat other people equally, while the second component asks a member country to treat foreigners and locals equally.

Freer trade

Lowering trade barriers is one of the most effective means of encouraging international trade. Trade barriers normally include customs duties (or tariffs) and nontariff measures such as import bans or quotas that restrict trade quantities selectively. From time to time other issues, such as red tape and exchange rate policies, have also been discussed in trade negotiations. Opening national markets can be beneficial, but it also requires adjustment. The WTO agreements allow countries to introduce changes gradually, through "progressive liberalization." Developing countries are usually given a longer time span to fulfill their obligations.

Predictability

Only with stability and predictability, can investment be encouraged, jobs be created, and consumers fully enjoy the benefits of competition: more choice and lower prices. The multilateral trading system makes the business environment more stable and more predictable. In the WTO, when member countries agree to open their markets for goods or services, they "bind" their commitments, which amounts to, with regards to goods, ceilings on customs tariff rates. A country can change its bindings only after negotiating with its trading partners, and may have to compensate them for any resulting loss of trade. The system also tries to improve predictability and stability by encouraging transparency at both national and international levels.

Fair competition

The WTO is sometimes described as a "free trade" institution, but that is misleading. The system does allow tariffs and, in limited circumstances, nontariff trade barriers. More accurately, the WTO is a system of rules dedicated to open, fair, and undistorted competition. The rules on non-discrimination – the most favored nation and the national treatment – are designed to secure fair conditions of international trade. So too are those on dumping (exporting at below cost to gain market share) and subsidies. The issues are complex, but the WTO rules try to establish what is fair or unfair, and how governments can respond to unfair trade practises by, for instance, charging additional import duties calculated to compensate for damage thus caused.

More benefits for the less developed

Over three-quarters of WTO members are developing countries and countries in transition to market-based economies. The WTO recognizes that these less developed countries should be given greater flexibility, trade concessions, and technical assistance within this multilateral trading system. At the end of the Uruguay Round 1986–94, it was decided that developing countries, particularly the poorest or the "least-developed" countries, should be given certain transition periods to adjust to the unfamiliar and, perhaps, difficult WTO provisions, that better-off countries should accelerate implementing market access commitments on goods exported by the least-developed countries, and that the WTO should seek increased technical assistance for the least-developed countries.

World Trade Organization agreements

The WTO's rules are illustrated in the agreements reached by the WTO member countries in negotiations over the years. The current set of agreements were the outcome of the 1986–94 Uruguay Round negotiations, and includes a major revision of the original GATT. Although the GATT was accepted as the WTO's principal rule book for trade in goods, the Uruguay Round has created new rules for dealing with trade in services, relevant aspects of intellectual property, dispute settlement, and trade policy reviews. The complete set runs to some 30,000 pages, consisting of about 30 agreements and separate commitments (called schedules) made by individual members in such specific areas as lower customs duty rates and services market-opening.

Goods

From 1947 to 1994, the GATT was the forum for negotiating lower customs duty rates and other trade barriers; the text of the agreement spelt out important rules, particularly the rule of non-discrimination. Since 1995, the updated GATT has become the WTO's umbrella agreement for trade in goods. It has a number of annexes dealing with certain sectors such as agriculture and textiles, and with specific issues such as state trading, product standards, subsidies and actions taken against dumping.

Services

Within the multilateral trading system, banks, insurance firms, telecommunications companies, tour operators, hotel chains and transport companies looking to do business abroad can now enjoy the same principles of freer and fairer trade that originally only applied to trade in goods. These principles appeared, as a result of the Uruguay Round negotiations, in the new General Agreement on Trade in Services after 1994. WTO members have also made individual commitments under the new agreement, stating which of their services sectors they are willing to open to foreign competition and how open those markets are.

Intellectual property

Intellectual property rights, including copyrights, patents, and trademarks, are now under protection in the multilateral global trading system. The rules for trade and investment in ideas and creativity appeared, as a result of the Uruguay Round negotiations, in the new Agreement on Trade-Related Aspects of Intellectual Property Rights after 1994. The rules state how intellectual properties, including copyrights, patents, trademarks, geographical names used to identify products, industrial designs, integrated circuit layout-designs and undisclosed information such as trade secrets, should be protected when trade is involved. Together, those three agreements – the GATT, the General Agreement on Trade in Services, and the Agreement on Trade-Related Aspects of Intellectual Property Rights – cover all three main areas of trade within the multilateral trading system.

Dispute settlement

The Uruguay Round negotiations also created a dispute settlement mechanism, which is specified clearly in the Dispute Settlement Understanding. Therefore, WTO member countries can now resolve trade quarrels through institutional channels and procedures, which is vital for ensuring the smooth flow of trade. They can, for instance, bring disputes to the WTO if they think their rights under the WTO agreements are being infringed in one way or another. Judgments by specially appointed independent experts are based on interpretations of the WTO agreements and individual countries' commitments to the WTO. The WTO encourages its member countries to settle their differences through consultation. Failing that, the member countries can follow a carefully mapped out, step-by-step procedure that includes the possibility of a ruling by a panel of experts, and the chance to appeal the ruling on legal grounds within the multilateral trading system.

Policy review

After the establishment of the WTO, the WTO General Council began to conduct regular reviews of individual countries' trade policies. This trade policy review mechanism is aimed at improving transparency and understanding of WTO member countries' trade policies and practises through regular monitoring, improvement of the quality of public and intergovernmental debate on the issues, and the multilateral assessment of the effects of policies on the multilateral world trading system. WTO member countries may also see the reviews as constructive feedback on their policies. Nevertheless, all WTO member countries must undergo the periodic review process, which normally contains reports by the country concerned and by the WTO Secretariat.

- **China's accession to the World Trade Organization**

China was one of the 23 original signatories of the GATT in 1948. After China's revolution in 1949, the government in Taiwan announced that China would leave the GATT system. Although the government in Beijing never recognized this withdrawal decision, nearly 40 years later, in 1986, China notified the GATT of its wish to resume its status as a GATT contracting party. Since then, China has tried very hard to negotiate with GATT (WTO) and its member countries about its entry to this multilateral trading system. The decision made by the Chinese government to rejoin the GATT was a result of China's market-oriented reforms initiated in the late 1970s, and a result of China's increased integration with the rest of the world since then.

In the last two decades of the twentieth century, China emerged as a major player in the global economy. From the late 1970s to 2000, China's foreign trade saw a 23-fold increase, and its share of total world trade saw a 6-fold increase times. By 2000, China had become one of the leading exporters and importers in the world. China also attracted record amounts of foreign direct investment over the period. By 2000, China had become the world's second largest recipient of foreign direct investment, following only the U.S.A. Meanwhile, with a remarkable increase in the number of Chinese firms investing abroad, by 2000 China had become the largest outward investor among developing countries. China also raised significant amounts of capital on international securities markets, through the sale of sovereign bonds and the listing of Chinese companies on overseas equity markets.

However, China's integration into the world economy was restricted by some institutional barriers. With high tariffs and nontariff barriers, some critical sectors of the Chinese economy, such as automobiles and agriculture, remained relatively insulated from international competition. The state controlled imports by imposing limitations on companies authorized to engage in imports; by imposing onerous inspection and other requirements on imported goods; by imposing technical standards to protect domestic industries; and by discriminating against imported goods in government procurement. On top of that, the service sector remained closed to foreign direct investment. All these were against WTO rules, and could be overcome with China's entry into the WTO. A more open China was also to the benefit of all member countries in the multilateral global trading system.

Like many of the countries applying for WTO membership, China had to implement economic reforms to transform its economy to take account of market mechanisms. China's accession process to the WTO was guided by a Working Party whose membership consisted of all interested WTO member governments. Initially, the Working Party on China's status was established under GATT in 1987 and it was concerned only with China's trade in goods. In 1995, it was converted to a WTO Working Party and its scope was broadened to include trade in services, new rules on non tariff measures and new rules on intellectual property rights.

A substantial part of China's accession process involved bilateral negotiations between China and WTO members. These were usually conducted privately, either at the WTO in Geneva or in countries concerned. The process also involved meetings, either informal or formal, of the WTO Working Party. While several areas of China's trade policies, such as schedules of market-access commitments on goods and services, were the focus of bilateral and multilateral negotiations, it was the responsibility of the Working Party to maintain an overview of how the negotiations were progressing and to ensure that all aspects of China's trade policies were addressed. By the end of 1999, China had completed negotiations with most WTO member countries, and was trying very hard to strike a deal with the U.S.A., the E.U. and Mexico, which was vital to China's accession to the WTO. China signed the agreement on WTO accession with the U.S.A. on 15 November 1999, with the E.U. on 19 May 2000, and with the Mexico on 13 September 2001, thus completing negotiations with all WTO member countries. On 11 November 2001, the Protocol on the Accession of the People's Republic of China was passed at the WTO ministerial conference in Doha, Qatar, and the WTO formally accepted China as a member of the WTO.

2 Basic rights and obligations

China began to enjoy the basic rights offered to all members of the WTO and had to fulfill its obligations to the WTO at the same time. These basic rights and obligations cover so many subjects that they cannot be covered fully here. This section, therefore, briefly addresses some of the general points of China's basic rights and obligations as a member of the WTO. It then highlights the details of China's commitments to the WTO on freer trade in goods and services.

Indiscriminate treatment

After the entry into the WTO, China began to enjoy the most-favored-nation treatment and national treatment in trading with all its partners within the multilateral trading system, that is, indiscriminate treatment. Therefore, some of the unfair treatment China experienced before its entry into the WTO have been abolished. For example, the U.S.A. has granted China "permanent normal trade relations" thus abolishing previous annual review practice. Furthermore, the E.U., Argentina, Hungary, Mexico, Poland, Turkey and Slovenia will abolish discrimination towards China's products, such as quantitative restriction and anti-dumping measures that are against WTO rules, in about five to six years.[1] In addition, according to the WTO Agreement on Textiles and Clothing, developed countries will abolish the quotas on textiles on 1 January 2005. Therefore China will enjoy this treatment together with other WTO member countries.

Developing country treatment

After the entry into the WTO, China began to enjoy developing country treatment in terms of greater flexibility, trade concessions, and technical assistance within the multilateral trading system. This treatment covers many aspects of the economy, including subsidies, safeguard measures, dispute settlement, and the adoption of international standards. Most importantly, China was given a reasonably long transition period to adjust to the unfamiliar and difficult WTO provisions in such areas as the role of the state in the economy, tariff and nontariff barriers to trade in goods, and the opening up of the service sector, as is shown below.

State trading, pricing, and subsidies

Through negotiations, the WTO allowed China to assign the trading right of some key products to state-owned trading enterprises. Products subject to state importing include grain, cotton, vegetable oil, sugar, tobacco, crude oil, processed oil, and chemical fertilizers, while products subject to state exporting include tea, rice, corn, soy bean, tungsten ore, tungstate, coal, crude oil, processed oil, silk, and cotton. However, China must ensure that import purchasing procedures of state trading enterprises are fully transparent and are in compliance with the WTO agreements. It must not take any measure to influence or direct state trading enterprises as to the quantity, value, or country of origin of the goods purchased or sold unless it has reached an agreement with the WTO. Furthermore, China must provide full information on the pricing mechanisms of its state trading enterprises for exported goods.

The WTO also allows China to control the price of some key products and services such as tobacco, edible salt, natural gas, pharmaceuticals, grain, vegetable oil, processed oil, cotton, chemical fertilizers, silkworm cocoons, gas for civil use, tap water, electricity, heating power, water supplied by irrigation projects, the entrance fee for tourist sites, sales price and rental fees of residential apartments, charges for education services, charges for transportation services, charges for professional services, charges for commission agency services, charges for settlement, clearing and transmission services of banks, charges for health-related services, and charges for postal and telecommunication services.

While China has had to abolish some subsidies, such as the priority in obtaining loans and foreign currencies based on export performance, the WTO has allowed it to keep some state subsidies that are not against the WTO Agreement on Subsidies and Countervailing Measures. These subsidies include the those from local budgets for loss-making state-owned enterprises, the preferential policies for the SEZs, the preferential policies for the Economic and Technology Development Areas, the preferential policies for the SEZ of the Pudong area of Shanghai, the preferential policies for FIEs, the policy loans from the state policy banks, the financial subsidies for poverty alleviation, the funds for technology renovation, research and development, the funds for infrastructure construction in agricultural water conservancy and flood protection projects, the tax and tariff refund for export products, the reduction and exemption of import duties for certain enterprises, the provision of low-price inputs for special industrial sectors, the subsidies to certain enterprises in the forestry industry, the preferential income tax treatment to high-tech enterprises, the preferential income tax treatment for enterprises utilizing waste, the preferential income tax treatment for enterprises in poverty-stricken regions, the preferential income tax treatment for enterprises transferring technologies, the preferential income tax treatment for disaster-stricken enterprises, and the preferential income tax treatment for enterprises that provide job opportunities for the unemployed.

Compliance with the basic rules of the World Trade Organization

As a WTO member, China has agreed to obey the WTO principles and comply with the WTO basic rules. For example, China must follow the non-discrimination rule. Foreign individuals and enterprises and FIEs are to be granted treatments no less favorable than those granted to other individuals and enterprises in respect of:

1   the procurement of inputs and goods and services necessary for production and the conditions under which their goods are produced, marketed, or sold both in the domestic market and abroad; and
2   the price and availability of goods and services supplied by national and sub-national authorities and public-owned or state-owned enterprises, such as transportation, energy, basic telecommunications, and other utilities or factors of production.

China must also follow the rule of uniform administration. First, the provisions of the WTO Agreement and the Protocol on the Accession of the People's Republic of China apply to the entire customs territory of China, including border trade regions and minority autonomous areas, SEZs, open coastal cities, Economic and Technical Development Zones and other areas where special regimes for tariffs, taxes and regulations are established (collectively referred to as "special economic areas"). Second, China must apply and administer in a uniform, impartial, and reasonable manner all its laws, no matter whether they are issued by the central or local governments, pertaining to or affecting trade in goods, services, trade-related aspects of intellectual property rights, or the control of foreign exchange. Third, the regulations, rules, and other measures issued by local governments at the sub-national level must conform to the obligations undertaken in the WTO Agreement and the Protocol on the Accession of the People's Republic of China. Finally, China must establish a mechanism under which individuals and enterprises can bring to the attention of the national authorities cases of non-uniform application of the trade regime.

Furthermore, China needs to follow the rule of transparency. To begin with, China undertakes to enforce only those laws, regulations and other measures pertaining to or affecting trade in goods, services, trade-related aspects of intellectual property rights, and the control of foreign exchange that are published and readily available to other WTO members, individuals and enterprises. China must also make available to WTO members, upon request, all laws, regulations and other measures pertaining to or affecting trade in goods, services, trade-related aspects of intellectual property rights, and the control of foreign exchange before such measures are implemented or enforced. In emergency situations, laws, regulations, and other measures shall be made available at the very latest when they are implemented or enforced. Second, China must establish or designate an official journal dedicated to the publication of all laws, regulations and other measures pertaining to or affecting trade in goods, services, trade-related aspects of intellectual property rights, and the control of foreign exchange. After the publication of these laws, regulations, or other measures in the journal, China must provide a reasonable period for comment to the appropriate authorities before such laws, regulations, and other measures are implemented, except for the laws, regulations and other measures involving national security, the specific measures setting foreign exchange rates or monetary policy, and the specific measures the publication of which would impede law enforcement. China must publish this journal on a regular basis and make copies of all issues of this journal readily available to individuals and enterprises. Third, China must establish or designate an enquiry point where, upon request from any individual, enterprise, or WTO member, all information relating to the laws, regulations, and other measures required to be published by the WTO may be obtained. Replies to requests for information shall generally be provided within 30 days of receipt of a request. In exceptional cases, replies may be provided within 45 days of receipt of a request. Notice of the delay and the reasons for it must be given in writing to the interested party. Replies to WTO members must be complete and represent the authoritative view of the Chinese government. Accurate and reliable information must also be provided to individuals and enterprises.

Most importantly, China has to follow the principle of freer trade, and all the WTO agreements on trade in goods, services, and intellectual property. With regard to trade in intellectual property, China promised to follow the Agreement on Trade-Related Aspects of Intellectual Property Rights immediately after the entry into the WTO. With regard to trade in goods and services, as is seen below, China has promised to abolish, step by step, some current practices that are not in line with the GATT and the General Agreement on Trade in Services.

• 3 Commitments to trade in goods

In 1947–94, trade in goods was the only concern in negotiations under the GATT, which concentrated primarily on lower customs duty rates and other trade barriers. Trade in goods remained the most fundamental issue under the WTO and, as such, was a key topic of negotiations between China and the WTO on China's accession. The overwhelming majority of the Protocol on the Accession of the People's Republic of China relates to China's commitment to freer trade in goods, including the right to trade, tariffs, nontariff barriers, tariff rate quotas, technical barriers to trade, and designated trading.

The right to trade

China has agreed to progressively liberalize the availability and scope of the right to trade, so that, within three years after accession, all enterprises in China shall have the right to trade in all goods throughout the customs territory of China, except for those goods that are subject to state trading in accordance with the Protocol on the Accession of the People's Republic of China.[2] Such right to trade include the right to import and export goods. All foreign individuals and enterprises, including those who do not invest or are not registered in China, shall be accorded treatment no less favorably than that accorded to enterprises in China with respect to the right to trade.

Immediately after the entry into the WTO, China would eliminate, for both Chinese and foreign investment enterprises, any requirements for export performance, trade balance, foreign exchange balance, and prior experience in importing and exporting as criteria for obtaining or maintaining the right to import and export.

For Chinese enterprises, China would gradually reduce the minimum registered capital requirement for obtaining the right to trade to RMB 5 million in year one after accession, RMB 3 million in year two after accession, RMB 1 million in year three after accession, and would eliminate the examination and approval system for obtaining the right to trade at the end of the phase-in period.

During the phase-in period, China would also progressively liberalize the scope and availability of the right to trade for foreign investment enterprises. One year after accession, joint venture enterprises with minority shares of foreign investment would be granted the full right to trade; and two years after accession joint venture enterprises with majority shares of foreign investment would be granted the full right to trade.

Tariffs

According to the Protocol on the Accession of the People's Republic of China, the average level of tariff rate would be cut from 14 percent to about 10 percent in 2005 (see Table 10.1). Specifically, the average level of tariff rate for agricultural products would be cut from 19.9 percent to 15.5 percent in 2004. The average level of tariff rate for 98 percent of industrial products would be cut from the current 13 percent to 9.3 percent in 2005. However, the average level of tariff rate for automobiles and parts and components of mobile vehicles would be cut from the current 80–100 percent to 25 percent and 10 percent in 2007, respectively. In 2005, all tariffs for information technology products will be abolished.[3]

Nontariff barriers

China has promised to abolish all nontariff measures, including import quotas, import licenses and import tendering, for more than 400 tariff lines

Table 10.1 Average level of tariff rate

Year	Average level for all products (%)	Average level for industrial products (%)	Average level for agricultural products (%)
2000	15.6	14.7	21.3
2001	14	13	19.9
2002	12.7	11.7	18.5
2003	11.5	10.6	17.4
2004	10.6	9.8	15.8
2005	10.1	9.3	15.5
2006	10.1	9.3.	15.5
2007	10.1	9.3	15.5
2008	10	9.2	15.1

Source: Annex 8 of the Protocol on the Accession of the People's Republic of China.

no later than 1 January 2005. These tariff lines mainly cover automobiles and key parts of automobiles, electromechanical products, and chemical products. During the phase-in period, China is progressively increasing the import quotas for these products each year (see Table 10.2).

Tariff rate quotas

According to the WTO Agreement on Agriculture, the WTO member nations should provide minimum market entry for agricultural products, that is, establish the so-called tariff rate quota system. Tariff rate quotas imply market entry opportunities, rather than import obligations. After entry to the WTO, China will use the tariff rate quota system to manage the import of key agricultural products and, to a lesser degree, some chemical fertilizers. The tariffs for the import of these products within the quota system are much lower than those outside the quota system. The implementation date for the final quota quantity will be no later than six years after the accession. During the transition period, the quantity of the quotas will increase progressively (see Table 10.3).

Technical barriers to trade

China must publish in the official journal all the criteria that, whether formal or informal, form the basis for technical regulations, standards or conformity assessment procedures. All China's technical regulations, standards and conformity assessment procedures have to comply with the Technical Barriers to Trade (TBT) Agreement immediately after its accession to the WTO.

China must apply conformity assessment procedures to imported products only to determine their compliance with technical regulations and standards in accordance with the WTO Agreement and the Protocol on the Accession of the People's Republic of China. Conformity assessment bodies will

Table 10.2 Nontariff measures subject to phased elimination for main products

	Quota category	Unit	Initial quota volume/value	Annual growth rate (%)	Phasing-out period
1	Processed oil	Million metric tons	16.58	15	2004
2	Sodium cyanide	Million metric tons	0.018	15	2002
3	Chemical fertilizer	Million metric tons	8.9	15	2002 (some upon accession)
4	Natural rubber	Million metric tons	0.429	15	2004
5	Tires of rubber used on automobiles	Million metric tons	0.81	15	2002 (some upon accession or 2004)
6	Motorcycles and key parts	Million pieces	286	15	Motorcycles 2004; key parts of motorcycles 2003
7	Automobiles and key parts	US$ million	6000	15	Cars 2005; other vehicles 2004; key parts of vehicles upon accession or 2003
8	Air conditioners and compressors	US$ million	286	15	Upon accession or 2002
9	Recording apparatus and key parts	US$ million	293	15	2002
10	Magnetic sound and video recording apparatus	US$ Million	38	15	Upon accession or 2002
11	Recorders and transport mechanisms	US$ million	387	15	2002
12	Color TV sets and TV tuners	US$ million	325	15	Upon accession or 2002
13	Crane lorries and chassis	US$ million	88	15	2004
14	Cameras	US$ million	14	15	2003
15	Wrist watches	US$ million	33	15	2003

Source: Annex 3 of the Protocol on the Accession of the People's Republic of China.

Table 10.3 Products subject to tariff rate quotas

Product	Tariff quota (mmt)	Share of state trading (%)	In-quota tariff rate (%)	Out-of-quota tariff rate	Date of implementation	Phase-in period for tariff quotas (mmt)
Wheat	9.636	90	1–10	Down from 71 to 65	2004	2002: 8.468 2003: 9.052
Corn	7.2	Down from 68 to 60	1–10	Down from 71 to 65	2004	2002: 5.85 2003: 6.525
Rice	5.32	50	1–9	Down from 71 to 65	2004	2002: 3.99 2003: 4.655
Soy bean oil	3.5671	Down from 34 to 10, and to nil in 2006	9	Down from 52.4 to 19.9, and to 9 in 2006	2005	2002: 2.518 2003: 2.818 2004: 3.118
Palm oil	3.168	Down from 34 to 10, and to nil in 2006	9	Down from 52.4 to 19.9, and to 9 in 2006	2005	2002: 2.4 2003: 2.6 2004: 2.7
Rape-seed oil	1.24	Down from 34 to 10, and to nil in 2006	9	Down from 52.4 to 19.9, and to 9 in 2006	2005	2002: 0.87 2003: 1.0186 2004: 1.1243
Sugar	1.945	70	Down from 20 to 15	Down from 60.4 to 50	2004	2002: 1.764 2003: 1.852
Cotton	0.894	33	1	Down from 54.4 to 40	2004	2002: 0.8185 2003: 0.8563
Wool	0.287	Nil	1	38	2004	2002: 0.2645 2003: 0.2758
Wool tops	0.08	Nil	3	38	2004	2002: 0.0725 2003: 0.0763
Chemical fertilizers	13.8183	Down from 50–51	4	50	6 years after accession	Initial year: 9.40

Source: Annex 8 of the Protocol on the Accession of the People's Republic of China.

Notes: 1. mmt refers to million metric tons. 2. Wool and wool tops are under designated trading rather than state trading. Designated trading of wool and wool tops will be abolished in three years after the accession. 3. Chemical fertilizers include diammonnium hydrogenorthophosphate (diammonnium phosphate), UREA, and NPK.

determine the conformity of imported products with commercial terms of contracts only if authorized by the parties to do so. China shall ensure that such inspection of products in order to comply with the commercial terms of contracts does not affect customs clearance or the granting of import licenses for such products.

Upon accession, China shall ensure that the same technical regulations, standards and conformity assessment procedures are applied to both imported and domestic products. In order to ensure a smooth transition from the current system, China shall ensure that, upon accession, all certification, safety licensing, and quality licensing bodies and agencies are authorized to undertake these activities for both imported and domestic products, and that, one year after accession, all conformity assessment bodies and agencies will be authorized to undertake conformity assessment for both imported and domestic products. The choice of these bodies or agencies shall be at the discretion of the applicant. For imported and domestic products, all bodies and agencies shall issue the same mark and charge the same fee. They shall also provide the same processing periods and complaint procedures. Imported products shall not subject to more than one conformity assessment. China shall publish and make readily available to other WTO members, individuals, and enterprises full information on the respective responsibilities of the conformity assessment bodies and agencies.

No later than 18 months after accession, China will assign the respective responsibilities to the conformity assessment bodies solely on the basis of the scope of work and the type of products without any consideration of the origin of a product. The respective responsibilities that will be assigned to China's conformity assessment bodies will be notified to the WTO's TBT Committee no later than 12 months after accession.

Designated trading

Designated trading refers to the government designating some enterprises to act on its behalf in the import and export of certain products. The difference between state trading and designated trading is that the former can remain after the accession while the latter has to be abolished no later than a date agreed by the WTO. According to the Protocol on the Accession of the People's Republic of China, China will phase out the designated trading within three years of its accession to the WTO.[4] At the end of the three years, all enterprises in China and all foreign enterprises and individuals will be permitted to import and export such goods throughout the customs territory of China.

4 Commitments to trade in services

As trade in goods was more liberalized than trade in services in China before the WTO accession, the negotiations between China and the WTO on China's WTO accession focused on a wide range of issues related to opening up the service sector. China's commitment to freer trade in services covers almost every service industry, but only the most important are highlighted in this section, including telecommunications, banking and other financial services, insurance, securities, distribution, tourism, education, transportation, and professional services.

Telecommunications

China's commitment to telecommunications covers both the value-added services[5] and the basic telecommunication services. For the value-added services, foreign service providers can only establish joint ventures, with foreign shares of no more than 30 percent of the total shares of a joint venture upon accession, no more than 49 percent of the total shares of a joint venture within the first year after accession, and no more than 50 percent of the total shares of a joint venture within the second year after accession. These joint ventures are limited to Shanghai, Guangzhou, and Beijing upon accession, and to an additional 14 cities within the first year after accession, and are not limited geographically at all within the second year after accession.[6]

With regard to the basic telecommunications services, foreign service suppliers are only allowed to establish joint ventures. For paging services, upon accession these joint ventures are limited to Shanghai, Guangzhou, and Beijing, with foreign shares of no more than 30 percent of the total shares of a joint venture. Within one year after accession, these joint ventures can be established in an additional 14 cities, with foreign shares of no more than 49 percent of the total shares of a joint venture.[7] Within two years after accession, the joint ventures can be established all over China's territory, with foreign shares of no more than 50 percent of the total shares of a joint venture. For mobile voice and data services, upon accession the joint ventures are limited to Shanghai, Guangzhou, and Beijing, with foreign shares of no more than 25 percent of the total shares of a joint venture. Within one year after accession, the joint ventures can be established in an additional 14 cities, with foreign shares of no more than 35 percent of the total shares of a joint venture.[8] Within three years after accession, the joint ventures can have foreign shares of no more than 49 percent of the total shares of a joint venture; and within five years after accession, the joint ventures can be established all over China's territory. For basic domestic and international services, within three years after accession, the joint ventures are limited to Shanghai, Guangzhou, and Beijing, with foreign shares of no more than 25 percent of the total shares of a joint venture. Within five years after accession, the joint ventures can be established in an additional 14 cities, with foreign shares of no more than 35 percent of the total shares of a joint venture.[9] Within six years after accession, the joint ventures can be established all over China's territory, with foreign shares of no more than 49 percent of the total shares of a joint venture.

Banking and other financial services

"Banking services" refer to:

1   acceptance of deposits and other repayable funds from the public;
2   lending of all types, including consumer credit, mortgage credit, factoring and financing of commercial transaction;
3   financial leasing;
4   all kinds of payment and money transmission services, such as credit, charge and debit cards, travelers' checks and bankers drafts (including those for import and export settlement);
5   guarantees and commitments;
6   trading of foreign exchange for own account or for account of customers.

For the foreign currency business, there will be no geographic restriction upon accession. For the local currency business, the geographic restriction will be phased out as follows:

1   upon accession: Shanghai, Shenzhen, Tianjin, and Dalian;
2   within one year after accession: Guangzhou, Zhuhai, Qingdao, Nanjing, and Wuhan;
3   within two years after accession: Jinan, Fuzhou, Chengdu, and Chongqing;
4   within three years after accession: Kunming, Beijing, and Xiamen;
5   within four years after accession: Shantou, Ningbo, Shenyang, and Xi'an; and
6   within five years after accession: all geographic restrictions will be removed.

For the foreign currency business, upon accession foreign financial institutions will be permitted to provide services in China without any restrictions as to their clients. For the local currency business, within two years after accession, foreign financial institutions will be permitted to provide services to Chinese enterprises. Within five years after accession, foreign financial institutions will be permitted to provide services to all Chinese clients.

Upon accession, there will be no restrictions for motor vehicle financing by non-bank financial institutions, and no restrictions for such financial services as the provision and the transfer of financial information, financial data processing, and software related to other financial services.

Insurance

Upon accession, foreign life insurers will be permitted to establish joint ventures with foreign shares of no more than 50 percent of the total shares of a joint venture, and will be allowed to provide individual (not group) insurance to foreigners and Chinese citizens in Shanghai, Guangzhou, Dalian, Shenzhen, and Foshan. Within two years after accession, they can also provide services in Beijing, Chendu, Chongqing, Fuzhou, Suzhou, Xiamen, Ningpo, Shenyang, Wuhan, and Tianjin. Within three years after accession, they can provide health insuance, group insurance, and pension/annuities insurance to foreigners and Chinese, and there will be no geographic restrictions on their services.

Upon accession, foreign non-life insurers will be permitted in the form of either a branch or a joint venture with 51 percent foreign ownership in Shanghai, Guangzhou, Dalian, Shenzhen, and Foshan. Within two years after accession, they can also be established in Beijing, Chendu, Chongqing, Fuzhou, Suzhou, Xiamen, Ningpo, Shenyang, Wuhan, and Tianjin, and they are permitted to provide all kinds of non-life insurance services to foreigners and Chinese alike. Within three years after accession, there will be no geographic restriction for them.

Upon accession, brokerage for insurance of large-scale commercial risks, brokerage for reinsurance, and brokerage for international marine, aviation, and transport insurance and reinsurance are permitted in the form of joint ventures with foreign shares of no more than 50 percent of the total shares of a joint venture in Shanghai, Guangzhou, Dalian, Shenzhen, and Foshan. Within two years after accession, they will also be permitted in Beijing, Chendu, Chongqing, Fuzhou, Suzhou, Xiamen, Ningpo, Shenyang, Wuhan, and Tianjin. Within three years after accession, there will be no geographic restrictions for them, and foreign shares can be increased to 51 percent of the total shares of a joint venture. Within five years after accession, wholly foreign-owned subsidiaries will be permitted.

Securities

Upon accession, foreign securities institutions can engage directly (without a Chinese intermediary) in the B shares business. Representative offices of foreign securities institutions in China may become special members of all Chinese stock exchanges.

Within three years after accession, foreign securities institutions will be permitted to establish joint ventures with foreign shares of no more than one-third of the total shares of a joint venture to engage directly (without a Chinese intermediary) in underwriting the A shares, underwriting and trading of the B shares and the H shares as well as government and corporate bonds, and the launch of funds.

Upon accession, foreign services suppliers will be permitted to establish joint ventures with foreign shares of no more than 33 percent of the total shares of a joint venture to conduct domestic securities investment fund management business. Within three years after accession, foreign shares can be increased to 49 percent of the total shares of a joint venture.

Distribution

For commission agency services and wholesale trade services (excluding salt and tobacco), foreign service suppliers can establish joint ventures to engage in the distribution of all imported and domestically produced products upon accession, except for: books, newspapers, magazines, pharmaceutical products, pesticides, and mulching films that will be permitted within three years after accession; and chemical fertilizers, processed oil, and crude oil that will be permitted within five yeas after accession. They will be permitted to have foreign majority ownership within two years after accession.

For retail services (excluding tobacco), upon accession foreign service suppliers will be permitted to establish joint ventures in five SEZs (Shenzhen, Zhuhai, Shantou, Xiamen, and Hainan) and eight cities (Beijing, Shanghai, Tianjin, Guangzhou, Dalian, Qingdao, Zhengzhou, and Wuhan) to engage in the retail of all products, except for: books, newspapers, and magazines that will be permitted within one year after accession; pharmaceutical products, pesticides, mulching films, and processed oil that will be permitted within three years after accession; and chemical fertilizers that will be permitted within five years after accession. Within two years after accession, foreign services suppliers will be permitted to establish retail joint ventures in all provincial capitals as well as Chongqing and Ningpo, and will be permitted to have foreign majority ownership. Within three years after accession, restrictions will be removed. However, for chain stores with more than 30 outlets that sell grain, cotton, vegetable oil, sugar, motor vehicles, books, newspapers, magazines, pharmaceutical products, pesticides, mulching films, processed oil, and chemical fertilizers, foreign majority ownership is not permitted. Within five years after accession, the equity limitation will be removed for chain stores with more than 30 outlets that sell motor vehicles.

For franchising and wholesale or retail trade services away from a fixed location, there will be no restrictions within three years after accession. Upon accession, furthermore, FIEs may distribute their products manufactured in China, and provide subordinate services including after-sales services.

Tourism

For hotels and restaurants, foreign services suppliers may construct, renovate and operate hotel and restaurant establishments in China in the form of joint ventures with foreign majority ownership permitted upon accession. Within four years after the accession, wholly foreign-owned subsidiaries will be permitted. Foreign managers and specialists who have signed contracts with joint venture hotels and restaurants in China shall be permitted to provide services in China.

For travel agencies and tour operators, upon accession foreign services suppliers are permitted in the form of joint venture travel agencies and tour operators in the holiday resorts designated by the Chinese government and in the cities of Beijing, Shanghai, Guangzhou, and Xi'an under the following conditions:

1   the travel agency and tour operator should mainly engage in the travel business;
2   its annual worldwide turnover should exceed US$40 million;
3   the joint venture should have registered capital of no less than RMB 4 million.

Within three years after accession, the registered capital requirement will be cut to RMB 2.5 million, and foreign majority ownership will be permitted. Within six years after accession, wholly foreign-owned subsidiaries will be permitted, and geographic restrictions will be removed. Joint ventures or wholly foreign-owned travel agencies and tour operators are not permitted to engage in the activities of Chinese traveling to foreign countries, including to China's Special Administrative Regions Hong Kong and Macao, and the Chinese Taipei.

Education

For educational services, joint schools with foreign majority ownership can be established upon accession. These joint schools can provide primary and secondary educational services (excluding national compulsory education), higher educational services, adult educational services, and other educational services (including English language training), but cannot provide special educational services such as military, police, political and party school education.

Foreign individual educational service suppliers may enter into China to provide educational services when invited or employed by Chinese schools and other education institutions if they possess a Bachelor's degree or above, an appropriate professional title or certificate, and two years' professional experience.

Transport

For international transport (freight and passengers), upon accession foreign service suppliers are permitted to establish shipping companies in the form of a joint venture under the following conditions:

1   Foreign shares should not exceed 49 percent of the total registered capital of the joint venture.
2   The chairman of the board of directors and the general manager of the joint venture must be appointed by the Chinese side.
3   The companies have to operate a fleet under the national flag of the People's Republic of China.

For international maritime cargo-handling services, customs clearance services, and container station and depot services, upon accession foreign service suppliers are permitted to establish joint ventures with foreign majority ownership. However, for international maritime agency services, upon accession foreign service suppliers are permitted to establish joint ventures with foreign shares of no more than 49 percent of the total shares of a joint venture.

For internal waterways transport, only international shipping in ports open to foreign vessels shall be permitted, and foreigners are not allowed to establish any kind of company to conduct internal waterways transport. For internal freight transportation by road in trucks or cars, foreign service suppliers are permitted to establish joint ventures with foreign shares of no more than 49 percent of the total shares of a joint venture within one year after accession; within three years after accession, majority foreign ownership will be permitted; and within six years after accession, wholly foreign-owned subsidiaries will be permitted. For freight transportation by rail, foreign service suppliers are permitted to establish joint ventures with foreign shares of no more than 49 percent of the total shares of a joint venture upon accession; within three years after accession, foreign majority ownership will be permitted; and within six years after accession, wholly foreign-owned subsidiaries will be permitted.

For storage and warehouse services, foreign service suppliers are permitted to establish joint ventures with foreign shares of no more than 40 percent of the total shares of a joint venture upon accession; within one year after accession, foreign majority ownership will be permitted; and within three years after accession, wholly foreign-owned subsidiaries will be permitted. For freight forwarding agency services, foreign freight forwarding agencies which have at least three consecutive years' experience are permitted to set up joint ventures with foreign shares of no more than 50 percent of the total shares of a joint venture upon accession; within one year after accession, foreign majority ownership will be permitted; and within four years after accession, wholly foreign-owned subsidiaries will be permitted. For aircraft repair and maintenance services, foreign services suppliers are permitted to establish joint ventures, but the Chinese side must hold controlling shares or be in a dominant position in the joint ventures.

Professional services

For legal services, one year after accession, foreign law firms can provide legal services only in the form of representative offices, and can engage in profit-making activities all over China's territory. However, they cannot employ lawyers licensed in China.

For accounting, auditing and book-keeping services, only certified public accountants licensed by the Chinese authorities can establish partnership or limited liability accounting firms in China. Foreign accounting firms are permitted to affiliate with Chinese firms and enter into contractual agreements with their affiliated firms in other WTO member countries. The licenses issued to those foreigners who have passed the Chinese national certified public accountants examination shall be accorded national treatment.

For medical and dental services, foreign service suppliers can establish joint venture hospitals or clinics with Chinese partners, with foreign majority ownership permitted. The majority of the doctors and medical personnel of the hospitals or clinics shall be of Chinese nationality. Foreign doctors with professional certificates issued by their home country shall be permitted to provide short-term (6–12 months) medical services in China after they obtain a license from the Ministry of Public Health.

For tax services, initially foreign service providers can only establish joint ventures, with foreign majority ownership permitted. Within six years after accession, foreign firms will be permitted to establish wholly foreign-owned subsidiaries. For architectural services, engineering services, integrated engineering services, and urban planning services, foreign service suppliers can only establish joint ventures, with majority foreign ownership permitted. Within five years after accession, they can establish wholly foreign-owned subsidiaries.

· 5 The impact on the Chinese economy and opportunities for investors

China's accession to the WTO will have significant impact on the Chinese economy. China's commitments to trade in goods and services will further open up the Chinese markets to foreign competitors. On the other hand, the world markets will further open to Chinese products after China becomes a member of the multilateral global trading system. However, the increased integration of China into the world economy after the WTO accession will affect different economic sectors and activities to different degrees and, therefore, provide more opportunities for foreign investors in some areas than others. This section highlights only some of the impacts and opportunities.

The most affected areas are the service sectors. Service sectors such as banking, telecommunications, securities, insurance, transportation, education, professional services, distribution, and tourism have been the least opened areas in China. The Chinese government considers these sectors as vital to the economy, and thus has subjected them to the control of the central and local governments. State-owned enterprises and various governmental entities have dominated these sectors. Under the monopoly of the state, these sectors are notoriously low in efficiency, high in cost and non-competitive in price. After accession, these sectors will open up to foreign investors to varying degrees. Foreign investors with sufficient capital, advanced technology, updated managerial know-how and competitive prices can venture into these sectors to compete with their Chinese counterparts. It is expected that foreign investors in these sectors will enjoy obvious advantages in terms of efficiency, cost, technology, and price, and thus have a greater chance of success in business.[10]

As for the trade in goods, the most affected sectors are those that were previously heavily protected through tariff and nontariff trade barriers. The automobile industry, for instance, will be under huge pressure after China's accession to the WTO. The current tariff rate for automobiles and parts and components of mobile vehicles is as high as 80–100 percent, and there are quantitative restrictions on the import of these products. Under such protection, the Chinese automobile industry is very weak, characterized by small-scale, out-of-date technology, of low quality and high price. When the quotas are removed in 2005, and the tariff rate is cut to 25 percent for automobiles, and 10 percent for parts and components of mobile vehicles in 2007, domestically produced motor vehicles and parts and components of mobile vehicles will face fierce competition from their foreign counterparts, and will be in a disadvantageous position in the competition. Foreign investors with sufficient capital and advanced technology may move into this sector to establish joint ventures for the production of automobiles, parts, and components of motor vehicles. Given the huge market for motor vehicles in general, and automobiles in China in particular, investment in this sector will have a very good chance of success. The same analysis applies, although to a less degree, to the domestic appliances sector with a tariff rate much higher than the average, such as color TVS (with a current tariff rate of 35–45 percent), refrigerators (with a current tariff rate of 35 percent), microwave radars (with a current tariff rate of 35 percent), and air conditioners (with a current tariff rate of 25 percent).

Another affected area is the textile industry and other labor-intensive industries. China's comparative advantage lies mainly in its huge amount of cheap labor resources. For a long time, China has taken advantage of this to produce labor-intensive goods and sell them on the international market. These goods have been discriminated against on the international market in the form of anti-dumping measures and nontariff measures such as the quota system. The E.U., Argentina, Hungary, Mexico, Poland, Turkey, and Slovenia have promised to abolish such discriminatory practises within about five to six years after China's accession to the WTO. Developed countries have also promised to abolish the quotas on textiles on 1 January 2005 within the WTO trading system. Therefore, China's textile industry and other labor-intensive industries are expected to grow rapidly in the years ahead, thus providing opportunities for foreign investors. Foreign investors may invest in these industries, take advantage of advanced technology and the network of international markets, and achieve success in business.

Further reading

Clarke, Donald C., "China's Legal System and the WTO: Prospects for Compliance," *Washington University Global Studies Law Review* 2, 2003, 97–118.

World Trade Organization, *The Protocol on the Accession of the People's Republic of China*, 2002. Visit the Web site of the WTO at www.wto.org.

Notes

1 See Annex 7 of the Protocol on the Accession of the People's Republic of China.
2 See Annex 2A of the Protocol on the Accession of the People's Republic of China for a list of these goods.
3 See Annex 8 of the Protocol on the Accession of the People's Republic of China for details of China's commitment to the reduction of tariff rate in agricultural and industrial goods.
4 See Annex 2B of the Protocol on the Accession of the People's Republic of China for details of the specified goods for which the designated trading will be phased out.
5 Value-added services include electronic mail, voicemail, on-line information and database retrieval, electronic data interchange, enhanced/value-added facsimile services, code and protocol conversion, on-line information and/or data processing (including transaction processing).
6 The 14 cities refer to Chendu, Chongqing, Dalian, Fuzhou, Hangzhou, Nanjing, Ningpo, Qingdao, Shenyang, Shenzhen, Xiamen, Xi'an, Taiyuan, and Wuhan.
7 The 14 cities refer to Chendu, Chongqing, Dalian, Fuzhou, Hangzhou, Nanjing, Ningpo, Qingdao, Shenyang, Shenzhen, Xiamen, Xi'an, Taiyuan, and Wuhan.
8 The 14 cities refer to Chendu, Chongqing, Dalian, Fuzhou, Hangzhou, Nanjing, Ningpo, Qingdao, Shenyang, Shenzhen, Xiamen, Xi'an, Taiyuan, and Wuhan.
9 The 14 cities refer to Chendu, Chongqing, Dalian, Fuzhou, Hangzhou, Nanjing, Ningpo, Qingdao, Shenyang, Shenzhen, Xiamen, Xi'an, Taiyuan, and Wuhan.
10 See the details of China's commitments to the trade in services illustrated above to assess investment opportunities for each of the service sectors.

11 The development of the western region

At the beginning of the twenty-first century, while moving toward greater international economic integration by joining the WTO, China was also seeking greater national economic integration by launching a grand project to develop its poorest interior region – the western region. In a sense, the WTO accession and the western region development project are two events that will be most significant in shaping the course of China's economic development in the first decades of the twenty-first century. It is essential, therefore, for foreign investors to understand the background and objectives of the project for western region development, the priorities the Chinese government has set for developing the western region, and the preferential policy treatments that the Chinese government has promised to offer to foreigners investing in the region.

1 Background and objectives

China's east coast region enjoys the locational advantage in terms of easy access to international markets, foreign advanced technology, foreign capital, and, most importantly, overseas Chinese communities in Hong Kong, Macao, and Taiwan. After the launch of the economic reform and the opening up in the late 1970s, therefore, the Chinese government kept granting preferential policy treatments to the coastal region in order to achieve rapid success in a locality in a relative short period. As a result, the east coast region developed very quickly, while the interior region has begun to lag behind in the last two decades or so. In recent years, the coastal-oriented development strategy and the resulting gap between the east coast and the interior region became a threat to social stability, national security, sustainability of rapid economic growth, and even environmental protection, which increasingly drew attention from the Chinese government. The Chinese government intended to resolve these problems by launching the project for western region development.

From east to west

On 19 January 2000, an Inter-ministerial Committee for Developing the western region of the State Council was set up in Beijing, with Premier Zhu

Rongji as the Chair. The formation of this high-powered committee showed the determination of the Chinese government to develop the poor and backward interior, and signified the beginning of a shift in focus of economic development from the eastern (coastal) to the western region.

China's 31 provinces and metropolitan cities are currently divided into eastern (coastal), central and western regions.[1] The western region includes 11 provinces and one metropolitan city. It accounts for 70 percent of China's land area, but only 29 percent of China's population and 18 percent of China's GDP. Here the physical environment is very harsh, and most of the land areas are covered by mountains, hills, plateaux, deserts, and dry lands. Transportation and telecommunication facilities are extremely underdeveloped. Until 1999, for instance, railway coverage was 26 km per 10,000 km^2 in this region while it was 153 km per 10,000 km^2 in the eastern region. To date there is no railway at all in Tibet. The poor telecommunication facilities can be seen by the low number of telephone sets and Internet subscribers. In 1999, for instance, there were about 400 telephones and one Internet subscriber per 10,000 people in the western region, while the figures in the eastern region were about 1,000 and 10, respectively.

Owing to the harsh physical environment and poor infrastructure, the western region could not make full use of its abundant natural resources and tourist resources, and has been the poorest region in China for centuries. To date, 90 percent of Chinese living under the poverty line are in the western region. The illiteracy rate is much higher in the western region (27 percent) than in the east coast region (14 percent). In Tibet and Qinghai, illiteracy rates are as high as 54 percent and 43 percent, respectively. The poverty and backwardness of the western region has been a major concern for Chinese leaders, even in the early years of economic reform when they focused their attention primarily on the east coast region.

In the early 1980s, Deng Xiaoping had proposed the idea of two stages of regional development, that is, the coastal provinces were to make use of their locational advantage to develop first, and they could then help the development of the interior provinces. During his southern tour in 1992, Deng further proposed that China should move from the first stage to the second, that is, shift the focus of reform and development from the coast to the interior, by the end of the twentieth century. The shift of focus of reform and development from the coast to the western region was, therefore, a well-planned move that had been under deliberation for more than a decade.

When Deng Xiaoping proposed reorienting development to the interior, his main concern was to "resolve the problem of widening disparities between coastal and interior regions."[2] Since then, however, other concerns have developed and further motivated the current westward drive, such as the separatist movements in minority nationalities that threaten national unity and security, the sluggish domestic demand that became worse during the Asian financial crisis, and the deterioration of the ecological environment that have caused devastating disasters along the Yangtze River and the Yellow River in recent years. China's current drive to develop its western region, therefore, has been initiated and promoted to achieve multiple goals.

Regional equality

The primary goal of the westward drive is no doubt to narrow regional economic disparities. Following the adoption of the reform and opening-up policies in 1978, China encouraged the coastal areas to utilize their locational advantage to achieve more rapid economic growth than other parts of the country. To this end, a series of preferential policy treatments was granted to coastal areas with regard to foreign investment, foreign trade, taxation and the establishment of the SEZs. As a result, coastal areas developed faster than their interior counterparts, and the disparities between coastal and interior regions has widened quite consistently in the last two decades.

From 1978 to 1999, the ratio of GDP per capita of the coastal region to that of the central region rose from 1.50 to 1.87, and the ratio of GDP per capita of the coastal region to that of the western region rose from 1.84 to 2.59. In the 1990s in particular, the disparities between coastal and western regions widened remarkably. Looked at in greater detail, the widening of the gap between the coastal and western regions is even more astonishing. The GDP per capita of the Qinghai Province as a percentage of that of Shanghai (the richest coastal metropolitan city) was 17 percent in 1978, but it fell to 10 percent in 1999. Consumption per capita of the Qinghai Province as a percentage of that of Shanghai fell from 54 percent in 1978 to 24 percent in 1999. By 1999, all western provinces were below the national average in terms of GDP per capita and consumption per capita.

Compared with the fastest-growing provinces such as Guangdong, Zhejiang, Jiangsu, Fujian, and Shandong in the east coast region, all interior provinces fell well behind in terms of the growth of both GDP per capita and consumption per capita. In 1978, four of the five coastal provinces lagged behind Qinghai in terms of GDP per capita, and all of them lagged behind Qinghai in terms of consumption per capita. From 1978 to 1999, however, GDP per capita in the five coastal provinces increased by eight–ten times while that in Qinghai increased by only three times. Over the same period, consumption per capita in the five coastal provinces increased by five–six times while that in Qinghai increased only doubled. By 1999, therefore, GDP per capita in the five fastest-growing coastal provinces had already been twice or three times as high as that in Qinghai, and consumption per capita in the five coastal provinces had all surpassed that in Qinghai.

The gap between the coastal and interior regions becomes more vivid if a comparison is made between an interior province and the "open" areas in southeast coastal China. In 1999, for instance, per capita GDP and per capita savings in 14 open coastal cities (Dalian, Tianjin, Qinhuangdao, Yantai, Qingdao, Shanghai, Wenzhou, Lianyungang, Fuzhou, Guangzhou, Haikou, Nantong, Ningpo, and Zhanjiang) were five times and eight times as high as those in Qinghai province, respectively, and per capita GDP and per capita savings of the four SEZs (Shenzhen, Shantou, Zhuhai, and Xiamen) were 12 times and 13 times as high as those in Qinghai province, respectively.

The widening regional disparities are antagonistic to the Communist ideology that still dominates the party and the government, and have caused much unhappiness for those living in the interior, who complain about the unfairness of the on-going reform and opening-up program.[3] The discontent gained strength in the years immediately following the Tiananmen Square Incident in 1989.[4] Were the increase in regional inequality not brought under control, not only would the on-going reform and opening-up program be under threat, but also the legitimacy of the current regime. The primary goal of the westward drive is, no doubt, to narrow the disparities between the east coast and the interior regions.

National security

Another motivation behind the westward drive is to ensure national security. The west is a region where China's minority nationalities live in compact communities. Fifty of the 54 minority nationalities in China, including the Uighur, the Tibetan, the Hui, the Yi, the Bai, the Hani, the Zhuang, the Dai, and the Miao, live in the western region. In fact, three of the nine provinces in the western region are autonomous regions dominated by minority nationalities, that is, the Xinjiang Uighur Autonomous Region, the Tibetan Autonomous Region, and the Ningxia Hui Autonomous Region. Owing to the ethnic diversity, the western region has experienced frequent ethnic conflicts in Chinese history, and has been a main concern for China's national security for centuries.

After 1978, the Chinese central government relaxed its control over local affairs in order to provide incentive for local authorities at various levels to accelerate reform, opening up and economic development. The Chinese central government also adopted a more liberal policy allowing the freedom of religious beliefs among minority nationalities. Along with the process of decentralization and liberalization, the movement toward greater autonomy or even full independence gained momentum in some of the minority areas in the western region. China's opening up to the outside world presented an opportunity for the separatists to work in concert with their supporters abroad.[5]

In the Xinjiang Uygur Autonomous Region, for instance, Muslim extremists have been demanding that Xinjiang become a separate Muslim state, independent of China. In February 1997, hundreds of Uighurs took to the streets in Yining, a city near the border between China and Kazakhstan, shouting "God is supreme" and "Independence for Xinjiang." They become violent when the Chinese government tried to crack down on the demonstration. The Chinese official media reported that ten people had been killed, but Uighur exile groups put the death toll at more than 100. After the crackdown, the Muslim extremists continued with murder, bombing and violent rampage against Beijing, and they were provided with weapons from the Uighur exile groups in China's neighboring countries. In January 2000, in Aksu, an isolated town in Xinjiang, several separatist militants were killed by the police.[6]

In the Tibetan Autonomous Region, separatist movements have posed an even greater threat. Ever since the Tibetan government led by the spiritual leader Dalai Lama fled abroad in 1959, the Tibetan Buddhism separatist movement has maintained its demand for independence. The exiled Tibetan government tried to make use of international forces against the Chinese government, and gained considerable support from extremist Tibetan Buddhists both inside and outside China. In September 1987, for instance, after the exiled Dalai Lama called for an independent statehood for Tibet, riots broke out in Lhassa in support of the spiritual leader. In the following two years, a series of protests in various forms was reported in Lhassa. The Tibetan separatist movements staged a violent rebellion in March 1989, in which scores of people were killed. The Chinese government had to declare martial law in Lhassa for more than a year. After that, although open violent opposition against the Chinese government subsided, covert separatist activities did not stop, as indicated by the escape of the 14-year-old Karmapa Lama, leader of the Kargyu sect of Tibetan Buddhism, to India in early January 1989.

Faced with the pressure of separatist movements, the Chinese government believes the best solution to the problem is to integrate further the minority nationalities into the rest of the nation. That is to say, the central government will help the western region catch up with other parts of the nation in terms of economic reform and development. The Chinese government hopes that along with the rise in the standard of living and the increased flow of commodities, resources and personnel across regions, the minority nationalities in the western region will become less dissatisfied with the government, and increasingly consider themselves, as part of a unified nation.

Growth momentum

A third motivation behind the westward drive is to provide new sources of economic growth. In the 1990s, the Chinese economy had changed from a "shortage economy" to a "surplus economy," characterized by overcapacity in production and low levels of private consumption. Excessive investment and increasing polarization contributed to the change. With few exceptions, more than half of the production capacity in domestic appliances lay idle; yet, more investments were pouring into this sector. On the other hand, most residents in poor areas could not afford to buy these commodities due to low income. As a result, overstocked goods increased enormously. The overstocked TV sets numbered, for instance, more than 3 million in the late 1990s.

The problem became worse during the Asian financial crisis. China's exports became less competitive due to the currency devaluation in neighboring countries. China's foreign trade growth rate turned negative in 1998, the first time in 16 years, and only picked up in late 1999 and early 2000. Goods that could not be sold in international markets flooded domestic markets, which were already under the pressure of weak consumer demand. After October 1997, consumer price fell for more than 28 successive months, and only showed signs of bottoming-out in February 2000. China had suffered from its most serious deflation in the reform period.

China adopted expansionary fiscal and monetary policies to boost domestic demand during the Asian financial crisis, but the policies did not achieve the effect expected. The decrease in both domestic and international demand led to a slowdown in economic growth, and the growth rate of GDP fell continuously in the late 1990s. The growth slowdown exerted pressure on employment, causing increased concern among policymakers. To resolve the problem of sluggish demand and growth slowdown, new policy initiatives had to be made.

Through the westward drive, China is trying to provide new sources of growth. The westward drive would increase the consumption capacity of residents in the most backward areas of the country. It has been estimated that nearly 90 percent of the Chinese people living under the poverty line are located in the western region, and they have extremely low levels of consumption capacity. Rural residents in the western region are particularly poor, and consume much less than their counterparts in the coastal region in major durable consumer goods, particularly domestic appliances. If the standard of living of residents in the western region were raised to the same level as their coastal counterparts, domestic demand would certainly increase considerably.

The westward drive would also entail a large number of public projects in infrastructure construction, which would not only yield employment opportunities but also provide a solid basis for sustainable economic development in the long run. Therefore, a consensus has been reached among Chinese leaders: the "grand strategy of developing the Western Region" will become an important measure to boost domestic demand and promote coordinated, sustained, rapid, and healthy development of the national economy.

Ecological protection

Finally, the westward drive was initiated to tackle deteriorating ecological problems in the western and the central regions arising from China's rapid economic development. China was so eager to achieve rapid industrialization and economic growth that it did not pay much attention to environmental protection. Under the policy of "taking grain as the key link," for instance, rural residents were encouraged to turn hillsides and grasslands into farmlands, causing ecological imbalance. The deterioration of the ecological environment has been particularly severe in the interior, and has led to serious consequences such as the desertification of lands, floods, and the drying up of rivers. In particular, the soil erosion and water losses in the upper and middle reaches of the Yangtze River and the Yellow River have caused frequent disasters in recent years.

In the Yangtze River floods in 1998, for example, about 3,000 people died, and 3 million people were left homeless. The floods also did tremendous damage to crops, and made subsequent summer crop planting on some of the most fertile farmlands along the Yangtze River virtually impossible. In addition, the floods killed thousands of livestock, inundated hundreds of thousands of hectares of farmland, and destroyed both farm machinery and irrigation infrastructure. In the three provinces of Hunan, Hubei, and Jiangxi alone, the floods completely destroyed more than 3 million hectares of crops and aquaculture, and severely affected 7 million hectares of cultivated land.

The Yellow River is more threatening than the Yangtze River, although it has not caused serious floods in recent years. The river remains a potential source of the most devastating floods due to its high silt content accumulated over the years. Millions of tons of yellow mud choke the channel, causing the river to overflow its banks and change its course. In the lower reaches of the Yellow River, the riverbed has actually become higher than the level of the surrounding countryside. Unlike the Yangtze River, the water of the Yellow River is only held by its levees shielding 120,000 km^2 of land. This means that more than 7.3 million hectares of farmland and a population of about 78 million are exposed to possible devastating floods. If the levees were broken in the rainy season, the damage could be much greater than that caused by the fateful floods of 1931, in which the death toll hit almost 4 million.

As a result of the water loss in its upper and middle reaches, in the meantime, the Yellow River has begun to run short of water in its lower reaches in the dry season in recent years. In 1972, the water level fell so low that for the first time in China's long history, the river dried up before reaching the sea. It failed to reach the sea for 15 days that year, and did so intermittently in the years that followed. Since 1985, it has run dry each year, with the drying up periods becoming progressively longer. In 1997, for instance, it failed to reach the sea for 226 days, and for a long stretch of time it did not even reach the Shandong Province, the last province it flows through en route to the sea. The drying up of the Yellow River has seriously affected agricultural and industrial facilities located along its lower reaches.

The Chinese government has spent huge amounts of effort and money to fight these disasters each year, but little progress has been made in easing the threat. A fundamental solution to the problem is to protect the ecological environment of the upper and middle reaches of both the Yangtze River and the Yellow River. Both rivers have their sources in Qinghai, a western province, and their upper and middle reaches in other western and central provinces. By pursuing ecologically sound development of the western region, the Chinese government hopes to eradicate the roots of disaster.

As can be seen from the above discussion, most of the goals in developing the western region are far from easy to achieve. The westward drive is, therefore, not a temporary policy move, but a long-term strategic reorientation that will continue well into the twenty-first century. The Chinese government is prepared to "spend decades or even a whole century of effort to build a western region marked by economic prosperity, social progress, stable lifestyle, national unity, and beautiful mountains and rivers."[7]

2 Priorities in development

Although the western region is very diversified, the region is in main characterized by harsh physical environment, poor infrastructure and rich natural resources. It is vital, therefore, to form appropriate strategies and priorities for the development of this region. The Chinese government has announced that the western region development project will focus on four aspects: infrastructure construction, ecological protection, industry structure adjustment, and development of science, technology and education.

Reprioritizing development

In the past, the Chinese government has given priority to resource exploitation in the richly endowed western region.[8] In the planning period, industrialization in the western region was based on the development of resource-related industries, particularly mining, metallurgy and the defense industry. In agriculture, the exploration of land resources focused on reclaiming wasteland, and rural residents were encouraged to build terraced fields up the hillsides following the model of Dazhai, a village in Shanxi Province once glorified in Mao's era. After 1978, along with the shift in focus of industrialization to the coastal region, China began to turn the western region into the supplier of natural resources and raw materials for the coastal region. As a result, resource-related industries bloomed, and the previous policy of land exploitation was not corrected. For various reasons, however, such resource-oriented development did not much benefit the western region, and at times did even more damage to the regional economy.

First, domestic prices were distorted. The domestic commodity prices of raw materials, grains, minerals and metals were brought down to a very low level to facilitate rapid industrialization in the planning period, and were among the last to be liberalized in the reform period. The coastal region benefited very much from the "unfair price" structure, but the resource-based western region was the loser. Second, the international prices of the products of raw materials, grains, minerals, and metal have been falling for many years, and the western region has faced increasing competition since China's opening up to world market.[9] Third, the Chinese economy had already turned from a "shortage" to "surplus" economy since the mid 1990s, and the decrease in domestic demand drove the domestic prices down. In 1998, for instance, the supply of metals and minerals well surpassed the demand, and domestic prices of these products fell 4–7 percent, a fall that was much greater than the price of other products. In fact, the oversupply of grains also posed similar problems. The western region has suffered tremendously.

On top of that, the exploration of resources in the western region was carried out without careful consideration for resource conservation and environmental protection. Hundreds and thousands of small-scale mines were built in the rural areas; and they produced mineral products of low quality to be sold at very low prices. Trees were felled, and hillsides and grasslands were turned into farmland. Water loss and soil erosion became worse year after year. As the Yangtze River and the Yellow River rise in the western region, the deteriorating environment there has resulted in devastating floods hitting provinces in the lower reaches of the rivers.

Faced with these problems, China had to reconsider the previous resource-oriented policy, and reprioritize development of the western region. As early as October 1999, Premier Zhu Rongji proposed four new priorities in developing the western region: infrastructure construction, ecological protection, industry-structure adjustment, and the development of science, technology, and education. Zhu's proposal was reconfirmed at the first meeting of the Leading Committee of Developing the Western Region of the State Council on 16–19 January 2000. The four priorities have become the main targets in China's drive to develop the western region and, therefore, they deserve particular attention.

Infrastructure construction

The first priority is given to infrastructure construction, which is believed to be the "foundation" (基础) of the development of the western region.[10] The decision was made in consideration of the extremely poor infrastructure in the region. As mentioned above, transportation and telecommunications are extremely underdeveloped in the western region, which make the region very hard to access. To develop the region, China first has to make the region accessible to investors.

According to the Chinese government, infrastructure construction will, first, focus on highways and roads at three levels. The first includes 15,000 main national highways and transprovincial main roads linked to the western region. The second level involves 185,000 km of roads connecting cities in the western region. The third level includes 149,000 km of roads in rural areas connecting 452 towns, 41,530 villages, and 972 production and construction corps in the western region that currently are not accessible by roads. All the highways and roads will be completed in ten years, and a total of 700 billion yuan will be invested.

In the meantime, the infrastructure of railways and airports will be strengthened. In the next five years, a total of RMB 100 billion will be invested in the construction of railways. The focus will be on railways linking individual provinces within the western region, railways linking the western region to the coastal region, and railways linking the western region to neighboring countries in central Asia such as Kirghizia and Uzbek.[11] In particular, a railway connecting Kunming and Singapore is currently under consideration. In addition, RMB 5 billion will be invested in the construction of 11 new airports and the upgrading of nine airports in the western region.[12]

Efforts will also be made to construct natural gas pipelines. For instance, a mega project called "piping the gas in the west to the east" commenced in 2001, with a total investment of more than RMB 120 billion. The gas pipelines will connect the Tarim Basin in Xinjiang Province, which accounts for 22 percent of China's reserve of natural gas, with Shanghai. The gas pipelines, spanning some 4,200 km, will cut across seven provinces (Gansu, Ningxia, Shaanxi, Shanxi, Henan, Anhui, and Jiangsu).

Furthermore, attention will be given to power networks, post and tele-communication networks, broadcasting and television stations, and water resource facilities. For instance, 17 million small-scale or miniature "rain containers" will be built in the western region, particularly in the upper reaches of the Yellow River, to resolve the problem of water loss. In the next three years, RMB 190 billion will be invested in the construction and renovation of power networks in the rural areas, particularly those in the western region.

Ecological protection

The second priority is given to ecological protection, which is considered as the "fundamental" (根本) in the development of the western region.[13] In the next ten years, an estimated RMB 200 billion will be invested in various projects of ecological protection. Most of the investment will be in the western region, particularly in the upper and middle reaches of the Yangtze River and the Yellow River. These projects will focus on constructing and protecting forests and grasslands to prevent soil erosion, water loss, and desertification.

The most important project is the so-called "turning farmlands back into grasslands" (*tuigeng huancao*) or "turning farmlands back into forests" (*tuigeng huanlin*) project. Two-thirds of the silt (sediment) that have accumulated in the Yellow River and the Yangtze River are from the hillside farmlands. Currently, there are nearly 20 million hectares of hillside farmland in the country, 70 percent of which is in the western region. To encourage farmers to turn this hillside farmland back into forests or grasslands, the Chinese government is offering 100 kg of grains, RMB 50 worth of nursery-grown plants, and RMB 20 worth of education and health subsidies for every *mu* of farmland that is converted back into grasslands or forests. This project is, therefore, also called "exchanging grains for forests and grasslands." In 2000, the project was carried out on a trial basis in 174 counties in the upper and middle reaches of the two rivers (located in the western region).

Another project is the so-called "enriching people by establishing eco-homelands." In the past, more than 30 percent of the firewood used by residents in the western region was obtained by cutting down trees, causing widespread deforestation. In addition, crop straws were used as a source of energy and, therefore, could not be used to fertilize farmlands. This resulted in deterioration of the quality of farmland. The new project involves the introduction of the technology and understanding of renewable energy resources developed in the coastal region, such as marsh gas, into the rural areas of the western region. Such alternative forms of energy are aimed at reducing reliance on firewood and, thus, preventing deforestation and soil deterioration. By 2003, a number of villages in seven western provinces (Shaanxi, Gansu, Ningxia, Qinghai, Yunnan, Guizhou, and Sichuan) have been selected as experimental units for this project.

A third project is to build up nature reserves and ecological protection zones. In the next five years, a total of six million hectares of nature reserves and ecological protection zones will be built in the western region, particularly in the Qinghai-Tibet Plateau, the headstream areas of the Yangtze River and the Yellow River, the mountain and valley areas in the southwest provinces, and the highland and desert areas in Xinjiang and Inner Mongolia. By 2005, the number of the nature reserves and ecological protection zones in the western region will have increased from the present 776 to 1,000, and account for 8.5 percent of China's total land area.

Besides these projects, a number of policy measures will be taken to ensure the preservation and protection of the ecological environment in the western region. In the upper and middle reaches of the Yangtze River and the Yellow River, for instance, mountain passes will be sealed, logging will be forbidden, and lumber markets will be closed down. To promote reforestation, the government plans to develop forestry under various forms of non-state ownership, such as a share-holding system, joint-stock cooperative system and private enterprises. In particular, the government will promote the household contract responsibility system. Any juridical persons will be encouraged to turn wastelands into forests, and be entitled to obtain the right to use the forest according to terms stimulated in the contract. The rights to use the forest will be inheritable and transferable. The holder of the rights will be entitled to receive income from the forest.

Industry-structure adjustment

The third priority is given to industry structure adjustment. This is considered as the "key" (关键) to developing the western region.[14] The outdated industrial structure is responsible for, among other things, the poor income of rural residents, the lack of economic advantage, and the low level of competitiveness in the western region. The western provinces have been asked to adjust their industrial structure in accordance with both their own natural conditions and the demand of domestic and international markets. In so doing, they have to develop their own geographically specific industries or geographically advantageous industries so that they can become more competitive in the domestic and international marketplace.

In agriculture, emphasis will be on geographically specific crops and plants, such as cotton, sugar, fruits, vegetables, herbs, and tobacco leaves. The production of "green" food and "health" products will be given particular attention. In the meantime, greater efforts will be made to develop animal husbandry, particularly cattle and sheep husbandry. Processing industries for geographically specific farm products and animal husbandry products will become key players in the western region. Given the ethnic diversity of the western region, the processing of ethnically specific products, such as Muslim food, also offers great potential for growth.

In resource exploitation, conventional resources with weak market demand, such as minerals and raw materials, will give way to new resources with strong market demand, such as natural gas and hydroelectricity. Currently, the western region accounts for 87 percent of China's reserve of natural gas, which is mainly located in the gas fields in the Tarim Basin, the Qaidam Basin, the Shanganning Basin, and the Sichuan Basin. The four gas fields will become centers of gas exploitation once the "piping the gas in the west to the east" project takes off. The western region also accounts for 70 percent of China's reserve of hydroelectricity, which is mainly located in Sichuan, Yunnan, Tibet, and Guizhou. These provinces have great potential to become centres of hydroelectricity exploitation. As for minerals and raw materials, the new strategy calls for "rational exploration and resource reservation," emphasizing a more sober and cool-headed approach in utilizing the resources.[15]

In the meantime, greater effort will be made to phase out traditional industrial enterprises that use excessive resources, employ outdated technology, have small production capacity, produce goods of low quality, and pollute the environment. In addition, similar enterprises in the coastal region will not be allowed to relocate to the western region. Instead, industrialization in the western region will focus on the development of new industrial sectors and the transformation of the traditional industrial sectors with the help of new technology. In particular, the western region is encouraged to develop high-tech industries, including IT industries, new materials science, aerospace, and machinery and equipment.

Finally, and most importantly, the western region is being asked to make use of its geographic advantage to develop tourism and related tertiary industries. There are seven world-class cultural heritage sites in this region earmarked by UNESCO. These sites are the Mogao Crottoes in Gansu, the

Qin Shi Huang Mousoleum in Shaanxi, the Valley of Nine Stockaded Villages in Sichuan, Huanglong in Sichuan, the Emei Mountain in Sichuan, the Li River in Yunnan and the Potala Palace in Lhasa, Tibet. In addition, the Three Gorges of the Yangtze River, the Figurines of Soldiers and Horses, and the Silk Route are also well-known tourist sites in this region. On top of that, 50 of China's 56 minority nationalities, such as the Uighur, the Tibetan, the Hui, the Yi, the Bai, the Hani, the Zhuang, the Dai, and the Miao, live in compact communities in this region. As a result of its cultural-historical sites, breathtaking scenery and ethnic diversity, the western region has attracted millions of tourists from all over the world. Currently, the region accounts for about 30 percent of foreign tourists in China, and has enormous potential to develop tourism and related tertiary industries.

The development of science, technology, and education

The fourth priority is given to the development of science, technology, and education. This is considered to be the "important condition" (条件) for the development of the western region.[16] Apart from a few exceptions such as Shaanxi Province, Sichuan Province, and Chongqing City, science, technology, and education are extremely underdeveloped in the western region. In 2000, for instance, most western provinces were below the national average in terms of number of patents produced, number of articles on science and technology published, share of high-tech products in exports, and number of university students. In the poorest provinces of Tibet and Qinghai, the illiteracy rate went as high as 54 percent and 43 percent, respectively. With the dawn of the knowledge-based economy, the western provinces will certainly be hampered by a lack of dynamic in its long-term growth. Due to its unique historical background, the western region has been asked to focus on the following areas in the development of science, technology, and education.

In areas with a large number of defence industries, such as Shaanxi Province, Sichuan Province, Guizhou Province, and Chongqing City, emphasis will be placed on making full use of the technology developed in the defence industries over the last few decades. The technology in aerospace, electronics, ship-building and automobile production in the defence industries in the western region is considered among the most advanced in the country, and can be used in a wide range of civil industries. Therefore, these western areas have been asked to develop the defence industry into high-tech centres, and promote the transfer of advanced technology from the defence industry to the civil industry.

In big cities with a large number of universities and research institutes, such as Xi'an in Shaanxi Province, Chengdu in Sichuan Province, and Lanzhou in Gansu Province, attention will be given to making full use of the human resources in their academic institutions. In Xi'an, for instance, there are more than 60 universities, including the famous Xi'an Transportation University, more than 4,000 research institutes, and more than 800,000 personnel in various science and technology fields. With these academic institutions and trained personnel, Xi'an enjoys unique advantage in developing science, technology, and tertiary education. The software park in Xi'an has, for example, developed into a software park of national grade, and has the potential to become the largest base for software development, software production, and software services in China.

In small cities, towns, and vast rural areas with a large number of the less educated, emphasis will be placed on making primary and secondary education universal. A number of projects will be started to achieve this goal. In June 2000, one project was initiated to encourage schools in the coastal region to help schools in the poorer areas of the western region; another project was initiated to encourage schools in large cities in the western region to help schools in the rural areas within the region. In the meantime, a distance education programme will be started in the western region, and a total of 70 million yuan will be invested in this project in 2000. In addition, a number of existing projects will be strengthened to train teachers in the poor areas in the western region.

Finally, but not exclusively, greater efforts will be made to introduce talent and advanced technology from other parts of the nation, as well as from foreign countries, into the western region. To encourage talent from the central and coastal regions to move to the western region, the central government has adopted a new policy of "no change in permanent residence, no change in identification, and freedom to go back." In the meantime, the central government has initiated a project to provide financial support for returned overseas scientists and technicians to conduct research in the interior. Individual western provinces have also begun to adopt special policies to attract domestic and foreign talent. A number of projects will be initiated to promote the cooperation in science and technology between the western region and other parts of the nation as well as foreign countries.

Zhu Rongji's four priorities in developing the western region are well designed, and they fit in quite well with the needs of the western region. The projects involved are, however, very demanding both financially and technically. Even with the full support of the central and local governments, the successful implementation of these projects will depend on how financial and other resources are mobilized in a rapidly commercializing society. The government can no longer rely on political mobilization, as it did in the past through political movements and campaigns, and has increasingly to turn to market forces.

3 Preferential policy treatment for foreign investors

To implement the ambitious project for western region development, the Chinese government cannot reply on state resources. As shown by the successful experience of the east coast region in the last two decades, foreign direct investment could play a vital role in providing not only financial resources but also advanced technology and management know-how. The Chinese government has made it very clear that foreign investors are encouraged to move into the western region, and it has announced a number of preferential policy treatments for them to do so. Local governments in the western region also compete for foreign investments by issuing attractive preferential policy deals. This section highlights the preferential policy treatments offered to foreign investors by both the central government in Beijing and the local governments in the western region.

Problems with state financing

China's ambitious drive to develop its western region involves a large number of projects, which require a huge amount of investment. The Chinese government has shown its determination to finance these projects, and has made a number of promises. The government has promised, for instance, to allocate 70 percent of the government-appropriated funds, 70 percent of the treasury bonds, and 70 percent of its foreign loans to projects related to the development of the western region. In the meantime, state-owned banks, such as the People's Bank of China and the State Development Bank, have also promised to prioritize their credit and loan services to projects related to the development of the western region, and to open a number of new branches in the western provinces. There are, however, problems associated with state financing.

To begin with, the financial power of the Chinese government declined along with rapid economic growth, as indicated by the decrease in the share of government revenue in GDP. From 1978 to 1999, for instance, the share fell from 31 percent to 13 percent. Most importantly, the financial power of the central government has also been declining, as indicated by the decrease in the share of central government in total government expenditure. From 1978 to 1999, for instance, the share fell from 47 percent to 29 percent.

In the meantime, the power of the Chinese government in intra-governmental fiscal transfer weakened. After 1978, China pursued a policy of fiscal decentralization, and granted preferential treatment to coastal provinces in terms of their fiscal contribution to the revenue of the central government. The fiscal decentralization provided financial incentives for coastal provinces to perform better, but it resulted in a weakening of the fiscal transfer to the poor interior regions. From 1978 to 1999, for instance, the share of the central region in total government expenditure fell from 34 percent to 22 percent, while the share of the western region in total government expenditure fell from 28 percent to 18 percent.

Furthermore, the government burden of debt increased rapidly. To meet the expanding financial need, the Chinese government borrowed money year after year, and found itself in an increasing amount of domestic and foreign debt. Up to 1999, for instance, although the official budget deficit was only about 2 percent of GDP, the accumulated domestic debt amounted to

21 percent of GDP, while the accumulated foreign debt amounted to 15 percent of GDP. To make things worse, the bad loans from state banks has increased rapidly owing to the poor performance of the state-owned enterprises, amounting to 25 percent of GDP in 1999. Added together, the total government burden of debt was about 63 percent of GDP. Such a burden of debt would not present a problem for a government with an increasing ratio of government revenue to GDP, but it would do for a government with a weakening financial power as in the case of China.

In addition to the financial limitations mentioned above, state financing in China faces the problem of corruption. In recent years, corruption was most common in state-financed public projects. Meanwhile, state financing tends to lead to inefficiency in government-funded projects. The state-owned enterprises have been the contractors of most government-funded construction projects, particularly the large ones, owing to the government preferential policy. Most of the state-owned enterprises are loss-makers and cannot survive without state subsidies, as indicated by the huge amount of bad loans from the state banks. As loss-making state-owned enterprises are the main receivers of state financing, inefficiency would be expected in the government-funded projects in the western region.

Faced with these problems, the Chinese government has decided to make full use of non-state financial resources in the development of the western region. Priority is given to foreign direct investment since it provides sufficient financial resources to undertake large-scale projects of infrastructure construction, ecological protection and high-tech industries. Foreign direct investment can benefit the receivers not only in financial terms, but also in terms of technology transfer. It can bring in advanced foreign technology and management skills to the backward western region. Past experience has showed that foreign direct investment has played a vital role in the rapid development of the coastal region, and the Chinese government was determined to replay the history in the western part of the nation by means of granting more preferential policy treatments to foreign investors in the western region.

Preferential policies from the central government

On 29 September 2001, the State Council issued the Circular on the Distribution of Suggestions Submitted by the western region Development Office of the State Council for the Implementation of Policies and Measures Pertaining to the Development of the Western Region. This document highlights the following preferential policy treatment that the Chinese government has granted to the western region.

FIEs engaged in industries encouraged by the government in the western region enjoy a reduced rate of enterprise income tax of 15 percent in the period 2001–2010. FIEs engaged in industries encouraged by the government refers to those whose main business falls into the industries covered by the Guidance Catalog of Industries with Foreign Investment and the Catalog of Advantageous Industries with Foreign Investment in the Middle and Western Regions and whose income from the main business is more than 70 percent of the enterprise's total income.[17] Upon approval by the provincial-level government, FIEs based in autonomous regions, prefectures or counties may be granted reduction or exemption of local enterprise income tax.

Newly established FIEs engaged in transport, power supply, water conservancy, the postal service, broadcasting, television, etc., in the western region are eligible for preferential policies of enterprise income tax reduction and exemption. In particularly, FIEs with an expected operation period of more than ten years are eligible for a two-year enterprise income tax holiday starting from the year of initial profit-making and a 50 percent reduction of enterprise income tax for the next three years following the tax holiday. Newly established FIEs in transport refers to those that provide transport services through highways, railways, civil aviation, ports, wharfs, and pipelines. Newly established FIEs in power supply refers to those engaged in the business of power generation, transmission, and distribution. Newly established FIEs in water conservancy refers to those engaged in the development of water conservancy and flood control, including the comprehensive harnessing of rivers and lakes, flood control and water-logging elimination, irrigation, water supply, water resources protection, hydropower generation, water and soil conservation, river course dredging, and the construction of riverbanks and sea walls. Newly established FIEs in postal services refers to those that provide all kinds of postal services. Newly established FIEs in broadcasting and television refers to those engaged in the business of broadcasting and television. If not subject to other prevailing regulations, the aforementioned FIEs are eligible for these preferential tax policies only when the income from their main business accounts for more than 70 percent of the enterprise's total income.

Foreign enterprises engaged in converting cultivated land back into forestry and pasture for the purpose of ecological protection are exempt from paying agricultural tax for their special agricultural products thus produced for ten years starting the year they generate the initial income, provided that the size of ecological forests accounts for more than 80 percent of the total area converted.

By analogy with tax exemption in railway and commercial airport construction, no tax for farmland occupation is levied for taking cultivated land to build state-level or province-level highways in the western region. This policy of tax-free farmland occupation is only applicable to the cultivated land occupied by highways and their two side trenches, and is not applicable to the cultivated land occupied by stockyards, road maintenance crews, checkpoints, engineering teams, and vehicle washing yards located along the highways. It is up to provincial governments in the western region to decide on any reduction or exemption of taxes for taking cultivated land to build highways other than those at state level and province level. If land that should have been used to build state-level and province-level highways is occupied for other purposes, it will no longer be eligible for exemption from farmland occupation tax, which should be paid starting from the occupation.

If FIEs in the western region engaged in government-encouraged industries or industries with a competitive edge need to import advanced technology and equipment to facilitate projects with their investment, these imports, except for those that are not exemptible according to the Catalog of Non-Tax-Free Imports for Domestic Investment Projects (revised in 2000) and the Catalog of Non-Tax-Free Imports for Foreign Investment Projects, should be exempt from tariff and value-added tax, provided that the imports are purchased solely with their investment. If FIEs engaged in projects that conform to the Catalog of Industries with Competitive Edge for Foreign Investment in the Middle and Western Regions need to import equipment to facilitate their projects, these imports should be exempt from tariff and value-added tax, provided that the imports are purchased solely with their investment.

Preferential policies from local governments

In addition to preferential policies offered by the central government, local governments at various levels (basically provincial and city levels) have also offered a number of preferential policies to FIEs moving into their localities. This happened because local governments now have more power to deal with local affairs than previously due to the process of decentralization after 1978. In particular, the fiscal reform in 1994 segregated the taxes collected by the local governments from those collected by the central government, thus giving local governments greater leverage in offering preferential tax treatment to foreign investors.[18] To compete in attracting foreign investment, individual provinces and cities in the western region try to provide more preferential tax treatment than their neighbors. In practise, therefore, preferential policy treatments to FIEs differ from one province to another and, sometimes, from one city to another. The following are a few examples.

With respect to income tax on FIEs and foreign enterprises, some provinces offer more preferential tax treatments to foreign investors than those offered by the central government. In Tibet, for instance, FIEs in a production industry enjoy a reduced tax rate of only 10 percent, and FIEs in energy, transport, agriculture, and animal husbandry further enjoy a tax exemption for five years and 50 percent of tax reduction for the following three years.[19] In Qinghai, export-oriented FIEs, technologically advanced FIEs, and FIEs in agriculture, animal husbandry, domestic commerce, foreign trade, tourism, transport, energy, and communication enjoy a 50 percent tax rebate. In Ningxia, FIEs in a production industry enjoy a tax exemption for three or five years. In Guizhou, FIEs in a production industry enjoy a *de facto* tax exemption for five years, and FIEs in energy, transport, water conservancy, public facilities, "green" industries, and tourism enjoy a *de facto* tax exemption for up to ten years.

Regarding the part of enterprise income tax collected locally, it is completely exempted indefinitely for all FIEs in some provinces such as Xinjiang, and for certain kinds of FIEs (such as technologically advanced FIEs, export-oriented FIEs, and FIEs in energy, transport, agriculture, and animal husbandry) in some provinces such as Shaanxi. In Chongqing and Ulubqi, FIEs in a production industry enjoy a tax exemption indefinitely, while FIEs in other industries enjoy a 50 percent tax reduction.

As for property tax, Gansu provides a 100 percent property tax rebate to FIEs in a production industry for five years, and FIEs in other industries for three years. In Xinjiang, all FIEs enjoy a tax exemption for five years. In Sichuan, FIEs in a production industry enjoy a tax exemption for up to ten years, while FIEs in other industries enjoy a tax exemption for three years. In Chongqing, technologically advanced FIEs, export-oriented FIEs and FIEs in forestry, energy, resource exploitation, transport, tourism, and ecological protection enjoy a tax exemption indefinitely.

In respect of vehicle and vessel license tax, Qinghai provides a tax exemption for all FIEs for ten years. In Sichuan, FIEs in a production industry enjoy a tax exemption for ten years, while FIEs in other industries enjoy a tax exemption for three years. In Gansu, FIEs enjoy a 100 percent tax rebate. In Chongqing, FIEs in a production industry enjoy a tax exemption for ten years, FIEs in other industries enjoy a tax exemption for three years, and technologically advanced FIEs, export-oriented FIEs, and FIEs in forestry, energy, resource exploitation, transport, ecological protection, and tourism enjoy a tax exemption indefinitely.

For city and township land usage tax, Xinjiang provides a five-year tax exemption for FIEs in agriculture, forestry, and animal husbandry, a ten-year tax exemption for FIEs in energy, water conservancy, and transport, and a 20-year tax exemption for FIEs using waste land and hills. In Gansu, FIEs are exempt from tax for a period ranging from five years to 15 years according the amount of capital they invest. In some counties, such as Yongdeng in Gansu, FIEs can use the land completely free of charge. In Qinghai, technologically advanced FIEs, export-oriented FIEs, and FIEs in agriculture and animal husbandry, domestic commerce, foreign trade, tourism, transport, energy, and communication enjoy a tax exemption indefinitely, while other FIEs enjoy a 50 percent tax reduction indefinitely.[20]

Further reading

Tian, Xiaowen, "Market Orientation and Regional Disparities in China," *Post-Communist Economies* 11 (2), 1999, 161–72.

Notes

1 The eastern region includes Liaoning, Beijing, Tianjin, Hebei, Shandong, Jiangsu, Shanghai, Zhejiang, Fujian, Guangdong, and Hainan. The central region includes Heilongjiang, Jilin, Shanxi, Henan, Anhui, Hubei, Hunan, and Jiangxi. The western region includes Xinjiang, Gunsu, Qinghai, Ningxia, Shaanxi, Tibet, Sichuan, Yunnan, Guizhou, Chongqing, Guangxi, and Inner Mongolia. The eastern region is along the coast and, therefore, is also called the coastal region. The central and western regions are in the interior and, therefore, are also called interior regions.

2 See *Selected Works of Deng Xiaoping* (Beijing: People's Press, 1993), vol. 3, p. 374.

3 See Hu Angang, *China Regional Disparities Report* (Liaoning: Liaoning People's Press, 1995).

4 See *People's Daily*, 23 February 1992.

5 See, for example, John Pomfret, "Separatists Defy Chinese Crackdown: Persistent Islamic Movement May Have Help From Abroad," *Washington Post*, 26 January 2000.

6 John Pomfret, "Separatists Defy Chinese Crackdown: Persistent Islamic Movement May Have Help From Abroad," *Washington Post*, 26 January 2000.

7 This quotation is from a talk by President Jiang Zemin during his visit to Xi'an on 17 June 1999. See Xinhua News Agency, 18 June 1999.

8 For instance, 50 percent of China's reserve of minerals is located in the five provinces in the western region (Xinjiang, Gansu, Ningxia, Qinghai, and Shaanxi).

9 Calculated at 1990 constant prices in US dollars, for instance, the commodity price of raw materials, minerals, and grains in 1999 were only 59 percent, 44 percent, and 45 percent, respectively, of those in 1970. Although the falling prices were accelerated by a decrease in demand during the Asian financial crisis, the long-term movement of changes in commodity prices was clearly not in favor of the products of raw materials, grains, minerals, and metals. Most of China's exports of raw materials, grains, minerals, and metals were from the western region directly or indirectly, and the falling prices for these products hit the western region badly.

10 *People's Daily*, 1 November 1999; *People's Daily*, 23 January 2000; and *People's Daily*, 5 April 2000.

11 The railways under construction include, for instance, double track lines between Baoji of Shaanxi and Lanzhou of Gansu, between Xi'an of Shaanxi and Hefei of Anhui, and between Zhuzhou of Hunan and Liupanshan of Ningxia and Gansu. There will be single track lines between Suining of Sichuan and Chongqing, between Da County and Wan County of Sichuan, between Wan County of Sichuan and Zhicheng of Hubei, between Taiyuan of Shanxi and Zhongwei of Ningxia, between Shenmu and Yanan of Shaanxi, and between Xi'an and Ankang of Shaanxi.

12 The 11 new airports are in Guangyuan, Mianyang, Panzhihua, Jiuzhaigou, Wanzhou, Tongren, Simao, Lincang, Zhongchuan, Erletai, and Kuche. The nine airports to be upgraded are Chendou Airport, Kunming Airport, Urumqi Airport, Xianyang Airport, Geermu Airport, Dunhuang Airport, Luzhou Airport, Beihai Airport, and Qimo Airport.

13 *People's Daily*, 1 November 1999; *People's Daily*, 23 January 2000; and *People's Daily*, 5 April 2000.

14 *People's Daily*, 1 November 1999; *People's Daily*, 23 January 2000; and *People's Daily*, 5 April 2000.

15 *People's Daily*, 24 January 2000.

16 *People's Daily*, 1 November 1999; *People's Daily*, 23 January 2000; and *People's Daily*, 5 April 2000.

17 See Chapter 3 for the details of the catalogs.

18 Currently, taxes collected by local governments or shared by local governments and central government include urban maintenance and construction tax, fixed asset investment orientation regulation tax, income tax on FIEs and foreign enterprises, farmland occupation tax, business tax, local enterprise income tax, individual income tax, urban and township land use tax, property tax, vehicle and vessel license tax, stamp tax, and agriculture tax (see Chapter 8 for details).

19 A production industry refers to an industry engaged in material production such as machinery, electronics, and textiles.

20 In general, the time limit of land usage is 40 years for FIEs in commerce, 50 years for FIEs in industry, 60 years for FIEs in agriculture, and 70 years for FIEs in real estate.

Table of Chinese legal documents

The Administrative License Law of the People's Republic of China

The Administrative Measures of the People's Republic of China on the Movement of State Currency Into and Out of Chinese Territory

The Administrative Measures on the Settlement of Foreign Exchange under Current Accounts

The Administrative Procedure Law of the People's Republic of China

The Administrative Reconsideration Law of the People's Republic of China

The Administrative Rules on Domestic Foreign Exchange Accounts

The Administrative Rules on Foreign Exchange Settlements, Sales and Payments

The Advertising Law of the People's Republic of China

The Announcement of the People's Bank of China Concerning Further Reform of the Foreign Exchange Control System

The Announcement of the People's Bank of China on the Implementation of Foreign Exchange Settlements and Sales at Banks by Foreign Investment Enterprises

The Arbitration Law of the People's Republic of China

The Catalog of Advantageous Industries with Foreign Investment in the Middle and Western Regions

The Catalog of Encouraged High-Technology Products for Foreign Investment

The China Chamber of International Commerce Mediation (Conciliation) Rules

The China International Economic and Trade Arbitration Commission (CIETAC) Arbitration Rules

The Circular on Relevant Issues Concerning Foreign Companies Limited by Shares

The Circular on the Distribution of Suggestions Submitted by the Western Region Development Office of the State Council for the Implementation of Policies and Measures Pertaining to the Development of the Western Region

The Circular on the Explanation of Several Articles in the Detailed Rules for the Implementation of the Law of the People's Republic of China on Wholly Foreign-Owned Enterprises

The Circular on the Prohibition of Business Activities by Pyramid Selling

The Circular on the Strengthening and Improvement of the Management of Foreign Investment Enterprises over the Drawing, Remittance, and Use of Funds Relating to Chinese Employees' Rights and Interests

The Civil Procedure Law of the People's Republic of China

The Commercial Bank Law of the People's Republic of China

The Company Law of the People's Republic of China

The Legislation Law of the People's Republic of China

The Measures on Economic Compensation for Breach and Termination of Labor Contracts

The Measures on the Administration of Foreign Experts in Foreign Investment Enterprises

The Measures on the Administration of Patent Agencies

The Measures on the Administration of Registration of Resident Representative Offices of Foreign Enterprises

The Measures on the Administration of Registration of Sole Proprietorships

The Measures on the Implementation of Administrative Punishment Regarding Copyrights

The Measures on the Liquidation of Foreign Investment Enterprises

The Measures of the People's Republic of China on the Administration of Registration of Partnerships

The Measures on the Registration and Administration of Collective Marks and Certification Marks

The Measures on the Registration of Computer-Software Copyright

The Measures of the Shanghai Municipality on the Administration of Securities Trading

The Notice Concerning Questions about the Procedures and Powers in the Interpretation of Administrative Regulations

The Notice on Standardizing the Behavior of Using E-Mail to Send Commercial Information

The Notice on the Relevant Issues Concerning the Conversion of Sales Methods by Foreign-Funded Pyramid-Marketing Enterprises

The Notice Regarding the Further Enhancement of the Clean-Up Work of Local Regulations, Local Government Rules and Other Policies and Measures on Labor Protection so as to Meet the Needs Arising from the WTO Accession

The Notice Regarding the Protection of the Lawful Rights and Interests of Consumers in Internet Economic Activities

The Organic Law of the People's Court of the People's Republic of China

The Partnership Law of the People's Republic of China

The Patent Law of the People's Republic of China

The Protocol on the Accession of the People's Republic of China

The Provisional Measures on the Administration of Business Behavior over the Internet

The Provisional Measures on the Administration of Foreign Exchange Registration for Foreign Investment Enterprises

The Provisional Measures on the Administration of Wage Incomes in Foreign Investment Enterprises

The Provisional Regulations of the People's Republic of China on Business Tax

The Provisional Regulations of the People's Republic of China on Consumption Tax

The Provisional Regulations of the People's Republic of China on Private Enterprises

The Provisional Regulations of the People's Republic of China on the Administration of Resident Representative Offices of Foreign Enterprises

The Provisional Regulations of the People's Republic of China on the Land Appreciation Tax

The Rules on the Recognition and Protection of Well-Known Marks
The Rules Regarding Several Questions on Litigious Jurisdiction of Foreign-Related
  Civil and Commercial Cases
The Securities Law of the People's Republic of China
The Several Opinions on the "Collective Consultation" of Wages in Foreign Invest-
  ment Enterprises
The Several Provisions Concerning Judicial Interpretations
The Sole Proprietorship Law of the People's Republic of China
The Trade Union Law of the People's Republic of China,
The Trademark Law of the People's Republic of China
The Trial Measures on Maternity Insurance for Enterprise

Table of cases

Useful web sites

China Foreign Investment Registration
www.wzj.gov.cn
China International Economic and Trade Arbitration Commission
www.cietac.org.cn
China Internet Information Center
www.china.org.cn
China Securities Regulatory Commission
www.csrc.gov.cn
Information Center of the Legislative Office of the State Council
www.chinalaw.gov.cn
Invest in China
www.fdi.gov.cn
Ministry of Commerce
http://english.mofcom.gov.cn
Ministry of Finance
www.mof.gov.cn
Ministry of Labor and Social Security
www.molss.gov.cn
Ministry of Land and Resources
www.mlr.gov.cn
National Copyright Administration
www.ncac.gov.cn
State Administration for Industry and Commerce
www.saic.gov.cn
State Administration of Taxation
www.chinatax.gov.cn
State Intellectual Property Office
www.cpo.cn.net
State-Owned Assets Supervision and Administration Commission
www.sasac.gov.cn
Supreme People's Court
www.court.gov.cn

Index